Practical Strategy

Structured Tools and Techniques

Practical Strategy
Structured Tools and Techniques

Geoff Coyle

University of Bath

FT Prentice Hall
FINANCIAL TIMES

An imprint of Pearson Education
Harlow, England • London • New York • Boston • San Francisco • Toronto • Sydney • Singapore • Hong Kong
Tokyo • Seoul • Taipei • New Delhi • Cape Town • Madrid • Mexico City • Amsterdam • Munich • Paris • Milan

Pearson Education Limited

Edinburgh Gate
Harlow
Essex CM20 2JE
England

and Associated Companies throughout the world

Visit us on the World Wide Web at:
www.pearsoned.co.uk

───────────────

First published 2004

ISBN 978-0-273-68220-2

British Library Cataloguing-in-Publication Data
A catalogue record for this book is available from the British Library

10 9 8 7 6 5 4 3
08 07

Typeset in 9.5pt Stone Serif by 30
Printed and bound by Ashford Colour Press Ltd, Gosport, Hants

The publisher's policy is to use paper manufactured from sustainable forests.

This book is dedicated to my adored grandchildren,
Alistair Geoffrey, Elizabeth Rose and Jonathan Stuart Coyle

Contents

3 Thinking about futures   47

4 Identifying strategic actions   85

13 Dealing with wish lists   223

List of figures

List of tables

Preface

What this book is about

The teaching and practice of strategy, whether it be of the business firm, a government department, national defence, or any other organisation, has two aspects. The first is a need to *understand* at a deep level the very idea of strategy and to realise that it has many facets. To meet that need there are numerous excellent textbooks with titles such as *Strategic Management, Marketing Strategy* etc. covering the whole gamut of strategy. These texts include case studies of strategy in practice, designed to deepen strategic understanding and to give practice in thinking about such problems. The style is generally descriptive and intuitive, which is as it should be to develop insight. Such texts are a vital component of degrees in business administration but they are also avidly read by practising managers and consultants.

The second need, though, is to be able to use practical tools and techniques to develop specific action plans that are as robust as possible against the uncertainties of the future into which a strategic choice will evolve. This book aims to meet that need by explaining and illustrating a process for developing *practical strategy* so as to complement the 'intuitive' approach to strategy.

The toolset for practical strategy evolved from much academic research into systematic methods for modelling *strategic* issues. Some of the resulting techniques are completely new, others were adapted from the existing strategy literature, while yet others are simply summarised as they stand. However, and more importantly, the research has been extensively tested and refined through numerous practical, real-world, applications. Software to support the practical strategy process is described in Appendix 1.

The end result is a structured approach and supporting techniques for:

- unravelling the complexity of a problem
- visualising different futures
- developing actions that are as robust as possible against future uncertainties
- designing an organisation to implement those actions
- assessing how that organisation can be brought into being
- producing a workable action plan.

None of the tools involves any mathematics; some need simple arithmetic but most of them involve no more than strictly logical thinking. That is as it should be because the problems of practical strategy and action planning are far too complex and subtle to be reduced to some sort of mathematical form; to attempt to do so would destroy the nuances of strategy. Instead, the tools form a logical sequence of simple steps that give a clear audit trail by which results can be understood and confidently used. Such clarity enables the results to be tested and, if necessary, *easily* revised. Again, that is as it should be in the practical world.

The tools are, individually, relatively simple to explain but rather harder to use, so the approach adopted here is to explain each technique in turn and then to illustrate it through an evolving case study. Other cases are covered in Chapter 14, so the book is designed to impart a good deal of synthetic experience and supporting examples. There are numerous other topics for the reader to tackle.

This book is not only about business strategy; civil servants and people in non-governmental organisations (NGOs), such as the major charities, face similar problems. The application of the tools to a major hospital appears in Chapter 13 and the management of an ecological system features in Chapter 14.

In the military field, strategic analysis, as far as this book is concerned, is not so much about how to fight a campaign, it is more a matter of the acquisition of military assets such as ships, aircraft, and a myriad others. In many ways, that is more difficult than business strategy because of the bewildering variety of assets to be acquired, the fact that they have long lifetimes, and because they interact with each other in very complex ways. The book's tools have been applied to, and in some cases were specifically developed for, military acquisition strategies.

Who should read this book?

The book has been designed to appeal to four main audiences:

- MBA students or final year undergraduates in business. For them, the book is designed to provide an elective course to supplement the core teaching of strategy.

- Another group is practitioners in business, industry, government, NGOs, defence, consultancy and, indeed, anyone concerned with the formulation and implementation of workable strategic plans. More senior people may wish to skim the book to see how the tools and techniques fit together and lead to implementable action plans. 'Worker bees' will need to study it more closely, perhaps a chapter at a time. Since each chapter covers a specific technique and illustrates it via a case study, they should then be able to apply each chapter's lessons to their immediate concerns, thus getting practical benefit from their reading. Such readers will also find benefit in the additional tools and techniques that are described outside the main case study.

- Thirdly, the book is intended to be useful on MSc degrees in Operational Research, Decision Sciences, Management Science, Systems, Military Studies, Environmental Studies, and the like. Its coverage of strategic analysis techniques might complement the teaching of 'standard' methodologies such as linear programming, queuing, and so forth. The methods described in this book are very much in the vein of 'soft' operational research and therefore fit well with an emerging trend in Operational Research.

For both the academic audiences, some guidance for teachers is given below and extensively on the website, available at **www.booksites.net/coyle**.

■ Finally, I hope that my academic colleagues teaching strategy in business schools, and elsewhere, will find useful complementary ideas in this volume.

How to read this book

The book falls into seven parts, though they are not numbered as such.

■ Chapter 1 stands alone as it sets the scene for all the rest by describing a framework for practical strategy. It might be read quickly the first time and revisited from time to time as the second group of chapters unfolds.

■ Chapters 2 to 7 deal with a series of steps which have been found to work well together in practice and which, for many problems, usually lead to a practical solution. Each chapter explains a technique and then illustrates it by application to an evolving case study.

■ Chapter 8 summarises the main ideas in those chapters, offers a checklist for using the tools, mentions some topics to which they have been applied, and challenges the reader with some suggested problems for analysis.

■ Those eight chapters are the core of the work but it should not be assumed that what is described is the *only* or even necessarily the *correct* way to analyse a strategic problem. Strategic issues are too diverse for any single method to work in all cases. Accordingly, Chapter 9 is a bridge to some more specialised, though still simple, techniques that deal with particular issues, such as stimulating technology development.

■ Chapters 10 to 13 deal with these additional tools but it should not be supposed that these are unimportant simply because they are not included in the main case study. They are, in fact, effective tools for some significant types of strategic problem.

■ Chapter 14 describes two case studies of applications of the strategic tool set to major problems. Study of those cases will give added insight into the use of tools for practical strategy.

■ Chapter 15 summarises the whole book. It discusses the management of practical work in the real world.

Reading all that in sequence is quite a load so you might start by reading Chapter 1 to get the outline of the book and then seeing how the techniques hang together by reading the Murray/Darling River Basin (MDB) case study in Chapter 14. To help you get started, the MDB case has outline explanations of what the techniques do; how they do it is fully explained in the preceding chapters. The MDB case is of a socio-economic, ecological and political problem but the practical strategy techniques can be, and have been, applied to almost any domain, be it business, government, defence, and many others, examples of which will emerge as the book unfolds.

Teaching practical strategy

Teaching this material can be immensely rewarding, both for the instructor and the student. I am regularly amazed at the scope and quality of the work produced by my MBA students at the University of Bath and elsewhere. They react with great enthusiasm not only to the techniques themselves but also to the challenge of working on a problem at the same time as they learn about the tools.

Teachers wanting to introduce this material to an MBA curriculum, probably as an option to follow a strategy course, or as a module in an MSc in Operational Research/Management Science, or in any other equivalent context, will, of course, have their own ideas and experience to draw on, and will have to do it in their own institutional context and with their own student cohort. It is certainly not for me to tell others how to teach this material, but some suggestions, based on experience, are included on the website.

The material available includes:

- a suggested timetable for an intensive one-week course, though that is easily adapted to run over a term or semester
- additional case studies to supplement the three full cases in the book (*Herrington-Jones* and those in Chapter 14)
- PowerPoint slides for all of the diagrams
- advice on running syndicates from the instructor's point of view
- comments on how one might teach the material in most of the chapters
- suggestions for research topics in practical strategy.

References

Choosing which references to cite in a book is partly a matter of an author's personal style. Some writers offer many references so that the reader can explore as fully as time allows. I have chosen to cite a limited number of sources, but only where they bear on the topic in question in a useful and accessible way. Each reference has its own bibliography to take you further into the topic in question.

Acknowledgements

No author writes a book without a great deal of assistance and, for me, that has come from many sources.

On the one hand are my consultancy clients, from whom I have learned much. The other invaluable source has been those research students who worked with me to develop some of these ideas and others who have tested them on case-based courses at the universities of Bath, Oxford, Cardiff, New South Wales, and at the Royal Military College of Science.

My academic colleagues David Faulkner (Oxford), Steve MacIntosh (Cardiff), Don MacNamara (Queens University, Ontario), Charles Newton (New South Wales) and John Powell (Bath) – in alphabetical order – gave me the impetus to develop this material as a book, excellent students with whom to work, and comment on the text. I thank them, while retaining responsibility for errors and opinions.

I am grateful to: Ian Rogers, a former student, who developed the first version of the example of an MOA for a large hospital as a third-year undergraduate project; and to Darcy Brooker, an MSc student at the Australian Defence Force Academy, who suggested and developed the first version of Table 15.1, though that has been adapted for Chapter 15. In addition the section on the Delphi method in Chapter 3 draws on the extended discussion of Delphi by T. J. Gordon in J. Glenn (ed.) *Futures Research Methodology*, Version 1, Washington, DC, The American Council for the United Nations University (ACUNU) 1999.

A big debt is due to Jacqueline Senior, Bridget Allen, Anita Atkinson, and the people at Pearson Education. They gave me much enthusiastic and highly expert help in converting the manuscript to the finished book. The backup material that Pearson Education provides for authors was invaluable.

I am deeply grateful to them all but, as in all my previous books, the real acknowledgement is to my darling wife, Julie, who made it all possible in ways that I cannot count.

RGC,
Shrivenham

Publisher's acknowledgements

We are grateful to the following for permission to reproduce copyright material:

Figure 1.1 derived from and Figures 3.1, 3.2, 14.5, Tables 14.8, 14.9, 14.11, 14.13 from 'Scenario thinking and strategic modelling', in Faulkner, D. and Campbell, A. (Eds) *Oxford Handbook of Strategy*, Oxford University Press (Coyle, R. G. 2003); Figures 2.2, 2.3 and 2.5 adapted from *Futures Research Methodology*, Version 2.0, American Council for the United Nations University (ACUNU), Washington DC, copyright of J.C. Glenn (Glenn, J.C. (ed) 2003); Figures 2.10, 2.11, 2.13, 2.14, 2.15 and 2.16 from 'The practice of system dynamics: milestones, lessons and ideas from 30 years experience', *System Dynamics Review*, 14 (4) (Winter), copyright 1998, © John Wiley & Sons Limited, reproduced with permission (Coyle, R.G. 1998); Figure 2.12 from *Systems Dynamic Modelling*: *A Practical Approach*, CRC Press (Coyle, R.G., 1996); Table 3.2 from *Scenario Planning. Managing for the Future*, copyright 1998, © John Wiley & Sons Limited, reproduced with permission (Ringland, G. 1998); Table 3.3 from *Scenario Techniques*, copyright of Ute von Reibnitz (von Reibnitz, 1998, p.45); Figure 3.3 reprinted from 'Field anomaly relaxation. The arts of usage', *Futures*, 27 (6), pp. 657-74, copyright 1995, with permission from Elsevier (Rhyne, R. 1995a); Figure 3.4, Table 3.4, Table 3.5, Figure 3.5 from 'A scenario projection for the South China Sea', *Futures*, 28 (3), pp 269-83, copyright 1996, with permission from Elsevier (Coyle, R.G. and Yong, Y.C. 1996); Table 4.1 from *Scenarios. The art of strategic conversation*, copyright 1996, © John Wiley & Sons Limited, reproduced with permission (van der Heijden, K. 1996, p 234); Table 4.2 from *Idon Scenario Thinking*, Idon Resources, (Galt et al 1997, p107); Figure 14.1 from MDBC (Murray-Darling Basin Commission), image used with the permission of the MDBC.

The section on impact wheels in Chapter 2, drawn from the discussion of Futures Wheels by Jerome C. Glenn (editor) *Futures Research Methodology*, Version 2.0, American Council for the United Nations University (ACUNU), Washington DC, copyright of J.C. Glenn

Whilst every effort has been made to trace the owners of copyright material, in a few cases this has proved impossible and we would be grateful to hear from anyone with information which would enable us to do so.

The keys to the practical strategy toolbox

What this chapter is about

- Strategic issues and problems.

- A structured process for practical strategy.

- Introducing the tools in that process.

- Asking strategic questions.

- Introduction to the *Herrington-Jones and Co* case study.

Introduction

This book covers a structured set of practical tools for coping with almost any type of strategic problem, by which we mean an issue so profound and far-reaching that it affects the very nature and future of an organisation. The tool set consists entirely of '*soft*' methods that do not involve any mathematics but, instead, depend on disciplined, imaginative thought.

This chapter sets the scene for what is to follow and covers five main themes:

1. An explanation of why *soft methods* are essential for strategic problems.

2. The simplification of complexity and the key idea of a *model as a tool for thought*.

3. A suggested *process of practical strategy* involving a connected sequence of steps suitable for many strategic problems.

4. The key issue of *formulating a strategic question* as a precursor to analysis.

5. The background to the next six chapters which form a *case study to illustrate the process and tools of practical strategy*.

First, we will look at two very different types of problem.

Tactical problems vs. strategic questions

Tactical problems

The XYZ Manufacturing Company makes two products, A and B. Every A produces £3 of profit and every B gives £4 profit. If everything that is made can be sold, there is a *clear aim* of deciding how many of A and B the company should manufacture each week in order to make the maximum profit, given the times required to make A and B at each manufacturing stage and the numbers of machines available.

Note that in this type of problem the broad, long-term issues have already been decided, such as what is to be manufactured, the equipment to be used, and even what business to be in. Within that strategy, the question of how many As and Bs to make each week, while clearly of great importance, is a *tactical* matter. In tactical problems the objective, such as calculating the amounts of different types of product to manufacture so as to maximise weekly or monthly profit, is unambiguous and the outcome can be measured.

Some tactical problems can be solved exactly. For instance, XYZ's problem can be expressed in precise mathematical form as a so-called linear program (LP) and the mathematics of linear programming will guarantee to find the optimum solution to XYZ's problem. In practice, LP is easily capable of handling very complex problems. The method is widely used to plan production in oil refineries and it is fair to say that if all the linear programs were suddenly to vanish, that industry would be in very deep trouble.

Improving customer relations is also a tactical problem set in a wider strategic context, though that type of problem cannot, of course, be solved mathematically.

Strategic questions

On the other hand ...

1. Mr Littleworth and Ms Thrupp are the senior partners in a law firm but the area of legal practice in which they have built a successful and thriving business employing numerous people might decline drastically within the next few years. What should they do?

2. The Defence Department of the Kingdom of Northumbria needs to upgrade its military capabilities but the full cost of its wish list of requirements is about 300% more than the likely defence acquisition budget over the next 10 years. What should they buy?

3. Overseas Carers is a large non-governmental organisation (NGO) involved in disaster relief in the Third World. The Republic of Cataclysmia has had a major natural disaster and several governments and NGOs are hastening to help. What role, if any, should Overseas Carers offer to play? How can they ensure that they will be able to provide aid in the next disaster to occur?

4. The Ministry of Transport in the prosperous country of Utopia has to arrange for a vastly expensive tunnel, and associated major road improvement schemes, to connect Utopia's markets to those of its equally prosperous neighbours. What is the most satisfactory long-term plan?

5. *Herrington-Jones and Co*, a major retail chain, needs to think ahead to the year 2010. What kind of business should it be by then and how will it reach that target?

6. The Murray Darling river basin covers a vast area of Australia and supports 40% of the nation's agricultural product. It has an important ecological role, though there are many endangered species and there are fears that the rivers might effectively be dead within 20 years. What strategies should the River Basin Authority pursue?

Except for the Murray Darling river basin, none of these is a real organisation, though there are many actual cases of each type. Fictional case studies are used throughout the book for three reasons:

1. In order not to seem to criticise or congratulate particular firms.

2. To encourage you to think about how illustrative examples might apply in your own organisation, or others you might encounter in your career.

3 Real practical strategy cases are usually very sensitive commercial issues and can take a lot of space to explain.

> Fictional cases are used in the book to make you think about *types* of problem, not specific instances.

Characteristics of strategic problems

Strategic issues share several characteristics (for variety, 'issues' and 'problems' are used interchangeably):

1. They address the very nature and future of the organisation and are truly *strategic*.

2. There may be *many stakeholders*. To give but two examples, what will suit Mr Littleworth may not be what Ms Thrupp would like, and within Overseas Carers one interest group wants to spend a large amount of money to help Cataclysmia *now*, while another argues that public education will be a better long-term strategy.

3. They have *imprecise objectives*; their solution has to be 'acceptable' and achieved at 'tolerable' cost within a 'reasonable' time. Such objectives are ambiguous and even conflicting. They certainly cannot be expressed in mathematics.

4. There is likely to be *no 'right answer'* to any such problem.

5. They are nearly always of *long duration* – actions taken (or postponed) now will have effects for years to come.

6. Because the problems are so important, they can neither be left to chance nor can sound decisions be made by arm-waving or rank-pulling. Some form of logical, traceable, practical, and above all, *imaginative*, analysis is needed.

7. Precisely because they are so complicated it will be necessary to simplify them, and *create a suitable model* to serve as a tool for thinking about the issues.

8. Because there cannot be a 'formula' for their solution, strategic models have to use *'soft' methods involving structured thought* and, maybe, some simple arithmetic.

9. The problems are so complicated that they are likely to *need several methodologies* to deal with different aspects. Unfortunately, the sheer variety of this type of problem means that methodology X, which works very well for problem Y, may be a complete waste of effort for problem Z. Good practical strategy work

is always flexible and creative, sometimes modifying a methodology so that it will better fit the problem at hand.

10. Even the most skilled analysis will not 'solve' the problem but it should *illuminate the judgement* that will ultimately have to be made about what to do in a given case.

In summary, truly strategic problems are so difficult, so very hard, that they cannot be handled using rigorous mathematics; only 'soft' approaches will get anywhere near to coping with them.

There is, of course, a useful role for mathematical models in strategic issues; one might, for instance, use highly sophisticated models to calculate the optimum number of checkouts in a supermarket or to predict river flows. These are important factors but they are aspects of operations, not the deep issues of what kind of business we should be in 2010, or how the river basin can be rescued if, in fact, it can be rescued.

Simplification and modelling

The concept of a model

We humans need to simplify in order to think effectively about the problems we face so a model is always a *simplified* representation of a real-world problem. Even the very sophisticated LPs used in oil refineries simplify the complex chemistry and economics of oil refining by assuming that oil refining can be treated as a set of linear functions. It is also assumed that the complexities of human behaviour in a refinery, and many other aspects, do not need to be taken into account in the production planning.

However, models are not built just for fun (though modelling can be enormously enjoyable and intellectually very taxing). They are built for a purpose, such as to increase production efficiency or, in our case, to help to address strategic problems.

Thus, a model always has three components:

Models:
- are designed for a purpose
- simplify reality
- involve assumptions.

1. It has a purpose, which is best expressed as a *question*, or a few questions, which it is *designed* to answer – *the model is a tool for thought about those questions*.

2. It is a *simplification* of reality, because reality is too difficult to think about.

3. In any case, much of reality is irrelevant to the problem – we do not need to allow for the size and shape of A and B in XYZ, we do not even need to know what A and B are, we only need to know how long they take to make and how much profit each unit earns. A model therefore embodies *assumptions* about what needs to be included and what can be excluded.

There are several corollaries to those points:

- A model needs to be carefully designed for its task; it cannot just be thrown together.
- A large part of the analyst's skill lies in judging which simplifications are reasonable and which are not, but assumptions need to be explicitly stated.
- Simplifying a real problem requires some intellectual courage and the temptation to add more and more detail in an illusory search for 'accuracy' must be resisted.
- Because it simplifies a problem, a model can never be 'right' – the art is to be just wrong enough to be useful.
- Models are not often transferable – something designed to answer one set of questions can only rarely be safely copied and used for another set.
- Large computer programs are not usually effective as models for strategic problems.
- Modelling is an art (and probably a fairly black art); it is *not* a science.

There is nothing new about the idea of a model. They have been in use, at least implicitly, since people started to think but, in modern times, modelling has come to be associated with the discipline of Operational Research (OR), of which linear programming is a component. A reasonably short definition is that OR is:

the application of systematic and rigorous methods of analysis to give practical support to decision making.

In those terms, the tools described in this book are methods for the support of *strategic* decision-making; they are fundamentally 'soft' OR.

Types of model

There are many types of model, all of which are useful for different purposes.

> Different types of model are needed for differing purposes.

The simplest type is a *physical* model, perhaps using wooden blocks to represent the machines when designing the layout of a factory. Other examples, which may be to scale, are the styling of a car body or to show an architect's design.

A second type is the *mathematical model*. Sometimes the equations can be solved by algebra/calculus as in linear programming of oil refinery production. If the equations are too difficult to solve, *simulation techniques* can be used, for example in queuing systems and military combat. Very large simulations of climatic models are used for weather forecasting. Even then, the model is still a simplification of reality.

A less obvious type of model is a *diagram*. For example, a map simplifies geography for the useful purpose of helping us to get from one place to another. Later in this book we shall encounter influence diagrams and force fields as diagrams of strategic problems.

An even more subtle form is the *qualitative model* which uses only words to simplify and understand something. One example is a stage play which simplifies human actions and emotions. We shall use qualitative approaches when we deal with field anomaly relaxation, viable firm matrices, and SWOT analysis.

A process for practical strategy

Basic ideas

The underlying ideas of this book are:

■ that strategic problems need to be dealt with systematically
■ that there is a set of effective techniques for doing so
■ that there is a logical process for using those techniques.

This section will describe that process and introduce a set of tools which will be explained in Chapters 2 to 7 and summarised in Chapter 8. The methods covered in those chapters have been found to work well in practice and to give a coherent approach to most problems in practical strategy, but they are not the only tools. Practical strategy problems are of great diversity, so Chapters 10 to 13 will deal with additional tools for use in important special cases. We will preview them in Chapter 9.

The stages in the process

The process for practical strategy works in stages corresponding to some of the principal tools, though, at this stage, these are no more than names for things to be studied later. Where tools are mentioned, they are in italics with a reference to the relevant chapter. The eight steps in the methodology are:

Step 1: Asking a strategic question

Strategic problems need to be simplified so that a model can be developed as a tool for thought, though, in this book, a 'model' will be a connected set of individual tools. We also stated that a model has to be designed to answer a relevant question (or perhaps a few questions). It follows that the first stage is to ask a good strategic question. (*Focus groups* later in this chapter)

Step 2: Coming to grips with the complexity of the context

The question does not exist in isolation so the model will need to take account of the context in which it will have to be answered. The context may be some or all of the internal workings of the firm, its external environment, and the objectives of stakeholders. The context is likely to be quite complicated and we shall need to make sense of it. Once that has been done, it will be easier to decide on the extent to which reality needs to be simplified as the basis for the model. (*Influence diagrams*, *Mind maps* and others Chapter 2.) The sense-making may also lead one to see the problem in a new light and help to rephrase the question. This is very valuable because getting a good question is critical to a successful analysis. Step 2 thus has a dual role, both to verify the question posed in step 1 and also to act as a bridge to subsequent analysis.

It is, though, sometimes necessary to reverse steps 1 and 2 and to unravel the complexity before a suitable strategic question can be posed.

Step 3: Thinking about the future

Strategic choices have effects far into the future and it follows that a choice made without regard to what the future might hold could well be imprudent or even reckless. Views about the future are usually called scenarios and it is essential for more than one to be developed. (*Delphi, Field anomaly relaxation* Chapter 3)

Step 4: Identifying robust strategic actions

To move the analysis forward, we have to get some ideas about action plans which are sensible with respect to the organisation's current strengths and weaknesses versus the threats and opportunities which might arise now and in the future. This seems like the well-known SWOT (strengths, weaknesses, opportunities and threats) technique but we shall treat it differently to overcome the serious inherent limitations of SWOT (also renaming it as TOWS) and hence generate a preferred action plan. (*TOWS and strategies* Chapter 4)

Step 5: Finding a viable organisation to implement the actions

Action plans have to be implemented within the organisation and that will imply changes to its concept and structure that it might or might not be able to achieve. (*The viable firm matrix* Chapter 5; depending on the problem this can also be called a viable policy matrix, or whatever is most appropriate)

Step 6: Evaluating actions against stakeholder objectives and assessing resource requirements

One aspect of the organisation's ability to adapt is how well the change proposed in step 5 meets the objectives of different interest groups within the organisation. Another factor is the resources which might be needed to make that change, or which might become superfluous because of it. (*Congruence analysis and Resource analysis* Chapter 6)

Step 7: Looking for obstacles to implementation and overcoming them

Finally, even when all these factors have been studied, there may still be obstacles to achieving the required change. The final technical stage in the process of using the tools for practical strategy is to assess how obstacles can be overcome. (*Force field analysis* Chapter 7)

Step 8: Drawing conclusions and assessing risks

The last step of all is non-technical; it is to judge how well the initial aim of the study has been met. Recall that we started with a question to be addressed; for example, 'what strategies should Littleworth and Thrupp [the legal firm discussed on page 4] adopt to continue to prosper given the possible, and relatively imminent, collapse of their traditional legal market?' We shall have answered that question if we have, using the six technical steps of the eight-step methodology (names of techniques in italics):

   Step 2 Unravelled the context (*influence diagrams, mind maps, and others*)
   Step 3 Studied what the future might hold (*field anomaly relaxation*)

Step 4 Identified robust actions (*TOWS and strategies*)

Step 5 Seen how the organisation would need to be configured to pursue those courses of action (*viable firm matrix*)

Step 6 Considered stakeholder objectives and resource requirements (*congruence analysis and resource analysis*)

Step 7 Overcome any obstacles (*force field analysis*).

In practice, the result may be one or other of two things.

The answer may be 'No'; we have failed to identify effective and workable action plans. Perhaps the resource analysis shows that some of the required assets will simply not be available; in such a case, the analysis would have to loop back to step 5 to see if there is a less demanding configuration for the firm. Maybe the obstacles cannot be overcome and one might revisit step 6 to try to find a more cunning plan.

It might even be necessary to redefine the question, and it is vital to realise that this is usually a good thing. No question is perfectly chosen at the first attempt and redefining it will usually immeasurably improve the quality of the work. Having to loop back to an earlier stage is not necessarily a waste of effort, as work in subsequent stages may not have to be repeated. In any case, much will have been learned about the problem and practical strategy is a learning process, not a formula.

The answer, though, is almost never an unqualified 'Yes'. It is far more likely to be 'Yes, but …'. The 'but' could, for example, be that there is a chance that one of the required resources might not be available precisely as or when we require. In other words, the plan will probably work but there are some gaps and uncertainties. It is worth going ahead with the plan, knowing the risks identified by the 'but'. The great practical virtue of this is that the risks have been identified quite precisely and they can then be monitored and managed as the plan unfolds.

The eight-step practical strategy methodology may be summed up as follows:

Step 1	A –	**Ask a strategic question**
Step 2	C –	**Come to grips with, or unravel, the complexity**
Step 3	T –	**Think about what the future might hold**
Step 4	I –	**Identify the actions required to deal with the question against the future's uncertainties**
Step 5	F –	**Find a viable organisation to implement those actions**
Step 6	E –	**Evaluate the acceptability to the stakeholders of the changes and assess the resource requirements**
Step 7	L –	**Look for obstacles, find ways of overcoming them and develop an action plan**
Step 8	D –	**Draw conclusions about the feasibility of the action plan and assess the risks.**

Picking out a letter from each gives the acronym **ACTIFELD***. This should help you to memorise the practical strategy steps, or the **ACTIFELD** methodology, but it can also be looked at in another way:

- **ACTI** focuses on the need to find *actions* to cope with the strategic question.
- **FELD** deals with the practicalities of making those actions work, in the *field*, so to speak.

Each step in **ACTIFELD** will be highlighted when we come to it.

A picture of the practical strategy process

It helps to grasp the totality of these ideas by studying a diagram, Figure 1.1, which matches the thought processes on the left-hand side, in which one step leads to another, with the eight-step methodology on the right.

The key points about the diagram are:

- At the extreme left-hand edge, the thought process moves from the internal problem into the external environment and then back into analysis of internal factors.
- The arrows connecting the tools for practical strategy to stages in the thought process point both ways. From right to left they suggest, for example, that focus groups help to define problems and hence to pose questions. From left to right implies 'in order to define a problem and pose a question, use a focus group'.
- On the left-hand side, the dotted lines leading from 'No' show the loop back to an earlier stage in the effort to improve the quality of the practical strategy analysis. Note that two of these are double-headed; resource problems may be so serious that one has to review the viability of the organisational design; or inability to overcome obstacles may take one back to congruence or resource analysis to see if there is some less difficult way of handling those issues. Both of these are tantamount to a 'No' answer emerging before the end of the study.
- Two of the return arrows lead to the stages of making sense of the context and study of the future. Return to these means that the inability to find a workable plan has arisen because we do not understand sufficiently well how the business 'works', techniques for which will be covered in Chapter 2, or we have not achieved a rich enough view of the future's possibilities, a topic we shall study in detail in Chapter 3.
- Note particularly that one of the return arrows points to the problem faced and the question to be asked. We will discuss this important point after we have considered the nature of a strategic question.

You should study the diagram – it is in effect a map for understanding the next six chapters. You should certainly revisit it from time to time; a good trick might be to photocopy it and use it as a bookmark.

Before introducing the case study that forms the background to the next six chapters, we start with step 1 of the eight-step methodology.

---

*the author's trademark

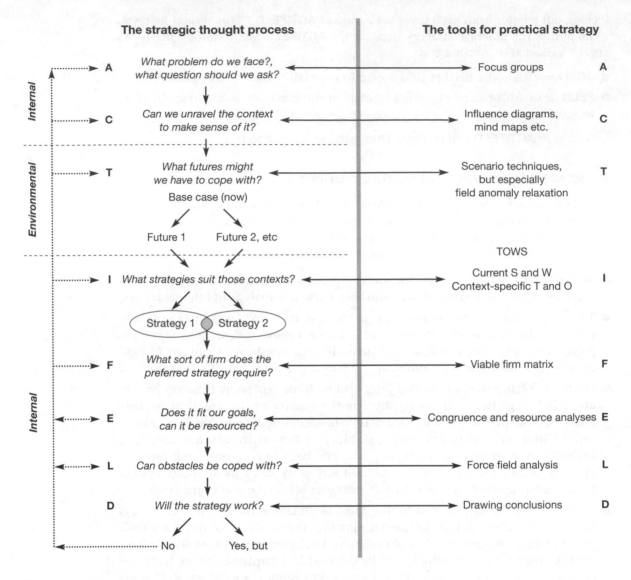

Figure 1.1 The practical strategy process

Source: derived from Coyle (2003)

Strategic problems and questions

What is a strategic problem?

A problem is 'any thing, matter, person etc. that is difficult to deal with, solve or overcome'. A strategy is 'a particular long-term plan for success, especially in business or politics'. For our purposes, we can combine these and define a *strategic problem* as:

> **Something which is difficult to deal with, *deeply* affects its owners, and requires a robust long-term plan if it is to be overcome.**

In those terms, problems are often easy to recognise. To give but a few examples:

- Hezekiah Bigwood and Co. has long been a dominant force in a retailing sector but has recently been overtaken as market leader by its rival, **Herrington-Jones and Co**, but there is also much takeover activity in the sector.
- Scatcherd and Son, once the unquestioned leader in another business sector, is encountering grave difficulties in competing with new entrants to that market.
- The rivers of the Murray/Darling basin may be effectively dead within 20 years.
- Littleworth and Thrupp, the law firm, may lose much of its market.
- The Northumbrian Defence Force's list of requirements for new military assets would cost 300% more than the defence budget.

All of these imply two characteristic questions: 'What should be done about it? Can anything be done about it?' Clearly, neither Hezekiah Bigwood nor Scatcherd and Son can be turned round overnight; maybe they will have to settle for a reduced role in their markets, although no chief executive would be happy with that. Ecological recovery in a river basin may require decades to achieve, even if it is still possible to do so. The Northumbrian armed forces will have to do the best they can with the money available. Perhaps Littleworth and Thrupp cannot survive the changed market, let alone continue to prosper.

A question is: 'a form of words used ... to elicit a response'; 'a point at issue'. We can rewrite that to define a *strategic* question as

> **a form of words used to *stimulate a solution* to a strategic problem.**

The key phrase in italics suggests that a good strategic question will help to generate a strategic plan; it will not simply state that there is a problem, neither will it be so vague as to be unhelpful. Thus, 'what should **Herrington-Jones and Co** do about the year 2010?' does not say why the firm is worried about 2010. Rewriting that as 'how can **Herrington-Jones and Co** continue to be pre-eminent to the year 2010?' is a little better but still says nothing about why they feel their dominance might be challenged. On the other hand,

> 'In the light of an ageing population and the possible growth of electronic shopping, how can **Herrington-Jones and Co** maintain a leading position by 2010?'

is much more helpful. It has the four factors that should exist in a strategic question:

1. *Why* is there a problem? – the population is ageing (as people get older their spending patterns might change) and electronic commerce might become a significant factor in retailing.
2. *What* is to be achieved? – maintaining a leading position in the sector.
3. *When* is it to be achieved (the relevant time horizon)? – by 2010.
4. *How* can the problem be solved? – a feasible strategy and supporting action plans to match the Why, What and When.

> A good strategic question involves *why, what, when* and *how*.

The action plans will usually stipulate *who* has to do something and *where* it has to be done. In total, these are the journalist's (and Kipling's) six questions; we shall meet them again in Chapters 11 and 12.

Whether or not the action plans satisfy the stakeholders is a vital issue and we shall deal with that at length under *congruence analysis* in Chapter 6.

The strategic question for the Northumbrian Ministry of Defence might be:

> 'In the light of budget limitations, what should our 10-year acquisition plan be in order to provide armed forces capable of carrying out tasks likely to be required by the government?'

Ideally, this would be under guidance as to what sort of tasks might be required and the solution would require heavy emphasis on step 3, forming views of the future. In practice, defence planning is not always so clearly guided. (In the 1930s the British government famously stipulated that the assumption should be that there would be no major war within 10 years.)

A strategic question should never be taken for granted and needs to be checked by writing its clauses again so that they correspond to the four criteria. This process is known as *parsing*. For the Northumbrian defence planning problem the parsing gives:

1. *Why* – the budget limitations.
2. *What* – provide armed forces capable of carrying out tasks likely to be required by the government.
3. *When* – 10 years.
4. *How* – by developing an acquisition plan to spend the available money to the best effect.

You should now pause before reading further and check that the strategic question posed for Littleworth and Thrupp on page 7 meets the foregoing criteria. You should also formulate and parse strategic questions for the Murray/Darling river basin and Overseas Carers.

ACTIFELD ## Asking strategic questions

An approach to asking strategic questions

If you answered the question at the end of the last section, you may have found that posing a strategic question is not always easy. If the question is made up on the spur of the moment and is not rewritten to parse it (you really cannot parse in your head), it is not likely to lead to a good analysis. It is very unlikely that one person can pose a good question as the 'why?' clause usually requires a range of views, experiences and insights.

Posing strategic questions is, in fact, a *group* activity and the obvious form of group discussion is the well-known brainstorm. These are usually not good for question formulation as the typical topic such as 'think of 50 ways of reducing traffic accidents' is intended to generate a blizzard of ideas about solving a problem, not to state the problem in the first instance. In practice, a more satisfactory approach is the focus group.

Focus groups

The concept of a focus group

A focus group (FG) brings together several people to discuss an issue in some depth and thus express their opinions about it. They have been much used to give a political party an informed view about some aspect of its (or its opponent's) election campaign. During the British election of 2001 the *Sunday Telegraph* newspaper commissioned its own FG to visit various constituencies and formulate reactions to successive developments in the campaign.

FGs differ from opinion polls because when someone is asked 'Do you think that Mr X would be a good prime minister?' there is no way of evaluating the reliability of the answer. The respondent may never have heard of Mr X and may have given no thought at all to his prime ministerial qualities, but is too embarrassed to admit that and will still give an opinion. Even when thousands of people are polled, they may not share the same definition of a 'good' prime minister.

The FG, on the other hand, can discuss the qualities of politicians at some length and each member can say how they view Mr X. An opinion poll is done on one day and the people questioned are usually not interviewed again, whereas the focus group keeps the same members for as long as necessary and can meet as often as required. The Labour government in Britain has used FGs continually throughout its tenure of office.

Running a focus group

There are two aspects to running a focus group: its membership, and how it manages its discussions.

The membership must be large enough to be *representative* but also small enough to allow the members to get to know each other well enough to speak freely, as well as to avoid endless discussion. The *Sunday Telegraph's* group had nine members, ranging from 20 to 58 years of age. The group must also be *objective*, with a range of views, and the *Telegraph's* group had two people who had been too young to vote in the previous election while the others had generally, or always, supported one or other of the major parties.

The idea behind *managing the discussions* of an FG is that, instead of simply asking 'How do you view the different parties?', the *Telegraph's* group members were asked to compare each party to a house. Labour (the governing party at the time) was described as 'gaudy, with too many Christmas trees'. The house of the Conservatives (who had lost the previous election very badly) was 'derelict' and 'it's a mess and *the question is should they try to renovate it or tear it down and rebuild from scratch*' (emphasis added; source: *The Sunday Telegraph*, 31 May 2001).

Focus groups and strategic thought

The italicised part of the previous quotation gives the clue as to how a focus group might help with the critical issue of verifying strategic problems and posing a good strategic question. Suppose the group was asked: 'If our company was a bird, what would it be?' Consider some answers: 'A kestrel, which hovers over the same spot hoping to find food'; 'A budgie which sits there and repeats what it is told'; 'An eagle which dominates its terrain and is dreaded by its prey' and so on. In each case, a corollary should emerge on the lines of 'such-and-such is bad about that and this-and-that is good, so the question is …'. Similarly, one might ask 'If our production department was a fish, what would it be?' or 'If our major (or minor) competitor saw us as a make of car, which would it be?' Corresponding strategic questions should emerge and an FG can be an effective way of defining strategic issues and posing precise questions to be addressed by the practical strategy tools.

Even when the FG has posed a question, it should still be parsed by some independent person and then reviewed again by the FG. This may seem like unnecessary work, but the effort of getting a good question will be amply repaid later in the analysis.

We shall argue in Chapter 15 that, as well as formulating the strategic question, the focus group also needs to be kept in being throughout the practical strategy project, to manage the process, and to evaluate the results.

Since the team members must be representative, objective, and free to speak their minds, a careful choice will have to be made between using in-house people, bringing in external sources, or a combination. External people would have to be paid and a cast-iron confidentiality agreement would be essential.

Setting up a focus group

Like all the tools for thought which this book will describe, focus groups are very easy to explain and much harder to carry out. Similarly, like much else in this book, it is inadvisable to do it completely in-house, and independent facilitation is often well worth its cost.

Changing the strategic question

When we discussed Figure 1.1, we noted that one of the return arrows pointed back to the question, and it is common in practical strategy for the question to change as the study unfolds. For example, on page 2 we mentioned that Littleworth and Thrupp faced a major change in their traditional market and that they wondered how they could cope with that. The implication was that they sought a survival strategy so the 'what?' clause of their strategic question would be to find such an action plan. On the other hand, we pointed out on page 11 that using the practical strategy tools might reveal no such plan and that perhaps Mr Littleworth and Ms Thrupp ought to sell out while they still can. It is obvious that an exit plan is not at all the same as one for survival, so the strategic question would have changed. When we study Littleworth and Thrupp in Chapter 14 we will find out whether or not that is the case.

For *Herrington-Jones and Co*, it may turn out that the cause for concern is not, or not only, the ageing population and e-commerce, it is also takeovers in the industry.

> Always keep the question visible and revise it if necessary.

If that is the case, the 'what?' may change from becoming dominant to continuing to exist. Perhaps the issues are so pressing that *Herrington-Jones and Co* cannot wait for 2010. In short, in any practical strategy work, it is essential to review the question as results unfold. It a sign of a good analysis, not a poor one, that the question changes as the work proceeds.

In practice, the question should always be written on paper or a whiteboard so that it can run alongside the other steps in **ACTIFELD**. As work moves through the successive steps, the question will either be confirmed as being the right one, or it will change. Sometimes the question is rephrased three or four times, in other cases the question is confirmed as being the correct one, the point being that it is always better to answer the right question than the wrong one.

However, changing the question usually does *not* require one to redo the work in previous steps. For instance, changing the strategic question does not affect what the future might hold. The effect runs the other way – thought about the future led to the question being rephrased but changing the question does not alter the future's prospects.

We now turn to the case study to be used to illustrate much of the next six chapters.

Herrington-Jones and Co 2010   CASE STUDY

Introduction

Two points need to be made before we get into the case material.

The first is that the case was developed by four students on an MBA elective at the Oxford Business School, under the author's guidance. The information is drawn from public sources, such as company reports and websites, but has been heavily revised and does not relate to any real firm. The aim is to make you think about practical strategy tools being applied to firms of this type, not to study in detail an actual analysis of a particular instance.

The second is that the case study is designed to lead you, in the following chapters, through the process of using some of the practical strategy tools but it is not intended to cover every detail or to be a perfect solution to this strategic problem. In fact, it is intended to make you work so that, for example, when we show a mind map for *Herrington-Jones and Co* in Chapter 2 it is no more than an illustration of that technique and you are challenged to improve it. You will have to do the same in other chapters. There is much information available to you from websites and so forth but it doesn't matter if you make guesses or simply invent your own data. The main thing is to become familiar with the tools for practical strategy so that you will be able to use them confidently in your own work.

Background to *Herrington-Jones and Co*

Herrington-Jones and Co is a very large and equally profitable food retailer in the UK. Its annual profits are hundreds of millions of euros and its turnover is billions. Over many years the company has grown both organically and by acquisition and now has hundreds of shops in Britain and throughout Europe and is expanding globally.

A substantial part of *Herrington-Jones's* current success can be attributed to a strong management team with a proven track record. *Herrington-Jones* strives to be highly customer focused and has developed a customer loyalty scheme and more recently an e-commerce home delivery programme. With a strong brand image *Herrington-Jones* is now trying to enter other retail sectors, though for the purposes of this case study you should focus exclusively on *Herrington-Jones's* core activity of food retailing (it could equally well be household goods, clothing, home improvement products, or, indeed, any of several other retail sectors).

Factors in *Herrington-Jones's* business environment

This business, like any other, operates in a complex environment and we shall have to explore that aspect for 2010 in Chapter 3.

For the moment, some factors affecting *Herrington-Jones's* strategic question are:

■ *Distribution*. A grocery retailer, which we have assumed *Herrington-Jones* to be, depends on the transportation of foodstuffs, between producers, outlets and consumers.

■ *Environment*. What *Herrington-Jones* sells can be affected by environmental degradation.

■ *Lifestyle*. Consumer lifestyles affect what is purchased.

■ *Technology*. Technology, especially IT, influences all levels of *Herrington-Jones's* business, from logistics, to supply chain, to marketing tools.

■ *Regulation*. Legislation, whether national or European, might significantly affect *Herrington-Jones's* business.

■ *Integration*. Many European Union (EU) policies are directed at economic and business matters.

■ *GDP*. The general economic climate is obviously important to *Herrington-Jones*.

Herrington-Jones's strategic question

A question for *Herrington-Jones and Co* was suggested on page 11 but, in the light of what we now know about the company, it may not be appropriate. Before going further, formulate and check what you regard as a better one.

Chapter summary

When I teach these methods, students sometimes ask: 'Is this the right way of using technique so-and-so?' I always reply that the right question is:

> 'Is technique so-and-so, *used in this way*, taking me forward, in a useful way, with my analysis of this particular strategic problem?'

If she answers, to herself, in the affirmative, then it is indeed the right way of using technique so-and-so. Of course, I never leave students to flounder, but it is a fine, and imperfect, art to judge when to give help and when to ask people to work it out for themselves; these techniques can only really be learned by self-guided study of a reasonably realistic problem.

The key to success in studying the next chapters is mental flexibility. Certainly, you need to learn the tools as they are explained but you will get nowhere with the real problems you will encounter in the outside world if you apply the tools slavishly. In short, as you read and, if possible, work in syndicates on problems of your own choosing, be alert to adapting techniques to problems, not the other way round.

Reference

Coyle, R.G. (2003) Scenario thinking and strategic modelling. In Faulkner, D. and Campbell, A. (Eds) *Oxford Handbook of Strategy*, Chapter 11, Vol. 1. OUP, Oxford.

Unravelling complexity

What this chapter is about

■ The strategic question has to be answered in relation to its context.

■ Contexts can be complex and we need to be able to come to grips with, or unravel, that complexity.

■ Unravelling complexity to make sense of contexts is an important skill in practical strategy.

■ There are four main types of tool for:
  – sorting out basic ideas
  – understanding the effects of trends and impacts
  – looking at the reasons behind problems
  – taking account of feedback effects.

Introduction

ACTIFELD

The strategic question has to be answered in the context within which the eventual action plan will have to work. The context is frequently *complex* as it usually includes both the internal workings of the organisation concerned and the external environment. It can be difficult to make sense of all that, so diagrams for sorting out complexity are the theme of this chapter.

The reason why we need diagrams is that the human mind works better with pictures when it needs to understand relationships, connections and effects. However, the variety of strategic problems is so great that we need different types of picture for different cases. The chapter therefore covers four main types of diagram:

1. *Mind maps* help to *sort out basic ideas* and identify the factors at work in a problem.

2. *Impact wheels* either depict the current *effects of trends, events or problems*, or show how historic forces have current impacts and, in turn, future consequences.

3. *Why diagrams* portray the *reasons behind problems* as a useful check on the strategic question.

IMPACT WHEELS [handwritten note]

... *back* and show how the causal mechanisms in a ... ...mic behaviour. This technique is explained at ... only because it is the most difficult to master, not because it is the most important.

It is not necessary to draw all these diagrams in every case; use whichever type or types of diagram you think will be most useful for your problem. Most people find mind maps very easy to draw, so a mind map will be used for *Herrington-Jones*, and in a case study in Chapter 14. You will, however, be challenged to draw other diagrams for some of those cases.

> Use whichever type of diagram is most helpful for your problem.

There are, though, many additional types of diagram, some of them little more than different names for the same thing. We cannot cover them all but some references are given at the close of the chapter.

Sorting out ideas

Mind maps

Mind maps (Buzan 1993) are an excellent way of teasing out factors in a problem or summarising the connections in evidence, and they are quite widely used by students to summarise lecture notes.

The essence of a mind map is to start with a central topic, which will stem from the strategic question. For the *Herrington-Jones* case, the initial topic is the factors likely to operate in the retail world in 2010, abbreviated to 'Retail 2010'. From that starting point, one can connect related ideas, and the relatives of those ideas, as a sort of expanding web. In Chapter 1 we reviewed some of the factors in *Herrington-Jones's* business and environment and those aspects are summarised and organised in the mind map in Figure 2.1.

Once you have checked that the *Herrington-Jones* map displays the factors from Chapter 1, you should do two things:

1. Revise the *Herrington-Jones* mind map to bring out your own ideas of the aspects of the business. Reviewing websites for similar, but real, businesses might be helpful.

2. Draw a mind map for the 'lecture' in Chapter 1.

Those exercises should give you an intuitive understanding of mind maps but there is no simple way to explain *how* to draw one; the only way to learn is to practise. What is certain, though, is that the map does not suddenly appear; it is the product of what might be a good deal of debate and discussion by the team members.

Decision-conferencing software can be used for mapping but I prefer to use a whiteboard as mind mapping is a thought process best used by a small team or syndicate. The group needs to have space to walk around, think, review and debate, changing the diagram as discussion progresses. When the group is satisfied, the diagram can be finalised using a graphics package. CorelDraw™ is excellent for that purpose.

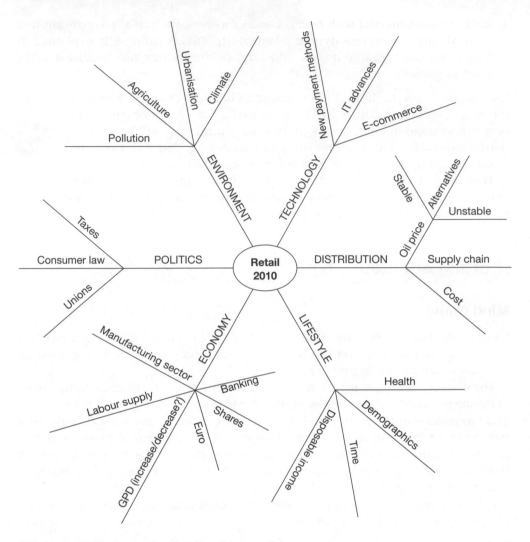

Figure 2.1 Mind map for the *Herrington-Jones* case

We now turn to a different type of diagram for sorting out ideas.

Impact wheels – making sense of trends and consequences

Basic ideas

Glenn (2003) has developed and described what he terms a 'futures wheel' as a means of understanding trends and their potential consequences. We shall use the term *impact wheel* since, for our purposes, they fall more naturally within the theme of sense-making than of forecasting and scenario development.

The essence of *impact wheels* is that one writes down the name of a trend or factor on an oval sticker; for instance, firms such as **Herrington-Jones** are faced by the growing cost of software and are increasingly dependent on it. One then similarly writes down the immediate consequences of that, the further consequences of *those* consequences and so on as far as necessity requires and patience supports. The ovals are then manoeuvred on the board until they start to form the spokes of a wheel. Primary consequences are placed near the original factor or trend, with secondary and tertiary ones further out.

Simple impact wheels

Figure 2.2 is an example of the simplest type of impact wheel (heavily adapted from the original cited by Glenn). It starts with the trend for **Herrington-Jones** to increasing cost of, and dependence on, software (for now, ignore the dashed ovals and the words in bold italic type). A primary impact (lower right) is more funds being needed for software and a secondary impact of that is the effect on other investment needs. Other primary impacts are on quality, costs, standards and productivity, all of which converge on the secondary impact on competitiveness. One might feel that competitiveness, for firms such as **Herrington-Jones**, is a very primary matter so, in impact wheels, the words primary and secondary really refer to the order in which things are written down rather than to their absolute importance. There are similar primary and secondary impacts in the other quadrants. You should study the diagram and, of course, revise as you see fit.

Of course, the impacts may affect one another – the secondary impact of loss of flexibility in developing in-house software may influence the primary impact of lack of standards. There is no objection to drawing links for such effects as long as the diagram does not lose its virtues of simplicity and clarity. Similarly, the hoped-for lower costs from software contractors should modify the primary impact of more funds required for software, but there is an ambiguity – what is the impact of '*lower*' costs on '*more*' funds? After we have examined influence diagrams later in the chapter, we will be able to show how impact wheels can be drawn to avoid confusions such as that.

The dotted ellipses and the words in bold italic, such as ***inevitability***, suggest that **Herrington-Jones** cannot sit idly by and do nothing about their software crisis. Inevitably, it will lead to the funding impacts. Further, if they do nothing, the primary and secondary impacts on competitiveness will come into play. In fact, the ***do nothing*** ellipse makes it clear that the real issue is not about software, it is about competing with other supermarket chains. Such ability to identify real problems is a valuable characteristic of these wheel diagrams and helps to confirm the strategic question for **Herrington-Jones**.

> Wheel diagrams can help to identify the real issues in a problem.

In fact, **Herrington-Jones** has the options of dealing with the problem internally, retaining IT consultants, or some combination of the two. Those possibilities are shown in the two remaining ellipses, depicting some of the trade-offs involved, such as one action needing more people and the other requiring fewer. You will see other trade-offs for yourself and you should refine Figure 2.2 or, even better, draw a wheel for a problem of your own.

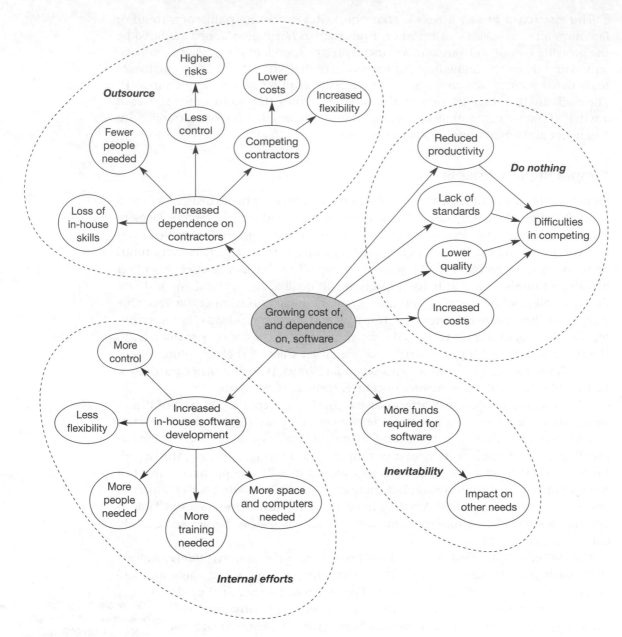

Figure 2.2 A simple impact wheel

Source: Adapted from Glenn's futures wheel, Glenn (2003)

The important property of all the types of diagram is to help you to put a complex issue onto one piece of paper.

For an identifiable 'client', such as *Herrington-Jones*, the wheel can connect impacts to policy options. For a more generalised problem where there is no identifiable decision-maker the wheel still does the immensely valuable service of putting on to one piece of paper the ramifications of a trend or event. That is true in different ways for all the diagrammatic techniques discussed in this chapter.

Structured wheels

There is a natural tendency for wheel builders to see mainly the aspects with which they are most familiar – economists might naturally concentrate first on the economic impacts, engineers on the technology and so on. One solution to that is the *structured wheel* shown in outline in Figure 2.3.

In that diagram, the trend or event is the achievement of European political integration and the primary and secondary impacts are depicted in general terms under six broad sectors. Note that some primary impacts fall on sector boundaries or overlap into other sectors. In other cases, a primary impact in one sector has secondary impacts in different domains of the issue. Dotted ellipses imply tertiary impacts, where it is necessary to consider them; as we have already pointed out, however, *there is no virtue in complexity for its own sake*. Of course, one might link one impact to another, as we discussed above, striking a careful balance between more detail and less visual clarity.

Of course, impacts may not be immediate and one might draw a large D on a link if there is a significant time delay. For instance, D_5 might denote an expected delay of five years.

You could now fill in some of the ellipses for the impacts in Figure 2.3 or draw your own wheel for that problem.

A structured wheel for Cardiff Bay

The elegant city of Cardiff is the capital of the Principality of Wales and, since devolution, the seat of the Welsh Assembly. During the nineteenth century it enjoyed considerable wealth as much of the coal and steel produced in South Wales was transported through Cardiff Docks. Since the 1950s both of those industries have declined; there is now only one working coalmine in South Wales. As a result, the docks area around Cardiff Bay experienced much poverty and social deprivation. With devolution, the construction of the Welsh Assembly building in the docks area and the building of the magnificent Millennium Stadium, Cardiff, and the Bay, is being regenerated and Figure 2.4 is a preliminary impact wheel for that socio-economic process.

The diagram is the work of three colleagues from the University of Cardiff at a seminar. They had literally five minutes of explanation of impact wheels and about 30 minutes in which to choose a topic and draw an initial wheel, which demonstrates how far one can get in a fairly short time with most of these diagrammatic techniques. Of course, the diagram is not a full analysis of Cardiff Bay and you are recommended to revisit this diagram after we have discussed influence diagrams later in this chapter.

Trend dynamics wheels

The next topic in impact wheels is to show how they can be related to time more clearly than by simply using Ds on links.

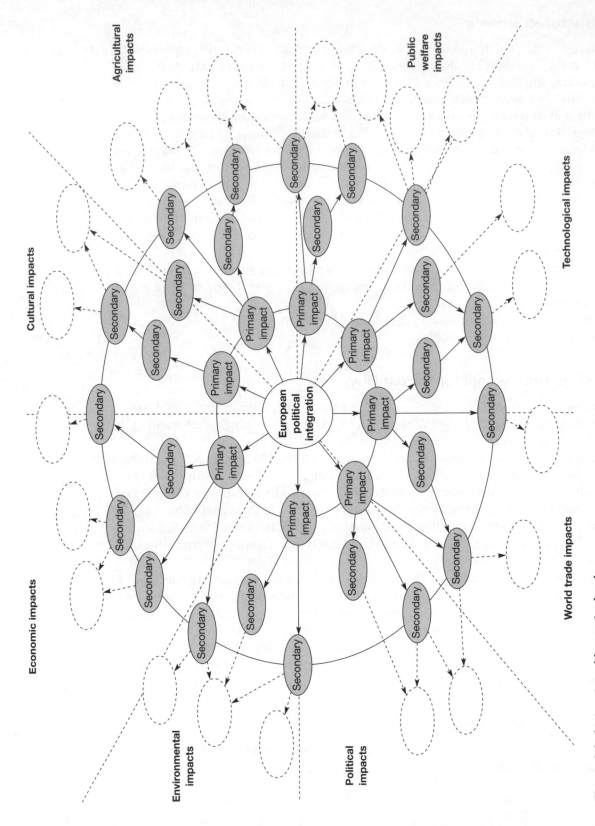

Figure 2.3 A structured impact wheel

Source: Adapted from Glenn's futures wheel, Glenn (2003)

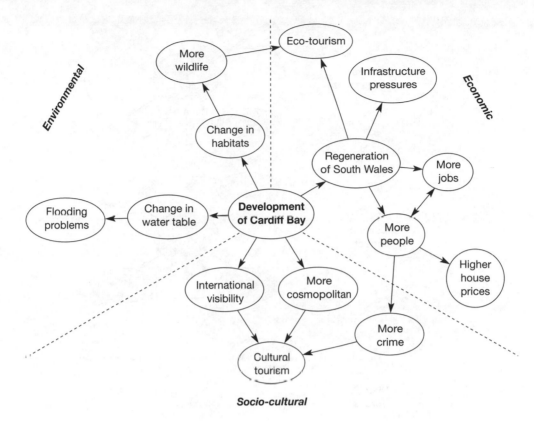

Figure 2.4 A structured wheel for Cardiff Bay

The concept is that the current event or trend may have had its origin in past events and impacts, and it, and some of its impacts, will create or drive a future event that will, of course, have its own impacts. That is more tedious to explain than it is to see in Figure 2.5.

This type of wheel can be useful in political cases, such as understanding the causes of terrorism and the consequences of actions taken against that scourge.

Convergent wheels

All the wheels we have so far looked at could be said to be divergent in that they relate an event or trend to the unfolding impacts it might have. Imagine, though, Figure 2.3, the structured wheel, redrawn so that the arrows point inwards and converge to an eventual event. Rename the eight sectors of the diagram as domains so that, for example, 'Technological impacts' in Figure 2.3 becomes the 'Technological domain' and so on. The secondary and primary impacts are similarly relabelled as 'events'.

This leads to a diagram, Figure 2.6, which shows how seemingly low-level events might lead to a larger effect, consequence or development. What were called tertiary effects in Figure 2.3 can now be seen as triggering factors, leading through events in a domain, or on a domain boundary, to initial effects and major impacts

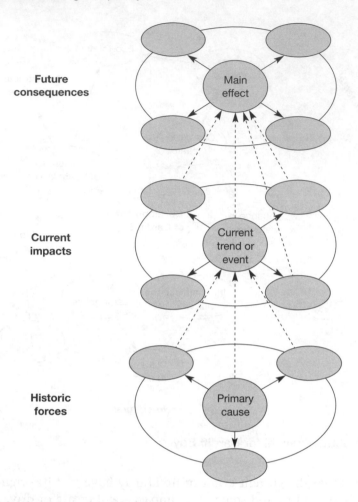

Figure 2.5 A trend dynamics wheel

Source: Adapted from Glenn's futures wheel, Glenn (2003)

to an ultimate effect or result. For example, while Figure 2.3 shows impacts *from* European political integration, the convergent wheel could show the influences that led to that integration in the first place, which might be an interesting tool for historians. As a policy analysis tool, the convergent wheel could be used to study events that might lead to a greater or lesser degree of integration.

Impact wheels and technology forecasting

One might use either a divergent or convergent wheel for the purpose of technology assessment and forecasting. The outer segments in a divergent wheel might still remain as the economic, environmental, social, or whatever impacts, though those categories are used here only for illustration – use whatever categories are helpful.

In a convergent wheel, the domains might themselves be areas of science or technology, such as biotechnology, neural computing and so forth, as the aim is to assess how progress, or lack of it, in a sub-area might lead to a wider effect in another domain of science or, indeed, the socio-economic consequences, for good

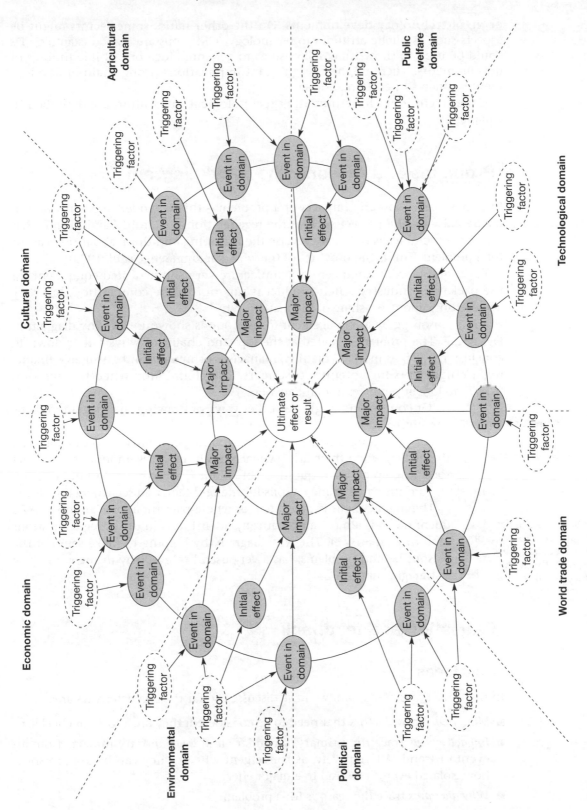

Figure 2.6 A convergent impact wheel

or ill, of technology developments. On the other hand, some sectors might be aspects such as public attitudes to technology (GM crops are a good example). Ds could be used to show time delays so as to get some idea of possible timings of developments. There might be significant implications if one chain of development is much slower than another.

Other techniques for stimulating technological innovation are described in Chapter 10.

Problems and reasons: the 'why' diagram

Impact wheels show the impacts of a problem – the dependence on software in Figure 2.2 – or of a project such as the regeneration of Cardiff Bay in Figure 2.4. Those are useful ideas but let us reverse the reasoning and think about the reasons for a problem. This is the province of the why diagram (Senge *et al.* 1999).

For example, XYZ Engineering manufacture very sophisticated equipment for the packaging industry. Their product is superior to the competition, but they achieve only about 5% share of the market. Why?

Some reasoning by a management focus group is shown in the why diagram in Figure 2.7. The problem is stated at the top, and chains of whys follow down to conclusions such as market volatility, management myopia and unsuitable financing arrangements for potential customers. The chains stop when the question 'why?' no longer produces a useful answer.

Of course, one might see other ways of drawing the diagram. Maybe the limited sales are a reason for the low appreciation of the product's quality, or it might be the other way round – customers cannot appreciate the quality when there are few machines in use. It is important not to get too hung up on such questions of detail; follow the main lines of argument, start from the three prime reasons for the problem, and see where they lead.

> Never allow detail to get in the way of thought.

The main benefit is the *gestalt*, or whole-pattern, appreciation of XYZ's dilemma and, almost automatically, identification of strategic questions requiring an answer. The why diagram, by helping to make sense of the reasons behind problems, has a very useful role to play in the revision of a strategic question.

> *Gestalt* means the insight or appreciation that emerges when you see the whole pattern, not just the separate parts.

Causation and feedback

Basic ideas

In the three types of diagram we have discussed so far the characteristics are:

- *Mind maps* show factors that need to be considered; they are a form of checklist.
- *Impact wheels* trace the primary, secondary and even tertiary impacts from an event or trend. Alternatively, as convergent wheels, they can be used to show how isolated events can lead to a major effect.
- *Why diagrams* trace the reasons for a problem.

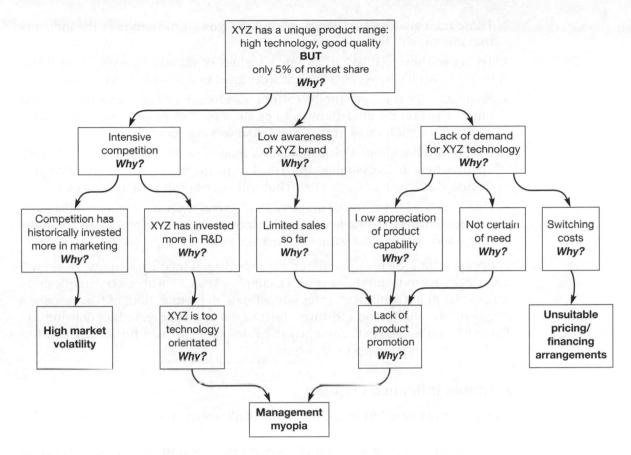

Figure 2.7 Reasoning with a why diagram

It is not necessary to use all diagrams for a given problem but, in a complex or novel case, it might be helpful to use a mind map to sort out initial ideas, and then move to a wheel diagram to try to sort out consequential impacts. If the reasons for a problem are unclear, the why diagram may help to make sense of them. We saw, though, that in the impact wheel one impact might feed back on another, and that there was the possibility of ambiguity about how one factor affected another. We will therefore now deal with *influence diagrams*, a technique that emphasises feedback and dynamics, which avoids ambiguity about effects and which, provided one exercises proper mental discipline, produces good, clear diagrams.

Concept of an influence diagram

An influence diagram (ID) represents, as its name implies, the influence that one factor has on another. On the face of it, then, an ID does not seem to be much different from mind maps, impact wheels or why diagrams but, in practice, an ID goes further than those diagrams do, and in several ways:

1. When we discussed the simple impact wheel in Figure 2.2 we identified ambiguities such as the impact of *lower* costs on *more* funds. IDs avoid that by rigorous rules for the definition of variables.

2. Those rules allow us to use plus and minus signs for the nature of the influence that one variable has on another.

3. Trying to show feedback in an impact wheel could lead to a very convoluted diagram. An ID, however, is explicitly designed to deal with feedback effects.

4. Feedback effects lead to the powerful idea of *feedback loops*, and the plus and minus signs on the links allow us to pick out *positive*, growth-producing, loops, and to distinguish those from *negative*, goal-seeking, loops.

5. IDs are the basis from which simulation models of the dynamics can be developed, where it is desirable and feasible to do so. Dynamic simulation is discussed at length in Coyle (1996) but will not be dealt with in this book.

6. Finally, IDs have the useful property that several mutually consistent diagrams can be drawn for the same problem to show it in more or less detail according to the audience and the point to be made.

These are strong claims to make for a simple diagrammatic technique so we will now justify them by means of several examples. We start with a very simple problem, explaining it intuitively. Later we will state the formal rules of IDs, describe a couple of case studies and end with a brief explanation of methods of drawing IDs. There will be some repetition when the rules are explained intuitively and formally, but that is intended to be helpful.

A simple influence diagram

Rich professors have lots of money in the bank which creates an inflow of £X per year depending on the balance and the interest rate of Y% per year offered by the bank (the interest is paid in monthly instalments for a smooth flow). For a given interest rate, the larger the balance, the greater the interest payments. As shown in Figure 2.8, those payments add to the balance so, provided one does not spend any money, the balance will continue to grow, very much as a snowball does. If the bank increases the interest rate the interest payments will be even larger. All the signs on the links are plus to show that as the factor at the tail of the arrow increases, so must the variable to which it points.

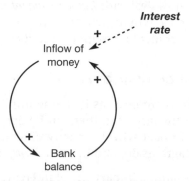

Figure 2.8 A positive feedback (snowball) loop

There is a closed chain of cause and effect from bank balance to interest payments and back to the balance, and that chain is called a *feedback loop*. Both of the signs on the links in that chain are plus so the loop as a whole is said to be a *positive*, or growth-producing, loop, and we have just explained how it increases the balance.

What happens if the bank *reduces* the interest rate to less than Y% per year? The answer obviously is that the lower interest rate leads to lower interest payments on a given balance. The balance will continue to grow, but it will do so more slowly. In other words, whenever the interest rate changes up or down the interest payments also change up or down; they move in the same direction as the changes in the interest rate and a plus sign is used to show change in the same direction.

Finally, the interest rate is shown in **bold italic** type to imply that it is a *pressure point* (or leverage point) in this simple system. The size of the interest rate governs how fast the balance will grow. A dashed line is used to show that it is external to the loop and, in fact, is external to the owner of the bank balance. Its changes are just something to be lived with and nothing can be done about them, other than to move the money to a more generous bank.

Someone in debt has a negative bank balance so the interest rate creates interest charges and the balance gets deeper and deeper into the red. The loop is still positive and is still producing 'growth' but it is now producing growth of debt, not of wealth.

Let us now make the case more realistic and look at this person's spending habits in Figure 2.9. We will assume that this account is for saving and extra spending, and that a separate account is used for regular income and routine expenses.

The upper part of Figure 2.9 is still the growth (or debt)-producing loop but the lower part is the spending loop. Let us consider two people.

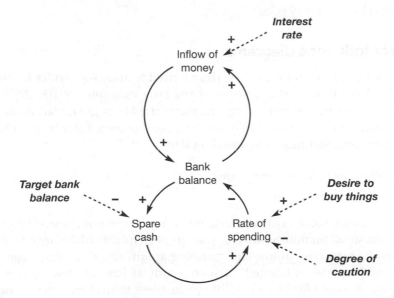

Figure 2.9 Positive and negative feedback

Fred is a cautious soul and has a target below which he does not want the balance to go. For a fixed target it is clear that the greater the balance, the more spare cash he has at any one time. If, however, he decides to increase his target balance then he will have less spare cash for a given balance. In other words, every time he changes his target, the spare cash changes in the *opposite* direction, and that is why we use a minus sign on that link. Like anyone else, Fred desires to buy things such as holidays (his normal spending for food and daily needs comes from another account) but, even with some spare cash, Fred is still careful about spending – some unforeseen need might crop up and, the greater his degree of caution, the less he will spend, perhaps foregoing the holiday, which gives another minus sign. Of course, whatever he spends, the balance will be reduced.

> Don't clutter up a diagram with superfluous detail.

It would not be *wrong* to show that the desire to buy things is influenced by advertising, peer pressure and so forth, but it is always necessary to decide whether extra detail really adds to insight or just clutters up the picture. We shall leave it as it is.

Figure 2.9 now has two feedback loops. The lower one goes from balance to spare cash to spending and back to balance. Its three links have two plus signs and one minus and the net effect of multiplying those three signs is minus, so the loop as a whole is said to be a *negative* or goal-seeking loop. It manages his spending by always seeking the goal of keeping Fred's actual balance at his target level.

Fred now has three pressure points – shown in bold italics – and he uses them to balance his finances against the uncontrollable pressure point of the bank's interest rate. If he gets the balance right, he will be solvent.

Joe, on the other hand, is profligate. He has no concept of a desired balance and has no sense of caution, so those pressure points can be deleted from the diagram. He does, however, like to buy whatever he sees, so his desire to spend is high. He effectively abolishes the negative, goal-seeking, loop and is soon deep in debt. The only control on him will be the bank cancelling his credit cards and refusing to honour his cheques (or checks).

Rules for influence diagrams

Before looking at some more realistic IDs we need to state some rules for them. You will find it hard to understand some of the later examples of IDs if you do not know these rules, but do not attempt to memorise them now; read through them and refer back to them as you study the later illustrations. Later in this chapter we will describe some techniques for building IDs.

The technique of influence diagrams

These rules *must* be followed:

1. A factor (factor means either a variable or a pressure point) *must* be capable of being measured unambiguously, at least in principle. Bank balance is, of course, counted in £ and the inflow and spending are in, say, £/month. Degree of caution could also be 'measured' in such words as low, moderate, very high or whatever, as could desire to buy things. In these terms Fred's degree of caution is high and his desire to spend is moderate. Joe's caution is zero and his desire

to buy is very high. (Fred must lead a quiet life and Joe is a fool. Is there a happy medium?) A name such as 'attitude towards spending' would not be satisfactory as it is not clear whether the attitude is cautious or spendthrift.

2. A plus sign is used on a link if the effect of the factor at the tail of the arrow is to move the factor at the head of the arrow in the same direction. This needs a little explanation. If interest rate increases then the inflow of money into the account will increase and conversely if the interest rate decreases. Clearly, changes in interest rate always change the inflow in the same direction. Changes in the inflow have to be thought about slightly differently as the inflow feeds a pool of money, very much as the flow in a stream feeds a lake. If the inflow increases, then the balance, or pool, of money will increase even more rapidly. If the inflow falls, the balance continues to grow but does so less rapidly, so the effect of changing inflow is still to move the balance in the same direction. Although a pool of water cannot be less than empty, a bank balance can go negative (be overdrawn or in debit) so, if the inflow becomes negative, the balance will start to fall. If the inflow is very negative, the balance will fall ever more until it goes into debit and the debit will get ever larger. The plus sign is still valid.

3. A minus sign has the opposite interpretation so, if degree of caution increases, perhaps to Ebenezer Scrooge dimensions, the rate of spending will fall, though it cannot go below zero. Similarly, the spending always drains the pool of money. If spending increases, the pool drains more rapidly and conversely if spending decreases.

4. The signs imply that you must always use only nouns in names and you should *never* use adjectives such as 'better' customer satisfaction – it is hard to say that you can have more or less of 'better'.

5. A feedback loop is a closed chain of cause and effect. A loop exists if it is possible to follow the arrows from one variable (pressure points are outside feedback loops) through others and get back to the starting point without going through any point more than once.

6. The signs on the links determine the overall sign, or *polarity*, of the loop as a whole. The polarity can be calculated by multiplying the successive signs on the links, recalling the school arithmetic that 'minus times minus makes plus'. It is easier and simpler to count the minus signs. If there is an even number of minuses (and 0 is an even number), the loop as a whole is *positive*, or growth-producing. If the number of minus signs is odd, the loop as a whole is called *negative*, or goal-seeking. Some people refer to negative loops as *balancing* loops but that is not desirable. A negative loop seeks a goal, such as helping Fred not to overspend, but there is no guarantee that his choice of pressure points will be successful and the balance may not be achieved.

7. Significant time delays (see below) are shown by a large D on the link, perhaps with a subscript to distinguish one delay from another.

Rules of good practice

The following 'rules' are guides to good practice. It is not mandatory to follow them but it is usually a good idea to do so.

1. Links should, wherever possible, be drawn as smooth curves to emphasise the circularity of feedback.

2. There should be as few points where arrows cross as possible and it is always worth redrawing a diagram to achieve that. Figures 2.8 and 2.9 are so simple that crossings can be avoided but, where they cannot, do not draw little bridges as is done in electric circuit diagrams.

3. Factors should not be enclosed in ellipses or boxes; it looks messy.

4. The sign should be close to the point of the arrow and so placed as to make it clear to which arrow it belongs.

5. Above all, a diagram must fit on to one piece of paper. Its whole purpose is to simplify reality as a tool for thought and that is lost if it is too big.

A more complex problem

Anglo-Consolidated Metals (AC Metals) is a major international mining company. It spends a lot of money to explore for new mineral deposits and, because its geologists are exceedingly expert, it is highly likely that they will eventually discover potentially valuable ore bodies. The end-point of their work is, though, only good indications of the ore body's probable size and geology. To convert the discovery into an operating mine takes a considerable time and requires further heavy expenditure to gain access to it (perhaps by sinking shafts), prepare it for mining and create all the processing plant and accommodation for the workers. The end result is called a mineable reserve, so the mine development expenditure transfers ore bodies from a pool of known, but as yet unused, discoveries into the reserves for an operating mine.

With large mineable reserves, production can be high but, as the mine produces, its mineable reserves are depleted and AC Metals would go out of business if it did not have discovered reserves from which to create new mines. Equally, AC Metals could not exist by simply discovering new reserves and not exploiting them (Coyle (1981) discusses the mining industry in more detail). The mineable reserves and the mine production rate interact to determine the remaining life of the operating mines, while the discovered but undeveloped reserves and the production rate similarly affect what might be called the 'life expectancy' of AC Metals.

As production occurs, the mines generate cash flow to feed AC Metals financial reserves. AC Metals can spend that money, if it is willing to do so, on exploration and mine development but a choice has to be made on the balance between these two options. (In practice, AC Metals' gold mines in, say, Ghana and Australia might be generating cash that is spent on exploration for diamonds in Canada and developing a new copper mine in Brazil.)

Once the mine is opened, the issue of production policy arises. The processing plant which converts mined ore into 'concentrate' that can be smelted to produce metal has to be designed to take ore containing a certain percentage of metal, within narrow margins above or below that figure. However, the actual percentage of metal usually varies considerably across an ore body, so the ore is mined from different parts of the ore body to get the desired input to the concentrator and to exploit the deposit as safely and fully as possible. This is not a simple matter for mining engineers to manage.

A complicating factor is that most metals are traded on the markets and prices can be unstable. One option for dealing with price variations is called high grading, which means to mine high-grade ore when prices are low and vice versa. Another possibility is to ignore the changes in price, within reason, and to minimise mining costs on the grounds that high-cost producers will be the first to close when prices are low. High-cost mines might have to mine high-grade ore when prices are high, as the only way to make a profit, and temporarily close down when prices are low.

All these factors are represented in Figure 2.10. Most of that diagram should be self-explanatory when compared to the above text. Some features need, though, to be explained.

■ The first is the links from discovered and mineable reserves to the percentage of investment devoted to exploration. The minus sign from ACM's life expectancy implies that large discovered reserves, relative to current production, lead to less exploration. What does the plus sign from remaining life of operating mines mean? What happens to the diagram if the words 'percentage on exploration', which are an arbitrary choice, are changed to 'percentage on mine development'?

■ The dashed line from price indicates that prices need not necessarily affect production and the +/–? implies that, if they do, they could do so in differing ways;

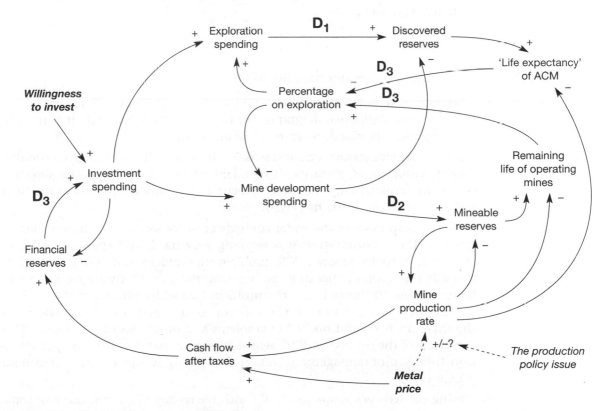

Figure 2.10 Anglo-Consolidated Metals

Source: Coyle (1998)

an increase in price might lead to increased production, it might create less output, or production might not be affected by price changes. Management might increase production when prices are high or they could choose to reduce it. Analysis of the diagram might shed light on that issue.

■ Finally, there are the five large Ds. D_1 and D_2 are the respective delays in discovery and mine development. D_1 is probably about 10 years and D_2 about five years. The D_3s are the planning delays within AC Metals, namely the time lags in their recognition of how much production capacity and discovered reserves they now have and thereby adjusting the percentage of investment devoted to exploration, and, on the left-hand side of the diagram, in making up their minds to invest. Those delays are perhaps about two years long.

You should study this diagram closely and even redraw it. One unresolved issue is that 'willingness to invest' is implicitly a constant pressure point, which does not seem very realistic. It is tempting to assume that expected prices have some effect on willingness to invest but it is an unfortunate fact that it is *exceedingly* difficult to forecast metal prices for more than a very short period ahead – perhaps a few months at most. On the other hand, the mineable reserves and the production rate govern, as we have seen, the remaining life of the operating mines and that might be an influence on investment willingness. Think about how the life expectancy might affect willingness to invest, and modify the diagram accordingly.

Before we investigate AC Metals a little further, it will be useful to study the purposes that are served by IDs.

The uses of influence diagrams

Influence diagrams have *five* uses.

Influence diagrams have five uses:

1. They put on to one piece of paper a view of a complex problem and, with a little practice, influence diagrams can be read as easily as text. It is hard to overemphasise the practical value of that attribute.

2. They can provide an agenda for discussion in which all the factors are simultaneously visible. In AC Metals' case we might visualise the CEO and the directors of finance, exploration, mine development and mining operations seeing their collective problem clearly displayed.

3. They can help to show the wider contexts of other work. For example, during 1999, UTILITY Corporation was working very hard, and spending a lot of money, to solve its apparent Y2K problem (the millennium 'bug'). Ostensibly this was a problem in checking computer hardware and software for Y2K problems, but the ID showed that the problem had wider ramifications, such as contingency planning in case Y2K was not fixed, together with the effects on the share price, current operating problems and numerous other aspects. This depiction of the context of Y2K helped to ensure that it got the proper attention from senior management, rather than being left to the IT department (Coyle 1998).

4. Tracing out feedback loops, as we did with the money diagrams, can give some insights into the factors governing the dynamics of the business.

5. Finally, but by no means least, the ID can be the basis from which a quantitative simulation model of the business dynamics can be developed, where it is necessary and feasible to do so.

Feedback in the AC Metals diagram

You should check for yourself that the AC Metals diagram puts a model of the business on to one piece of paper and could be an agenda for debate. It covers the third point by putting the production policy issue into a wider context. Three of the feedback loops are shown in Figure 2.11.

The growth loop, shown in a broad solid line, is positive. Production generates cash flow that can be spent on expanding production, with a total delay, $D_1 + D_2$, of about seven years. It has a common link from development spending to mineable reserves with the corporate policy loop by which AC Metals attempts to get a balance between discovered reserves and productive mines. This is a negative or goal-seeking loop with a delay of about seven years. The connection between the two loops is the drain loop by which, as fast as production takes place, mineable reserves fall. The strategic implication of these loops is that the choice of how much money to spend on exploration will be a key factor as, if the mines are alternately starved of, or flooded with, cash, the growth loop will not, so to speak, get into its stride and there will be less abundant cash for both needs.

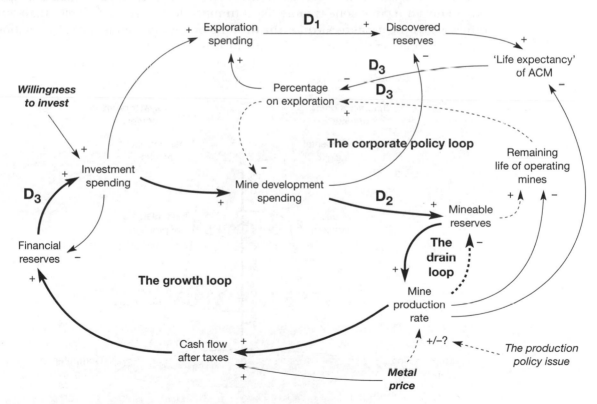

Figure 2.11 Some loops in Anglo-Consolidated Metals
Source: Coyle (1998)

These, though, are not the only loops in Figure 2.11. There is another loop that produces growth in discovered reserves (with a very long delay) and another policy loop. In fact, there are quite a few loops altogether and you should trace them out and try to understand their relationships with the business dynamics and the policy issues. There are no 'right' answers, but the ID is there to help you to make sense of this business and its strategic problems.

The 'cone' of influence diagrams

Influence diagrams are sense-making tools but sense can be made at different levels of detail for a given problem. In AC Metals, for example, the directors of exploration, mining and finance may need diagrams such as Figures 2.10 and 2.11 to unravel the complexity of their related tasks. The manager of a particular mine may need to make sense of production operations at a finer level of detail but the board of directors need a wider view, perhaps because they have to borrow money from the banks (recall Figures 2.8 and 2.9) or manage AC Metals share price. In short, it is necessary, desirable and feasible to draw more than one diagram for the same problem to meet different purposes. The amount of detail in a diagram will depend on the purpose; the names of the variables may change to meet the sense-making needs of different audiences but it is essential that the diagrams be conceptually consistent one with another.

> It aids understanding to draw more than one influence diagram for the same problem.

This idea is shown in Figure 2.12, the 'cone' of diagrams. Each shaded ellipse represents an ID (the cone is more like a trumpet; level 4 is much larger than any other as it is the detail needed for the fifth use of IDs, the building of a simulation model, a topic which is not dealt with in this book). The four levels relate the points of view of sponsor and analyst. Figures 2.10 and 2.11 are at about level 2 as

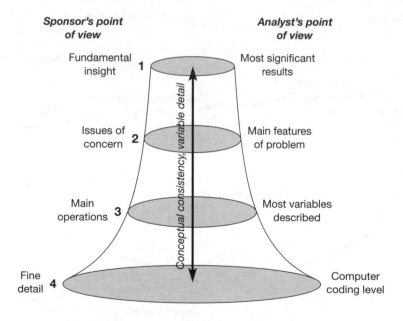

Figure 2.12 The 'cone' of influence diagrams
Source: Coyle (1996)

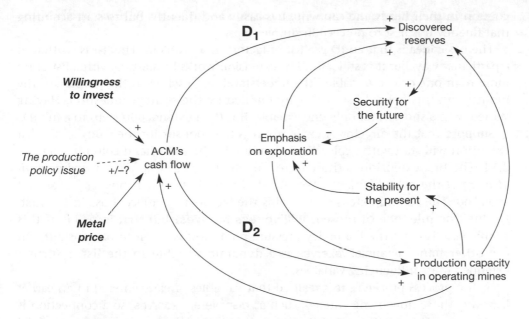

Figure 2.13 Level 1 view of AC Metals

Source: Coyle (1998)

the analyst has dealt with the issue of concern, the balance of investment between mines and exploration, and has shown the main features of the problem.

In a practical study, *work always starts at level 2*. It may then proceed to 3, to make sense of more detail, or even to 4 if a simulation model is needed. The study *ends at level 1*, when the most significant results are summarised and the overall insights are conveyed by means of a small and elegant diagram.

This is illustrated in Figure 2.13 to give what we might call a 'board's eye view' of AC Metals which might be used to brief financial analysts or, and maybe more importantly, be an annex to the agenda for a board meeting as it shows the fundamentals of the company in a clear and vivid fashion. Some of the variable names have changed from Figure 2.10, but the loops shown in Figure 2.11 are still there in more aggregated form (find them).

It is, of course, futile to debate in detail whether an ID is at some level or other. The four levels are only broad ideas. It would be fatuous to talk about level 3.5.

Techniques for building IDs

We have discussed IDs at some length, mainly because they shed some light on the dynamics of problems, and strategy is fundamentally a problem in business dynamics. Once one has mastered the syntax, IDs are as easy to read as text and when you know how to do it they are very easy to draw. How, though, are IDs drawn? That is the topic to which we now turn.

There are three methods for building IDs, two of which are best used as a precursor to a simulation model and do not concern us in this book. The third, *list extension*, is good for sense-making and is the one we shall use. People with much experience of IDs tend to use all three methods intuitively as a stimulus to what goes on in their heads and can write IDs easily and fluently, but to start acquiring that fluency it is best to proceed in simple steps.

The basic idea is that an ID is a list of factors in a problem. The list is written in a particular way, but it is still a list. List extension works by starting with a list of no more than one or two variables, the understanding of which is the purpose of the model, and this 'model list' is usually implied by the strategic question. Having started with a short list of only one variable, it is then extended in steps to a full ID.

Suppose that the director of exploration is the sponsor for the study so the list extension will start with exploration spending in the right-hand column of Figure 2.14. The first extension is those factors in the problem that *directly and immediately affect* the model variable. We already know that one of those is investment spending. The second extension contains the factors that affect those in the first. In this example, one of those is **willingness to invest** but that is, as far as this simple case is concerned, a policy pressure point and is taken to be constant. On the other hand, financial reserves is a dynamic variable so the list is further extended to its influencing variables.

As the process proceeds, it is realised that variables already entered in an earlier list drive those now being entered, such as discovered reserves, so a connection is made from right to left, a note being made that there may be a long delay involved (we know that there is).

You should now do two things.

1. Complete Figure 2.14, stopping each chain when you reach a pressure point, such as metal prices. In most cases, the result rapidly becomes a mess, with many links crossing, and it is essential to spend the time to redraw the diagram to get a smooth picture, such as Figure 2.10, with as few crossing links as possi-

Fifth extension	Fourth extension	Third extension	Second extension	First extension	Model list

Figure 2.14 List extension for ACM

Source: Coyle (1998)

ble. In practice, about four or five extensions are usually sufficient to get a good diagram, at least at level 2. For a really complex problem, such as the Angolan model in Coyle (1998), it is worth doing two or three separate list extensions for different aspects of the problem and then combining them into a final diagram.

2. Attempt list extension for a problem of your own – there is no substitute for practice and no amount of studying examples will really help you.

What, though, would have happened in this case had the finance director been the sponsor of this work and his model list had been cash flow after taxes? The answer is not very much, as list extension should have led to a diagram recognisably similar to, though probably not identical with, Figure 2.14 and thus to Figures 2.10 and 2.11. List extension is usually a good solution to the 'two-analyst problem', which means that two analysts who are equally skilled, imaginative and diligent should come up with at least closely similar models of the same problem. Redraw Figure 2.14 with the finance director's model list as a starting point and see if you agree.

Finally, it is exceedingly important to realise that a 'good' ID *cannot* be drawn on a PC. One of my most useful pieces of 'equipment' is a large pad of artist's paper on which I scribble, erase and redraw until I am satisfied with the diagram. At that stage I draw a legible version using a graphics package. Drawing an ID is a thinking task and the mind and hand need to be free of the demands of icons and software. Trying to save time or effort by doing both of those at once does not give good results.

Applications of influence diagrams

It is virtually impossible to describe all the applications of influence diagramming or to identify problems of business or socio-economic dynamics to which they cannot be applied. All we can do is to mention, under a few broad headings, a very small sample of problems to which IDs have been applied:

health care: psychogeriatic hospital management, unintended consequences of community care, management policy for a large general hospital

defence analysis: counter-insurgency warfare, tri-service air defence, sea control

business dynamics: Year 2000 problems of a major utility company, R&D in a high-technology engineering company, policy in a leading insurance company, staff planning for a management consultancy

socio-political issues: the drugs 'industry', the civil war in Angola

public services: air traffic control, the air travel industry

Each of these categories could be multiplied many times, especially in business dynamics and defence analysis; in fact, the range of applicability is limited only by the imagination and ingenuity of the analyst and his or her patience in working at the problem until a 'good' diagram emerges. What, though, constitutes a good diagram? There is a good deal more to influence diagrams than we have been able to cover in this chapter, but some aspects of an effective diagram are described below.

- Have the purpose and the target audience for the diagram been carefully chosen? It would be ineffective to use a diagram drawn at level 4 for a level 1 purpose.
- Are the factors (variables and pressure points) that it includes consistent with that purpose?
- Are the variables capable of being easily explained to the target audience, are they capable in principle of being measured and can they vary over time? A variable such as 'Security for the future' in Figure 2.13 might be highly relevant to a top-level audience. It might be measured in tons of metal in known reserves, though what those tons provide is security.
- Is the diagram neat and tidy, with a minimum number of lines crossing?
- Can feedback loops be clearly seen?
- Does the diagram fit easily on to one piece of paper? Big diagrams are not good diagrams.
- The objective of influence diagrams is to support thought about policy analysis, so are the pressure points at which policy is applied clearly shown in the diagram? (Recall the pressure points in the money diagrams, Figures 2.8 and 2.9.)
- If it is a level 1 diagram, does it capture the most significant insights and was it drawn *after* careful analysis?
- Can the diagram be redrawn to be one level lower or higher without losing conceptual consistency?
- Do I understand the diagram myself before I try to explain it to someone else, or to write about it?

The car lifetime problem

Before closing this chapter we pose one additional problem for you to think about and as practice in influence diagramming.

Thirty or more years ago I bought a new car and was exceedingly angry that, within 18 months, it had rusted to the point that there were holes in the front wings. By contrast, I recently traded in a car that had given 14 years of excellent service and still had not a mark on it. Its replacement has a *12-year* warranty on the bodywork and there are many similar models. Clearly, manufacturers do not expect to have to pay out on those guarantees and, in short, cars now last a lot longer than they used to.

We need, then, to make sense of the question: 'What might be the consequences for the motor industry, the motoring public, and society at large, if cars last a lot longer than they once did?' Note, though, that this is not the strategic question as such, but making sense of the complexity might help us to rephrase the strategic question of the Minister of Transport so as to make sure that we are answering the right question, not rushing ahead with the wrong one.

At first glance, the answer is that fewer cars will be built because there will be less need for replacement cars but, on the other hand, there will be a larger pool of good second-hand cars available. So, the willingness to buy new and used cars comes into it and that might be affected by the cost of motoring. However, if a car lasts a long time its capital cost can be spread over a longer period. Of course, road congestion increases motoring costs and the government might react to congestion either by building more roads or by increasing the availability of public transport.

However, there are probably quite a few aspects of which sense might have to be made and, as an exercise, you should do five things (and you will learn nothing if you look too soon at the tentative solution on the next page).

1. Spend some time, perhaps half an hour, writing down a list of some of the factors that you can visualise, from common sense and general experience, as likely to be relevant. Perhaps a mind map or an impact wheel will help to organise your thinking.

2. Draw a list extension with a model variable such as, perhaps, numbers of cars in use. It is, though, important to choose the model variable you think is important and not just follow these suggestions. Remember the rule that the extensions are the factors that directly and immediately affect the variable being extended. The number of cars in use is 'driven', so to speak, by cars being built, scrapped, or written off in accidents. You may want to take into account that my new car has a high degree of accident protection, and additional attractions such as air conditioning, which are the result of much research and development by its maker. Spend an hour or so on this task.

3. Now draw your diagram again so that it meets the criteria for a good diagram, such as neatness and tidiness, set out above.

4. At this stage you should look at the 'solution' in Figure 2.15, bearing in mind that its title is 'A tentative diagram'. (The dotted line in Figure 2.15 means that I think that the availability of public transport has little effect on the willingness to buy cars. You may not agree.) Your version may not look like mine but that does not mean that mine is 'right' and yours is 'wrong'. You can probably take the best features of both and produce a better diagram to make more sense of this problem.

5. Finally, you should trace out some of the loops and think about what they imply.

We referred earlier to the possible ambiguities in impact wheels, such as the impact of *lower* costs on *more* funds in Figure 2.2. Fortunately, the syntax of influence diagrams, with its emphasis on defining variables so that they can, in principle, be measured, offers a way out of that difficulty. This can be seen in Figure 2.16, which is Figure 2.4 with the variables redefined so as to be measurable; further, that allows plus and minus signs to be used.

This is not to say that an impact wheel should be transformed into an ID. Each has its own uses; in this case (even though Figure 2.16 should be revised as an exercise) the wheel helps to make sense of the issues in the redevelopment of the Bay area, such the regeneration of derelict industrial sites. If, for instance, regeneration leads to such high house prices that many people can no longer afford to live there and are forced to commute long distances, the redevelopment will not have achieved all its aims.

To refine your sense-making skills, try to form a syndicate with some colleagues or fellow students to work out some of the issues and, perhaps, develop a mind map or an ID for this important and highly practical problem.

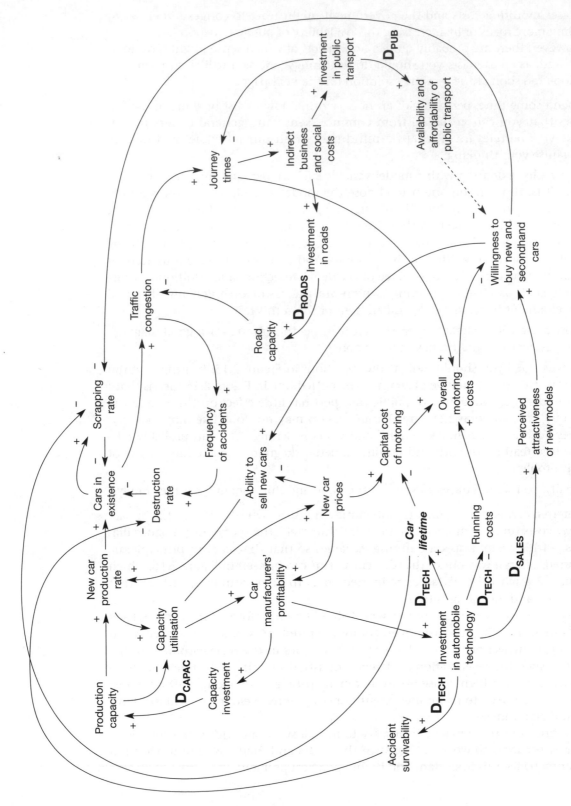

Figure 2.15 Tentative diagram for effects of car lifetime

Source: Coyle (1998)

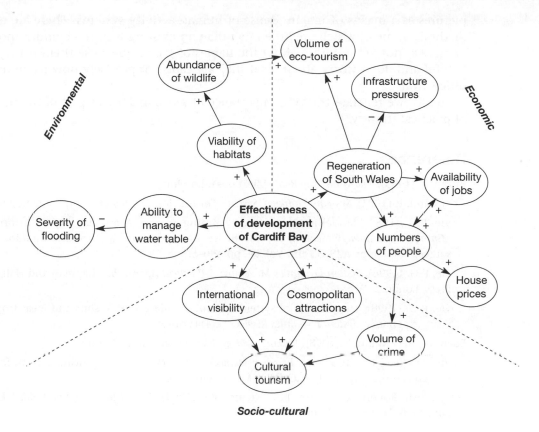

Figure 2.16 A signed structured wheel for Cardiff Bay
Source: Coyle (1998)

Chapter summary

This has necessarily been a long chapter and it will require a good deal of effort to master all its ideas. They are easy to read about, but being able to use them requires some practice. None of them is rocket science once you get used to them but they are a great help in making sense of complexity.

The four techniques we have described each have their strengths and limitations (write down what you think they are). Sometimes one diagram will suffice to make sense, for other problems it may be needful to use more than one. For instance, a mind map is a good way to identify factors in a problem. An impact wheel can show the effects that those factors have on one another; a signed wheel might be even clearer. Wheels do not, however, show dynamics clearly, so, if dynamics seem to be important, an influence diagram would be a natural next step. There is, however, no virtue in drawing diagrams for the sake of it and part of the art of sense-making is to know when to stop.

One of the difficulties of writing about this subject is that there is a plethora of diagramming techniques. For example, Eden and Ackermann (1998) describe cognitive maps and their oval mapping technique. Checkland (1981) describes rich pictures as a means of making sense of human activity systems. There are other methods, some of which are little more than an existing technique under another name. Do not get hung up about the names of techniques; use them if they are helpful and don't worry about what they are called or precisely how technique X differs from Y.

Finally, we reiterate the vital importance of sense-making as part of the process of practical strategy.

References

Buzan, T. (1993), *The Mind Map Book*. BBC Books, London.

Checkland, P. (1981), *Systems Thinking, Systems Practice*. John Wiley and Sons, Chichester.

Coyle, R.G. (1981), Modelling the future of mining groups. *Transactions of the Institute of Mining and Metallurgy (Sect A)*, 90, A81–8. See also papers by Coyle and Montaldo, same source, Vol. 93, pp A28–33 and Vol. 94, pp A90–5.

Coyle, R.G. (1996), *System Dynamics Modelling: A Practical Approach*. Chapman and Hall/CRC Press, London.

Coyle, R.G. (1998), The practice of system dynamics: milestones, lessons and ideas from 30 years experience. *System Dynamics Review*, 14(4) (Winter).

Eden, C., Ackermann F. (1998), *Making Strategy*. Sage Publications, London.

Glenn, J.C. (ed.) (2003), *Futures Research Methodology*. Version 2.0. American Council for the United Nations University (ACUNU), Washington, DC.

Senge, P.M., Roberts, C., Smith, R.B., Kleiner, B.J. (1999), *The Fifth Discipline Fieldbook*, 8th edn. Nicholas Brealey, London.

Thinking about futures

What this chapter is about

- Strategic plans have to unfold into the future, perhaps many years hence.

- Trusting to luck and ignoring what the future might hold is rash, even reckless.

- The human mind cannot *know* the future but *can think logically* about what it might be.

- The theme of the chapter is, therefore, *the art and practice of intelligent thought about the unknowable future*.

- Several futures methodologies are explained but the main emphasis is on:
  - the Delphi method
  - morphological approaches for identifying all imaginable possibilities and eliminating those that are logically contradictory.

Introduction

This chapter deals with step 3 of the practical strategy methodology (the **T** in **ACTIFELD**) – the art and practice of thinking intelligently about the future. It is about forecasting what *might* happen in the future, but not about predicting what *will* happen.

AC**T**IFELD

It is a long chapter because, while the aim is to lead to one particular method of forecasting, field anomaly relaxation (FAR), and to show how it can be used to develop scenarios, we first have to show why forecasting is important in practical strategy. In addition, while FAR is an effective approach to generating scenarios, *it is not the only one*, and it cannot fully be understood without knowing about other approaches that are, in any case, useful in their own right. Some of the other methods will be explained only in outline and most attention will be given to the use of *scenario thinking* – generating more than one view of the future. The chapter closes with a summary of 'the art of the long view', a guide to further reading and, of course, *Herrington-Jones's* scenarios.

The coverage of FAR starts on page 63 but it is recommended that you do *not* skip to that point, otherwise you may not fully see the subtlety of FAR when you encounter it.

When you have completed the study of *Herrington-Jones* and the **ACTIFELD** sequence after Chapter 7, you might come back to this chapter and think about how some of the other scenario techniques might, or might not, also be applicable to the type of problem that *Herrington-Jones* faces.

Is the future a foreign land?

It is tempting to think of the future as a foreign land about which we know little; the implication being that the future will happen and, when we get there, we will just have to cope with the changes as best we can. However, suppose that in 10 years' time you were to say, 'If only I had known 10 years ago that X was going to happen, I would have done A. As it was, I assumed that Y would come about and so I did B, which turned out badly because it wasn't suitable when X happened.' Even worse, you might have to say, 'Since I didn't even think about what *could* happen, I just went ahead and did B.' In short, ignoring the future's possibilities could be rather risky and possibly expensive or even dangerous.

To emphasise the point, van der Heijden (1996) shows that the oil industry lost billions of dollars after the 1973 oil crisis. The reason was simply that the industry as a whole was so used to steady growth that the possibility of a decline in demand was not conceived of. Shell, however, claim to have avoided the worst effects through their use of scenario thinking to sensitise the minds of their management about what the future might hold.

You should now think of some examples in which your firm, government agency or non-profit organisation got into difficulties because of failure to think about the possibility that the future might be unlike the present and recent past.

Only racing tipsters and fortune tellers are prepared to say what *will* happen and one might be unwise to bet the firm by basing strategic choices on such predictions. However, a reasonable person might say, *in the present*, 'I can see plausible reasons why X or Y *might* happen in the future. A would be good with X, and B with Y, but I am not happy about the risk of gambling on one choice. It would be sensible to try to find some alternative, C, which might not be ideal but will still be reasonably good if either X or Y happens. C would be *robust* against the future's uncertainties. Even if there is no C and I have to choose A or B, then at least I'll have assessed the business risks I might be running. *I'll be prepared for change.*'

This chapter therefore has three themes:

1. Truly strategic choices will have to be lived out in a future which is as yet unknown. While some problems might involve futures of about 5 or 10 years, other instances might call for thought about more distant futures, perhaps 20 years ahead. Distant futures tend to occur with major engineering or very high-technology projects. For example, new types of aircraft tend to take 10 or 15 years to design and build.

2. Not to think about what the future might hold and whether a contemplated strategic choice might be wise in view of that is, at best, careless. At worst, it is reckless.

3. Happily, it *is* possible to think with intelligent discipline about the changes that might occur in the future and to get some idea of its possibilities.

The message is that the future does not have to be a foreign land, into which one ventures unaware of its variety and risks, provided that one has a set of ideas and tools for thinking systematically about the future.

Futures methodologies

Figure 3.1 shows several tools for futures thought. The diagram is read from the bottom up, but the fact that something is higher up the page does not mean that it is more important or useful; the order is for ease of explanation. The diagram is effectively a map for this chapter and its labels are headings for several subsequent sections. You might photocopy it and use it as a bookmark for this chapter.

The left-hand side shows approaches which are passive towards change, or which share any risks due to change with others. These are easy to explain.

Under *passive approaches*, one hopes that change will not happen or, if it does, that it will be small enough to ignore. Failing that, reliance is placed on being able to cope – a firm of accountants, for example, knows that tax legislation changes frequently and cannot be predicted precisely, but the firm can rely on its expertise to continue to advise its clients in the changed environment. This 'do nothing' strategy is sometimes perfectly acceptable as not all change is dramatic and not everything can be foreseen. *Perhaps the first step in 'futures studies' is assessing whether the effort is necessary*.

> The first stage is to decide why a futures study is needed.

Sharing risk as a means of dealing with change is the basis of the insurance industry. One assures against certainties, such as death, and insures against possibilities, such as theft of one's car or loss of a ship at sea. However, the Lloyd's of London insurance market was nearly destroyed by failing to anticipate that there might be a series of massive claims.

The rest of the diagram deals with the anticipation, or *forecasting*, of change and will form the bulk of the rest of this chapter.

Projection and modelling

Trend projection, or econometric modelling, uses data from the past to explore the future. For example, the UK Treasury, in common with most other finance ministries, uses a very powerful computer to process huge quantities of data on many aspects of the economy over many previous years in order to make projections of, for instance, inflation for the next few years.

> Econometric methods are based on past data and current trends.

Despite being strictly based on factual data, the track record of econometric projections is poor. The Treasury forecast for inflation made at the end of 1997, when

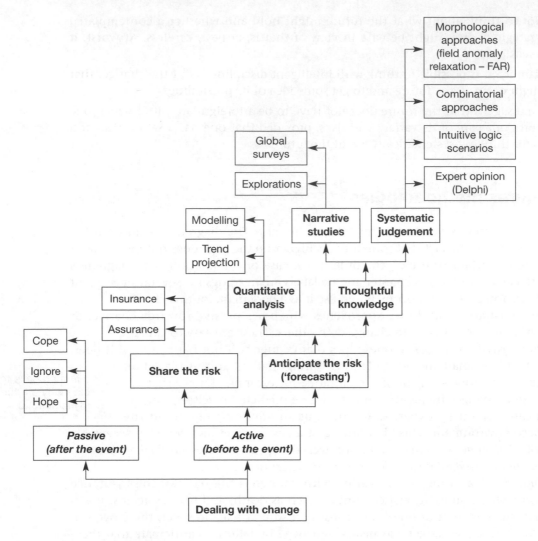

Figure 3.1 Futures methodologies

Source: Coyle (2003)

inflation was 2.6%, projected a 90% chance that it would be between 1% and 4.5% by the middle of 2000. The government's target was 2.5% but actual inflation was 3.5% in May 1999, about at the top of the range of 90% chances for that time, and within only 15 months of the projection being made.

In assessing a futures methodology it is essential to grasp what basic assumption it makes, as that will govern how far ahead it can forecast with reasonable reliability.

The basic assumption of econometric forecasting is that past trends continue into the future so its limit of credibility is *as far as recent trends can be pushed into the future*. Its track record suggests that that is not very far.

The *modelling approaches* include *system dynamics*, a method of modelling and studying the interactions of the causal processes in a system as they play them-

Assess a forecasting methodology by:
- its basic assumption
- how far into the future that assumption holds.

selves out over time (Coyle 1996). The best-known use of system dynamics in futures studies is *The Limits To Growth* (Meadows 1972). That model represented the world's social and economic behaviour over a period of 200 years in terms of a set of presumed key variables, such as population, pollution, capital, natural resources and quality of life. Clearly, modelling the world involves uncertainties about data and causal processes but the uncertainties are not necessarily fatal, as it is not intended to predict precise events, just broad patterns of behaviour.

The inherent assumption of that type of approach is that present causal processes do not change in the future so its limit of credibility is *as long as current causal processes can be expected to last*. System dynamics is very widely used for modelling corporate strategies, where the limit of credibility is usually between 5 and 15 years.

> Modelling approaches are based on projecting current causal processes into the future.

The modelling approaches require the very complex forces in society or technology to be reduced to equations. For futures studies, that may be too great a simplification, so there is apparent advantage in making use of the ability of human judges to cope with subtleties and nuances.

We now turn to the right-hand side of Figure 3.1 and consider methods based on systematic human judgement, starting with the narrative studies.

Narrative studies

A narrative study is usually a full-length book with its author's carefully researched views on some aspect of the future. Its limit of credibility is *as far as human judgement and imagination can stretch into the future*. There is a voluminous and growing literature from which only a few sources have been selected to indicate the main types, though other works are cited for further reading. The reading of narratives is, in fact, an essential part of the forecaster's art. They feed the imagination, and the essence of futures thinking is the imaginative visualisation of plausible possibilities.

> Narrative studies exploit human knowledge, imagination and judgement.

There are two types of narratives, *explorations* and *global surveys*, though these are not mutually exclusive and it is futile to debate into which category a given narrative falls; the distinction is mainly for ease of discussion.

An *exploration* can seem somewhat speculative and might, therefore, be too easily dismissed. For example, a respected scientific journalist, Berry (1995), using the views of reputable scientists, discusses what life might be like 500 years hence. He presents a reasoned basis for the statement that 'perhaps comparatively early in the 21st century, hundreds of thousands of people will have the chance to fly into space'. As a plausible possibility, what are the implications of this forecast for long-term research and development in an aerospace company? Might such a firm find itself saying, 'If only we had imagined that mass space travel might plausibly happen we would have done ...'?

Of course, if a firm did invest in developing space capabilities, that might have the *self-fulfilling* effect of making the forecast become reality. On the other hand, if it regarded the forecast as unrealistic and did nothing, the effect might be *self-negating*. There is thus an intimate connection between forecasts and strategic actions. The point is not whether the forecast is 'right' or 'wrong', but whether it is useful.

> Forecasts can be self-fulfilling or self-negating. Their main purpose is to be useful.

Similar sources, though there are many others, are *The Future Now. Predicting the 21st Century* (Gribbin *et al.* 1998), and *The Next World War* (Adams 1998).

Global surveys differ from explorations in the sense that they take a much wider view and are presented as a connected chain of argument as opposed to a collection of topics. They are not necessarily global in the sense of dealing with the whole world, though that is sometimes the case. They are global in the sense of exploring at some length the wide ramifications of a topic.

To give but one instance, *The World in 2020* (Macrae 1994) is the first true scenario to be encountered in this chapter, as it is *a story about the future*. Macrae, with copious notes and references, and in 300 pages, reviews where the world stands now and then discusses such driving forces as demography, resources, the environment, trade and finance, technology, and government and society. That leads him to an assessment of where the world might stand in 2020 by regions such as North America, Europe and East Asia. His conclusion is that, by then, the world will be a better place, though he fears difficulties after that.

Other sources are *The Clash of Civilisations* (Huntington 1997), *The Coming War with Japan* (Friedman and Lebard 1993) and *Preparing for the 21st Century* (Kennedy 1993). A fascinating variant on this narrative form is *Virtual History, Alternatives and Counterfactuals* (Ferguson *et al.* 1997), in which a group of distinguished historians explore the debate about whether it is legitimate to speculate on what might have been. A typical topic is 'What if Britain had stayed out of the First World War?' This is not, of course, futures studies but such excursions of the imagination can be a useful stimulus to 'thinking outside the box'.

The fundamental assumption of narrative studies is that perceptive and knowledgeable people can, by studying a large amount of information, form judgements about the future. It may be no accident that both Berry and Macrae are senior journalists, whose profession is to study and interpret disparate sources of information. It is important for futures analysts to keep abreast of such narratives as a source of information, insight into the thought of others, and to broaden one's own perceptions.

However, the global survey type of narrative has two weaknesses.

The first is that they tend to be about 300 pages long. How, then, should one react if, halfway through, one sees what might be a mistake, or an interpretation one cannot agree with? For instance, Huntington (1997, p. 246) states that the first 'intercivilisational' war was the Soviet Afghan War of 1978–89, but were the Crusades or the Fall of the Roman Empire earlier examples? Are these slips of the pen that do not matter, or do they undermine confidence in the whole argument? This poses the difficult choice between continuing to accept an argument in which one has found flaws, of rejecting a vast amount of otherwise careful work, or of attempting to repeat the whole exercise oneself. None of these choices is palatable, so the reader of narratives should study them critically, seeking for gems and sifting out dross.

> Narratives have to be read carefully – look for gems and avoid dross.

The second limitation of most global surveys is that they are a single chain of reasoning leading only to one view of what the future might hold. However, we argued earlier that strategic decisions ought to be robust against a *range* of future possibilities, and a global survey which gets closer to that is *Russia 2010 and What It Means for the World* (Yergin and Gustafson 1994). They create four possible future 'Russias' to which they give imaginative names such as 'Muddling Down' and 'Two

Headed Eagle'. Further (p. 135), they link these into a diagram of scenario pathways into the future (from 1994), showing the potential for moves into two extreme cases of totalitarianism and decentralisation, or via a middle road, but with all paths ending at a single future condition of 'Capitalism Russian-style'.

This is very close in spirit to some of the methods to be considered later. The difference is that Yergin and Gustafson's study is founded on what might be called 'learned judgement' and leads to one outcome. We shall examine structured methods, drawing on judgement, but leading to several plausible futures.

To sum up, the last sentence of Macrae's book is the justification shared by all these narratives: 'The more we can understand about the way the world is changing in the run-up to 2020, the greater the chance we have of securing its future.' However, narratives are usually the work of only one or two people, so we now turn to methods dependent on the systematic judgement of a number of people, starting with the well-known Delphi method.

The Delphi method

Introduction to Delphi

The basic assumption of Delphi is that a panel of experts are able to make more realistic judgements about some aspect of the future than could a group of lay people. It is so called for the Delphic oracle of Ancient Greece, though that is no more than a memorable name for the technique as the two Delphis have nothing in common.

> Delphi draws together the collective knowledge and insight of a group of experts.

The method is that a group of people chosen for their presumed knowledge of the topic are asked to respond to a well-designed questionnaire giving their views on when a selection of technological developments might take place: by, for instance, 2005, 2010, 2015, 2020, 2025, later than 2025, or never. There might be numerous questions. Loveridge *et al.* (1995) is an example of a wide-ranging technology-forecasting Delphi. Applications of Delphi to other problems are described below.

The Delphi process

The key components of Delphi are:

- The number of respondents should be at least 30 to 40.
- They *must* be assured of anonymity.
- There will be feedback of their assessments in summary form, so that they can revise their judgements.
- Last but not least, there will be a research team to plan the exercise, pre-test the questions and analyse the results.

After the first questionnaire, or 'round', of Delphi, the results are summarised by quartiles; perhaps a quarter of respondents judged that technology X would be achieved before 2015, half thought between 2015 and 2025, while the remaining quartile was later than 2025 or never. When these data are sent back to the experts for a second round, people with opinions at the extremes of the range are able either to revise their views in the light of any apparent consensus or, and far more usefully, explain the reasons for their assessments, though still anonymously. For instance, someone might argue that X will never happen because it is too expensive, or because technology Y is superior to X and is already near to fruition.

The ideal Delphi process can extend to a third round in which the research team summarise the reasons for the judgements of extreme values (while preserving anonymity) and again feed them back to the panel for further assessment. Those results can be fed back in a fourth round for final assessment. This permits the reasons to be debated; maybe someone else knows why X will not be too expensive. In theory the process can be continued to as many further rounds as the respondents' patience and workload can stand, but four rounds is usually the limit. In practice, two rounds are often all that the respondents will tolerate.

As Gordon elegantly puts it, 'Delphi is a controlled debate. The reasons for extreme opinions are made explicit, fed back coolly and without rancour. [consensus may emerge but] the reasons for disparate positions become crystal clear. *Planners ... can make judgements based on these reasons and their own knowledge and goals*' (emphasis added). He adds that the number of respondents is usually too small for Delphi to produce statistically significant results. The only thing that it does is to summarise the views of the respondents, though, because they are experts, those views should be useful to planners. We will return later to the importance of the italicised comment.

> Delphi should be a controlled debate, not a statistical exercise.

Variants of Delphi

There are numerous variations on the basic Delphi approach of asking people to assess when something might be expected to have happened. It should be borne in mind that Delphi, *like every other technique described in this book*, needs to be used imaginatively. There is no standard form and, when designing a Delphi exercise, the variant most likely to produce helpful results should be used. The variants listed below are not even the only possibilities and you should feel free to invent others. However, there is no virtue in using variants just for the sake of it; making the questionnaire too complicated is likely to produce a poor response rate from the panel.

Some possibilities are listed below.

'Standard' reasons

Even a two-round Delphi is fairly costly and time-consuming, so it can sometimes be helpful to provide a list of possible reasons for extreme values in a 'when might this happen?' Delphi. Some possibilities for very late answers are: 'fundamentally impossible', 'far too expensive', 'would require worldwide collaboration', and so on. Of course, in the second round, respondents could argue why something is not too expensive, so the standard reasons simply initiate the debate. A reason for a very early answer might be 'this has already happened', which would give a very useful sanity check that the Delphi questions are well chosen, as a poor question might have slipped through the pre-Delphi in which questions should have been tested. There should always be room for other reasons to be written in.

Degree of expertise

No matter how carefully the panel members have been selected, it is impossible for them to be equally expert in every possible aspect of the topic the Delphi is addressing. It may therefore be useful to add an extra item for each question: 'State your degree of expertise.' This can range from 5, for someone actually working on technology X, down to 1 for someone who has vaguely seen it mentioned in the newspapers. Answers with expertise below, say, 3 might be discarded.

'If this happened?' Delphis

Another, and very useful, form of Delphi is to ask 'What would be the significance of X happening by 2025 (or some other date)?'. The scale can be from 5 for highly significant to 1 for trivial. This form is good for assessing non-technological questions such as political or socio-economic trends; for example, the X could be 'successful control of population growth'. For such cases, the following three variants can be used collectively, possibly also using some of the previous ones.

Likelihood of occurrence

The likelihood of X happening by the stated date can be rated from 5, practically certain, to 1, impossible (or has already happened).

Degree of confidence

This can apply to either or both of significance and likelihood, with 5 corresponding to certainty on the part of the respondent, down to 1 for the answer being no more than a guess. Two 5 ratings, for example, would mean that I am certain both that it will be significant and that it will happen. Other pairs of ratings have corresponding meaning.

Parameter estimates

Delphi can also be used to estimate parameter values for simulation models. In such a case, there is no attempt to reach consensus or to debate reasons, so the panel can be only a few people. All estimates are tested in the model to assess its sensitivity to the range of possible parameter values. If several people each make estimates for a number of parameters, all combinations have to be tested, which can be quite laborious.

Policy implications of Delphi

Developments in technology, politics or socio-economics can be significantly harmful or they might be beneficial, which raises all sorts of possibilities, some of which are summarised in Table 3.1. (You should extend the table to as much detail as you think is helpful.)

The policy issues in cases B to D might be addressed by another Delphi to pose questions about courses of action that might have the desired effects or which might be counter-productive, or even a waste of effort. A better approach might, however, be the military appreciation (Chapter 12) for identifying courses of action to achieve an aim and producing action plans to implement those courses. Despite its name, the appreciation is *highly* applicable to all sorts of problems, not just military campaigns.

Table 3.1 Policy implications of Delphi

Nature of possible development	Likelihood	Confidence (about likelihood)	Policy implication
Highly beneficial (and high confidence of significance)	High	High	**A** – Monitor developments to give warning of decreasing likelihood.
	Low	High	**B** – What can be done to increase the likelihood?
Seriously harmful (and high confidence of significance)	High	High	**C** – What can be done to reduce the likelihood?
	Low	High	**D** – What can be done to prevent the likelihood increasing?

Selection of Delphi panellists

We have described three distinct types of Delphi question: 'When might something happen?', 'If it happened by a certain date, would it matter?', 'If it would matter (for good or ill), what can be done about it?' and it is evident that each of these questions calls for its own type of expertise. Somewhat simplifying, the knowledge domains are, respectively, science and technology, social science/economics, and policy planning and management. It follows that the panellists must be carefully chosen to match the question and Gordon discusses this at some length. Anyone planning to conduct a Delphi exercise will find his comments very helpful.

Summary on Delphi

The basic assumption of Delphi and its variants is that humans can make assessments of the future. As with narratives, its limit of credibility is *as far as human judgement and imagination can stretch into the future*.

The benefit from a Delphi study is the summary of the debate between experts. The reasons for all views, not just the extremes, are explored and synthesised to give a good picture of the problems in question. The Delphi output gives reasons why something might happen much sooner or much later than had first been assumed; as with all approaches to study of the future, it sensitises people to the future's uncertainties. Table 3.1 links that to policies and actions which might be necessary.

The main benefit from Delphi is the controlled debate in which the reasons for divergent views emerge and are debated.

There are five weaknesses to Delphi:

Like any other futures method, Delphi has weaknesses as well as strengths.

1. It can be very time-consuming to organise and conduct.
2. There is no way of knowing how much time and thought respondents have put into preparing their answers.
3. Although the purpose of Delphi is debate, there may be a tendency to follow the peer group and converge on a consensus answer.

4. Delphi does produce reasons for the divergent opinions but the guarantee of anonymity makes it hard to trace the source of the reasons; the 'audit trail' is not plain.

5. Without doubt by far the greatest weakness of Delphi is that usually no context, or overall pattern of socio-economic circumstances, is specified to provide a backdrop against which the respondents are to make their judgements. For instance, a world generally characterised by 25 years of tranquillity, prosperity and optimism is not at all the same as one of hostility, poverty and pessimism. The potentials for technology, or other, development in those two worlds might be grossly different in those two cases. In short, the Delphi questions should always be phrased in terms such as 'given a world like *this* how do you assess the development of technology X?'. Depending on the willingness of the respondents, the question might be repeated for a world like *that*. Later in this chapter, under field anomaly relaxation (FAR), we will study a means of generating suitable contexts.

Delphi is a very widely used methodology for thinking about futures but, like every other such method, it has strengths and weaknesses that need to be understood before deciding on whether or not to use Delphi in a given problem. Nonetheless, a well-conducted Delphi can be a valuable addition to the futures armoury and it should not be dismissed as being no more than organised opinion polling.

Finally, Delphi produces statements *about* the future, not explanations of how that future came about. It does not produce true *scenarios*, a term which we must discuss before going further.

Scenarios as stories of the future

The term 'scenario' is often used to mean a picture of some point in the future, but that is not very helpful. For example, 'a scenario in which Australia is a republic' describes a condition but does not explain how it came about. It does not consider other possible paths such as Australia becoming a dictatorship, remaining a monarchy or ... . Similarly, simply saying that *Macbeth* ends with him being killed gives no understanding of the complex motives and events leading to that outcome.

> A scenario is a story about the future, not a statement about a point in time.

Just as a play or a novel is a story about unfolding events, a scenario is 'a predicted sequence of events'. Responsible forecasters, however, never claim to predict so we will modify that to:

> **A scenario is a justified and traceable sequence of events which might plausibly be imagined to occur in the future.**

Just as a novel is a story in which time passes, its purpose being to entertain, a scenario is a story about the future, its purpose being to stimulate strategic thought and to guard against betting the firm on one expectation. To pursue the theatrical analogy, scenarios are *rehearsals for the future* (Schwartz 1996). Ringland (1998) calls scenarios '*a well-developed memory of the future*'. A scenario should, therefore, be a story describing a path into the future, not a description of an end state.

Unfortunately, both senses are used in the futures literature, even by authorities on the scenario process. We will distinguish between the two meanings when it is necessary to do so by calling them *story scenarios* and *end-state scenarios*. Where no distinction is made, 'scenario' in this book will mean a story scenario.

Just as a novel is not true, the probability of any forecast of the future turning out to be exactly correct in every detail is about zero. However, just as a good novel has the valuable and practical effect of deepening one's insights into the variety of human behaviour and motivations (the now neglected works of C.P. Snow are a case in point) so the futures scenario has the valuable and practical effect of deepening the strategist's insights into the variety and complexity of the world into which his decisions must unfold. As we have seen, a scenario may be self-fulfilling if its attractions are such that people actively seek to make it come about. Equally, it may be self-negating if its horrors make one try to avoid it. The true value of a scenario is whether anyone changes their behaviour or decisions as a result of reading its story.

A novel, however, is only one story about the time in which its characters live. Strategic thinking requires more than one story about the future in which decisions must live. The stories in the scenario set are required to be equally plausible *but there must be no suggestion that one scenario is more or less probable than another*.

We must now turn to the *systematic judgement* approaches and, in the following sections, consider some forms of scenario development.

In essence, there are four approaches to scenario development:

1. *'Drivers'* of change.
2. *Intuitive logic* in which the scenario is derived by consideration of the significant uncertainties but without the use of a formal analytical process.
3. *Combinatorial approaches* which consider all possible combinations of the extremes of uncertainty, retaining only those which are strongly consistent.
4. *Morphological approaches* in which the scenario team eliminates anomalies from a description of a social field and develops time-line scenarios from the remaining consistencies.

All of these approaches depend *fundamentally* on imagination and insight. The combinatorial and morphological methods have some similarities but also important differences. In all cases, the basic assumption, *and the limits of credibility*, are the same as Delphi's.

'Drivers' of change

The concept of this approach is that one can identify significant aspects of a socio-economic system and attribute to them the ability to shape the future. For instance, it might be judged, perhaps after debate between a number of knowledgeable people, that factors such as demographic change, economic globalisation, technological development, resources, and perhaps three or four more similar forces will drive the future. From those ideas, the next step is to generate some end-state scenarios by considering combinations of the drivers.

In the extreme, two of the 'drivers' are selected and represented on two axes as in Figure 3.2.

This is, of course, simplistic in the extreme. It is possible to distinguish between the four scenario spaces in only a vague, impressionistic sense. It is not clear where one scenario starts and another ends. The point where the axes cross is, presumably, some sort of medium/medium case, but that is excluded from the four extreme positions. Interactions with, and effects of, the discarded drivers are ignored. It is not even evident why the two axes cross at their centres and at right angles.

> The 'two-drivers' approach looks easy but has *serious* weaknesses.

The other weaknesses of the 'drivers' approach are:

- There are difficulties of definition. Terms such as globalisation are easy to use but harder to define in other than broad senses. Saying that it means that industry is becoming more global is a tautology. Saying that 50% of industry is global or that industry is 50% global is meaningless.

- Interactions are ignored. For instance, globalisation, whatever that is, and technological development may not be independent.

- The main weakness is the difficulty of separating cause and effect. Globalisation may be a result of deeper change in other socio-economic factors such as progress in air travel and computing. It may, of course, have effects on those factors and maybe even others.

While the drivers approach has been widely used, that is probably to be regretted and, *especially when used in this simplistic fashion*, it cannot be considered to be a good way of generating either end-state or story scenarios.

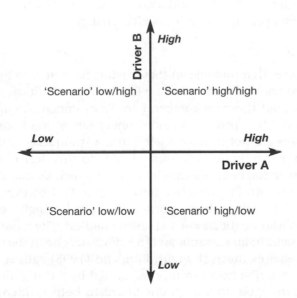

Figure 3.2 'Drivers' on two axes
Source: Coyle (2003)

Intuitive logic scenarios

These are best known from pioneering work in the Shell Oil company (properly called Shell Transport and Trading).

The Shell scenario process

Shell Oil was the first business to use this type of scenario in business and have put much effort into learning how to develop them. Indeed, two prominent figures in forecasting worked at Shell (Schwartz 1996; van der Heijden 1996). Their wisdom and experience can be summarised only briefly; the serious student must read the originals.

Broadly, their scenario writing is based on conversation and study of data. They emphasise that creating scenarios is an art of shared imagination and insight; indeed, their books are respectively entitled *Scenarios*: *The Art of Strategic Conversation* and *The Art of the Long View*. The key idea is that a scenario is a kind of strategic 'wind tunnel' in which the ability of a strategic decision to 'fly' in the variety of circumstances an uncertain future might hold can be tested. Just as a wind tunnel for testing a supersonic fighter might be unsuitable for an airliner, so, they propose, must the scenario be appropriate to the decisions in question.

> Intuitive logic scenarios are also called strategic conversations.

In outline, the Shell process is as follows (Schwartz 1996).

The decision

The focus of effort must, in Schwartz' view, be on the decision context, such as whether or not to build a billion-dollar oil facility, and a scenario cannot be developed in isolation. The first step, therefore, is to select the key factors in the immediate environment that will influence the success or failure of that decision; customer behaviour, perhaps, or technological change.

Driving forces

The significant forces that impinge on those factors have now to be identified. They can be categorised under the well-known PEST acronym: Political, Economic, Social and Technological, but they add another, E for Environmental. Other factors might be resources and conflict; perhaps included under Environment or perhaps treated separately. The keys are not to force oneself into a straitjacket and not to consider the whole world, but only those factors relevant to this decision context. Under these headings some forces are essentially constant, such as that the adult population 20 years hence can be predicted quite accurately. However, there might be critical uncertainties, such as the proportion of adults in single-person households and those couples who might choose to remain childless. The constant factors must, of course, be the same in all scenarios and the differences lie in the uncertainties.

This process requires much thought; Ringland (1998) calls it 'intuitive logic'. Galt *et al.* (1997) describe how it can be supported by writing ideas on hexagons, which can be rearranged on a magnetic board to help to identify themes and group them into patterns.

Finally, driving forces are ranked according to their importance for the decision and their uncertainty. Some might be discarded so that one ends with a few factors which are both important for this decision and are uncertain.

Writing the story

A novel has a theme, such as love or adventure, and the scenario story requires a broad logic or theme. Schwartz suggests several ideas such as 'Challenge and Response'. Perhaps London's position as a centre for financial services is challenged by Frankfurt and Tokyo; what are the drivers and uncertainties affecting the viability of a strategic response? Other themes are 'Winners and Losers' and 'Infinite Possibility'. The point is not what these themes are but to emphasise the imaginative act of getting into the deepest essence of the decision and thinking, as it were, of the type of wind tunnel which will test its ability to fly.

It is extremely important to think of a simple, memorable, name for each scenario which will immediately call to mind its essence. For example, Ringland (1998) describes the Mont Fleur scenarios, developed at the time of negotiations for transition to inclusive democracy in South Africa, and her Table 3.2 makes it clear that the descriptive name strikingly encapsulates each scenario.

It is important to note that there are *four* Mont Fleur scenarios, because that is what the issues required. By contrast, there is a temptation to have three scenarios, calling them Best Case, Worst Case, and Business as Usual. The names are not imaginative and there is an assumption that things might get better or worse or they might not change. What if things could only get better or they could only get worse? The idea of Business as Usual implies no change, and that is one description of the future which, by definition, is rather implausible. *The key is to have as many or as few scenarios as the uncertainties around the decision require and to describe them by strikingly memorable names.*

> Avoid calling your scenarios 'best case', 'worst case' and 'business as usual'.

Implications

The final stage of the Shell process is to assess the implications of a scenario, and techniques for doing so are described in the rest of this book, though those

Table 3.2 The Mont Fleur scenario names

Scenario number	Summary	Descriptive name
1	Negotiations do not achieve a settlement – non-representative government.	*Ostrich*
2	Transition not rapid and decisive – government that emerges is incapacitated.	*Lame Duck*
3	Democratic government's policies are not sustainable, collapse inevitable.	*Icarus*
4	Government policies sustainable – South Africa can achieve democracy and growth.	*Flight of the Flamingos*

Source: Ringland (1998)

approaches derive from other work and are not necessarily those used in Shell. Having assessed the implications, Schwartz argues that *leading indicators* have to be established as a means of identifying which scenario is closest to the truth as time passes. Since, however, the value of a scenario lies in making people think, and no scenario claims to be a prediction, the value of those indicators is not clear.

Scenario cases

An excellent way of developing the mindset needed for scenario thinking is to study examples. Ringland (1998) and Galt *et al*. (1997) have case studies of their own, and others' work. There is, moreover, no single ideal way of developing scenarios and Ringland, in particular, describes ways in which different organisations have developed their own approach and learned how to use it.

Combinatorial scenarios

Von Reibnitz (1988), as with all scenario workers, emphasises that scenarios are an act of imagination and judgement, but supports their development by a process which first searches all combinations of the uncertainties and then eliminates those which are not internally consistent.

The initial idea is shown in Table 3.3. In this instance, the client in question has identified numerous factors in the problem, only a few of which are shown in Table 3.3. Each is allowed to have two extreme conditions, such as high and low,

Table 3.3 Consistency matrix

		1 New technologies a	b	2 GNP a	b	3 Structural change a	b
1. New technologies	(a) Success		x				
	(b) Flop						
2. GNP	(a) Growth	2	0		x		
	(b) Decline	0	1				
3. Structural change	(a) Success	2	−1	2	−1		x
	(b) Flop	−1	2	0	2		
4. Unemployment rate	(a) Higher	0	1	0	2	0	1
	(b) Lower	1	0	2	−1	1	0

Source: von Reibnitz (1988 p. 45)

success and flop, and so on. The client then makes judgements such as 'GNP growth is consistent with success in new technologies'. In this case, the consistency is deemed to be strong and is given a rating of 2, moderate consistency being rated at 1. However, it is judged that flop in structural change would not be consistent with success in new technologies, which is rated at –1. Von Reibnitz's method does allow for strong inconsistency, rated at –2, but she states that this is rarely used in practice. A rating of 0 means no effect. A consistency matrix can be as large as required and, apparently, more than 100 factors can be considered.

Simply by looking at Table 3.3 it is clear that a combination of success with new technology, growth in GNP, successful structural change and lower unemployment does not involve any contradictions; all the numbers are positive. Similarly, failure of new technology, declining GNP, failure of structural change and higher unemployment do not involve any negative ratings and hence is also consistent, albeit very different from the previous instance. Von Reibnitz uses a proprietary computer program to test all the possible combinations for their consistency.

Von Reibnitz's approach also tests what she terms internal stability, though without giving details of the method. She states that, typically, out of 1,000 combinations only about 30 are strongly consistent and, of those, only about 15 will be stable and, of those, a few will appear which are consistent, stable, and very different from one another.

Her approach, like all the methods described in this chapter, has strengths and weaknesses. It has the advantage of exploring a large number of possibilities before selecting only a few, as opposed to pre-selecting only a few for detailed exploration. Its concept of identifying and avoiding logical contradictions is powerful and is very close to the morphological methods discussed below. Its weakness is that each factor is limited to only two extreme conditions; GNP either rises or falls, it does not remain unchanged. Many factors can be dealt with, whereas the morphological methods are restricted to not more than seven. That may or may not be a strength of von Reibnitz's approach, as the limit of seven arises from the inability of humans to grasp more than that number of factors at once and hence to see an overall picture. When the combinatorial approach handles, say, 100 factors it will not be possible to form an appreciation of the complete pattern of circumstances. A final weakness is that it seems to be difficult to trace a path from the present into the futures her technique picks out.

Morphological scenarios – field anomaly relaxation (FAR)

Introduction

The starting point of FAR comes from a social science theory to the effect that we all live within 'fields' of interactions with other people and events. For example, someone's personal 'field' might include such factors as interest rates on the mortgage, pleasure in one's garden, a choice between going on holiday to a favourite place or buying a new car, an interest in genealogy and so on for myriads of aspects such as the fact that Aunt Mabel's cat had kittens last week but one died. A person's field is infinitely fine-grained, even down to the detail of why the kitten died.

This notion is used in *morphological forecasting*, morphology meaning 'the form and structure of anything'.* The principles are that the logical structures within social fields will govern the possible future states that might emerge, and that connections between those feasible states will suggest conceivable paths into the future. FAR should thus generate story scenarios, not just end-state pictures. Clearly, though, Aunt Mabel and her cat have to be ignored and a coarse-grained field has to be composed using broader aspects such as economic growth, political stability and so forth. The first word in FAR thus means the simplified *field* of relationships for the societal or business environment in which policy has to be made. Like all simplifications of reality it is a model, the intention of which is to give a tool for rational and systematic thought about the future's possibilities.

> Morphology means 'the form and structure of anything', in this case of the future.

Each of the components of the field must have several conceivable conditions; economic growth might be high, low, stagnant, and so on. The idea is to create 'filing space' for all plausible possibilities. One of the possibilities for the political aspect might, for instance, be 'instability' and it is easy to see that a politically unstable world could not, at the same time, have high economic growth. Such an incongruous world could not be believed to exist, either now or in the future, so the anomalies can be eliminated from the field, hence the name *field anomaly* relaxation, for this scenario approach. FAR differs from von Reibnitz's method in that GNP, for example, is not restricted just to growth or decline but might also be allowed to be unchanged, grow slowly, decline very rapidly, or whatever is needed. We shall explain relaxation below but it does *not* mean the process of eliminating anomalies.

FAR also differs from the intuitive logic approach in that it is not directed to supporting a specific decision. Rather, it aims to provide a backdrop of internally consistent futures as contexts for policy formulation and decision-making. The contexts should not normally be tailored to any specific decision, as was the case with the Shell process. Rather, they should be potentially applicable for broader policy-making and decision analysis across the organisation as a whole by providing consistent and coherent views of the future. FAR aims to illuminate the strategic questions discussed in Chapter 1, not to answer them.

> FAR gives a set of consistent futures as a context for decision-makers.

The method is due to Rhyne (1981, 1995a) who applied it to a wide range of social fields in which business and governmental policies might have to live. His account of its application to problems of Indonesian defence in the 1970s (Rhyne 1995b, published 20 years after the work) is a masterpiece of scenario thinking, especially for its painful honesty about all the things that went wrong in the management and organisation of the project. More recent applications are to regional problems in the South West Pacific (Coyle and McGlone 1995) and the South China Sea (Coyle and Yong 1996). It has also been used in several confidential applications in the writer's consultancy work for governmental and commercial clients. Since it involves a very systematic procedure it requires to be described at greater length than the intuitive logic of the Shell approach.

---

*We shall have much more to say about morphological methods in Chapter 10, where references will be given.

The FAR approach to scenarios has a number of attractive features:

- It is fundamentally based on imagination, insight and judgement exactly as in the Shell process.

- It gives a clear audit trail of the logic underlying the scenarios it produces.

- All conceivable options are examined before discarding those which are infeasible, as is the case with von Reibnitz's approach.

- The scenarios are true scenarios in that they are traceable paths into the future.

- It generates as many or as few scenarios as the case calls for and is not restricted to only two or three pre-selected themes.

You should evaluate these features in the ensuing discussion and, critically important, form your own assessments of FAR's weaknesses *vis-à-vis* those of the methods already considered.

The FAR process

The FAR process works best with a small study team doing the detail, supported by a steering group of decision-makers. It is a four-stage process, as shown in Figure 3.3. Step 1 requires the development of some kind of imaginative view of the future into which the decision must unfold. Step 2 is very much as the Shell process and requires one to identify the critical uncertainties and their ranges of possibility, expressed in a matrix. Step 3 eliminates the anomalies after which, in step 4, the surviving configurations can be strung together to form scenario outlines.

FAR is cyclic in that the scenarios developed in step 4 will, ideally, make one think more deeply about the future and hence lead to another iteration of the FAR cycle, leading to better scenarios. This convergence towards a satisfactory solution is called relaxation in engineering, hence the full name of field anomaly *relaxation*. In practice, the first cycle may produce such good scenarios that the added effort may not be worth while. In any case, decision-makers may require the scenarios urgently as a basis for judgement and time may not be available for a second cycle.

Whether there are one or two iterations, the process ends by using the scenario outlines as the plots around which stories of the future can be written. FAR leads to a collection of short stories rather than one extended narrative. In use by the author it typically leads to about four scenarios, though Rhyne's work often gave rise to about 10.

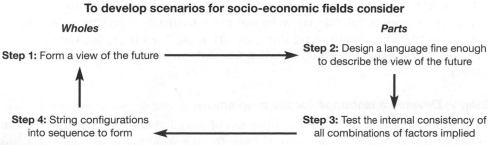

To develop scenarios for socio-economic fields consider

Wholes   *Parts*

Step 1: Form a view of the future ⟶ **Step 2:** Design a language fine enough to describe the view of the future

Step 4: String configurations into sequence to form ⟵ **Step 3:** Test the internal consistency of all combinations of factors implied

Figure 3.3 The FAR Cycle (after Rhyne)
Source: Rhyne (1995a)

A worked example of FAR

We now illustrate that process using the South China Sea case study which sought to develop unofficial scenarios as contexts for policy-making on Singapore's trade and defence relationships with, and economic support for, other nations in the region.

Step 1: Visualise the future

This is best done by asking five or six members of the steering group to write short essays in which they imagine what the future might be like in the South China Sea region. They might be allowed to choose their own themes or they might be given guidance, such as 'write about a gloomy future'. That does not necessarily mean that one aims at a gloomy scenario, the purpose is to tease out the factors the essayists see as significant in the region's future and it may turn out that a gloomy scenario will not emerge from the final analysis.

> Writing essays can be a good way of visualising the future to start the FAR process.

The same process works well whether the context is the socio-economic field for a business firm, the industry in which it operates, or transport planning for a city. It is, however, vital that the essayists work independently and that they draw on deep knowledge of the problem domain using whatever data and information are available. The end result is a narrative, somewhat on the lines of Macrae's work, though *much* shorter.

Teasing out the factors is most easily done using mind maps (Chapter 2). These allow one to string together individual comments by the essayists into a picture of the things they mentioned. Not uncommonly, they make the project team think of other aspects. The mind map for the South China Sea appears in Figure 3.4.

The radiating branches in Figure 3.4 show that China, economic growth, and so forth are themes in the essays and hence are aspects of the problem. One need not use those branch labels exactly; they are only a convenient way of abstracting ideas from the texts of the essays. Instead, one seeks a *gestalt* appreciation of the web of factors: in other words, a 'perception of a pattern or structure possessing qualities as a whole that cannot be described merely as a sum of its parts'. This is the most imaginative step in FAR and may need two or three tries before the right language can be found.

It is very important that the main themes, or sectors as they are called in FAR, be arranged to make a memorable acronym, ESPARC in this case. Thus, the Economic dimension is first only because it is first in ESPARC, not because it is the most important sector. ESPARC has now become a word, otherwise meaningless, which is a meta-language for this problem. *It is also important that each sector name is supported by thorough documentation of what is meant by, say, China's attitude.*

Finally, it is essential that there be not more than seven sectors as that is the maximum that the human mind can grasp. That limit led to Japan, mentioned in the mind map, being discarded as not sufficiently important to justify a sector of its own.

Step 2: Develop a language for the problem

Each sector is broken down into a collection of so-called factors. These are the fine detail of sector behaviour and are chosen to give what we earlier called 'filing space' for all plausible possibilities. *Each factor is, again, supported by explanatory*

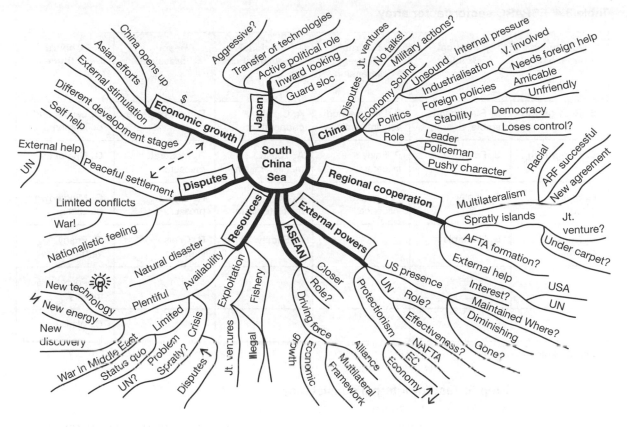

Figure 3.4 The South China mind map
Source: Coyle and Yong (1996)

documentation, even though it is summarised in a pithy phrase in the matrix. In this case, the end result is shown in Table 3.4. There is no theoretical limit to the number of factors for each sector but experience suggests that seven is a convenient, though not overriding, maximum.

The sequences of the factors in the columns of Table 3.4 are chosen simply for convenience. In the Economic dimension column, for instance, the progression from E_1, Rosy growth, to E_4, Negative growth, has no greater significance than that it makes for easy reading of the filing space of possibilities for the economic aspects of the problem. Further, and this is the vital point, the arrangement in the columns does *not* mean that a factor can only change to the next adjacent state. Again using E as the example, if the current condition is E_2, Fair growth, then, if things get better, the only possible move is to E_1, but if they get worse, the move could be to either E_3 *or* to E_4. Similarly, if China's attitude now is C_3, then it could change to C_1, C_5 or C_6, and does not have to move via C_2 or C_4. In short, the identifying numbers on the factors are no more important than the labels of files in a filing cabinet. Reading one file in a cabinet does not force one to read only the adjacent file. *In FAR, the numbers are only labels and have no other significance.*

Table 3.4 ESPARC sector/factor array

Economic dimension E	Political Stability S	External Power dimension P	Regional coop/Alliance A	Resource pressure R	China's attitude C
E_1 Rosy growth	S_1 Strong and stable	P_1 Effective and very influential	A_1 Close cooperation	R_1 Low pressure	C_1 Leader and policeman
E_2 Fair growth	S_2 Fairly stable	P_2 Fairly influential	A_2 Loose multilateralism	R_2 Moderate pressure	C_2 One of us
E_3 Stifled growth	S_3 Shaky	P_3 Limited influence	A_3 No multilateralism	R_3 High pressure	C_3 Minds own business
E_4 Negative growth	S_4 Unstable		A_4 Enmity	R_4 Crisis situation	C_4 Pushy, verbally
					C_5 Forceful, military
					C_6 Warlike

Source: Coyle and Yong (1996)

Step 3: Test for internal consistency

A 'world' for the South China Sea can be described by taking one factor from each sector. For example, $E_2S_2P_3A_2R_2C_3$ can be appreciated, in the gestalt sense, as a world in which self-help is under way – study the table to see this. The use of ESPARC and its subscripts is, at first, confusing, but one rapidly becomes fluent in the meta-language so that $E_2S_2P_3A_2R_2C_3$ takes on a meaning of its own.

Unfortunately, Table 3.4 has 4,608 combinations of ESPARC, and that number of possible worlds is far too large to be useful. In a larger case, 7 sectors and 7 factors would give 823,543 combinations. What makes FAR work is the gestalt appreciation that one could not conceive of a world in which the economic dimension was E_1, Rosy growth throughout the region and, at the same time, China was warlike, C_6. That is an anomalous world and eliminating it from the problem reduces the number of worlds to 4,416.* The whole FAR process is supported by the software described in Appendix 1.

The end result is shown in Table 3.5 in which 0 denotes a combination which is manifestly inconsistent, 1 indicates probably inconsistent, 2 is probably consistent, and 3 means certainly consistent. Eliminating those with scores of 0 and 1 leaves 91 survivors. When these are examined as whole patterns, using the gestalt criterion of 'could I imagine a world like that?', a further 15 were eliminated. This is supported by the consistency ratings. With six sectors, there are 15 pairwise combinations, all of which have to be reasonably consistent for the configuration as a whole to be consistent. Of course, if any one of the pairs is inconsistent, the

---

*There are 192 combinations in the SPAR columns (4^3*3) and 24 in E and C. When the pair E_1 and C_6 is eliminated, 23 of those remain, or 192 of the total have been eliminated. In a 7×7 matrix, eliminating the first anomaly removes 16,807 combinations.

Table 3.5 The ESPARC sector/factor pair matrix

	$S_1\ S_2\ S_3\ S_4$	$P_1\ P_2\ P_3$	$A_1\ A_2\ A_3\ A_4$	$R_1\ R_2\ R_3\ R_4$	$C_1\ C_2\ C_3\ C_4\ C_5\ C_6$
E_1	3 2 0 0	2 2 2	3 2 1 0	3 3 1 0	1 3 2 1 1 0
E_2	3 3 1 0	2 2 2	3 3 1 0	3 3 1 0	3 3 3 1 1 0
E_3	1 2 3 1	2 2 2	1 1 3 3	1 2 3 1	1 1 3 3 1 1
E_4	0 1 3 3	2 2 2	0 1 2 3	1 1 3 3	1 1 2 3 3 3
S_1		3 2 2	3 2 1 0	3 2 0 0	1 3 2 0 0 0
S_2		2 3 2	2 3 1 0	2 3 1 0	2 3 2 1 1 0
S_3		1 2 3	1 2 3 1	1 2 3 2	1 1 2 3 1 1
S_4		0 1 3	0 1 3 3	1 1 3 3	1 1 2 3 3 3
P_1			2 2 2 1	3 2 1 1	2 3 3 1 1 1
P_2			2 2 2 1	3 3 2 1	3 3 3 2 1 1
P_3			2 2 2 3	3 3 2 2	3 3 2 3 3 3
A_1				3 2 1 0	1 3 2 1 0 0
A_2				2 3 2 1	3 3 3 3 3 1
A_3				2 3 3 2	1 1 3 3 2 1
A_4				0 1 3 3	1 1 2 3 2 2
R_1					1 3 1 1 0 0
R_2					2 3 3 1 1 0
R_3					3 1 1 3 3 1
R_4					1 1 1 2 3 3

Source: Coyle and Yong (1996)

whole configuration is inconsistent. If the maximum possible score for a given pair is 3, the maximum for a six-member configuration is 45 and any configurations scoring less than, say, 35, can be eliminated.* This process is analogous to von Reibnitz's approach.

Further study of the surviving configurations shows some pairs which are such similar 'worlds' that they can be clustered into one. The combinations of closely comparable configurations are denoted as $E_2S_{1/2}P_{2/3}A_2R_2C_2$ for configuration F, and similarly elsewhere in the tree. The end result is that there are 26 clusters.

Step 4: Form scenarios

The 26 clusters are not themselves scenarios but are the bricks from which scenarios are constructed and that is the stage of FAR most demanding of imagination and patience. The technique is to write each cluster on a Post-It sticker with an identifying letter *and* a few words which characterise that cluster. A few examples are 'ASEAN (the Association of South East Asian Nations) starting to take shape', 'End of disputes over South China Sea (SCS) resources', 'Worldwide energy crisis

*The reason for this apparently arbitrary step is that a 6-member configuration has 15 pairs. If 5 of them are strongly consistent and rated at 3, but 10 are only moderately so, rated at 2, the configuration *as a whole* becomes suspect. Clearly, 5 threes and 10 twos come to 35.

sparks severe tensions over the oil resources of the SCS' and so on. The stickers are then simply manoeuvred on a board until they fall into sequences, always applying the gestalt appreciation of 'Can I see *this* world leading to *that* one?' This process may take a week or so, not of full-time effort but of sessions looking at the board and intervals of other work while the ideas filter through the minds of the study team.

It is essential that the stickers and their labels be large enough to be legible while one walks round the room and thinks. Developing the sequences on a computer is bad practice, though the results should, of course, be recorded using a graphics package.

For the South China Sea, the end result is shown in Figure 3.5 in which there are four groups of paths. The solid lines indicate transitions which the team could visualise with confidence, and the dotted lines are transitions which were seen as less plausible.

For example, there are plausible paths to P, though, beyond that, if the less plausible transitions do not occur, the state P will simply continue with Asia never fully developing its own identity. State C might be reached fairly quickly from A, or more slowly via B. State S is a resource crisis elsewhere in the world and, since assessing the plausibility of that is somewhat beyond the frame of reference of this study, it is shown as a 'wild card' which would be the triggering agent of a move from a rather unpleasant world, R, to even less attractive cases such as Z and M. The message in this case is that Asia is unlikely to cause its own catastrophe but may be forced into one by events elsewhere. Note that three of the configurations are not used. The reason is that, though they are internally consistent, there seemed to be no path by which they could be reached.

Writing text scenarios is now easy. Each configuration in the tree has, it will be recalled, a few words describing its essence. For example, those for A, C and N are:

A – Situation in South China Sea (SCS) as in 1994.

C – Self-help in process – ASEAN Regional Forum and other multilateral framework taken off; but still an uncertain time depending on China's next move.

N – Cooperation among regional countries and external power(s) to bring about a stable climate in the face of an unpredictable China; disputes in SCS remain low in profile.

That might now be written as the first part of a short story of the future:

> 'The first years after 1994 saw a growing trend to self-help through the aegis of the ASEAN Regional Forum and other multinational mechanisms, though there was still uncertainty about China's intentions. Thereafter, China's unpredictability continued to be a concern but, because her own needs for economic development and political stability made her continue to mind her own business, it was possible, though progress was slow, to improve cooperation and develop stability. Fortunately, disputes, especially those involving the Spratly islands, remained low-key.'

Use the configurations to write story scenarios.

You should now write the rest of the story.

The short stories are an audit trail in the sense that they provide a sequence by which, say, end condition α might be reached. The audit trail both explains the logic and is a means by which the scenario, in both senses of a path and an end condi-

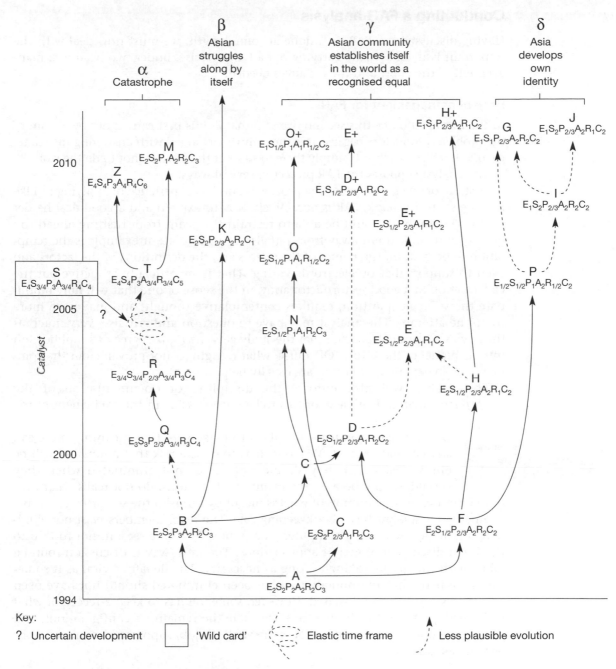

Figure 3.5 The South China futures tree

Source: Coyle and Yong (1996)

tion, can be challenged, revised and improved upon. *As with all scenarios,* the stories do not have to be true; their purpose is to sensitise strategy formulation to the uncertainties of the future. Their value will lie in making decision-makers think about the robustness of their choices in the face of the future's vagaries, and not seek the illusion of an optimal decision.

> The value of scenarios, regardless of the technique, is to sensitise people to the future's possibilities.

Conducting a FAR analysis

Having discussed the FAR technique at some length, we must now deal with the important issue of actually carrying out a FAR exercise, under two headings: management of the effort and the resources needed.

Project management for FAR

In the introduction to this section, we said that FAR is best carried out by a team of the problem proprietors because it is they who are charged with answering the strategic question. The analyst is simply there to support the process, not to do the work.

The analyst supports the FAR project in several ways.

First, he or she knows what the process is and has experience of applying it. Like much else in this book, FAR is deceptively easy to explain and a good deal harder to do. The analyst should be able to restrain the team from rushing ahead too quickly and guide them away from pitfalls. A *very* important example is the temptation to brainstorm the names of the sectors and the definitions of the factors and even to support that by electronic voting. That is superficially attractive but the construction of a good sector/factor array, in the sense of one that will fully illuminate the strategic question, requires contemplative thought and may need more than one attempt. The analyst may have to question and criticise, very much as the devil's advocate, to ensure that the study gets the right degree of simplification into its model of the future. Of course, what is 'right' is not provable but the comments of an experienced person are usually helpful.

The analyst will also enforce the discipline of documentation of the sector/factor matrix. It is easy for this to be pushed aside in the excitement of the analysis (and FAR is a vastly enjoyable process) and the analyst sometimes has to badger the team members to make sure that meanings are clear, shared, and explicit. Without that, there is a risk that anomalies will be eliminated when they should not be, or not eliminated when they should, simply because the members of the team do not realise that they have differing understandings of what is meant by terms in the sector/factor array.

> Document the process to make sure that meanings are clear and shared.

Finally, the analyst has a bookkeeping role. The team members *must* not eliminate anomalies by using a computer. That tends, for some reason, not to lead to thorough discussion of gestalt appreciations. The ideal way is discussion round a table, with the debate taking as long as necessary. The debate is vital as it sometimes happens that an anomaly that has been eliminated should not have been and it may need to be reinstated. However, someone has to keep a record of what is decided, perform the eliminations, calculate the remaining configurations, and print them out for review, and that is the analyst's job, supported by suitable software (Appendix 1).

Resources for FAR

Rhyne, who invented FAR, states that a full two-cycle FAR takes not less than about six months with one or two analysts full-time, a team of perhaps four problem owners working certainly not less than half-time on average and a supervisory group of senior people meeting as necessary. All told, that is something in the region of 100 or more person-weeks of effort. The author's experience is that FAR does not need to be anything like so resource-intensive. The South China Sea effort described earlier required about eight person-weeks in all for one cycle, both to do the analysis and write the report. As a rough guide, one might say that a one-cycle FAR ought to be able to be done within not more than 8–10 person-weeks of effort, with a second cycle, if it is necessary, requiring somewhat less.

Even eight weeks of effort is not trivial but it does not seem an undue expenditure given the importance of the strategic issues addressed. Nonetheless, few organisations are willing to commit to that degree of expense for results which will not be available for some months. We have to live in the real world and accept that, manifestly unsatisfactory as it might be in theory, it is often necessary to do the best one can in much less time. We therefore turn to a simplified version of FAR which has been found to work better than one might have expected and is certainly better than doing nothing at all to think about the future.

Simplified FAR

One of the attributes of a good analyst is the ability to produce at least some kind of results by the time at which they are needed and not to pursue rigorous perfection which will be too late to be of practical use. A complementary skill is, of course, to explain the caveats attached to a 'quick and dirty' study in such a way as to give the user a sensible understanding of the trustworthiness of those results.

In terms of FAR, this may mean that a rough study has to be carried out within a few days as opposed to the ideal of some months. No one suggests that such an approach is fully satisfactory; the point is that it is somewhat more satisfactory than doing nothing to think about the future.

Simplified FAR depends on building outline time lines by finding a few consistent futures, as opposed to eliminating all the inconsistencies and forming scenarios from the remaining consistent configurations. Simplified FAR uses the following steps:

1. Form a sector/factor array in the usual fashion with as much documentation as time permits but, at the very least, explanation of what the sectors (columns) mean.

2. Find a consistent configuration which represents the current situation. (In any FAR, simplified or full-scale, if none of the configurations represents the present, there is a *fundamental* flaw in the sector/factor array.) Write a short description, in 5–10 words, of what that condition represents, record it on a yellow sticker and place it at the foot of a whiteboard or flipchart. Call it the 'base configuration'.

3. Find two or three consistent, but different, configurations which are believable, in the *gestalt* sense, as conditions for the end of the time horizon being used. In practice, three are often easily found. Again, write short descriptions on a yellow sticker and put them on the board. Space them apart across the board from 'worst' to 'best'; the yellow stickers should state clearly why they are bad, good, or in between. 'In between' does not necessarily mean halfway between good and bad. It might, for instance, mean 'pretty good' or 'rather worrying'.

4. Find a few more consistent, believable, configurations as intermediate states, and record them as before.

5. It should now be easy to connect these six to eight stickers into credible time lines. If it is not, revisit steps 3 or 4.

This simplified version of FAR is used on the author's one-week practical strategy course described in Chapter 15 and on the instructor's website. The justification is that one week is all that is available, and, within that time, the course has to cover *both* thought about the future *and* tools for thought about what to do once one has a vision of some future prospects. In short, the course has to cover most of the first seven chapters of this book and just under two days can be devoted to FAR. Nonetheless, crude and over-simple as it might be, the simplified approach works well, as will be seen from the case studies in Chapter 14.

Extended FAR

Usually, in a FAR sector/factor array, a factor is not constrained to move only to the adjacent condition but can change to any other value in its column. In some cases, though, such as some corporate modelling studies, the sector/factor matrix can be so written as to preclude large movements. For that condition, Powell and Coyle (1997) have developed an approach which they call EFAR, for Extended FAR. It relies on defining the sector/factor matrix in such a way that the factors in a given sector form a natural progression, as it were, 'up and down' a scale. An example is the company's share price, the filing space for which is, say, £2.50, £3.00, £3.50 and so on up to £5.00. Share prices for large companies do not normally change in large steps so, if the present price if £4.00, the only feasible moves are by one step to £3.5 or £4.5 or, just possibly, by two steps.

EFAR works by first eliminating anomalies, as in standard FAR. The next step is to define rules such as that no one factor can move more than two steps at a time or that there can be no more than four steps in total across the whole sector/factor array. Given such pragmatic judgements, the surviving configurations can easily be grouped into clusters from which sequences and scenarios can be developed.

Before using EFAR, be careful to check that its assumptions are valid for your problem.

Applications of FAR

The FAR method has been applied to a range of problems and it is not restricted to the geopolitics of regions such as the South China Sea. A few examples, mainly unpublished, are: corporate strategy in an aerospace company; management buy-out in a high-technology firm; the future of a school district; regional economic development; national park development policies; planning the reconstruction of a nation's mining industry; management of border controls between two countries; and in several military planning applications. More case studies using simplified FAR are described in Chapter 14.

Normative scenarios

The customary basis of scenario work is to appraise the future's possibilities, the conclusion being, in effect, 'Here is what might plausibly happen. You, Decision-Maker, would be prudent to be aware of these possibilities and make sure that your decisions are robust against them.' The principle is that the future is something to be lived with but that not much can be done to make it any different.

There is, however, no reason in principle why scenario thinking cannot be used to shape the future, though Wood and Christakis (1984) are among the few to have shown how that might be thought about. Their case study describes the use of several futures techniques, including FAR, to study planning and economic development in the North Piedmont region of Virginia. One of their main concerns was to develop a means by which concerned citizens could take part in the planning process.

Their FAR analysis generated two futures for the North Piedmont region of Virginia which we will simply identify as good and bad, from their point of view. Although in scenario work there should be no concept that one future is more probable than another – they should, in Rhyne's phrase, be 'comparably plausible' – Wood and Christakis regard bad as most likely to happen. Both good and bad are described by the equivalent of an ESPARC configuration and simply by comparing the sector/factor array descriptors of the two cases they were able to arrive at a set of planning gaps, one for each of the seven sectors in their array. A similar, but subtly different, approach is used in the viable firm matrix (Chapter 5).

The art of the long view

The essence of the matter is that human decisions have long-lasting effects. To give but one example, the decision in 1947 by the then British government to set up a National Health Service which was universal and free at the point of use has had dramatic effects on the health of the British people and on their expectations and attitudes. When the NHS was founded the following statements were true: medicine was simple and cheap; people were exhausted by war, poor, deferential and grateful for what they received; the word of doctors was law. Fifty-odd years later none of those things is true. The NHS, once a source of admiration, is now the subject of deep concerns.

In short, the uncertainties of technology, society or politics call for one to rehearse the future so that choices can be more robust against its vagaries. To be sure, no one can predict, and forecasts cannot be accurate, especially if they become self-negating, but the underlying assumption of the whole effort is that one would be imprudent not even to try to think intelligently about the unknowable future and to practise the art of the long view.

Story scenarios are rehearsals of the future.

Of course, economic and statistical analyses have a role to play in data handling and interpretation but taking a long view is fundamentally an art requiring thought and imagination. Such a qualitative approach seems to some people to be highly speculative and difficult to justify, though the reasoning behind the process is supported by the use of good documentation and clear audit trails. Since the results can be explained and justified, they can be improved as better insights emerge, and become more acceptable to policy-makers and analysts.

Perhaps the intellectual and pragmatic bases for these approaches can be summarised in three points:

1. The consequences of policies and decisions can be very long-term and the uncertainties of the future in which they will have to fly can be so severe that a policy-maker would be imprudent to the point of recklessness not even to try to rehearse the future.

2. It is not required that one forecast be more probable than another – the members of a set of scenarios should be comparably plausible – still less that it be 'right'. The purpose of scenarios as stories about the future is to make people think more deeply so as either to justify or to modify their decisions.

3. The qualitative nature of the scenario process is not only because we are not smart enough to think of mathematical ways of building scenarios. It is because all the truly important problems are so hard (difficult) that they can only be addressed by 'soft' methods which stimulate creative thought.

The final word is that futures thinking is, as we have repeatedly remarked, *fundamentally* an act of imagination and vision. Galt *et al.* (1997) use the striking phrase 'an intense exercise of imagination and judgement'. These tools and techniques are, therefore, no more than aids to imagination. They are a guard against ODIDTOT, which is the strategist's nightmare – 'Oh Dear (or other expletive), I Didn't Think Of That.'

Further reading

Reading scenarios which others have written is only part of the story and it is also necessary to try to monitor driving forces which might affect the field for which one is trying to forecast. Schwartz (1996) coins the delightful phrase 'information hunting and gathering' and devotes 40 pages to describing what he monitors.

Few may have the time to emulate him but one excellent source is *The Economist* for its coverage of politics, science, business and world affairs. A related source is the same publication's annual series, *The World in 200X*. The academic literature appears in *Futures*, *Foresight*, and others such as *Technological Forecasting* and *Social Change*.

A deeper understanding of the art of the long view is given by some of the sources cited here. If one only has time to read a few, one would be Macrae's *World in 2020*, not so much for what it says but for the style of the narrative form. Other scenario writers are Schwartz, van der Heijden and Ringland.

 CASE STUDY   ## Simplified FAR at *Herrington-Jones*

Introduction

In Chapter 1 we posed a strategic question for **Herrington-Jones** and asked the reader to test and revise it. In Chapter 2, we showed a mind map for **Herrington-Jones** and, again, asked you to enhance it. It is now time to show the **Herrington-Jones** FAR analysis but, yet again, you will be asked to improve it.

The first stage is to derive a sector/factor array from the mind map constructed earlier but the main drivers and factors behind *Herrington-Jones's* business identified in the map need to be refined and redefined. Ideally this would be the first step in an iterative, two-cycle FAR but, with the pressure of time in what can be assumed to be a consultancy exercise, it will not be possible to perform a second iteration. You, however, might well enjoy constructing an improved sector/factor array.

Refining the main aspects of *Herrington-Jones's* mind map

Distribution

Herrington-Jones is a grocery retailer, using road, sea, and perhaps rail transport systems to transport foodstuffs from the producers (perhaps overseas) to the outlets, and from the outlets to the consumer. *Herrington-Jones's* business might be severely affected by a breakdown of one of these distribution systems. The cost of fuel is an obvious consideration.

Environment

The strong relationship between the environment and agricultural production is self-evident. The products sold by *Herrington-Jones* might be severely affected by environmental degradation.

Lifestyle

Consumer lifestyles affect, are even defined by, the choice of products purchased. For this exercise consideration is limited to two main elements, the broad aggregate of income level, and leisure time. Other factors influencing consumer choice might emerge during the FAR and be included in a second iteration.

Technology

Technology, in the sense of IT, is vital in this highly competitive business sector and the ability to manage IT, and to exploit further developments, is therefore a significant aspect of this business.

Regulation

Legislation, whether from the national government or from the European Union, could affect *Herrington-Jones's* business. In this simplified FAR, legislation might be described as pro-consumer or anti-consumer. The first implies stringent environmental rules and strict food safety standards. An anti-consumer environment suggests minimal state intervention on behalf of the consumer.

Integration

The UK is currently an active member of the European Union (EU), the most powerful trading bloc in the world, but has not yet joined the Euro currency. Many EU policies are directed at economic and business matters and, whether the UK fully integrates with the EU or not, the issue seems to be significant to the future of *Herrington-Jones's* business.

GDP

The general economic climate is obviously important to *Herrington-Jones*.

The sector/factor array

These seven categories form the acronym DELTRIG, a meaningless but pronounce-able word giving a meta-language to illuminate *Herrington-Jones's* strategic question. That word provides the basis for the sector/factor array in Table 3.6.

Feasible contexts

The sector/factor array is now utilised to develop a set of plausible future contexts. In this case we use simplified FAR, which is not ideal, but is often all that can be done under pressure of time. The simplified approach usually leads to good results and, in this case, it identifies the base case and produces three plausible future contexts which emphasise interesting differences. It is essential that you highlight the elements of each context and study the sector/factor array in detail to see how that provides the narrative description of each context.

At this stage, we simply summarise the contexts, a base case for 2001 and three plausible end states for 2010. After that, we can write short stories as scenarios leading from the base case to each end state.

Table 3.6 DELTRIG sector/factor array for *Herrington-Jones*

Distribution D	Environment E	Lifestyle L	Technology T	Regulation R	Integration I	GDP G
D_1 – Major increase in distribution costs	E_1 – Total collapse of sustainable agricultural environment	L_1 – Greater income and greater leisure time	T_1 – High digital convergence, high efficiency gains	R_1 – Extreme pro-consumer	I_1 – EU/euro integration, super-state, no barriers	G_1 – Negative growth
D_2 – Slight increase in distribution costs	E_2 – High pollution and climate change, major negative agricultural impact	L_2 – Greater income but less leisure time	T_2 – Medium digital convergence and medium efficiency gains	R_2 – Moderate pro-consumer	I_2 – EU/euro integration, national autonomy, no barriers	G_2 – Zero growth
D_3 – Slight decrease in distribution costs	E_3 – High pollution, minimal agricultural impact	L_3 – Less income and less leisure time	T_3 – Low digital convergence but efficient increase from IT implementation	R_3 – Minimal regulation	I_3 – EU integration, UK out of Euro, no barriers to trade	G_3 – Low growth
D_4 – Lower distribution costs	E_4 – High pollution increases efficiency of crops in EU	L_4 – Less income and greater leisure time	T_4 – Low digital convergence, low efficiency gains from IT implementation	R_4 – No regulation	I_4 – EU integration, UK out of Euro, barriers to trade	G_4 – Medium growth
	E_5 – Low pollution, minimal agricultural impact			R_5 – Anti-consumer regulation	I_5 – Collapse	G_5 – High growth

Base case 2001 – $D_3E_3L_2T_1R_3I_3G_3$

Despite pressure for greater European integration, the EU is still a free trade zone with sovereignty largely retained by member states. The UK remains outside the trial run of a common European currency. European economic growth is low, and consumers generally have disposable income but little leisure time. Better management of distribution has reduced costs, but very significant cost savings from digital convergence have yet to be realised. Global pollution has noticeable impacts on agriculture. Food scares have led to moderate amounts of consumer and environmental regulation.

Context 1 – 2010 – $D_1E_2L_4T_1R_1I_1G_2$: European superstate

Most legislation originates from the European government in Brussels, with only regional matters being decided in national parliaments. Ineffective environmental protection has led to high levels of pollution worldwide, with significantly diminished agricultural productivity and higher food prices. To control pollution the European government has imposed extremely strict regulations. That has caused a major increase in distribution costs which have offset the efficiency gains from digital convergence. There is stringent consumer protection legislation and a powerful European Food Safety Agency. The European economy as a whole is stagnant, and consumers on average have less disposable income and more leisure time.

Context II – 2010 – $D_4E_2L_2T_1R_4I_5G_5$: Après moi le déluge

The European Union has been dissolved, with new trade barriers between European countries. The UK has good economic growth thanks to rapid growth in its main trading partners, the USA and Asia. Agriculture is now entirely marginal in the UK. Attempts to control pollution have been abandoned because of public reluctance to bear the associated costs. Consumers have good disposable income and little leisure time. Increases in world food prices and the costs of new trade tariffs are counteracted by cheaper and more efficient distribution of food products.

Context III – 2010 – $D_1E_5L_2T_2R_1I_2G_4$: Green shoots

Global pollution has been much reduced by effective regulation. Although technological breakthroughs have reduced the use of internal combustion engines, the gains from digital convergence have been limited and distribution costs have risen. The UK has joined the euro, but European member states have retained their political autonomy, and the European Union operates mainly as an integrated economic zone. The UK, like the rest of Europe, has medium economic growth, and consumers have more disposable income and less leisure time. Despite low world food prices, increased distribution costs and strict food safety regulations within Europe are pushing food prices up.

Summary on the *Herrington-Jones* contexts

It is interesting that the end-state contexts overlap in some ways; contexts do not have to be mutually exclusive in all respects, their purpose being solely to illuminate the strategic question. In this case, the implication of the overlap may be that it will be possible to develop reasonably robust strategies for *Herrington-Jones*. With only three end states, there is little point in drawing a tree from the base case to them.

Despite the extreme simplicity of this FAR analysis, it will be seen in later chapters how it leads to strategies for *Herrington-Jones* when the other tools for practical strategy have been applied.

Scenarios to 2010

We now use the base case and the end states to write short story scenarios with plausible explanations of the progression from one to the other.

Scenario for Context I – European superstate

Between 2000 and 2005 European integration progressed swiftly. The UK and all other current members of the European Union joined the euro, as did Switzerland and the Central European states of Poland, the Czech Republic and Hungary. The currency and the political and economic apparatus to support it developed quickly. The European Parliament adopted considerable powers from the European Commission after a hard-fought campaign to make the EU democratic and representative of the people. A European Defence Force was developed to counter a potential threat from an unstable and resurgent Russia.

To support integration the EU raised barriers to trade which led to a stand-off with other major trading blocs such that international agreement on a wide range of issues ground to a standstill.

The US economy continued to grow and the economic development of developing countries moved quickly without any concern for the environment. Consequently, pollution reached the highest recorded levels, with freak weather conditions. Man-made disasters, including terrorism and radiation contamination in the former CIS, made matters worse. The EU began to implement legislation to counter this, although large industries fought the move as the proposed legislation would increase costs of transportation and distribution. As global pollution started to get out of control the European Green Party was formed and immediately attracted a large voting bloc across the EU.

The EU Central Bank and the European Parliament wanted the full costs of integration to be borne quickly so that integration could be completed by 2015. To support this, the EU started a campaign for all revenue raising to be taken away from national government and put into its own hands. As a consequence, an economic slowdown was predicted by 2010 as the economies of the EU struggled to align themselves with each other. The EU continued to promote a minimum wage policy so that there was a growing equality of wage levels across Europe, albeit at a low general level. People were increasingly asked to work less and less to maintain the number of jobs.

The pace of technological change increased with the development of wireless applications and digital convergence. Consumers could order their shopping from their mobile phones and a growing number started to do so. In response, *Herrington-Jones* started to push its delivery services and began implementing smart technology throughout its value chain, including huge databases on individuals' weekly and daily purchasing habits.

Scenario for Context II: Après moi le déluge

The continued low value of the euro and the dominance of the UK and US economic models, combined with uneven growth across continental Europe, corruption in the EU Commission, the failure of reforms to GATT, as well as a rapidly enlarged EU which now includes the countries of Central Europe, led to friction and recrimination between the main countries. The German public harked back to the days of a strong Deutschmark and French public opinion became increasing nationalistic.

The financial demands of the EU continued to increase at an alarming rate and the move towards closer political, foreign policy, defence and economic union started to polarise opinion throughout Europe. Political leaders throughout Europe struggled to maintain the dream of a united Europe as jobs were lost to the Far East and the USA. The main policies on the agenda were ways in which the Eurozone could be stabilised and the main parties promoted protectionist policies. Individual members came under increasing pressure to consider domestic issues over and above EU issues.

The US economy continued to grow and the economic development of developing countries moved quickly without any concern for the environment. Consequently, pollution reached the highest recorded levels, with freak weather conditions. Man-made disasters, including radiation contamination in the former CIS, made matters worse. The EU began to implement legislation to counter this, although large industries fought the move as the proposed legislation would increase costs of transportation and distribution. The European Green Party was formed and immediately attracted a large voting bloc across the EU.

The pace of technological change increased with the development of wireless applications and digital convergence. Consumers could order their shopping from their mobile phones and a growing number started to do so. In response, *Herrington-Jones* started to push its delivery services and began implementing smart technology throughout its value chain, including huge databases on individuals' weekly and daily purchasing habits.

Scenario for Context III: Green shoots

Using the two previous scenarios, with their similarities and differences, as examples, you should now write your own story scenario for the progression towards Context III.

Summary on the *Herrington-Jones* scenarios

This very simplified FAR, applied quite quickly, has produced a base case, three future contexts and three scenarios. As will be seen in later chapters, it provides a good basis for strategy development for this illustrative case. In the case studies in Chapter 14, we shall encounter other applications of simplified FAR, some of which lead to quite complex futures trees.

Chapter summary

The theme of this chapter is that the future does not have to be a foreign land but can be explored logically and intelligently.

The unifying theme for the chapter is that it would usually be reckless for decision-makers to treat the future as a foreign land and to hope that they can cope with it when they get there. That is, though, *sometimes* a reasonable stance as future change may not be dramatic and can be handled as it arises, as was the case with the accountancy firm handling changes to tax law. In other cases, the risks of change can be shared, always bearing in mind the awful lesson of the near-collapse of the Lloyd's insurance market. In general, though, the cope or share strategies are of limited application and, to avoid the danger of wandering unknowing into a strange and foreign land, some form of futures research can be invaluable and is intellectually possible.

It may be possible, but it is not perfect, and any forecasting methodology must be probed for its assumptions, perhaps the most profound of which is *how far can this approach be stretched into the future?* We argued that methods which are based on projections from past data do not reach very far, and that causal model techniques, which involve the assumption that causal processes do not change, are only reliable for perhaps 10 years, though they are very useful in business policy analysis. Qualitative futures techniques, such as Delphi and FAR, are limited by the extent to which human ability to grasp a problem, and then apply insight and imagination, can stretch into the unknowable future.

A futures project therefore involves four questions:

1. What is it about the future that is a cause for concern?
2. Can we rely on being able to cope with whatever comes along?
3. If not, how far ahead do we need to forecast?
4. Which of the three approaches, trend projection, quantified modelling or systematic human thought, is most appropriate?

We have argued that, for truly strategic issues, characterised by broad, sometimes conflicting, objectives and long time-scales, the imaginative, disciplined thought underlying FAR is most likely to be useful, though Delphi also has a role to play for some types of problem.

The value of FAR lies in its morphological structure and the ensuing requirement to create filing space for all reasonable possibilities. Eliminating the anomalous combinations creates as many or as few scenarios as the problem calls for and avoids the trap of focusing on a few pre-selected options. The surviving configurations are the basis from which true story scenarios can be created as rehearsals for the future.

The keys to success are:

- the willing exercise of imagination
- avoiding an illusory search for comfort by over-dependence on quantitative data – by definition, data relate to the past and we need thought about the future

- the ability to work fruitfully with other people in the team, using the framework of FAR to turn what might have become an argument into a discussion
- wide reading to help to sensitise one's mind to the future's vagaries and possibilities.

References

Adams, J. (1998), *The Next World War*. Random House Publishers, London.

Berry, A. (1995), *The Next 500 Years. Life In The Coming Millennium*. Headline Book Publishing, London.

Coyle, R. G. (2003) Scenario thinking and strategic modelling. In Faulkner, D. and Campbell, A. (eds) *Handbook of Strategy*, Chapter 11, vol. 1. OUP, Oxford.

Coyle, R. G. (1996), *System Dynamics Modelling: A Practical Approach*. Chapman and Hall/CRC Press, London.

Coyle, R. G., McGlone, G. (1995), Projecting scenarios for South-east Asia and the South-west Pacific. *Futures*, 26(1), 65–79.

Coyle, R. G., Yong, Y. C. (1996), A scenario projection for the South China Sea. *Futures*, 28(3), 269–83.

Ferguson, N. (ed.) (1997), *Virtual History, Alternatives and Counterfactuals*. Picador Press, London.

Friedman, G., Lebard, M. (1991), *The Coming War with Japan*. St Martin's Press, New York.

Galt, M., Chicoine-Piper, G., Chicoine-Piper, N., Hodgson, A. (1997), *Idon Scenario Thinking*. Idon Ltd, Pitlochry, Perthshire.

Glenn, J (ed.) *et al.* (1999), *Futures Research Methodology*. CD ROM, American Council for the United Nations University, Washington, DC.

Gribbin, J. (ed.) (1998), *The Future Now, Predicting the 21st Century*. Weidenfeld and Nicolson, London.

Huntington, S. P. (1997), *The Clash of Civilisations and the Remaking of World Order*. Simon and Schuster UK Ltd, London.

Kennedy, P. (1993), *Preparing for the 21st Century*. HarperCollins Publishers, London.

Loveridge, D., Georghiou, L., Nedeva, M. (1995), *United Kingdom Technology Foresight Programme Delphi Survey*. Policy Research in Engineering Science and Technology, University of Manchester.

Macrae, H. (1994), *The World In 2020*. HarperCollins Publishers, London.

Meadows, D. H. *et al.* (1972), *The Limits to Growth*, UK edn. Earth Island Press, London.

Powell, J., Coyle, R. G. (1997), A network-based approach to strategic business planning. *Journal of the Operational Research Society*, 48, 367–82.

Rhyne, R. (1981), Whole-pattern futures projection using field anomaly relaxation. *Technological Forecasting and Social Change*, 19, 331–60.

Rhyne, R. (1995a), Field anomaly relaxation. The arts of usage. *Futures*, 27(6), 657–74.

Rhyne, R. (1995b), *Evaluating Alternative Indonesian Sea-Sovereignty Systems*. Institute for Operations Research and the Management Sciences, Linthicum, Maryland.

Ringland, G. (1998), *Scenario Planning. Managing for the Future*. John Wiley and Sons, Chichester.

Schwartz, P. (1996), *The Art of the Long View*. John Wiley and Sons, Chichester.

van der Heijden, K. (1996), *Scenarios. The Art of Strategic Conversation*. John Wiley and Sons, Chichester.

von Reibnitz, Ute (1988), *Scenario Techniques*. McGraw Hill Book Company, Hamburg (translation from German). Only available from the author at 1842, Ave. des Templiers, F 06140 Vence, France.

Wood, W. C., Christakis, A. N. (1984), A methodology for conducting futures-oriented workshops. *Technological Forecasting and Social Change*, 26, 281–97.

Yergin, D., Gustafson, T. (1994), *Russia 2010 and What It Means for the World*. Nicholas Brealey Publishing, London.

Identifying strategic actions

What this chapter is about

■ Asking a good strategic question, unravelling the context and generating scenarios are only the first steps in practical strategy.

■ We now need to develop action plans that are as robust as possible against future uncertainties.

■ Simple matrix tools can be used to evaluate action plans or decisions that have already been proposed.

■ However, we need to think about strengths, weaknesses, opportunities and threats (SWOT) in order to identify the actions to be evaluated.

■ Conventional SWOT does not help very much, as it has serious limitations.

■ A variant on SWOT overcomes those drawbacks and leads, almost automatically, to imaginative and comprehensive action plans.

Introduction

In the previous three chapters we showed how to pose strategic questions, unravel complexity and develop scenarios, so we now turn to those parts of the practical strategy toolbox which address the vital question:

'We understand the issues and we have the scenarios, so what do we do?'

In short, we have to identify appropriate actions and strategies and work out how they can be implemented in the practical world. This is not trivial and it will need four chapters to cover the next four steps in **ACTIFELD**:

■ **I** – identifying actions and strategies in relation to contexts – this chapter

■ **F** – finding an organisation able to implement the actions – the viable firm (or policy, or organisation) matrix (VFM) in Chapter 5

- **E** – evaluating how the changes fit with the interests of stakeholders, and assessing the resource implications – congruence and resource analysis in Chapter 6
- **L** – detecting and overcoming obstacles to change – force field analysis in Chapter 7.

Let us now address the first question, the relationship between strategies and contexts.

Formulating and evaluating strategies

There are, in principle, two ways in which one can relate strategies to scenario contexts.

1. Suppose that some competing strategies have already been formulated. In such a case, the question is how well or badly the strategies might play against end-state scenarios.

2. Use the scenario contexts as the starting point and work out the strategies appropriate to those contexts. If more than one context is used, it might be possible to find strategies likely to be robust against the future's uncertainties.

The next two sections, *A simple matrix technique* and *The Idon Scenario Matrix*, describe techniques used in the first case. The remainder of the chapter deals with the second method. As ever in this book, there is no single 'right' way of tackling the problem of relating strategies to scenarios. On balance, the second approach is probably to be preferred if time, resources and *politics* permit. For instance, if a set of actions and strategies are already being proposed by powerful interests in the organisation, one is likely to get nowhere by asking for time and resources to develop new ones. We have to live in the real world and, in the circumstances just described, the first method – assessing existing strategies against scenarios – may be all that is possible and would certainly be better than *not* assessing the strategies for their robustness against the future.

If the situation is less constrained by politics or other factors, then formally developed scenarios, using, perhaps, the FAR approach from the previous chapter, and explicitly analysed strategies, using the method described later in this chapter, are likely to give more satisfactory strategic results. The strategy formulation method is very simple and does not require extensive resources.

A simple matrix technique

Van der Heijden (1996) uses a deceptively simple table of the consequences of the Mont Fleur scenarios discussed in Chapter 3. His approach is to rate strategic options against scenarios by using multiple plus and minus signs to indicate how much better or worse each option is assessed to be, relative to carrying on with the present policy. The 'do nothing' option should always be considered when evaluating strategic choices because another strategy is not automatically better than the present one; that is clearly the case in the Lame Duck scenario. (Recall that these are end-state scenarios, not the more useful story scenarios.) His assessments are shown in Table 4.1 in which a blank indicates no advantage or disadvantage relative to 'continue as is'.

> Always remember to consider the 'do nothing' strategy.

Table 4.1 Scenario/Option matrix

	Ostrich scenario	Lame Duck scenario	Icarus scenario	Flamingos scenario
Withdraw	+		–	– –
Continue as is				
Short-term investments	–		+ +	+
Long-term investments	– – –	– –		+ + +

Source: van der Heijden (1996, p. 234)

Van der Heijden stresses strongly that the object is not to decide which option should be accepted; in fact it is clear from Table 4.1 that none of the strategic options is fully robust against all the future's uncertainties. The aim is to stimulate work towards improving the options for action. It is also clear that the world of the Flamingos is so attractive that effort might be devoted to help to bring it about so that long-term investments might prosper.

Table 4.1 says nothing about how the options were selected in the first place, though van der Heijden mentions the use of SWOT – strengths, weaknesses, opportunities and threats, which will be the subject of most of the rest of this chapter and which we shall see later for *Herrington-Jones*, and in the cases of the Murray/Darling River Basin and Littleworth and Thrupp in Chapter 14.

The Idon Scenario Matrix

A variation on this by Galt *et al.* (1997) is the Idon Scenario Matrix, Idon being their trademark. Space does not permit a full explanation but the framework is shown in Table 4.2; the reader should turn to the source for a full account.

Starting with a blank matrix, the first stage is to identify the scenarios and, by some means, the decision options; these are written in the top row and the left-hand column. The matrix will handle as many scenarios and options as desired and is not limited to four and three as in this example. One then takes each decision option in turn and works across the rows, asking the question 'What would be the consequences of pursuing option 1 in scenarios A, B ...?' This is the meaning of 1A and so on which stand for 'this could cause problems unless we ...', or 'to get the best out of this we would have to arrange to ...'. Once a row has been completed, the key step is to rephrase its option as a very specific choice that will be as robust as possible in the range of scenarios. The final stage is to work down each column and identify the core competences needed in each of the scenarios and then to identify the robust competences.

Table 4.2 Idon Scenario Matrix

	Scenario A	Scenario B	Scenario C	Scenario D	
Decision option 1	1A	1B	1C	1D	Robust option 1
Decision option 2	2A	2B	2C	2D	Robust option 2
Decision option 3	3A	3B	3C	3D	Robust option 3
	Competence A	Competence B	Competence C	Competence D	Vital, or robust, competences

Source: Galt *et al*. 1997, p. 107

The SWOT method and its limitations

The conventional SWOT method

A common initial step in developing actions and strategies is the well-known method of creating a table of strengths, weaknesses, opportunities and threats – so-called SWOT analysis.

Identifying the SWOT factors can be achieved by simple brainstorming, but some sort of framework is often useful. A common one is PEST; political, economic, social and technological factors are considered in turn. Some people add another E for environmental aspects. There is even an acronym of SEPTEMBER, which has the huge drawback that no one can remember which E is which, so people can end up talking about different things at the same time. Other headings might be the management team, distribution facilities, IT skills and so forth. Perhaps the most effective technique is to use the principal factors from the mind map, make up from them an unambiguous acronym and display that prominently on the whiteboard when the SWOT analysis is performed.

The limitations of SWOT

'Conventional' SWOT has serious drawbacks.

However, SWOT has, in practice, three serious drawbacks.

The *first* is that, unless the exercise is well managed, the numbers of strengths, weaknesses, opportunities and threats which people identify can be very considerable, even verging on the unmanageable. Considerable care may be needed to boil the ideas down to a sensible number, perhaps by combining similar items or rejecting those that are manifestly trivial. As a rough guide, an overall total of up to about 30 or 40 strengths, weaknesses, opportunities and threats can be coped with; more than that number is likely to lead to difficulties in making sense of the ideas.

Secondly, SWOT often leads to disagreement, which can be heated, about whether a given item is, say, an opportunity or a weakness. For instance, in the case of Littleworth and Thrupp, in Chapter 14, it is a fact that some of the senior people are near retirement age. That is a weakness because of the loss of experience but it is also an opportunity to bring in new blood. It is better to forget the arguments and recognise that a given item can appear more than once in a SWOT table.

Finally, the *third*, and the most serious, weakness of SWOT, as it is conventionally practised, is that it leaves unanswered the vital question of *'so what do we do now that we have a SWOT table?'*

The method explained in this chapter avoids the second problem because, as we shall see, it does not even matter very much where in the table a given item is placed, as it will always be considered. The method also solves the third problem as it is explicitly designed to deduce actions and strategies from the SWOTs.

ACT**I**FELD

TOWS and strategies

Basic ideas

The alert reader will have noticed that SWOT has turned into TOWS. The reason is that it seems that the process works better by first thinking about the threats and opportunities of the external world before considering the internal weaknesses and strengths. There is no real evidence for that; it is just an impression from experience. In the rest of the book we shall use TOWS, but it does not matter if you use SWOT.

The essence of the method is very simple; the TOWS table is used to compare, contrast and combine the Ts, Os, Ws and Ss, in various ways, so that action plans which, say, use one of the strengths to exploit an opportunity emerge more or less automatically. That is easy to say, but, like most of the tools for practical strategy, is rather harder to do, so we will demonstrate it by using a simple example followed by one that is much more profound, and finishing with the *Herrington-Jones* case study.

First, we must deal with a more or less philosophical problem.

Are TOWS absolute or relative?

This can be a source of debate and confusion but, as ever, going back to first principles in the dictionary can help to resolve the matter in a practical way. We find (*Collins English Dictionary*):

- strength – something that is regarded as being beneficial or a source of power
- weakness – state or quality of being weak
- opportunity – favourable or advantageous *combination of circumstances*
- threat – an indication of imminent harm [by implication from some person or *circumstance*].

The words in italics suggest that we should see the Ss and Ws as inherent in the organisation and the Os and Ts as arising from the environment or context. For problems involving immediate action in the current 'world' the Os and Ts are in the present environment and a futures study is not necessary. For other problems involving evolution over time, a futures study will be needed and the Os and Ts will depend on the forecast context – *a context being a coherent configuration derived from a FAR sector/factor matrix*. As we shall see in the **Herrington-Jones** case at the end of the chapter, there are three contexts, each with its own set of slightly over-lapping Os and Ts. By contrast, the Ss and Ws are **Herrington-Jones's** present position and are, therefore, kept constant and tested against the different Os and Ts. The end result is strategies to move **Herrington-Jones** into the future that are as robust as possible against those three forecast futures.

TOWS and strategies: a worked example

The case problem and the context

The case study deals with research and development (R&D) strategies for the development of a military unmanned ground vehicle (UGV) which is, as its name suggests, a ground vehicle which can carry out tasks with little or no human control. An unattended sensor is somewhat like that; it sits in place and reports enemy movements or other events. A UGV, however, has to be able to move. Although this case study has a military flavour, the same principles might be applied to any other high-tech R&D effort.

First, we pose a strategic question:

'Find an immediate action plan to ensure that recent R&D applicable to UGVs can be exploited.'

This is simple to parse: *why* – by implication the R&D might be wasted; *what* – ensure that it is not wasted; *when* – in the imminent future; *how* – by developing a plan of action to exploit available technology in a useful way. The problem is fairly straightforward so we probably do not need to unravel its complexity and, since the problem is imminent, we can omit the futures exploration. In short, it is not always necessary to go through the full **ACTIFELD** methodology. It is a very flexible process and it is important to realise that it can be bent to suit particular needs.

> ACTIFELD is a very flexible process – adapt it to fit your problem. Don't adapt the problem to fit the process!

The first step is shown in Table 4.3, which is a conventional TOWS table with a total of 12 items. Study the table but do not worry about where these facts came from, just accept them for this example. Revise the table if you wish, maybe O_3 should be T_4; technology is changing so fast that no one can keep up. Note also that the three Ws, seen in isolation from the Ts, Os, and Ss, might be enough to kill the whole project. It is one of the advantages of the TOWS method that it avoids such blinkered thinking.

The critical step, which makes this method work, is shown in Table 4.4. It is very simple and consists only of moving the weaknesses and strengths to one side so as to make space in which to work, and then *comparing items from the original TOWS boxes*. Table 4.4 is an example of the deduction made by comparing S_2 and T_2, and the process of comparisons is completed in Table 4.5, which contains a total of 10 actions.

Table 4.3 The TOWS for the UGV problem

External threats	External opportunities
T_1 Other nations also doing research and development	O_1 National and international research agreements exist
T_2 Lack of recognised need for UGVs	O_2 Increasing number of UN operations
T_3 Collaborative research threatened by industrial recession	O_3 Speed of technological development
Internal weaknesses	**Internal strengths**
W_1 Reduced funding	S_1 Strong research and development base
W_2 Lack of confidence in UGVs	S_2 Some technology already available
W_3 High cost to develop advanced technology	S_3 Machines needed to compensate for reduced manpower

Table 4.4 Starting to deduce actions

	External threats	External opportunities
	T_1 Other nations also doing research and development	O_1 National and international research agreements exist
	T_2 Lack of recognised need for UGVs	O_2 Increasing number of UN operations
	T_3 Collaborative research threatened by industrial recession	O_3 Speed of technological development
Internal weaknesses W_1 Reduced funding W_2 Lack of confidence in UGVs W_3 High cost to develop advanced technology		
Internal strengths S_1 Strong research and development base S_2 Some technology already available S_3 Compensation needed for reduced manpower	**Strengths vs. threats** Use demonstrator vehicle to create awareness (S_2,T_2)	

Table 4.5 The complete action set

	External threats	External opportunities
	T_1 Other nations also doing research and development	O_1 National and international research agreements exist
	T_2 Lack of recognised need for UGVs	O_2 Increasing number of UN operations
	T_3 Collaborative research threatened by industrial recession	O_3 Speed of technological development
Internal weaknesses W_1 Reduced funding W_2 Lack of confidence in UGVs W_3 High cost to develop advanced technology	1. Deploy simple vehicles to generate user need (W_2,W_3,T_2) 2. Transfer funding to UGV research to avoid losing technological advantage (W_1,W_4,T_1,T_3)	5. Build simple vehicles to gain user confidence (W_2,O_2) 6. Develop national and international R&D links (W_1,O_1) 7. Look for technology transfer from other research areas (W_3,O_3)
Internal strengths S_1 Strong research and development base S_2 Some technology already available S_3 Compensation needed for reduced manpower	3. Use demonstrator vehicle to create awareness (S_2,T_2) 4. Emphasise benefits of collaborative research (S_1,T_3)	8. Continue strategic research (S_1,O_3) 9. Build vehicles using available technology for UN-type operations (S_2,S_3,O_2) 10. Develop national and international R&D links (S_1,O_1,O_3)

It is of great practical significance that the TOWS process, used imaginatively, has led to exactly the right collection of actions needed for this problem. We now have a complete basis for an action plan, rather than the incomplete plan that we might first have thought of.

The final step, which is the main strength of this approach, is to notice that some of the actions are closely similar to one another. For example, actions 1, 3 and 5 all relate to vehicles to demonstrate UGV technology, while item 9 uses similar wording but in the context of a UN operation. There are other similarities.

> **Group the related items to develop action plans.**

The end result is:

Actions 1+3+5+9 → Develop a simple vehicle based on available technology and suitable for UN operations
  (some sort of surveillance vehicle to monitor remote borders?)

Actions 4+6+10 → Promote international links and collaboration
  (UN orientation achieves that)

Actions 2+7+8 → Continue research with emphasis on technology transfer
  (links with, say, oil/nuclear/chemical industries for surveillance of hazardous environments?)

The final action, or strategy, is very clear, straightforward and, above all, *justified* by the analysis. There is an audit trail of logic that is both easy to justify and to revise if further TOWS items are identified or existing ones cease to apply.

This case study used pairwise comparisons of the TOWSs but in later examples we shall see how, once one studies the matrix and absorbs it, comparisons are made from more than two boxes.

Finally, one could carry this method further and do 'second-order' TOWS analyses for the communications systems for the UGV, its suspension, transmission and so forth. In R&D planning that can be very valuable as it can give a coherent design and development plan for what can, after all, be a complex undertaking involving many specialised disciplines. If they work to a commonly understood strategy which has been derived 'top-down' from the underlying need, the result may be more satisfactory and the process easier to manage.

> Don't limit yourself to comparing things in pairs. Look at items in all parts of the table.

Promoting e-commerce

CASE STUDY

Introduction

This case study is intended to show a much more complex TOWS analysis. It will also suggest some ways in which the analysis of large problems can be organised. It contains a lot of detail and you will have to study it closely. It will come in stages and you will be asked to work out some of the steps for yourself before looking at the 'answer'.

Background

Consumer e-commerce offers people the opportunity to buy from the Internet, or from digital television, products and services they would otherwise have bought from shops, supermarkets, travel agents etc., or even not bought at all. Consumer e-commerce has many apparent attractions, such as ease, convenience, the wide range of products that can be made available and, probably, reduced cost. Indeed, some supermarket chains now offer e-commerce services in conjunction with their existing shops. Some e-commerce businesses seem to be prospering, others have not yet been successful, and it seems fair to say that, as yet, e-commerce has not been as successful as its proponents might have hoped.

There are certainly some obvious difficulties. Consumers may be worried about security of credit card transactions over the Internet. How can after-sales service be ensured? How will items be delivered? Many people have neither the skill nor the equipment to use the Internet. On the other hand, there is strong governmental support for e-commerce. Young people who are used to computer games are now becoming consumers themselves. The prospects of lower prices and, for busy people, being able to shop from home are attractive.

What then, are the strategies for promoting e-commerce in the near future and who might have to implement them? It is unlikely that we shall find some single action, as with the UGV case, and it is possible that the 'solution', to the extent that such a complex problem can be 'solved', will be quite wide-ranging.

To answer that question, a group of colleagues, knowledgeable about e-commerce, spent about half a day at a working seminar to apply TOWS to it. Before describing the results of their efforts we must first consider the important issue of managing and organising such a venture so as to get the best results from it.

Organising a TOWS analysis

Some of the points to be made here may seem obvious after they have been made but they are vital to a successful outcome from using the time of busy people.

The whole point of TOWS is to draw out the shared knowledge of concerned people and an away-day, working seminar, study period, or whatever you choose to call it is an excellent and easy way of doing that. It is essential that the study be done away from the office in pleasant and well-fed surroundings. Mobile phones must be turned off and preferably left behind.

This kind of thinking is best done away from the office.

However, the participants know about a problem domain, not an analysis technique, so getting to feel comfortable with the technique will be a key factor. In this instance, the UGV case study was explained; it is simple and, as the problem was unfamiliar to them, the participants had no preconceptions about its details and could concentrate on the ideas.

There is, however, a considerable gap between UGVs and, in this case, consumer e-commerce, so a second key factor is to produce a simple illustration of TOWS for the problem in question. Common sense and a little background reading will usually supply enough knowledge to produce an illustrative TOWS matrix intended only to show that the ideas of the UGV TOWS can be replaced with terminology from the new problem domain. The example should help the participants to get their ideas running freely. Preparation for the away-day may take a day or so but it is time well spent as input to the exercise.

It is important to have enough participants to form at least two syndicates each of four or five people, as one group cannot generate sufficient diversity of ideas. In this case, there were three syndicates of four, each group having people from diverse backgrounds, the cross-fertilisation of ideas within the group being an ingredient of success. We shall consider the management of syndicate work in Chapter 15 but, briefly, the facilitator has to make careful judgements (or inspired guesses) about when to leave a syndicate to work things out for themselves and when to offer advice and guidance. Syndicate work is going well when the facilitator is ignored when he or she enters the room. It is also important for syndicates to allocate time to each phase of their work and to move to the next phase when time is up.

The TOWS tables, and the actions deduced by the syndicates, are collated after the exercise; the final result of indicated strategies has to be developed by the facilitator and all these results fed back to the participants. The results can be discussed at a short meeting, but, in the ideal world, they should be the input to a second away-day. This is similar to the two-stage FAR analysis described in Chapter 3, though, as in that case, a second round of TOWS is not always possible, given the demands on the time of busy people.

The e-commerce TOWS table

The final TOWS table, collated from the syndicate results, is shown in Table 4.6. You will need to study it carefully as there are 37 TOWSs; about at the limit of manageability, though inevitable for a wide-ranging problem such as this. They include technological, economic and social (such as W_6, the fear that large numbers of people might be excluded from the e-revolution, and T_1, resistance and cynicism) factors. There are business implications, such as small-to-medium enterprises lacking the necessary capabilities (W_{11}), and traditional stores using IT to fight back against e-commerce (T_7). There are legal considerations and the political factor that the government wants to promote e-commerce and has raised £22 billion from the sale of mobile telephone licences. TOWS analysis is a very effective,

Table 4.6 The consumer e-commerce TOWS table

Threats	Opportunities
T_1 Consumer resistance and cynicism	O_1 Nintendo generation grows up
T_2 Worries over delivery and after-sales support	O_2 Existing network of law and regulation
T_3 Fears over data security	O_3 Companies cannot afford to lose market share
T_4 High-profile bad experiences	O_4 Rapid development of technology with unforeseeable advances
T_5 'Show-stoppers': viruses and fraud	O_5 Business-to-business e-commerce spreads e-knowledge
T_6 Non-convergence over standards	O_6 Potential for cheaper goods
T_7 In-store improvements via technology	O_7 Potential for time-saving via home delivery
	O_8 Potential for transparency of price/information
	O_9 Availability of £22 bn from mobile telephone licence sale

Weaknesses	Strengths
W_1 Lack of user e-skills	S_1 Strong government support
W_2 Limited ownership of PCs and modems	S_2 Good benchmark companies with trusted brands
W_3 Limited payment systems, especially for young people, but parental concerns	S_3 Tradition of retail innovation
W_4 Poor distribution systems	S_4 Strong creative community
W_5 Lacks social interaction	S_5 Relatively good cable infrastructure
W_6 Fear of emergence of social exclusion	S_6 Competitive market in telecomms and digital TV
W_7 Cost of telephone calls	S_7 Enlightened attitude to regulations and auctions
W_8 Limited public access points	S_8 Developments in search engines
W_9 Slow growth in digital TV	S_9 Capability for highly-targeted marketing
W_{10} Lack of e-skills to set up e-store fronts	S_{10} Entrepreneurial culture
W_{11} Lack of awareness, especially in small to medium enterprises	

and simple, framework for thought, especially in its ability to help people to identify *all* of the ramifications of a complex problem.

TOWS and actions

The deduction of the actions suggested by the TOWS is shown in Table 4.7, which is spread over pages 97 and 98. It is important to notice that the actions are *not* deduced from simple pairwise comparisons of the TOWS headings. As one studies the table one sees combinations from three or even four of the TOWS headings, such as action 11. Again, you will need to study the table closely, as there are a total of 29 actions but, before that, you will learn much by creating an empty table, as was done in Table 4.4, and then deducing your own actions. Do not be deterred if you think you know nothing about e-commerce – common sense and imagination will take you a long way to success.

Note that some of the actions, such as 3 – research into electric vehicles, are very similar to the UGV technology strategy problem. There are similar cases in Table 4.7, not only in technology, where a second-order TOWS might be carried out to develop a specific action plan.

TOWS and strategic areas

For a problem with such wide social, economic, legal and technical ramifications as this one, it is not to be expected that there will be a single clear outcome as there was for the UGV case. We will expect to see a number of strategic areas emerge when actions are grouped by their similarities.

The strategic areas are shown in Table 4.8, which is the main result of the whole exercise. It is important to realise that Table 4.8 can be read in several complementary ways. None of them is the 'right' way; the different ones just give alternative perspectives on the problem. All the viewpoints are needed for a complete understanding of the indicated actions and strategies.

- *Firstly*, the table can be read from left to right. Thus, the first row states that actions 1, 9, 16, 2, and 11 combine into strategic area A; promotion of awareness of, and access to, e-commerce. Similarly, 19, 20, 22 and 10 fall under area E, creation of a legal framework and protection against abuse.

- The *second* way to read it is down the right-hand column. This shows that there are seven strategic areas. This result, that there are *seven* broad areas, as opposed to any other number, is of considerable importance. Unstructured thinking about this problem might have missed one or more of these areas. (Of course, you should be producing your own version of this analysis.)

- In some ways it is most illuminating to take the *third* view, and read the table from right to left. This now shows that to achieve area A, for example, it is necessary to do all five of the actions listed. It might be a waste of money to combine actions 2 and 16 and put 10,000 PCs, with free Internet access, into places people visit, such as post offices, libraries, doctors surgeries and so on, if action 1, provision of on-the-spot training, and action 11 are not also implemented. Even these four actions might achieve only a passing benefit if action 9, continued education, is not also performed. Similar ideas apply for the other areas.

Table 4.7 Deduction of actions from the e-commerce TOWS table

	Threats	**Opportunities**
	T_1 Consumer resistance and cynicism	O_1 Nintendo generation grows up
	T_2 Worries over delivery and after-sales support	O_2 Existing network of law and regulation
	T_3 Fears over data security	O_3 Companies cannot afford to lose market share
	T_4 High-profile bad experiences	O_4 Rapid development of technology with unforeseeable advances
	T_5 'Show-stoppers': viruses and fraud	O_5 Business-to-business e-commerce spreads e-knowledge
	T_6 Non-convergence over standards	O_6 Potential for cheaper goods
	T_7 In-store improvements via technology	O_7 Potential for time-saving via home delivery
		O_8 Potential for transparency of price/information
		O_9 Availability of £22 bn from mobile telephone licence sale
Weaknesses	1. Promotion of user-friendly training experience to broaden acceptance (T_1, W_1, W_2, W_6, S_1)	9. Promote continuing education – school to university to develop familiarity (T_1, O_1, W_1, W_6)
W_1 Lack of user e-skills	2. Invest mobile telephone licence money to give free access at POs, surgeries, Lottery points (T_1, O_9, W_1, W_2, W_6, W_7, W_8)	10. Develop new systems/regulations on payment with proper safeguards (O_1, O_2, S_7)
W_2 Limited ownership of PCs and modems	3. Safer delivery vehicles – research into electric vehicles (T_2, O_7, W_4, S_1, S_7)	11. Skilled presentation of benefits of e-commerce (T_1, O_6, O_7, O_8, W_6, S_4)
W_3 Limited payment systems, especially for young people, but parental concerns	4. Promotion of training in small to medium enterprises (W_{11}, O_3)	12. Get retailers to offer 0800 numbers (O_7, W_4)
W_4 Poor distribution systems	5. Promote growth and simplicity of use of digital TV (T_1, O_4, W_6, W_9, S_4, S_5, S_6)	13. Develop network of safe delivery points (O_7, W_4)
W_5 Lacks social interaction		14. Develop interactive digital TV to give a safe environment for small to medium enterprises (O_5, W_9, W_{11}, S_6, S_8)
W_6 Fear of emergence of social exclusion		
W_7 Cost of telephone calls		

▶

Table 4.7 Continued

Weaknesses

W_8 Limited public access points

W_9 Slow growth in digital TV

W_{10} Lack of e-skills to set up e-store fronts

W_{11} Lack of awareness, especially in small to medium enterprises

Strengths

S_1 Strong government support

S_2 Good benchmark companies with trusted brands

S_3 Tradition of retail innovation

S_4 Strong creative community

S_5 Relatively good cable infrastructure

S_6 Competitive market in telecomms and digital TV

S_7 Enlightened attitude to regulations and auctions

S_8 Developments in search engines

S_9 Capability for highly-targeted marketing

S_{10} Entrepreneurial culture

Threats

6. Support and training to set up e-store fronts (W_{10}, O_3, O_5)

7. Traditional stores fight back (T_1, T_4, T_6, T_7, W_1, W_5, S_3)

8. Reduce costs of PCs, modems and digital TV (O_9, W_2, W_9)

18. Benchmark companies use creative skills to innovate and promote benefits of e-commerce (T_1, O_6, O_7, O_8, S_2, S_3, S_9)

19. Develop suitable (trans-national) guarantees (T_2, S_1, S_7)

20. Improved techniques for data protection, plus appropriate legal framework (T_3, S_7, S_8)

21. Pay serious attention to learning from experience and produce objective guide to best and worst Internet sites (T_4, S_4, S_7, S_8)

22. Develop and publicise smart regulation and suitable penalties against 'show-stoppers' (T_5, O_2, S_7)

23. Improved protection against 'show-stoppers' with global early warning (T_5, O_4, S_8)

24. Partnership to promote open standards (T_6, S_2, S_3)

25. Need for policy choice on balance between traditional and e-commerce (T_7, O_3, O_6, O_7, O_8)

Opportunities

15. Stimulate virtual communities with intelligent agents to mimic human behaviour (O_1, W_5, S_4, S_8)

16. Development of intermediaries (POs, district nurses?) to provide real-time price comparisons (T_1, O_5, O_8, W_1, S_2)

17. Ensure that 'walled gardens' do not hamper in small to medium enterprises (O_2, W_{10}, W_{11})

26. Develop personalised searches to ease meeting of individual needs and wants (O_6, O_7, O_8, S_4, S_8, S_9)

27. Monitor technology to ensure that useful new developments are exploited (O_4, S_5, S_6)

28. Ensure that UK firms are not hampered in achieving international market share of e-commerce (O_3, S_1, S_2, S_7)

29. Create environment to support start-ups (O_1, O_9, S_7, S_{10})

Table 4.8 The e-commerce TOWS deductions developed into strategic areas

	TOWS deductions rearranged and grouped	Broad area or strategy
1 9 16 2 11	Promotion of user friendly training to broaden acceptance Promote continuing education – school to university to develop familiarity Development of intermediaries (Post Offices, district nurses?) to provide real-time price comparison Invest mobile telephone licence money to give free access at Post Offices, surgeries, Lottery points etc. Skilled presentation of benefits of e-commerce	A. Promote awareness of, and access to, e-commerce
8 12 18 21 5	Reduce cost of PCs, modems and digital TV Get retailers to offer 0800 numbers Benchmark companies use creative skills to innovate and promote benefits of e-commerce Pay serious attention to learning from experience and produce objective guide to best and worst Internet sites Promote growth and simplicity of use of digital TV	B. Ensure that expectations raised by A will come to fruition
3 15	Safer delivery vehicles – research into electric vehicles Develop network of safe delivery points (supported by 16 – Development of intermediaries)	C. Make the logistics work
27 26 15 23	Monitor technology to ensure that useful new developments are exploited Develop personalised searches to ease meeting of individual needs and wants Stimulate virtual commodities with intelligent agents to mimic human behaviour Improve protection against 'show stoppers' with global early warning	D. Prepare for the future by promoting, finding or funding technology and ensure protection of system
19 20 22 10	Develop suitable (trans-national) guarantees Improved techniques for data protection plus appropriate legal framework Develop and public:se smart regulation and suitable penalties for 'show stoppers' Develop new systems/regulations on payment with proper safeguards	E. Create a legal framework to enable the system to work and to guard against criminal abuse and personal folly
4 6 17 24 29 14	Promotion of training for small to medium enterprises Support and training to set up a-store fronts Ensure that 'walled gardens' do not hamper small to medium enterprises Partnerships to promote open standards Create environment to support start-up Develop interactive digital TV to give a safe environment for small to medium enterprises	F. Create conditions for widespread e-business and avoid commercial exclusion of small to medium enterprises
7 25 28	Traditional stores fight back Need for policy choice on balance between traditional and e-commerce Ensure that UK firms are not hampered in achieving international market share of e-commerce	G. Formulate an even-handed overall strategy to achieve benefits of new modes while giving due weight to existing interests

■ Finally, the *fourth* view is also from right to left, but this time in terms of organisations. Under area A, this implies that implementing that set of actions would require effort from the health services, the Post Office company, the local government councils which control schools, and so forth. Some details emerge, such as a contract between the government and an advertising agency to perform action 11, skilled presentation of the benefits of e-commerce. Even more subtle is the idea that, next time the licence to operate the national lottery is awarded, the applicant would have to show how they would provide Internet access in parallel with the lottery computers. This view also shows that there may be no existing agency able to carry out a particular action. For instance, who is going to do action 27, monitoring technology? Should whoever does that also do action 18? How will they do it and who should pay for it? Such seeming minutiae are, in fact, the necessities of successful strategic action, and the simple TOWS approach has, with a minimal effort, pointed them out fairly exactly.

In this problem, each of the 29 actions appears in only one strategic area but it is perfectly permissible for a given action to arise under more than one area. In fact, a given agency or organisation could well be involved in more than one strategic area and therefore have to coordinate with the different groups of actors in those areas.

CASE STUDY · TOWS and strategies at *Herrington-Jones and Co*

Introduction

We now continue with the *Herrington-Jones* case by applying the TOWS and strategies technique to identify robust actions for the company. In Chapter 1 we assumed that *Herrington-Jones* is a food retailer, in Chapter 2 we developed an outline mind map for factors in its business sector, and in Chapter 3 we formulated scenarios for 2010. We also assume that *Herrington-Jones* is ambitious to be the number one retailer in the European Union. These assumptions are easy to change to give another exercise to help you to hone your skills. Note, though, that this TOWS analysis has to be very future-orientated.

Herrington-Jones's SWOT analysis

The company perceives itself as having strengths and weaknesses, and also as facing opportunities and threats. By definition the strengths and weaknesses are intrinsic to *Herrington-Jones* but the opportunities and threats will arise in the future contexts revealed by the FAR analysis to be plausible and internally consistent. Since there are three future contexts we shall repeat the TOWS analysis three times with the aim of identifying strategies that will be as robust as possible against the uncertainty of a range of plausible futures.

Strengths

Herrington-Jones's strengths are considerable in several aspects of the business.

- *The brand*. **Herrington-Jones** is a household name in the UK and the value of its brand is expected to assist, to some extent, any project that **Herrington-Jones** might attempt.

- *Size*. **Herrington-Jones** has an established presence in almost every town and city in the UK, and in many European cities. This gives a very large customer base and these two dimensions of presence and customers are connected in a positive feedback, or virtuous cycle, that feeds and sustains the growth of **Herrington-Jones**.

- *Supply chain management*. The widespread presence of **Herrington-Jones's** shops causes complexity in managing inventory and distribution channels. **Herrington-Jones** has, however, created advantages specific to the business by its success in managing this complex supply chain. This is a major strength.

- *Information technology (IT) and electronic-commerce*. IT is at the core of managing **Herrington-Jones's** large network of stores and the company is very competent in this field. It has made large strides towards integrating consumer electronic commerce into its established business and is ahead of its rivals in this respect.

- *Established international expansion strategy*. **Herrington-Jones's** growth in Eastern European countries has given it some experience of breaking into a new market. This will be one of **Herrington-Jones's** strengths in tackling future threats from competition and taking advantage of growth opportunities.

- *World-class management*. **Herrington-Jones's** numerous experienced managers have enabled it to achieve its current leadership position in the UK retail market. This strength sustains **Herrington-Jones's** advantageous position in its aspiration to be the number one retailer in Europe.

Weaknesses

Of course, **Herrington-Jones** perceives some weaknesses.

- *Poor brand strength outside the UK*. One of **Herrington-Jones's** problems in attempting to achieve dominance over the European retail market is that its brand recognition is not strong beyond the United Kingdom.

- *Low margins*. Currently, the retail business has low margins and high turnover, not so much of a weakness of **Herrington-Jones** as a characteristic of the whole retail sector. Changes in business practices and the blurring of traditional boundaries between business sectors may make it a serious weakness to be forced to accept these traits as inherent to the industry.

- *Weak presence in the EU*. Under the assumed objective, **Herrington-Jones** has to grow into the EU states and it does not, as yet, have the penetration it needs to create a virtuous cycle whereby scale feeds growth that in turn provides economies of scale, and so on, as is the case in its UK business.

TOWS analyses for different contexts

We now need to apply these strengths and weaknesses against the threats and opportunities specific to the three plausible future contexts. This is done in the next three sub-sections, and Tables 4.9 to 4.11, each of which is headed with the name of one of the scenarios for *Herrington-Jones* which were deduced in Chapter 3. Note that the strengths and weaknesses cells are the same in each case but the threats and opportunities vary to a greater or lesser degree as the contexts change. Each table is followed by the strategic insights that emerged from the comparisons of the TOWS elements.

Context I: European superstate

Table 4.9 *Herrington-Jones's* **TOWS for Context I: European superstate**

	Threats T_1 Competitors T_2 E-commerce T_3 Changing consumer need T_4 Regulation T_5 Pollution	Opportunities O_1 Expansion UK, Europe O_2 New products GM/organic O_3 IT + e-commerce + supply O_4 Lifestyle – more time/less money
Weaknesses W_1 Low brand value outside of UK W_2 Low margins W_3 Low EU penetration	1. W_1,W_3,T_1,T_3, a small fish moving from a small pond to a large one needs developing brand outside the UK 2. W_2,T_1,T_2, O_3, improve strength of value chain 3. W_2,T_4,T_5, promote on green platform as a Trojan horse	8. W_1,W_3,O_1, acquire brands in mature markets and develop brands in developing markets 9. W_2,O_2,O_4, move into higher-margin organics or cut costs by using GM crops 10. W_2,O_3, value chain efficiency drives profits
Strengths S_1 Brand in the UK S_2 Size in UK S_3 Supply chain management S_4 IT e-commerce S_5 Established international expansion strategy S_6 World-class management	4. S_1,T_4,T_1, in order not to lose existing base maintain home brand strength 5. S_1,S_2,T_3,T_5,T_6, lower risk through international exposure, develop strong international managers 6. S_4,T_1,T_2, first mover advantage – harness technical efficiency gains (roll out profitable model overseas) 7. S_3,S_4,T_4,T_5, use IT & supply chain management to distribute goods pollution free	11. S_1,S_2,S_6,O_1, use current strength to increase market share throughout Europe, including UK 12. S_3,S_4,O_4, customise high-margin services for new lifestyle requirements (auto-recurring purchases) 13. S_1,S_2,O_2, use brand to set new trends in competing in the new niche market 14. S_3,S_4,O_4, customer segmentation and spillover effect of distribution and database

Strategic insights for Context I:

1, 3, 4, 5, 6, 11, 14: Expand into the EU while maintaining UK strength.

2, 6, 10, 14: Technology should open up new opportunities both in value added services and the back-office operation of value chain management.

3, 9, 12, 14: The customer will be the driver of change in what can be sold; keep an eye on current trends, expect their evolution and be prepared for them.

Generally speaking, the EU may end up being one superstate but the customers will be slower to conform and only broad trends will be in common.

Context II: Après moi le déluge

Table 4.10 *Herrington-Jones's* **TOWS for Context II: Après moi le déluge**

	Threats	Opportunities
	T_1 Competitors T_2 E-commerce T_3 Changing consumer need T_4 Pollution T_5 Value of time	O_1 Expansion UK, Europe O_2 New products GM/organic O_3 IT + e-commerce + SCM O_4 Higher disposable income O_5 Decreased distribution costs
Weaknesses W_1 Low brand value outside of UK W_2 Low margins W_3 Low EU penetration	1. W_1, W_3, T_1, T_3, develop brand outside the UK 2. W_2, T_1, T_5, offer time-saving services to increase margin 3. W_2, T_4, O_3, move to higher margins through promotion on green and fair trade platforms	8. W_1, W_3, O_1, acquire brands in mature markets and develop brands in developing market 9. W_2, O_2, O_4, move into higher-margin organics or cut costs by using GM crops 10. W_2, O_3, O_5, lower transportation costs and increased value chain efficiency allows for increases in profit margins
Strengths S_1 Brand in the UK S_2 Size in UK S_3 Supply chain management S_4 IT e-commerce S_5 Established international expansion strategy S_6 World-class management	4. S_1, T_4, T_1, prevent entry by maintaining home brand strength 5. S_1, S_2, T_3, T_5, reduce risk through international exposure, develop strong international managers 6. S_4, T_1, T_2, O_3, first mover advantage, harness gains from value added services, and roll out profitable model overseas 7. S_3, S_4, T_4, use IT & supply chain management to distribute goods pollution free	11. S_1, S_2, S_6, O_1, use current strength to increase market share throughout Europe, including UK 12. S_3, S_4, O_4, customise high-margin services for new lifestyle requirements (auto-recurring purchases) 13. S_1, S_2, O_2, use brand to set new trends for competing in new niche markets, for example organic products 14. S_3, S_4, O_4 exploit database to identify customers' exact needs and customise service provision

Strategic insights for Context II:

1, 4, 5, 8, 9, 11, 13: Brand strength, its creation and maintenance will be critical to the success of *Herrington-Jones* in its European expansion.

2, 3, 12, 14: Customers will not be shopping for basic reasons; the customer will become a more complex entity that needs to be watched carefully and provided with more than a 'shopping experience'.

2, 6, 7, 9, 10, 14: Technology will cut costs and enable the provision of wider services.

Context III: Green shoots

Table 4.11 *Herrington-Jones's* TOWS for Context III: Green shoots

	Threats	Opportunities
	T_1 Foreign competitors T_2 Competitors promote green policies T_3 Changing consumer preferences T_4 Tightening regulation T_5 Food scares	O_1 Increased market share in UK, expansion into Europe O_2 New products GM/organic O_3 E-commerce not delivering on its promise O_4 Consumption patterns – more money/less time
Weaknesses W_1 Low brand value outside of UK W_2 Low margins W_3 Low EU penetration	1. W_1, W_3, T_1, build brand outside the UK 2. W_2, T_2, T_4, switch to 'green' distribution channels and reposition to build a green brand 3. W_2, T_4, T_5, O_4, adopt high quality standards (above those demanded by regulation) to overcome negative customer perceptions and justify higher margins	8. W_1, W_3, O_1, acquire brands in mature markets and develop brands in developing markets 9. W_2, O_2, O_4, S_1, move into higher-margin organics or cut costs by using GM crops 10. W_2, O_3, longer-term R&D and trial runs to leverage eventual gains
Strengths S_1 Brand in the UK S_2 Size in UK S_3 Supply chain management S_4 IT e-commerce S_5 Established international expansion strategy S_6 World-class management	4. S_1, S_2, T_1, T_4, T_5, invest in maintaining home brand strength and market share 5. S_1, S_2, T_1, T_2, T_3, T_4, T_5, reduce risk exposure by expanding abroad 6. S4, T3, maintain e-commerce development strategy in expectation of longer-term benefits from customer management 7. S_3, T_2, T_3, use supply chain management and e-vehicles for environmentally friendly distribution of goods	11. S_1, S_2, S_6, O_1, use current strength to increase market share throughout Europe, including UK 12. S_1, S_2, O_2, use brand to set new trends in competing in the new niche markets 13. S_4, O_3, O_4, customer database can be used immediately to improve individual marketing for conventional business model

Strategic insights for Context III:

1, 4, 8: Expansion and brand strength are tied to each other and should be approached in tandem.

2, 3, 9, 12: The customers' preferences will shape the evolution of the industry and the ability to track these changes and anticipate their change will determine degree of success.

6, 7, 10, 13: Technology infrastructure should be ready to meet the growth of the industry and its requirements.

Conclusion – strategies for *Herrington-Jones and Co*

Three robust strategies emerged from this analysis:

1. **European expansion**: acquire retail brands in mature European markets and develop retail brands in new European markets, with the aim of capitalising on learning scale efficiencies.

2. **E-commerce**: invest in infrastructure, exploit gains from first mover advantages in efficient supply chain management, position to provide competition both on cost and tailored value-added services.

3. **Lifestyle**: build up responsive and detailed customer database to monitor changing customer needs and take advantage of segmentation of the consumer market to cherry-pick attractive segments. Augment the focus on value by providing 'more than just a mere shopping experience'.

You should recall, though, that the strategy recommendations are based on scenarios from one cycle of the FAR method. One of the main strengths of FAR is that it is an iterative procedure, and that a more useful and imaginative set of scenarios could be created by another FAR cycle if time and resources permit.

We can suggest some of the thoughts that might well influence a second sector/factor array.

First, the factors in the 'Technology' sector focus exclusively on data processing and the Internet. Novel transport technologies, and technologies related to food production (GM foods), might be equally important and could be included as additional factors. Second, it is not clear to what extent the 'Integration' sector plays a useful role. Perhaps different regional customs (with regard to both types of food and consumer habits) are more important than political changes regarding the significance of national borders. Finally, there is the question of the nature of relations with suppliers. Clearly, free market competitive bidding for contracts by suppliers (i.e. a spot market for inputs) on the one hand, and networks of long-term relationships between *Herrington-Jones* and its suppliers on the other, will be appropriate to different external circumstances. Moreover, different products might also be suitable to different supplier relationships. For instance, an emphasis on high-quality organic produce might imply that a business model based on networked suppliers is preferable.

As exercises

You might now, as a syndicate exercise, repeat the *Herrington-Jones* FAR and then the TOWS analysis. Alternatively, you could usefully repeat this analysis for Tom Tiddler and Son who own a small chain of shops in Devon and Cornwall (a region of England which is a very popular holiday destination with a strongly seasonal trade) and are seeking to defend their position from encroachment by *Herrington-Jones* into the larger towns.

Chapter summary

The I step in **ACTIFELD** is actually quite straightforward, though, like all the rest of **ACTIFELD**, it is easier to explain than it is to do. Studying examples helps, but the only way to learn it is to apply it, preferably in a syndicate, to a problem that interests you. That 'study-and-then-apply' method is the key to the outline course structure on the instructor's website.

The key to the approach is the simple idea of building a SWOT or TOWS table in the usual way, and then making space to compare the TOWSs, initially in pairs, such as Ts against Os but, as insight deepens, taking items from three or even four cells in the TOWS table. People seeing this for the first time often say that it is the single most powerful step in **ACTIFELD** and that they will never do SWOT in the usual way again. I disagree that there is any single most powerful step in **ACTIFELD** – the steps hang together as a whole. I agree with the second comment; the 'usual' way of doing SWOT often gets nowhere as it can become bogged down in argument about whether something is a T, O, or whatever. Even without that, there is the problem of 'SWOT, so what?' (pun intended).

The TOWS and strategies approach is intended to overcome those problems but to make it work some skills are needed:

- The first is not to worry too much about which of the TOWS categories X belongs in. You have to be sensible about this; if X is manifestly a weakness, it would be silly to put it down as an opportunity. Apart from that, however, as long as X is at least roughly in the right place, it will be considered when its time comes.

- Secondly, be prepared to recognise that something can be in more than one cell in the matrix. The retirement of senior staff could well be both a weakness and an opportunity.

- The third skill is to focus on the aim, which is to identify strategies; the TOWS table is a means to that end, but not the end in itself. Don't, therefore, waste time on debating the table but, as soon as it is reasonably acceptable, get on to the real work.

Finally, the real work is to identify the actions and group them into strategic areas, and the keys here are:

- Start by looking at pairwise comparisons of the cells in the matrix but try to free your imagination to search for triple and quadruple comparisons.

- Be careful to compare like with like and opposite with opposite. For instance, like with like involves senior staff leaving. The relevant actions might be to get them to write down some of their experience before they leave, and to get the new staff to work alongside them for a while. The opposite relationship might be to use a company's strength in IT to counter a competitor's customer loyalty scheme.

- Avoid having a large number of TOWS elements supporting one action. That might suggest that the TOWS matrix is double-counting similar effects and it might need to be revised or simplified.

■ Make sure that everything in the TOWS table has been used at least once. If some item has not been used, is it trivial or is there a fault in the matrix or the deductions?

These tips and tricks will help, but the fundamentals for success are the free range of imagination, combined with the use of the discipline and clarity of the approach to help to turn unconstructive arguments into fruitful discussions.

References

Galt, M., Chicoine-Piper, G., Chicoine-Piper, N., Hodgson A. (1997), *Idon Scenario Thinking.* Idon Resources, Pitlochry, Perthshire.

Van der Heijden K. (1996) *Scenarios. The art of strategic conversation.* John Wiley and Sons, Chichester.

Finding viable organisations

What this chapter is about

■ The actions identified by TOWS and strategies have to be implemented by an organisation.

■ The *viable firm matrix* (VFM) is used to find the organisational structure that is *viable* and can implement the identified strategies.

■ The VFM can be applied in three ways:

(a) to differentiate between different firms in a given market area

(b) as a rapid analysis tool giving a shortcut in the full **ACTIFELD** process

(c) in its designed place within a full analysis.

■ The VFM can be applied in all three ways to any type of organisation, changing the name 'VFM' to match.

Introduction

The use of TOWS to develop action plans and strategies raises the question of whether or not the firm or other organisation is so structured as to be able actually to implement the plans. To address that, we turn to the use of the viable firm matrix (VFM).* Throughout this chapter we shall use the VFM for business examples but the same idea can be applied to any type of organisation, with a change of name. For example, in Chapter 14 for the Murray/Darling River Basin case, the VFM becomes a VPM, a viable policy matrix. In a military case, it might be a viable force matrix, and so forth in other instances. As with all of the techniques in this book, ideas should be used flexibly – the main thing is to adapt the tool to the problem, not to bend the problem to fit the tool.

ACTIFELD

---

*Although VFM is not a trademark, the author asserts that he is the originator of this idea.

To demonstrate that flexibility, we will show three ways of using the VFM. They are:

■ as a means of differentiating between firms in a given business area

■ as a short cut in the **ACTIFELD** methodology in order quickly to identify strategic options.

These two uses will help you to understand the principles and flexibility of the VFM before we turn to the third use:

■ the VFM's proper place in the **ACTIFELD** process, shown with the aid of the *Herrington-Jones* case study.

We will review those variants of the VFM at the end of the chapter and suggest numerous examples for you to use as practice.

The principle of the viable firm matrix

The VFM shows all the conceivable firms in a business sector.

The basic principle of the VFM is very simple; a matrix of all conceivable firms of the given category is developed. We might, for instance, define all imaginable car manufacturers, management consultants, or, as with *Herrington-Jones*, food retailers.

One might equally well identify all the possible ways in which a country might run its foreign policy, a defence force might be configured or, as in the case study in Chapter 14, all the options for setting up and running the Murray/Darling River Basin Commission.

You can also develop viable 'firm' matrices for any other type of organisation.

Whatever the problem type, some of those organisational structures involve impossibilities; for instance, a specialist manufacturer of sports cars could not sustain a high volume of production. Those anomalies can be avoided, so as to find firms that *could* exist, the viable firms.

The VFM is a form of morphological analysis in that it considers all the conceivable shapes and forms of business firms of a particular type. To that extent, the VFM has many similarities to field anomaly relaxation (FAR), which was referred to as morphological forecasting in Chapter 3. However, FAR and the VFM have *important and subtle differences*. FAR uses the feasible configurations as stepping-stones to develop paths into the future, while the VFM helps to find the feasible firm that could implement the action plans identified by the TOWS analysis. One could say, 'Our firm currently looks like *this* but to implement the plan it would have to look like *that*' – the VFM is a type of gap analysis. In essence, FAR is an *exploration* tool while the VFM is a tool for business *evaluation* and *design*.

Before explaining how to build a VFM we will consider an example.

An illustration of the VFM

Table 5.1 is an illustrative VFM for all conceivable firms of management consultants. At this stage we only want to show the basic ideas of the VFM, though, in a later section, we shall apply those ideas to the problems of a particular business.

Table 5.1 The viable firm matrix for the management consultancy sector

REPUTATION R	CLIENTS I	COMPETENCES C	PEOPLE E	FACILITIES F	OWNERSHIP O	MARGINS M
R_1 One of very few firms seen as consultant of first recourse	I_1 Numerous established blue chip and government clients with plenty of contracts for foreseeable future	C_1 Wide range of skills at cutting edge	E_1 Top quality people actually seek employment. High overall work load. High pay	F_1 Prestigious accommodation and latest equipment. Reserves for several months	O_1 Owned by few people. Not many employees. Problems of succession	M_1 Able to command top fees without argument. Highly profitable
R_2 Regarded as being in the top tier of the consultancy industry	I_2 Several major established and potential clients and steady stream of available work	C_2 Balanced portfolio at good level of expertise	E_2 Fairly easy to recruit and retain good people. Average workload. Better than average pay	F_2 Reasonable accommodation and equipment. Not dependent on overdraft	O_2 5–10 partners/ shareholders. Fairly large staff. Succession usually not a major problem	M_2 Fees higher than most but seen as reasonable. Quite profitable
R_3 Reputation growing steadily but not yet in the major league	I_3 Access to a few major clients but contracts intermittent and hard to get	C_3 Portfolio evolved by historical accident	E_3 Not easy to recruit and retain good staff. Some variability in work load. Average pay	F_3 Reasonable accommodation and equipment but cash flow needs constant attention	O_3 Many partners or co-ownership by all senior employees. Large staff. Planned succession	M_3 Fees governed by competition and regulated by major clients. Modestly profitable
R_4 Regarded as one of numerous minnows in the wider market	I_4 Client base in small local/regional firms	C_4 Concentration on 2 or 3 skills areas	E_4 Filling slots with warm bodies. Below average staff quality and pay	F_4 Fair accommodation and facilities. Relationship with bank needs careful management	O_4 A few people loosely associated/ not incorporated on a fairly full-time basis	M_4 Fees governed by accepted scales
R_5 Reasonable reputation in a local/regional market	I_5 Work very hard to obtain and spasmodic	C_5 No really solid or unique expertise.	E_5 Recruitment spasmodic and unplanned	F_5 Operating from individuals' homes with basic equipment	O_5 Ac-hoc collaboration by a few people as need arises	M_5 Margins cut to bone in attempt to get work

The matrix has seven columns, each for a different aspect of that type of business. There should be no more than seven columns, as we aim, as we did with FAR, at a *gestalt*, or whole-pattern, appreciation of the business, and experience indicates that seven is the maximum number of factors that can simultaneously be carried in the mind. The columns are arranged to give a meaningless but pronounceable word, so that **R**eputation is first in the acronym, not first in importance.

The rows, as with FAR, are intended to give 'filing space' for all the possibilities that can reasonably be envisaged under that heading. For example, and since we are talking about management consultants in general, there are firms which are able to command top fees without argument from the client, M1. On the other hand, there are others at M5. Similarly, the C column describes a range of competences. It just happens that this matrix has five rows in each column but there is no requirement for all the columns to have the same number of rows. Use as many or as few as are needed for filing space. The entries in the row do not have to be arranged in descending order from 'good' to 'bad'. In fact, for **O**wnership it is hard to say what is good or bad. *As with FAR, it is very important that the column headings and the row entries be clearly documented, as well as being summed up in a short phrase in the matrix.* You should write that documentation for the tables in this chapter as an exercise in doing so.

Experience shows that, in general, seven is about the maximum number of rows that can conveniently be handled. If there are fewer than about three rows the problem may not have been thought about with sufficient imagination. (We will consider the formulation of a VFM in more detail in the next section.)

This matrix has seven rows each with five possibilities, so the number of conceivable consultancy 'firms' seems to be 5^7 or 78,125. However, it is instantly obvious that a firm with $F_4O_1C_4E_3$, a small business with limited facilities and recruitment problems, cannot achieve $M_1I_1R_1$ and be at the top level in this business; an attempt to do so would simply not be viable. It is essential that you study the matrix and satisfy yourself about this point before going further.

Table 5.2 takes the argument a little further by highlighting the cells corresponding to two viable firms. BigLeague Consultancy Associates is shown in ***bold italics*** and a smaller firm, Gessit, Prayhard and Sine, is in **bold**.* These are very different firms but each, *in its own way*, is a viable business. Again, study the table carefully and find at least one more configuration for a viable consultancy business.

The phrase above in italics makes it clear that 'viable' does not mean large, successful or even prosperous. Gessit is simply not the same business as BigLeague. It is smaller, has fewer people, is not as profitable and, in short, it is a much smaller fish in a rather different pond, but none of those things mean that Gessit is about to go out of business. It is a viable firm in its niche and its three owners are probably very pleased with themselves and their lifestyles.

> 'Viable' does *not* mean large, successful or prosperous.

You should, of course, revise Table 5.1 if you do not think it is a sufficiently good representation of the consultancy world (Maister 1993).

It is important to realise that, in this VFM, the R, **R**eputation, column is the output or result that these two very different firms achieve. For Gessit, Prayhard

---

*Professor Pat Rivett coined this delightful name for a firm of slightly dubious accountants.

Table 5.2 Two hypothetical consultancy firms: 'Gessit, Prayhard and Sine' (bold characters) vs. 'BigLeague' (bold, italic)

REPUTATION R	CLIENTS I	COMPETENCES C	PEOPLE E	FACILITIES F	OWNERSHIP O	MARGINS M
R_1 *One of very few firms seen as consultant of first recourse*	I_1 *Numerous established blue chip and government clients with plenty of contracts for foreseeable future*	C_1 *Wide range of skills at cutting edge*	E_1 *Top quality people actually seek employment. High overall work load. High pay*	F_1 *Prestigious accommodation and latest equipment. Reserves for several months*	O_1 *Owned by few people. Not many employees. Problems of succession*	M_1 *Able to command top fees without argument. Highly profitable*
R_2 Regarded as being in the top tier of the consultancy industry	I_2 Several major established and potential clients and steady stream of available work	C_2 Balanced portfolio at good level of expertise	E_2 Fairly easy to recruit and retain good people. Average workload. Better than average pay	F_2 Reasonable accommodation and equipment. Not dependent on overdraft	O_2 5–10 partners/shareholders. Fairly large staff. Succession usually not a major problem	M_2 Fees higher than most but seen as reasonable. Quite profitable
R_3 Reputation growing steadily but not yet in the major league	I_3 Access to a few major clients but contracts intermittent and hard to get	C_3 **Portfolio evolved by historical accident**	E_3 **Not easy to recruit and retain good staff. Some variability in work load. Average pay**	F_3 Reasonable accommodation and equipment but cash flow needs constant attention	O_3 **Many partners or co-ownership by all senior employees. Large staff. Planned succession**	M_3 Fees governed by competition and regulated by major clients. Modestly profitable
R_4 Regarded as one of numerous minnows in the wider market	I_4 **Client base in small local/regional firms**	C_4 Concentration on 2 or 3 skills areas	E_4 Filling slots with warm bodies. Below average staff quality and pay	F_4 **Fair accommodation and facilities. Relationship with bank needs careful management**	O_4 A few people loosely associated/not incorporated on a fairly full-time basis	M_4 **Margins governed by accepted scales**
R_5 **Reasonable reputation in a local/regional market**	I_5 Work very hard to obtain and spasmodic	C_5 No really solid or unique expertise.	E_5 Recruitment spasmodic and unplanned	F_5 Operating from individuals' homes with basic equipment	O_5 Ad-hoc collaboration by a few people as need arises	M_5 Margins cut to bone in attempt to get work

and Sine to become a competitor to BigLeague the cells in all the other columns would have to be changed from the profile emphasised in bold type to that in bold italic, and that would be quite a challenge.

Digressing for a moment, this idea of viable policies can be applied in many circumstances. For instance, in a governmental case, some of the columns in a viable *policy* matrix might be the range of policy options that could be considered for implementation in different circumstances. For instance, Australia's possible immigration policies might be 'Open doors to all comers', 'Encouraged immigration' (such as the £10 passages offered in the 1950s), 'No immigration allowed', 'Immigration only for people with necessary skills', etc. Any of these could be implemented if the government chose to do so; the question is what would be the most appropriate in the wider context of a viable Australia matrix. Other columns in that matrix might refer to industrial development, social welfare and so on, and it is evident that there might be policy failures if, perhaps, the immigration and industrial development policies are inconsistent. Develop similar ideas for a viable common agricultural policy for a viable European Union, or any other similar example you choose.

Developing a VFM

As with just about everything else in this book, a VFM looks deceptively simple after it has been developed, but formulating one is not a trivial task, neither is it one to be done in a hurry and without thought. It is very unlikely that the first version of a VFM will, at an intuitive level, 'feel' right, neither is it likely that it will be an effective analysis tool. That usually arises if the VFM has not been developed using a sensible method but, even when it has, it is often necessary to revise the VFM after the first attempt to use it.

There are five approaches to building a VFM:

| There are five ways of building a VFM – be careful about how you use some of them. |

1. The first, and worst, is by brainstorming the factors in the business. That usually leads to a profusion of factors, often far too many to handle, and to a lot of argument (which can get quite heated) about what to leave out.

2. A second method, which is slightly better because it is a little more organised than brainstorming, is to list factors on a board and then to try to develop them into a matrix. The reason that both of these tend to fail is because they assume that the matrix will somehow emerge from the debate.

3. A third approach, which can sometimes work well, is first to concentrate the discussion on the principal factors in the business, which will be the column headings in the matrix, and then to develop the matrix rows. The risk is that a column will be missed out, in which case the matrix will be inadequate from the beginning.

4. The fourth, and usually the best method, is to use a mind map to get the principal factors, with the tendrils in the map helping to identify the entries that will go into the rows. This seems to be rather like the third method but the discipline of drawing the map seems to focus the discussion more effectively than is the case with the third approach.

5. Fifthly, it is rather tempting to try to avoid all that work and thought and copy an existing matrix. While it is true that studying existing matrices is a good way to learn the ideas, that temptation should be *firmly* resisted. An existing VFM was developed to help to answer a particular strategic question but your problem will have a different question so you have to formulate your own VFM. If two problems are closely similar you may finish up with similar VFMs. For example, the VFM in the case of Littleworth and Thrupp in Chapter 14 is somewhat similar to the VFM we are going to study next, but it is also different in several respects.

It would be nice, in a textbook, to be able to state that one method is always better than any other. However, as we are dealing with the ways in which groups of human minds interact to perform a task, that is really not possible.

The people best qualified to develop the VFM are often the focus group who, we have suggested, should be guiding the whole practical strategy exercise. They have seen the study evolve and should be intimately familiar with the business and be fairly comfortable with the tools for strategic thought. Finally, though, we reiterate that the first VFM is likely not to be fully satisfactory and, if time permits, should probably be revised.

> The VFM should be developed by the project's focus group.

Evaluating strategic options with the VFM

Having examined the first use of VFMs, for evaluating businesses, we now move to the second use, *rapid exploration of strategic options*.

Petroleum Associates Inc. (PAI) provides high-quality consultancy services to the oil industry, most of its clients being in the second tier of size for oil firms. PAI has developed some very sophisticated mathematical models for the general economics of the oil industry, for optimal purchase of crude oil on the spot market (where oil is traded on a daily basis), efficient planning of refinery production (using the linear programs mentioned in Chapter 1), and cost-effective exploitation of new oil fields. They are a reputable and fairly profitable firm. They do some work for other process industries such as bulk chemical manufacturing, but that is not a major feature of their business. PAI belongs to the four people who started it, and it employs about 30 analysts and support staff.

However, PAI's monitoring of their clients has raised fears that their established business might undergo rapid change. There are possibilities that the demand for PAI's type of consultancy may increase, though perhaps only temporarily, but PAI are more worried about the oil firms developing some in-house analytical capabilities instead of hiring PAI, or that disillusion about the assumptions needed in modelling such complex problems (review modelling in Chapter 1) might lead to major, but fairly unpredictable, changes in the kinds of work that oil companies might in future require, with related concerns about whether or not PAI could meet those different needs. The only good sign is that these changes in the oil industry will not happen overnight and will probably take place over the next two or three years, so at least PAI has some time in which to adjust its strategic posture.

A suggested VFM for firms such as PAI is shown in Table 5.3. It requires close study, as it is rather different from the previous VFMs, the differences being due to the facts that we now wish to analyse a particular firm in the context of the nature of its business, and that we can exploit the inherent flexibility of this tool to adapt it to a new task.

The table has seven columns arranged to make the acronym TECRAMO. (Of course, a VFM does not have to have seven columns; somewhere between five and seven is usual.) In this case, though, the columns are also arranged into three related groups of market potential, company characteristics and corporate posture, named within an added row at the top of the table. This is to allow us to exploit the differences between FAR and the VFM – we shall not be trying to eliminate options but, instead, seeking for viable configurations that might enable business objectives to be achieved. That mode of analysis is the reason why one of the columns is filing space for objectives or outcomes that companies such as PAI might try to achieve. Those range from rapid growth to bare survival. Of course, no firm wants to struggle to survive but it might be the only viable option.

PAI's present configuration is shown in Table 5.3 in bold type. They have a steady flow of oil work, T_2; they get some non-oil work, E_4; they concentrate on an established skill set, C_3; have some recruitment problems (as do many consulting firms), R_3; are well respected, A_4; don't do much marketing, M_6; and are doing quite nicely, O_3; though they hope for some growth, O_2. It is quite legitimate to colour two cells in a matrix if the definitions do not quite capture what is required. If you find that you are doing that very frequently, it is a sign that the matrix requires revision.

However, PAI's potential strategic problem is quite serious, as indicated by the two matrix cells in bold italic in the T column. If the oil studies market changes dramatically, what options are open to them? The number of possible 'firms' in Table 5.3 is $6^6 \times 7 = 325,692$ but attempting to stay at $O_{2/3}$ would not be possible with $T_{5/6}$ and E_4. There are, perhaps, two options.

One is to try to maintain at least O_3, in bold italic type in the O column. With $T_{5/6}$, that seems to require a move through E_3 to reach E_2. That cannot be achieved with the existing marketing strategy and a progression to M_2 and then to M_5 (recall that the rows are not arranged in ascending or descending order, they only give filing space). To move in that way, PAI cannot rely on C_3 but must get to C_2. They might reasonably hope that these moves will lead to A_3 and then A_2, which might improve the human resources position from R_3 to R_2.

PAI now have the outline for a two-stage strategy. It is a bold one as it involves attempting to develop a new business while the established one collapses around them. To understand the strategy, photocopy Table 5.4, a plain copy of the VFM, and highlight the cells for the existing business, and those required for this bold strategy, in different colours. That will give you an appreciation of the gaps to be filled in order to implement that strategy. In Chapter 6 we will look at some gap-analysis tools but it is evident that this bold strategy will be rather challenging.

Doing the first thing that comes to mind, this bold strategy, could be very rash and Table 5.3 can be used to look at other options. One is to retrench the business, with PAI's principals seeking to protect their own positions as best they can. They could reason that T_5 or T_6 will happen, but that there will still be enough work for

Table 5.3 The VFM for Petroleum Associates Inc. (present – bold, future – *bold italic*)

Market potential		Company characteristics			Corporate posture	
Traditional oil industry market T	Scope for Expansion in other markets E	Skill and Capability base C	Human Resource position R	Corporate reputation and Attitude A	Marketing policy M	Strategic Objective O
T_1 Worries over economic volatility bring some growth in oil consultancy market	E_1 Excellent. Seen as having ideal solutions to client needs in a wide range of cases	C_1 Wide range of skills at cutting edge. Skill base retained by recruitment of people with those skills	R_1 Highly qualified people see employment with firm as a good career step. Very high quality of work. High motivation and pay	A_1 One of the very few firms seen as an analytical consultant of first recourse in any market area and for most types of problem	M_1 Actively seek business wherever it can be found and regardless of what it is	O_1 Aim for rapid growth in size and value
T_2 Steady flow of work	E_2 Very good. Seen as having ideal solutions to client needs in a range of niche markets	C_2 Planned and actively managed portfolio of skills with strong attention to training for skill development	R_2 Fairly easy to recruit and retain good people. Consistently good work quality. Above average motivation and pay	A_2 A well-known and respected firm with a good client base in both market areas	M_2 Actively seek business wherever it can be found but only if it fits a selected range of skills	**O_2 Aim for some growth in size and value**
T_3 Volatility (up and down) in frequency and volume of work for next few years	E_3 Reasonable. Proposals mainly meet client needs but serious competition from other solutions	**C_3 Consciously chosen, but limited, portfolio with recruitment of people with those skills**	**R_3 Not easy to recruit and retain good people. Some variation in work quality. Average motivation and pay**	A_3 Reputation and client base growing steadily but not yet in the big league	M_3 Concentrate on a well-established market segment	***O_3 Aim to remain pretty much the same size and value***
T_4 Steady flow of work at significantly reduced level	**E_4 Limited. Some contracts because of unique skills**	C_4 Concentration on 2 or 3 skill areas, real expertise and careful training of new recruits	R_4 Filling slots with warm bodies	**A_4 Good reputation but not widely known outside its traditional market**	M_4 Careful attention to existing customers, some effort at getting new ones	O_4 A smaller firm, designed to be survivable in difficult and changed circumstances
T_5 Major clients develop some in-house studies capabilities	E_5 Poor. Able to offer only one or two skills with poor support	C_5 Concentration on 1 or 2 skills areas with no skill development	R_5 A core team supplemented by extensive use of associates	A_5 One among many small firms of reasonable quality	M_5 Constant monitoring of both markets to exploit established reputation	O_5 Seek survival (and possibly some growth) by merger/partnership with complementary firm
T_6 Disillusion with modelling leads to major changes in petroleum consultancy market	E_6 Very slight. Skills not seen as relevant outside oil industry	C_6 Small, but unique with world-class skills	R_6 A few highly expert individuals	$A6$ Small firm, weak reputation outside limited client base	**M_6 Rely on reputation and contacts to bring in work**	O_6 Keep struggling to exist by pursuing expedients
					M_7 Promise anything to a few existing clients	

Table 5.4 A plain VFM for Petroleum Associates Inc.

| Market potential | | Company characteristics | | | Corporate posture | |
Traditional oil industry market T	Scope for Expansion in other markets E	Skill and Capability base C	Human Resource position R	Corporate reputation and Attitude A	Marketing policy M	Strategic Objective O
T_1 Worries over economic volatility bring some growth in oil consultancy market	E_1 Excellent. Seen as having ideal solutions to client needs in a wide range of cases	C_1 Wide range of skills at cutting edge. Skill base retained by recruitment of people with those skills	R_1 Highly qualified people see employment with firm as a good career step. Very high quality of work. High motivation and pay	A_1 One of the very few firms seen as an analytical consultant of first recourse in any market area and for most types of problem	M_1 Actively seek business wherever it can be found and regardless of what it is	O_1 Aim for rapid growth in size and value
T_2 Steady flow of work	E_2 Very good. Seen as having ideal solutions to client needs in a range of niche markets	C_2 Planned and actively managed portfolio of skills with strong attention to training for skill development	R_2 Fairly easy to recruit and retain good people. Consistently good work quality. Above average motivation and pay	A_2 A well-known and respected firm with a good client base in both market areas	M_2 Actively seek business wherever it can be found but only if it fits a selected range of skills	O_2 Aim for some growth in size and value
T_3 Volatility (up and down) in frequency and volume of work for next few years	E_3 Reasonable. Proposals mainly meet client needs but serious competition from other solutions	C_3 Consciously chosen, but limited, portfolio with recruitment of people with those skills	R_3 Not easy to recruit and retain good people. Some variation in work quality. Average motivation and pay	A_3 Reputation and client base growing steadily but not yet in the big league	M_3 Concentrate on a well-established market segment	O_3 Aim to remain pretty much the same size and value
T_4 Steady flow of work at significantly reduced level	E_4 Limited. Some contracts because of unique skills	C_4 Concentration on 2 or 3 skill areas, real expertise and careful training of new recruits	R_4 Filling slots with warm bodies	A_4 Good reputation but not widely known outside its traditional market	M_4 Careful attention to existing customers, some effort at getting new ones	O_4 A smaller firm, designed to be survivable in difficult and changed circumstances
T_5 Major clients develop some in-house studies capabilities	E_5 Poor. Able to offer only one or two skills with poor support	C_5 Concentration on 1 or 2 skills areas with no skill development	R_5 A core team supplemented by extensive use of associates	A_5 One among many small firms of reasonable quality	M_5 Constant monitoring of both markets to exploit established reputation	O_5 Seek survival (and possibly some growth) by merger/partnership with complementary firm
T_6 Disillusion with modelling leads to major changes in petroleum consultancy market	E_6 Very slight. Skills not seen as relevant outside oil industry	C_6 Small, but unique with world-class skills	R_6 A few highly expert individuals	$A6$ Small firm, weak reputation outside limited client base	M_6 Rely on reputation and contacts to bring in work	O_6 Keep struggling to exist by pursuing expedients
					M_7 Promise anything to a few existing clients	

a small number of people if it is T_5 and that people of their expertise will be able to develop new consultancy services if it is T_6. They feel that E_4 can be maintained, and that O_4 is a viable objective. They would rely on their expertise to achieve C_6, move to R_6 or R_5 and attempt to maintain A_4. They could no longer rely on M_6 and would have to adopt M_4, M_3 being too risky. To be sure, this will involve converting full-time employees to associates (R_5), but some of them could be brought back if T_4 happens. This seems safer, as they still have O_5 in reserve. None of the principals wants O_6/M_7 so, if O_5 failed, they would sell out while they could.

Highlight this strategy and think about the adjustments that might be needed to deal with the gaps it reveals.

Are there any more viable strategies that might be considered? If the answer is yes, then strategic thinking has been deepened for PAI. If it is no, a stark choice has been identified.

We now turn to the formal use of the VFM as a sequel to TOWS analysis by considering a VFM for *Herrington-Jones*.

Herrington-Jones's viable firm matrix   CASE STUDY

At the end of Chapter 4, three robust strategies emerged from the *Herrington-Jones* TOWS analysis:

1. **European expansion**: acquire retail brands in mature European markets and develop retail brands in new European markets, with the aim of capitalising on learning scale efficiencies.

2. **E-commerce**: invest in infrastructure, exploit gains from first mover advantages in efficient supply chain management, position to provide competition both on cost and tailored value-added services.

3. **Lifestyle**: build up a responsive and detailed customer database to monitor changing customer needs and take advantage of segmentation of the consumer market to cherry-pick attractive segments. Augment the focus on value by providing 'more than just a mere shopping experience'.

Tables 5.5 and 5.6 interpret those strategic moves into VFM terms. They represent, respectively, what *Herrington-Jones* looks like now, as a very viable business in present-day conditions, and the configuration required to be the number one European retailer in 2010. The description in each row is now done with a one-word description supplemented by a short phrase.

A notable feature of Tables 5.5 and 5.6 is that *Herrington-Jones's* management team is a critical factor. It is at T_1 now and that performance must not be allowed to slip. Noticing that issue might lead us to do a new strategic analysis to ensure that *Herrington-Jones* can maintain its management quality. Posing an appropriate strategic question and going through the **ACTIFELD** methodology for that question would be an excellent case study to help you to build your knowledge of these tools for strategic thought.

Table 5.5 *Herrington-Jones's current position (in bold)*

Product expansion P	E-commerce E	Channel C	Purchasing Network N	Company Objective O	Brand value B	Management Team T
P_1 – *Expand.* New range of services and retail products	E_1 – *Lead.* Proactive e-commerce strategy and development of new technology	C_1 – *Drastic.* New distribution channel like home delivery or depots	N_1 – *Expand.* Scale allows leading price negotiations with manufacturers	O_1 – *Rapid.* Growth through acquisition and rollout of new outlets in EU	B_1 – *Leader.* High brand equity leader in sector and ability to stretch	T_1 – *Strong.* **Highly successful management team continue growth**
P_2 – *Stretch.* **New retail food and non-food products**	E_2 – *Adopt.* **Early adoption of new IT and distribution technology**	C_2 – *Expand.* Existing channels with several store formats	N_2 – *Partner.* EU expansion and group buying enable semi-competitive purchasing	O_2 – *Moderate.* Funding available for limited new outlets within EU	B_2 – *Tier 1.* Solid brand, level with other leading retailers	T_2 – *Distracted.* Loss of focus with new entrant and revert to following industry leader
P_3 – *Moderate.* Expand into limited niches	E_3 – *React.* Match leading rivals	C_3 – *Reduce.* **Revert to single efficient mega-store format**	N_3 – *Limited.* **Low buyer power with low margins**	O_3 – *Organic.* **Growth through reinvestment of retained profits**	B_3 – *Established.* **Second tier with some negative connotations**	T_3 – *Weakened.* Lose key people and short-term poor management
P_4 – *Steady.* Concentrate on established three-tier segmentation	E_4 – *Fail.* Recognise trend but inefficient implementation with low value		N_4 – *None.* No network buying threatens survival	O_4 – *Survive.* Share valuation halts expansion for lack of capital	B_4 – *Negative.* Poor image in both quality and service	T_4 – *Poor.* Management failure in critical business issues
P_5 – *Reduce.* Single home brand range	E_5 – *Lose.* No understanding of new business and distribution models			O_5 – *Downsize.* Share collapse causes divestment of some outlets		

Table 5.6 Viable firm matrix required to be the number one retailer in Europe (in bold italic)

Product expansion P	E-commerce E	Channel C	Purchasing Network N	Company objective O	Brand value B	Management team T
P_1 – *Expand.* New range of services and retail products	E_1 – *Lead.* **Proactive e-commerce strategy and development of new technology**	C_1 – *Drastic.* **New distribution channel like home delivery or depots**	N_1 – *Expand.* **Scale allows leading price negotiations with manufacturers**	O_1 – *Rapid.* **Growth through acquisition and rollout of new outlets in EU**	B_1 – *Leader.* **High brand equity. Leader in sector and ability to stretch**	T_1 – *Strong.* **Highly successful management team continue growth**
P_2 – *Stretch.* **New retail food and non-food products**	E_2 – *Adopt.* Early adoption of new IT and distribution technology	C_2 – *Expand.* Existing channels with several store formats	N_2 – *Partner.* EU expansion and group buying enable semi-competitive purchasing	O_2 – *Moderate.* Funding available for limited new outlets within EU	B_2 – *Tier 1.* Solid brand, level with other leading retailers	T_2 – *Distracted.* Loss of focus with new entrant and revert to following industry leader
P_3 – *Moderate.* Expand into limited niches	E_3 – *React.* Match leading rivals	C_3 – *Reduce.* Revert to single efficient mega-store format	N_3 – *Limited.* Low buyer power with low margins	O_3 – *Organic.* Growth through reinvestment of retained profits	B_3 – *Established.* Second tier with some negative connotations	T_3 – *Weakened.* Lose key people and short-term poor management
P_4 – *Steady.* Concentrate on established three-tier segmentation	E_4 – *Fail.* Recognise trend but inefficient implementation with low value		N_4 – *None.* No network buying threatens survival	O_4 – *Survive.* Share valuation halts expansion for lack of capital	B_4 – *Negative.* Poor image in both quality and service.	T_4 – *Poor.* Management failure in critical business issues
P_5 – *Reduce.* Single home brand range	E_5 – *Lose.* No understanding of new business and distribution models			O_5 – *Downsize.* Share collapse causes divestment of some outlets		

Notice that, unlike PAI's VFM, there is no column for the objectives. The objective of being number 1 in Europe has been stipulated and the analysis in this case is to see what has to be done for that aim to be achieved. When we do the remaining steps in the **ACTIFELD** approach, it might turn out that the aim cannot be achieved. In that case, we might have to loop back to an earlier stage in the analysis, as we discussed in Chapter 1, especially Figure 1.1. That might lead us to a different VFM which included objectives, to help us to analyse *Herrington-Jones* from a different standpoint.

We reiterate, yet again, that there is no standard way of using these tools. They have to be applied imaginatively and flexibly.

Finally, as far as *Herrington-Jones* is concerned, you may disagree with the assessments and with the matrices. That is perfectly legitimate and you should feel free to revise them.

Chapter summary

The VFM can be used in three ways.

The VFM, simple though it seems to be *after* it has been formulated, is quite a subtle tool that, as we have seen, can be used in three ways.

1. It is a means of evaluating viable firms or their competitors in a given business area or, in other contexts, exploring possible structures for a government agency, a defence force, or whatever. That use was illustrated for consultancy firms in Tables 5.1 and 5.2.

2. The VFM can be used so as to explore, quickly, some strategic options as was shown in Table 5.3. That method is a shortcut in the **ACTIFELD** methodology as it does not follow FAR and TOWS. It is for a problem that is immediate, so the futures exploration in FAR can be omitted, and it is drastic, so one needs to get some quick ideas about the strategic possibilities. Knowing what those options are, one could then use TOWS to see what actions would be needed to implement the least unfavourable.

3. The VFM can be used in its proper place in the **ACTIFELD** methodology, after a strategic question has been posed, complexity has been unravelled, TOWS have been evaluated and it is necessary to design an organisation that can implement the TOWS actions. We showed that full-scale use in Tables 5.5 and 5.6 for the *Herrington-Jones* case study.

We chose to show those uses through VFMs for professional services firms (an area much neglected in the management literature, with the notable exception of Maister (1993)), and *Herrington-Jones*, an assumed food retailer.

There is, though, no formal step that, as it were, 'maps' the TOWS results into the VFM and there are two reasons for that.

1. The TOWS analysis was an act of imagination, intuition and common sense and the VFM was, similarly, an imaginative and sensible view of what businesses in a given domain might look like. Identifying the existing firm, and the firm required to implement the TOWS strategies, in the VFM also calls for intuition and common sense but experience shows that, provided the VFM has been well

thought out, the step is not difficult. If it does prove hard to reflect the TOWS outputs in the VFM it likely that the VFM is unsatisfactory. Of course, if the existing business cannot be highlighted in the VFM, then the VFM is useless and needs drastic revision.

2. As we pointed out in Chapter 1, practical strategy is *fundamentally* incapable of being reduced to a set procedure, let alone a formula.

Now that you have studied the VFM in detail you will appreciate that there is, in fact, a *fourth* way of using it and that is as a training/familiarisation aid to help newly recruited senior managers understand the business. The *gestalt*, whole-pattern, picture that the VFM gives of the organisation's perception of its objectives and capabilities should be quite illuminating for a newcomer. Bearing in mind that the VFM shows the organisation's posture within a business sector – management consultancy or whatever – using the VFM to show that new manager the positioning of the sector's leaders, direct competitors and aspiring 'thrusters' might suggest all manner of business issues (obviously, it would probably confuse the issue to try to put all these onto one VFM!). This might be an effective way to verify the TOWS items.

One might even take this idea further and use the VFM to portray more vividly the four types of business in the well-known BCG matrix or to shed detailed light on Porter's equally well-known five forces.

Turning from those issues, there are two key success factors in using VFMs.

The *first* is to be able to change the mindset when moving from TOWS and strategies to the VFM so that, instead of thinking 'What do we need to do?', think about 'What kind of organisation could do those things?' That change of viewpoint is what was meant when we said that the **ACTI** in **ACTIFELD** corresponded to the *actions* to tackle the strategic question, whereas the **FELD** relates to making those actions work *in the field*, so to speak.

> Tho first success factor is to change the mindset.

The *second* is to be scrupulously honest in the assessments; wishful thinking will defeat their purpose. The focus group should be able to provide the right degree of imagination in developing a VFM and the proper objectivity in its use. The objectivity is critical when using a VFM for business evaluation and, especially, when a VFM is used, as it clearly can be, for competitor analysis. That can be done in two ways; the obvious one is to position a competitor in a VFM as a way of evaluating their viability or lack of it. The second is to try to assess where they see us in the VFM, though it would be quite a conundrum if where we think they see us is not the same as where we see ourselves. What might that imply? The first method might suggest strategic moves we might make; the second might allow us to predict their moves.

> The second success factor is *scrupulous* honesty in the assessments.

You now need to reinforce your understanding of all this by developing some VFMs for other types of business, or other organisations, always drawing a mind map as a way of getting into the VFM.* Do not worry if you know nothing about the cases suggested. There is much information on the websites of real organisations and in their annual reports. If you do not have time to do that research, you can always invent things. The point is not to do real analysis, but to master the art of the VFM. In doing so, you may well find other ways to use this technique.

---

* *Note to instructors*: this type of exercise can be set as an examination question and the whole **ACTIFELD** analysis of a chosen or stipulated theme is good term paper or course project.

Two suggestions are:

- Change *Herrington-Jones* from a chain of food supermarkets to a chain of home improvement (DIY) shops.

- You will see a lot of *Herrington-Jones* trucks on the roads but those vehicles are actually owned by MoveStuff, a national haulage business with contracts with companies such as *Herrington-Jones* to meet their national transport needs on a continuous basis. Develop a VFM for all possible mass-haulage firms.

Some other possibilities for exercises are:

- the charity sector in which NGOs such as Overseas Carers function
- the manufacturing sector in which the XYZ company from Chapter 1 operates
- Greyhound buses
- universities
- hospitals
- city governments.

You will think of many others but the key idea is not to do a VFM for, say, XYZ specifically, it is to build a matrix for all possible manufacturing businesses in XYZ's sector – the production of high-quality power tools, for instance – and then see what XYZ needs to be in order to be viable in that sector, perhaps as market leader, a niche operator or whatever.

Reference

Maister, D. H. (1993), *Managing the Professional Services Firm*. Free Press Paperbacks, New York.

Evaluating strategic moves

What this chapter is about

The viable firm matrix has shown the organisational transition needed to implement strategic actions. That move has to be assessed by:

■ how well it satisfies the *aspirations of stakeholders*, and

■ the *resources needed* to make it come about.

There are two practical strategy tools for those tasks:

■ *congruence analysis*, and

■ *resource analysis*.

Introduction to congruence and resource analysis

In Chapter 5, we studied the viable firm matrix and saw how it is used to differentiate between firms (or any other organisation), identify strategic options, and to design the organisation that should be able to implement a chosen strategy. It was stressed that a VFM is an *organisational evaluation* and *design* tool. That is, though, only the first step in strategic implementation and we must now address two other aspects.

ACTIF**E**LD

The *first* is how well the identified strategies or viable strategic options fit with the aspirations of the different stakeholders in the situation. This is called *congruence analysis*. For instance, in the case of Littleworth and Thrupp, the legal firm, Mr Littleworth is near to retirement age while Ms Thrupp is far from it and a strategy that is congruent with his aspirations might not fit at all well with what she wants to achieve.

Congruence analysis is highly political (with a small p) as it relates to the preferences, and even the ethical constraints, of the people and groups involved in strategic choices. That is as it should be. Practical strategy is, at its very roots, concerned with bringing about change in a situation, and that is *fundamentally* political. In democratic elections the competing parties seek to persuade the voters that their proposals for change will

Congruence analysis handles the vital political aspects of change.

best meet the aspirations of most of the people. Investors in ethical investment funds seek to make money, but prefer not to do so by owning shares in firms that deal in products of which they do not approve; perhaps benefiting from the profits of a tobacco company would not be *congruent* with their beliefs.

Congruence analysis is a vital part of the practical strategy process and cannot be neglected.

The *second* method covered in this chapter deals with the practical details of the resources needed for strategic implementation. It may be that the strategy which emerged from TOWS and led to the identification of a viable firm, or some strategic options which came from the quick use of the VFM (as with the oil consulting firm), will require additional resources of people, machines, money or whatever, or there may be existing resources that will not be needed with the new strategy. Not surprisingly, this is called *resource analysis*.

> Resource analysis deals with the practical details.

As with just about everything in this book, the ideas are very simple, but the practice is a little more difficult and is best studied by means of examples and best of all by syndicate work to apply the tool to an interesting problem.

An example of congruence analysis

Background

We will use the strategic options for Petroleum Associates Inc. (PAI), the consulting firm discussed in Chapter 5, to illustrate congruence analysis and you will recall that study of PAI's VFM suggested two possibilities. To help you to follow the argument, the plain VFM for PAI is shown again in Table 6.1.

One of PAI's options is the bold one of trying to stay at O_3, maintaining their present size and value despite the likely drastic reduction in their existing business. PAI's owners reasoned that, in order to stay at O_3, they needed to try to reach E_2, seen as having good solutions to problems outside the oil business. That would require the M_5 marketing strategy, monitoring both markets to exploit their reputation. However, reputation depends on performance so it would be needful to improve their portfolio to C_2, a planned and actively managed skill set supported by good training. That posture should lead to A_2, a well-respected firm with a good client base in two markets, and C_2/A_2 might reasonably be expected to improve the recruitment position to R_2, though some additional actions might also be necessary to achieve R_2.

PAI's other option is to retrench the business, choosing O_4 as the objective, a choice that is viable with a posture of C_6, R_6 or R_5, and A_4. They could no longer rely on M6 and would have to adopt M_4, M_3 being too risky. It is *vital* to your understanding of what follows to trace this out in Table 6.1.

Table 6.1 The plain VFM for PAI

Market potential			Company characteristics		Corporate posture	
Traditional oil industry market T	Scope for Expansion in other markets E	Skill and Capability base C	Human Resource position R	Corporate reputation and Attitude A	Marketing policy M	Strategic Objective O
T_1 Worries over economic volatility bring some growth in oil consultancy market	E_1 Excellent. Seen as having ideal solutions to client needs in a wide range of cases	C_1 Wide range of skills at cutting edge. Skill base retained by recruitment of people with those skills	R_1 Highly qualified people see employment with firm as a good career step. Very high quality of work. High motivation and pay	A_1 One of the very few firms seen as an analytical consultant of first recourse in any market area and for most types of problem	M_1 Actively seek business wherever it can be found and regardless of what it is	O_1 Aim for rapid growth in size and value
T_2 Steady flow of work	E_2 Very good. Seen as having ideal solutions to client needs in a range of niche markets	C_2 Planned and actively managed portfolio of skills with strong attention to training for skill development	R_2 Fairly easy to recruit and retain good people. Consistently good work quality. Above average motivation and pay	A_2 A well-known and respected firm with a good client base in both market areas	M_2 Actively seek business wherever it can be found but only if it fits a selected range of skills	O_2 Aim for some growth in size and value
T_3 Volatility (up and down) in frequency and volume of work for next few years	E_3 Reasonable. Proposals mainly meet client needs but serious competition from other solutions	C_3 Consciously chosen, but limited, portfolio with recruitment of people with those skills	R_3 Not easy to recruit and retain good people. Some variation in work quality. Average motivation and pay	A_3 Reputation and client base growing steadily but not yet in the big league	M_3 Concentrate on a well-established market segment	O_3 Aim to remain pretty much the same size and value
T_4 Steady flow of work at significantly reduced level	E_4 Limited. Some contracts because of unique skills	C_4 Concentration on 2 or 3 skill areas, real expertise and careful training of new recruits	R_4 Filling slots with warm bodies	A_4 Good reputation but not widely known outside its traditional market	M_4 Careful attention to existing customers, some effort at getting new ones	O_4 A smaller firm, designed to be survivable in difficult and changed circumstances
T_5 Major clients develop some in-house studies capabilities	E_5 Poor. Able to offer only one or two skills with poor support	C_5 Concentration on 1 or 2 skills areas with no skill development	R_5 A core team supplemented by extensive use of associates	A_5 One among many small firms of reasonable quality	M_5 Constant monitoring of both markets to exploit established reputation	O_5 Seek survival (and possibly some growth) by merger/partnership with complementary firm
T_6 Disillusion with modelling leads to major changes in petroleum consultancy market	E_6 Very slight. Skills not seen as relevant outside oil industry	C_6 Small, but unique with world-class skills	R_6 A few highly expert individuals	$A6$ Small firm, weak reputation outside limited client base	M_6 Rely on reputation and contacts to bring in work	O_6 Keep struggling to exist by pursuing expedients
					M_7 Promise anything to a few existing clients	

The congruence analysis technique

PAI's problem

The issue that congruence analysis addresses is how well or badly these options rate against the preferences of the interested parties, and a simple way of handling that is shown in Table 6.2 for PAI's first, bold, option.

The 'from' and 'to' definitions from the VFM are listed at the left, and that copying is essential as it ensures that everyone has the same understanding of what is being discussed (we shall consider the practice of congruence analysis after we have explained what it is). One then has as many columns as are needed for the interested parties, or stakeholders. In this case, we have three, respectively for the four people who own PAI, for their 30 employees, and for their existing clients. Including the clients may seem paradoxical, but not all of them want to go in-house, and some might be persuaded not to if they perceive PAI to be a viable business offering good services.

The final step is to rate each row in the columns to reflect a perception of how much each party likes or dislikes that aspect. Since these are qualitative assessments of preferences, we use a simple scheme of pluses and minuses (rather as was done in Table 4.1 for the relative attractiveness of different strategies *vis-à-vis* the Mont Fleur scenarios for South Africa). Three pluses mean 'like it very much', two pluses mean 'like it quite a lot', and one means 'like it a little'. The scale goes down to three minuses, for the opposite meanings. A blank entry means 'don't care one way or the other'.

Before explaining the plus and minus entries in Table 6.2, we need to make it clear that the assessments are those of the owners of PAI, as it is they who have to

The problem owners make the assessments in congruence analysis.

decide between the two options. They can judge how well or badly they themselves would like each of the two but they also have the difficult task of assessing (or guessing) the preferences of the employees and the clients. There might, perhaps, be some discreet conversations with the external stakeholders but the owners can hardly go to the employees and say 'How would you like it if we cut the business back to a small core?' The answer would be predictable and would trigger a lot more trouble than PAI's owners need. Politicians have to make the same kind of judgements about potentially unpopular initiatives, some of which are abandoned because it is perceived that an announcement that the government was even thinking about X would be too damaging. In short, only the holders of power can ultimately make the strategic choice but they must take into account other legitimate stakeholders who, if they have different preferences, might make or mar the contemplated decision.

Congruence analysis forces judgements to be explicit.

Congruence analysis is, of course, highly subjective precisely because it summarises opinions and assessments (or guesses). Its advantage is that it forces those assessments to be made clear and it displays them plainly. We will discuss the interpretation of the assessments at the end of the example.

First, we need to explain Table 6.2.

The first row says that the owners don't like this option very much as, having struggled to build up the existing business, they do not really want another battle

Table 6.2 Congruence analysis for PAI's first option

From	To	Attractiveness from the perspective of:		
		Owners	Employees	*Existing* clients
O₂ Aim for some growth in size and value	*O₂ Aim for some growth in size and value*	– –	+	
C₃ Consciously chosen, but limited, portfolio with recruitment of people with those skills	*C₂ Planned and actively managed portfolio of skills with strong attention to training for skill development*	– –	++	– –
R₃ Not easy to recruit and retain good people. Some variation in work quality. Average motivation and pay	*R₂ Fairly easy to recruit and retain good people. Consistently good work quality. Above average motivation*	++	++	++
A₄ Good reputation but not widely known outside its traditional market	*A₂ A well-known and respected firm with a good client base in both market areas*	++	+	– –
M₆ Rely on reputation and contacts to bring in work	*M₅ Constant monitoring of both markets to exploit established reputation*	– –		–

to survive (they have done a VFM to assess the strength of the likely competition in other markets). They think that the employees would like the attempt to stay in business, but the clients probably don't care what PAI's objectives are.

The reasons for the second row's ratings are that the employees might be quite attracted by the idea of learning new, and portable, skills. The owners do not, therefore, like the idea of a huge and expensive effort that might simply be wasted if the employees take their new skills with them. It is important not to see congruence analysis as an exercise in filling in a form, and also to be willing to change assessments after further thought. The owners at first quite like the C_3/C_2 transition and rate it +. When they study the employees' preferences, they change their minds and make it – –.

Finally in this row, the *existing* clients might not be happy at the likely loss of attention from PAI. In the third row, everyone likes the idea of good, well-trained people. Work out for yourself the apparent reasons behind the rest of the ratings. After you have done that, and preferably in syndicate discussion, try to put yourself in the shoes of PAI's owners and make your own assessments of these issues.

As we have seen, though, PAI's owners have identified two strategic options (and you may have found another if you did the exercise in Chapter 5), so Table 6.3 is the congruence analysis for retrenching the business. This time, we will explain these illustrative assessments by working down the columns, rather than across the rows. In practical use, you should use both methods as a cross-check on your understanding.

Table 6.3 Congruence analysis for PAI's second option

From	To	Attractiveness from the perspective of:		
		Owners	Employees	*Existing* clients
O_2 Aim for some growth in size and value	*O_4 A smaller firm, designed to be survivable in difficult and changed circumstances*	–	– – –	
C_3 Consciously chosen, but limited, portfolio with recruitment of people with those skills	*C_6 Small, but unique with world-class skills*	++	– – –	++
R_3 Not easy to recruit and retain good people. Some variation in work quality. Average motivation and pay	*R_5 A core team supplemented by extensive use of associates or R_6 A few highly expert individuals*	+++	– – –	+
A_4 Good reputation but not widely known outside its traditional market	*A_4 Good reputation but not widely known outside its traditional market*	–		
M_6 Rely on reputation and contacts to bring in work	*M_4 Careful attention to existing customers, some effort at getting new ones*	+		+

In essence, the owners are not too happy with O_4, going back to being the small firm they were when they started PAI, they like C_6 as they will be able to practise their own skills instead of having to spend a lot of time on management, and $R_{5/6}$ avoids all the recruitment trouble. A_4 seems to them to be a little restrictive and M_4's attraction is the positive interaction with the clients. The owners judge that the employees would hate the whole idea, for obvious reasons, but the existing clients might quite like the prospect of dealing with top-quality people and getting some marketing attention.

Interpreting the congruence analysis tables

We have the results, but what do they mean? How can we interpret them into meaningful actions?

Don't add the pluses and minuses to get the overall 'score'.

On the face of it, one might add up plus and minus ratings and 'calculate' the net effect but a little thought shows that to do so would be pretty meaningless as the trade-offs would be between very different factors. For instance, in Table 6.2 there are two minuses against O_2, an objective, but they do not cancel out two pluses against R_2, a human resource issue.

Aim for a *gestalt* appreciation of the whole pattern.

The preferred approach is the *gestalt*, whole-pattern, viewpoint of the web of factors that we used with field anomaly relaxation in Chapter 3. To remind you, *gestalt* means 'perception of a pattern or structure possessing qualities as a whole that cannot be described merely as a sum of its parts'. In other words, one has to look at a congruence analysis table as a whole.

For Table 6.2 the picture that emerges, *from the owners' standpoint*, is that while there are things that would be nice if they happened (R_2 and A_2), the discontents are too great (O_2 and C_2) and there is little to maintain the support of the existing clients. Table 6.3, on the other hand, has the drawback that it takes the owners back to square one, but that is outweighed by its other attractions and the possibility of continued business with at least some of the existing clients. Retrenching the business seems, on balance, to be the better preferred of the two options.

Although the plus and minus ratings are the judgements of the owners, it is worth looking at the implications of the employees' presumed preferences, which are that retrenchment is deeply unattractive to them, but there are things that they might like about the bold option. Perhaps, then, there is a third possibility: a management buy-out by the employees. It is a characteristic of many of these tools for practical strategy that they sometimes suggest a possible strategic action that had been overlooked until then; they might equally well be called *tools for strategic imagination*.

> The tools for practical strategy can suggest an option that had previously been overlooked.

Congruence analysis in practice

There are two aspects of the use of congruence analysis; the first is some practical tips and the second is its subtleties.

The first practical point is that the people who should do it are normally the focus group monitoring the practical strategy process. The second is that one has to think carefully about which stakeholders to include. Some obvious possibilities are the management group, employees, customers, shareholders, suppliers and, where it is relevant, the regulatory authority (where an authority exists it would probably be very unwise to exclude it!). It is usually a good idea to write a short explanation of why an interested party has been included and some statement about that entity's assumed preferences. It is tempting to have too many stakeholders, but more than about four or five makes it hard to use the gestalt appreciation. The upper limit for gestalt is seven in FAR but there the appreciation is of a one-dimensional configuration of items, one from each row. In congruence analysis, the table is two-dimensional and it has to be appreciated as a whole.

Congruence analysis is much more subtle than it looks. At first sight it might be dismissed as being no more than a set of guesses (we deliberately used that word earlier), and therefore of no value. However, consider the alternative and imagine PAI's owners trying to decide what they would prefer to do and how that might be influenced by the preferences of other parties (and this issue of preferences cannot be ignored in practical strategy). It is easy to see that, lacking the framework which congruence analysis provides, the discussion might rapidly degenerate into an argument, and perhaps a very heated one. On the other hand, if the congruence analysis concept is used not only with imagination but also with common sense, reasoned debate becomes possible about why one person rates a factor as two pluses while the rest of the group sees it as a minus. The issue might be resolved by a vote but it would be far more fruitful to explore the reasons for the extreme views. That, you will recall, was the essence of the Delphi method discussed in Chapter 3 and congru-

> Congruence analysis makes it possible to have a reasoned debate about preferences.

ence analysis is best seen as a Delphic approach to preference evaluation. In short, its main value is in being a good way to turn an argument into a discussion. That is probably true of many of the techniques described in this book.

Resource analysis

Introduction

Resource analysis deals with the gaps between the resources available at present and those that would be needed to implement a proposed strategy. The collection of gaps is an indicator of the ease or difficulty of implementing a strategic option and should, therefore, affect the final choice of what is to be done. In this section we will study an example of resource analysis, think about how its results are interpreted, and look at various ways of measuring gaps. Later in the chapter we will study *Herrington-Jones's* resource analysis.

> 'Resources' can include intangibles such as organisational culture.

The key to understanding resource analysis is that the resources are not just the obvious things such as machines, financial reserves, or numbers of people. 'Resources' also includes apparent intangibles such as the corporate culture, attention to customers and, indeed, anything that makes the business, or other organisation, viable; a resource gap of too little attention to customers may be as critical to success as too few machines, and filling a resource gap does not necessarily cost money. Of course, some resources might be in surplus: too many machines, perhaps.

It can also *sometimes* happen in resource analysis that the gaps between the current and the proposed firms are so large, or so numerous, that they cannot be filled. This means that an option, which appeared to be viable in the viable firm matrix, is not, in practical terms, viable at all. The reason for this apparent contradiction is that the VFM finds viable combinations of *written definitions*: such-and-such a combination of marketing, human resources and so on *appears* to be viable when expressed in words but might turn out not to be so when examined in detailed resource requirement terms. Perhaps the VFM should be called the *apparently* viable firm matrix, but we will stick with the simpler term as the true significance of the VFM is that it points attention to possibilities that seem to be worth detailed analysis and does not waste time and effort on obvious impossibilities.

An example of resource analysis

Let us stay with the problems of PAI but we will imagine not only that it has become clear to a group of the leading employees (we will call them the Group) that the owners are thinking of cutting the business back to a small core, in which case all the employees will lose their jobs, but also that someone has leaked the confidential VFM to the Group. Studying the VFM leads the Group to believe that with more dynamic and less complacent management the bold strategy is viable and they approach the owners with a plan to buy the business: a so-called management buy-out, or MBO.

We shall now study the problem from the Group's point of view as they start to negotiate the price, and other terms, such as an agreement to prevent the owners from competing with PAI within, say, five years. It is obvious that the resources the Group will need to invest, especially the monetary ones, will affect the price they can afford to pay for the business, and the scale of any other problems is an indicator of the business risks they will face. If the likely risks turn out to be too great, they might feel that it would be wise to withdraw from the MBO negotiations and look for other jobs. Resource analysis is intended to guide them to the answers to those questions (it is a sad fact that many MBOs do fail and maybe resource analysis could have avoided some of those disasters).

To explain resource analysis we will start with a fragment of the analysis, shown in Table 6.4 for the gaps between C_3 and C_2 (in Tables 6.4 and 6.5 the text definitions of factors such as C_3 and C_2 have been abbreviated to make the tables fit the pages). The Group feels that C, as a category, is too broad and therefore breaks it down into four sub-categories. (The blank row containing '???' is there to encourage you to add extra categories if you wish. You may, of course, feel that some of these sub-categories are not suitable. Perhaps recruitment brochures are too trivial to worry about. As always in this book, you are challenged to do your own analysis.)

> Break resources down into sub-categories, but only if it helps you to think.

Each sub-category is rated on a scale from 0 to 4, in which 0 means non-existent now, or irrelevant in the proposed strategy, 1 means poor, 2 means average, 3 is above average and 4 corresponds to excellent. 'Average', and the others, mean *relative to general standards in similar or competing businesses.*[*] (We shall discuss other definition systems when we have completed this example.)

The gaps in the right-hand column are easy to interpret, for instance, 'Our brochures need some improvement', 'We have ignored recruitment in the past, but

Table 6.4 A fragment from the MBO resource analysis

Sub-category	From	To	Resource gaps
	C_3 **Limited portfolio, recruit for those skills**	C_2 *Managed portfolio with good training*	
Availability of recruitment brochures	1	2	1
Activity in graduate recruitment	0	3	3
Provision of training	1	3	2
Research into new techniques	0	3	3
???			

---

[*]Obviously, what might be excellent for a consultancy in the Republic of Cataclysmia, mentioned in Chapter 1, could be grossly inadequate in London, New York or Melbourne.

now we need to be more active than most other firms', 'We have to get our training up to better than the average for *similar* consultancies'. All of these sub-categories will involve some expenditure but the training row has been emphasised as it will involve substantial expense. If the Group have their wits about them they will know what the better firms do; they have to match that, and they should be able to estimate the cost of doing so.

The total of the gaps in Table 6.4 is 9, and although that number is fairly meaningless in itself because it is the sum of different things, it does show that the C category will require some serious management attention from the Group, and the spending of some money, if the MBO goes ahead.

The end result for all the categories is shown in Table 6.5. Three sub-categories are now in bold type to show that they are likely to be expensive; estimated costs could be pencilled in against those rows. Three more items have gaps of 3, to show that they will need serious management attention, and a further three have gaps of 2, suggesting causes for concern. There are some gaps of 1, which might denote aspects that cannot be ignored but are not high priority. Finally, two items show no gaps.

How might the Group interpret these results? The significantly costly items might provide a basis for rational negotiation with the owners on the price to be paid for the business. The management attention sub-categories will show them what they are taking on. The overall gestalt appreciation is a more accurate picture of the viability of the MBO than the apparent viability from the VFM. Resource analysis is a cross-check on the VFM and the two approaches go hand-in-hand.

Resource analysis is a cross-check on the VFM thinking.

What should the Group decide to do? Is the MBO going to work or are the management problems so large that it will be impossible to deal with them? Bearing in mind that these people will have to borrow heavily and probably put their homes on the line, are the financial risks reasonable or are they too great? The final judgement will be for them to make, but it will have been made on the basis of comprehensive thought and coherent analysis, and that is the main value of resource analysis.

You should now do a resource analysis for the owners' other option of retrenching the business.

The importance of definitions

On the 0 = non-existent to 4 = excellent scale one has to be careful about definitions. For example, for a small firm, production capacity might, on a superficial view, be rated at 4, excellent, because the firm has just the right amount of capacity to handle a small volume of business. But suppose that the strategy being analysed called for a major expansion of output. That requires a 4 in production capacity, which the firm already seems to have, but it is obvious that the two 4s are not the same thing: the scale seems to be misleading.

Make sure that scales are not misleading.

The key to the apparent dilemma is to define the sub-category as 'ability to handle production volume'. For the small firm, that is 1, poor, because it can only handle small volumes. The expansion strategy calls for 4, so the scale is now working properly.

Table 6.5 Complete resource analysis for management buy-out

Sub-category	From	To	Resource gaps
	C$_3$ **Limited portfolio, recruit for those skills**	C$_2$ *Managed portfolio with good training*	
Availability of recruitment brochures	1	2	1
Activity in graduate recruitment	0	3	3
Provision of training	**1**	**3**	**2**
Research into new techniques	0	3	3
???			
	R$_3$ **Not easy to recruit. Average motivation and pay**	R$_2$ *Fairly easy to recruit good people. Above average motivation*	
Pay and conditions	**2**	**3**	**1**
Career management	0	3	3
Working environment	3	3	0
Quality and modernity of IT	3	3	0
Attendance at professional conferences	2	3	1
???			
	A$_4$ **Good reputation in traditional market**	A$_2$ *Good client base in both market areas*	
Attendance at industry gatherings	1	3	2
Publicity in and articles in trade journals	1	3	2
???			
	M$_6$ **Reputation and contacts bring in work**	M$_5$ *Monitoring of both markets*	
Skills in preparing and presenting proposals	2	3	1
Market research	**0**	**3**	**3**
Client monitoring and after-care	2	3	1
Attendance at trade fairs	1	3	2
???			

You need to keep this kind of consideration in mind if resource analysis is not to lead you astray.

Other definition systems for resource analysis

Tables 6.4 and 6.5 used simple definitions for the scale from 0 to 4, ranging from non-existent to excellent, relative to general standards in the industry concerned. That is easy to use, but what other systems exist for defining the meanings of resource gaps?

Table 6.6 shows four possibilities, all based on scale values of 0 to 4:

1. The first is the system we have already used: 'relative to others'.

2. The second, comparative, scale has two columns. The left hand is the availability of the current resources and the right hand is the resources required for the proposed strategy. The advantage of this scale is that it does not require comparisons with other firms or organisations in the same business area: sometimes no fair comparison can be drawn, as in the case of public monopolies or the Royal National Lifeboat Institution. The 'comparative' system of definitions is quite subtle as it works in two ways. On the one hand, if X is now a major strength and is also critical to future strategic success, then there is no problem. Similarly, if there are currently major weaknesses in X but X is not really important to the proposed strategy then, again, there is no gap. What, however, happens when X is currently rated at 1 but should be 4 in the future? It is the *left-hand* column that provides the answer: something that is now a major weakness, quality control, perhaps, is critical to success in the proposed strategy, and it should not be too hard to work out what needs to be done to achieve that. The TOWS technique might be helpful in doing so.

3. The third column is fairly self-explanatory, though you might want to qualify the definitions so that 'occasional' means 'twice a year', or whatever.

4. The last column has some purely illustrative financial figures which need to be changed to suit the problem; what is major investment for Joe, a self-employed builder, might not even rate as petty cash for **Herrington-Jones**.

It is important to realise that it is the numbers that are used in the resource analysis and that the words in Table 6.6 serve only to give meanings to those numbers.

It is obvious that one sub-category might be rated on a different system from another and Table 6.7 is a simple example of how that might be done. If differing systems are used it is usually a good idea to state explicitly which one applies in each case (which system of definitions would you use for research into new techniques?) but it is up to you to judge whether the complication of summing the gaps in different columns (on the right-hand side) is beneficial. Does the added detail help, or does it confuse the gestalt appreciation? Perhaps emphasising some of the rows is all that is needed. The answer will depend on the circumstances and one's personal style of thinking, but try to avoid an illusory concept that more detail means increased 'accuracy'. There is no virtue in complexity for its own sake.

Table 6.6 Some alternative definition systems for resource analysis

Scale value	Relative to general standards	Significance: current situation relative to proposed strategy		Senior management attention required	Monetary implications
		Current situation	Significance for proposed strategy		
0	Non-existent or not relevant	Non-existent	Not relevant	None – runs itself	Petty cash (£1,000/year)
1	Poor	Major weaknesses	Not really important	Rare	Routine maintenance (£5,000/year)
2	Average	Some weaknesses	Nice to have, but not critical	Occasional	Regular updating of facilities (£100,000/year)
3	Above average	Few deficiencies	Serious problems if not achieved, but not fatal to success	Frequent	Moderate investment (£500,000 every few years)
4	Excellent	Major strength	Critical to success	Constant	Major investment (£5 million as one-off)

A variant of resource analysis for a particular need

Do not assume that these four categories will cater for all resource analysis problems – you should be prepared to develop (and justify) your own scale when necessary; Colonel Brian Hall of the Australian army has kindly provided an interesting example of the creation of a variant on resource analysis to meet a particular need. The topic chosen by the team of which Hall was a member was strategies to ensure that the relevance of the Snowy Mountains Hydroelectric System (SMHES) could be maintained to the year 2030. Having applied the full **ACTIFELD** methodology, the team encountered an obvious difficulty when it came to resource analysis as, quite clearly, the SMHES is unique and its sub-category performances cannot be compared to the general standards in its industry, as we did with PAI. (There are, of course, vast hydroelectric systems in the USA, Russia, Argentina and elsewhere but they are not comparable for all manner of reasons.)

> Create your own rating system if necessary.

The concept evolved by the team (after some debate) is shown in Table 6.8, though that table is only a small fragment of the full SMHES resource analysis. The first four columns are the standard resource analysis format with the usual categories, sub-categories and gaps rated on the 'significance' scale from Table 6.6.

Table 6.7 An illustration of multiple systems

Sub-category	Scale	From	To	Management attention gaps	Money gap	Other gaps
		C_3 Limited portfolio, recruit for those skills	C_2 *Managed portfolio with good training*			
Availability of recruitment brochures	Relative	1	2			1
Activity in graduate recruitment	Management	0	3	3		
Provision of training	**Money**	1	3		**2 (or X million)**	
Provision of training	Management	1	3	2		
Research into new techniques	?	?	?	Which gap?		
???						

Table 6.8 A dual-rating system (adapted from Hall)

Sector	Sub-category	From	To	Gap	Score	Total
Supplying water	Storage capacity	3	4	DH1	9	
	Extent of distribution	3	4	MM1	4	
	Efficiency of water management	3	4	EL1	1	14
Supplying hydro-electricity	Generating capacity	2	3	MM1	4	
	Role in distribution management	2	3	ML1	2	6
Research and development	Skill in R&D management	2	4	EM2	4	
	Comprehensiveness of R&D investment plan	2	4	EM2	4	8

The variant proposed by Hall is in the last three columns and involved two steps. The *first* is to treat the gap as having three components:

1. its magnitude, that is, the difference between the two numerical ratings in a given row

2. the inherent problems of closing that gap, defined as E for easy, M for moderate and D for difficult

3. the resources (of whatever type) needed to close the gap, defined as L for low, M for medium, and H for high.

To understand this, consider the first sub-category: increasing storage capacity. The gap is 1 point on the scale, but it is very difficult to obtain the relevant planning permission and to solve the engineering design problems, and it is also certain to be very costly. That gives a rating of DH1, the **H** being in bold type to show that is a financial component. On the other hand, the water management sub-category is rated as EL1; the task is not very difficult and should not require much managerial effort.

The *second* part of this variant is shown in the last two columns of Table 6.8. It assigns numbers so that E = 1, M = 2, and D or H = 3. These are multiplied together and then multiplied by the numerical difference to get the final score, so that DH1, for instance, is translated as (D = 3)*(H = 3)*1 = 9. Finally, the sub-category scores are summed in the last column. Thus, using this very simple and clear approach, a gestalt appreciation of the whole problem is easy to make. In broad terms, and for this fragment of the analysis, solving the water supply problem is about as big a task as dealing with the other two combined.

The cleverness of this idea is that it allows for *non-linear effects*. It may, and probably will, be much harder to close a gap from 3 to 4 than to close a gap between 1 and 2. It might be simple to close a gap of 1 point but rather hard to close one of 2 points. Multiplying by the number of points then gives a feel for the overall magnitude of each task.

It is easy to see how this system could be extended, and some possibilities are to:

- extend the scale to allow for Very Difficult, Very Large resources, and so on

- change the weightings so that E stays at 1, but M = 3, D = 9 or whatever

- weight the categories so that if, say, supplying water is believed to be much more important than research and development, then the category totals could be multiplied by, say, 3 and 1. The first total would become 42 and the second would stay at 8. The effect – the numbers 42 and 8 – is a blend of the magnitude of each task and its importance. Depending on the situation, that may be a helpful indication of its true significance or it may confuse two different things.

It is always important not to overcomplicate scoring systems in an attempt to make them more 'scientific'.

We shall now see how congruence analysis and resource analysis can be applied to **Herrington-Jones**.

CASE STUDY	**Application to *Herrington-Jones and Co***

Herrington-Jones's strategy

You will recall from Chapter 5 that *Herrington-Jones's* strategy had three main components:

1. **European expansion:** acquire retail brands in mature European markets and develop retail brands in new European markets, with the aim of capitalising on learning scale efficiencies.

2. **E-commerce:** invest in infrastructure, exploit gains from first mover advantages in efficient supply chain management, position to provide competition both on cost and tailored value-added services.

3. **Lifestyle:** build up a responsive and detailed customer database to monitor changing customer needs and take advantage of segmentation of the consumer market to cherry-pick attractive segments. Augment the focus on value by providing 'more than just a mere shopping experience'.

Herrington-Jones's congruence analysis

You are challenged to put yourself into the shoes of *Herrington-Jones's* senior managers trying to deduce how these strategic components will 'fit' the aspirations and objectives of different stakeholders. Some obvious points of view are those of the senior managers themselves, the board of directors, middle managers, other employees, the financial markets, existing customers, suppliers and, perhaps, the Competition Commission. Would you be wise to try to consider all of these? If not, which might you decide to ignore, and why?

What might be the aspirations of each of the groups you decide to include? In practical congruence analysis it is essential to write a short pen-picture of a typical member of each group so as to ensure that the people doing the analysis have a shared view of what they are analysing. It will be misleading and pointless simply to put down some plus and minus signs without any real thought.

This exercise is best done in a group, being careful to take the Delphi approach of debating the reasons for extreme views. That will give practice in both congruence analysis and Delphi.

Herrington-Jones's resource analysis

A resource analysis for *Herrington-Jones* appears in Table 6.9.

This would now be a good point at which to review the *Herrington-Jones* case study from Chapter 4, TOWS, and Chapter 5, the VFM, to draw all these threads together. On review, you may disagree with the assessments and with the matrices. That is perfectly legitimate and you should feel free to revise them.

Table 6.9 *Herrington-Jones's* resource analysis

Sector	Sub-category	From:	To:	Gaps
Brand value		B_3 – *Established.* Second tier with some negative connotations	B_1 – *Leader.* High brand equity. Leader in sector and ability to stretch	
	Corporate visibility	2	4	2
	Positive association	3	4	1
	Trust	3	4	1
	Perception of quality	4	4	0
	Perception of value	3	4	1
	Marketing skills 3	4	1	
	Knowledge of market	2	4	2
Growth objective		O_3 – *Organic.* Growth through reinvestment of retained profits	O_1 – *Rapid.* Growth through acquisition and rollout of new outlets in EU	
	Availability of capital	1	4	3
	Acquisition strategy	3	4	1
	Knowledge of foreign markets	3	4	1
Purchasing network		N_3 – *Limited.* Low buyer power with low margins	N_1 – *Expand.* Scale allows leading price negotiations with manufacturers	
	Supplier relationships	1	4	3
	Partner relationships	2	4	2
	Understanding of foreign market	3	4	1
	Contacts within industry	3	4	1
E – commerce		E_2 – *Adopt.* Early adoption of new IT and distribution technology	E_1 – *Lead.* Proactive E-commerce strategy and development of new technology	
	Ability to adapt	4	2	2
	Capital investment in infrastructure	2	4	2
	Management commitment	3	4	1
	Trained staff	4	2	2
	Understanding of new technology	2	4	2
Channel		C_2 – *Expand.* Existing channels with several store formats	C_1 – *Drastic.* New distribution channel like home delivery or depots	
	Management commitment	4	4	0
	Capital investment in infrastructure	2	4	2
	Understanding of consumer	3	4	1
	Understanding of new technology	3	4	1

Chapter summary

We have now examined two more techniques from the practical strategy toolbox. They follow from the viable firm matrix, which generated a description of a viable firm that ought to be able to implement actions from TOWS, or other suggested strategies. The purpose of congruence and resource analysis is to establish whether or not the business that seemed to be viable from the text definitions of the VFM is really able to survive in the cold light of people's preferences and objectives, and the harsh reality of resource needs.

Congruence analysis is a checklist of a more-or-less-objective strategy against human values and preferences. We commented on the first page of this chapter that bringing about change of any sort, which is what the tools for practical strategy aim to do, is an intensely political act, and the best strategic analysis in the world will be futile if it ignores the politics. Congruence analysis is an attempt to evaluate the political, or preferential, factors in an organised, systematic way intended to make as sure as one can that nothing significant, and no relevant interest group, has been ignored. It is a checklist for the human factors. Of course, its assessments are themselves subjective – they cannot be otherwise – but any hope of implementing a strategy is very likely to be forlorn if congruence analysis is omitted.

Resource analysis is also a checklist process. One of its virtues is that it forces people to identify clearly what has to be done – the sub-categories – but does not list every conceivable factor. Make judgements about what is trivial and what is significant.

A second virtue is that the rating systems, simple though they are, again compel assessments to be made about the ease or difficulty of coping with the issues. Resource analysis cannot, however, prevent wishful thinking that some problem is easy to solve when, in fact, it is very hard. The best protection against that is the Delphi debate, mentioned under congruence analysis, which explores the extreme judgements; Joan thinks X is easy but Fred feels that it is hard, so why do they hold those opinions? Like congruence analysis, resource analysis should be a good way of clarifying the issues and turning what could otherwise be a heated argument into a productive discussion.

And finally, it may happen that congruence or resource analysis shows that the apparently viable firm is not acceptable to interest groups or that its resource demands cannot be met. In such a case, one loops back to the VFM to find another configuration that will work, or to TOWS for less demanding strategies and actions.

For instance, in Chapter 4 the TOWS analysis for the unmanned ground vehicle (UGV) suggested that the development of a demonstrator vehicle might be a good idea. For that project, we might omit the VFM step and go straight to congruence and resource analysis. If the conclusions were that the demonstrator vehicle was likely to be a step too soon from the standpoint of a particular stakeholder, or that the resource demands were excessive, one might revisit TOWS and deduce that a more practical step was to hold a conference to explore the issues more fully.

Obstacles, remedies, plans and decisions

What this chapter is about

- The first six steps in **ACTIFELD** took us up to evaluating stakeholder views and assessing resource implications.

- We are now close to an answer to the strategic question.

- We need to make one last check on the practicability of the emergent actions.

- That is done by cooking obstacles and designing remedies using *force field analysis*.

- This calls for a change of mindset to make sure that we have checked the proposed actions from a different viewpoint.

- The end result will be an explicit corporate plan of action.

- The plan will show where risks exist and that will lead to the final decision.

Introduction

We have now covered most of the steps in the **ACTIFELD** methodology so, while its full practical working will be discussed more fully in the next chapter, it is worth giving you a brief reminder of it before we deal with its last, and critical, step.

The tools for practical strategy described in the previous six chapters dealt with: **A** – asking a good strategic question; **C** – coming to grips with, or unravelling, the system's complexity; **T** – thinking about the future's possibilities; **I** – identifying strategic actions; **F** – finding a viable organisation to implement that plan; **E** – evaluating the acceptability of the proposed changes to the various stakeholders (congruence analysis), and assessing the resource requirements.

At any one of those steps the outcome might, in a real case, be *'this is not going to work'* and, as we pointed out in Chapter 1, that might lead us to rephrase the strategic question. If, for instance, no strategy for long-term growth can be found, the strategic question might become one of

Remember continually to check the strategic question.

short-term survival, and that would be a fundamentally different issue. An important aspect of the **ACTIFELD** steps is continually to test the strategic question, either confirming it as correct or revising it if necessary, on the common-sense basis that it is better to answer the right question than to answer the wrong one. In some instances, the analysis might mean that we have to loop back to an earlier stage, though that is less usual than redefining the strategic question.

For instance, in the *Herrington-Jones* case the complexity could be understood or unravelled, the future could be foreseen (in so far as that ability is given to mortals), clear actions emerged from TOWS, a viable firm could be designed, and the resource implications, though challenging, were not infeasible (we assume that the congruence analysis you did for yourself showed that the aspirations, objectives and ethical requirements of *Herrington-Jones's* various stakeholders were satisfied). The successive steps confirmed that the initial question was the right one.

ACTIFELD

Force field analysis checks the plan from a balance of forces point of view.

There remains one final methodological step – the **L** in **ACTIFELD** – before we come to D, the decision on whether or not to go ahead with the proposed strategy. The **L** step involves a final check of the strategic plan to find out whether or not obstacles within the system or in the external environment can be overcome. In essence, it studies the balance (or lack of it) between two sets of forces, one of which is trying to move the organisation in the direction it needs to go, while the other might be holding it back. This study of the balance between actions and restraints is called *force field analysis*, or FFA for short.

The concept of force field analysis

Force field analysis evaluates a strategy in terms of three components:

1. Are there *restraints* on the ability to achieve the objective?

2. What *actions* could bring it about?

3. Finding the *balance* between actions and restraints.

The results of FFA then lead to a fourth item:

4. Developing a *corporate plan* with *performance milestones*.

We will look at the details later, but the basic idea is shown in Figure 7.1. The vertical axis shows an objective to be achieved; in this simple instance it is to improve the proportion of 11-year-old children who can read fluently, and show understanding of, some standard piece of prose. The *current level* is that 60% can achieve that standard. The *desired level* is that 90% should reach that standard; realistically, that is not 100% as there will be some children with learning or other difficulties who cannot reach it. The *feasible level* recognises that, even with the best will in the world, we might not be able to do all that we might wish; there might be some proportion of pupils who, through illness or truancy, have missed too much school time, and there will be others who are simply not interested in learning to read. Perhaps the feasible level is 80%, which is not ideal but would be a worthwhile improvement on current performance.

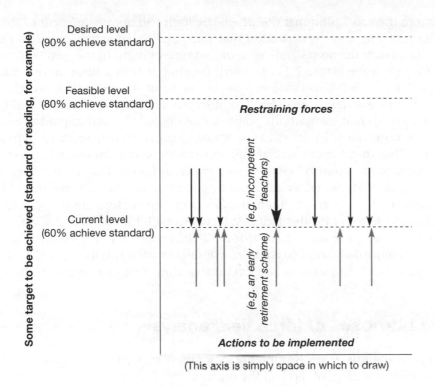

Figure 7.1 The concept of force field analysis

The vertical axis should be labelled in some suitable way. In this simple case we have used percentage values but, when we apply FFA to *Herrington-Jones*, we will use configurations from the firm's VFM. You should use whatever labelling system is most useful for the problem you are dealing with. The axis obviously cannot be drawn to scale for VFM configurations but, even when the axis is labelled using numbers, it should not be drawn to scale.

> Don't bother about accurate scales – leave space to work in.

It is more important to have space in which to work than to appear to be using accurate measurements. Similarly, the horizontal axis gives space to work in.

The rest of the diagram is completed with downward-pointing arrows for the *restraints* that might prevent the target being achieved and with upward-pointing arrows for the *actions* to be implemented. We will discuss where the actions and restraints come from, and the layout of the forces, below but for the simple example in Figure 7.1, we will imagine that a restraint is the presence of some incompetent teachers. The countervailing action is

> FFA helps you to check for implicit assumptions.

a premature retirement scheme to get rid of them, the implicit assumption being that the contract of employment makes it very difficult to dismiss teachers for incompetence, so it is easier to buy them out. Careful identification of implicit assumptions is always important, but much more so in FFA as its analysis may lead to assumptions, or cherished illusions, being challenged.

Even this very simple example makes an important point: the restraint arrow for the poor teachers is a good deal wider than the action arrow for the retirement scheme. This implies that the restraint is much more powerful than the action, leading to the conclusion that the scheme by itself will not be sufficient to solve the teacher problem, and the deduction that some additional action(s) will be needed. We will consider the deep significance of that type of result in the next section.

Before we leave Figure 7.1 it is worth looking at it in a little more detail. For instance, at the left-hand side two restraints point to one action, which might mean that one action overcomes two obstacles or that two obstacles nullify the action. Next to that, two actions point to one obstacle, which might have equivalent interpretations. In other cases, actions and restraints seem to bypass one another. That might mean several different things: maybe an obstacle is not being dealt with, or an action is being wasted, or perhaps an action is a cunning way of bypassing an obstacle, rather than meeting it head-on. We will give some tips for conventions to show these different cases later, but these examples should show you that FFA is a very flexible tool that leaves scope for much imagination.

We have seen the basic idea of force field analysis, but before we go on to explain in more detail how to *do* it, we will discuss what it is *for*. This will take very little space, but the ideas are so important that they deserve a section of their own.

The purposes of force field analysis

Force field analysis serves two interlocking purposes. First, it is a *'sanity check'* that the strategic objective of moving the organisation from one VFM configuration to another will not encounter any insuperable obstacles. Assume that, in this example, the presence of some incompetent teachers was identified as a weakness in the TOWS analysis, and an early retirement scheme was thought of as one of the actions required. However, it might just be assumed that the retirement scheme would solve that aspect of the problem, so FFA is a useful check for over-simple assumptions. The FFA technique, and it is scarcely rocket science, of drawing broad and narrow arrows (something discussed in the next section) to represent the perception of the respective powers of the restraint and the action has helped us to realise that tackling the teacher problem requires more than the retirement scheme. In this role, FFA performs a 'belt and braces' role by guarding against assumptions that the resource analysis has correctly and fully dealt with all the factors involved in the configuration change.

> FFA is a 'sanity check'.

Second, and more importantly, it is a *further stimulus to creative practical strategy*. In practical work it is virtually certain that something will have been overlooked in the earlier phases of using the tools for practical strategy; FFA should help to identify the extra ingredients and the example of increasing reading standards is an instance of that. In the teaching example, perhaps ideas such as retraining, changing the implicit assumption and having new contracts to make dismissal easier, better teaching materials, or whatever, will now emerge as factors that had not previously been imagined. Perhaps, even, the teacher problem was identified in TOWS, but it was not adequately considered and no one thought of an early retirement scheme. Of course, FFA cannot guarantee that new ideas will emerge, but it gives a last chance for them to do so.

> Study of the force field can stimulate creative thought.

In short, force field analysis offers a quick visual check of the robustness and apparent holes in the ability of an organisation to achieve its desired goal.

The technique of force field analysis

Having looked at what FFA does, it is now time to consider some of the details of the technique.

The first point to make is that, like all the methods we have examined in this book, FFA is deceptively simple. In practice it can be very subtle and highly effective but *it needs to be used with imagination.*

A natural question is to ask where the FFA arrows come from. The answer is that they do *not* automatically follow from either the TOWS actions, the congruence analysis of the politics, or the resource analysis sub-components. One reason for that is that there will usually be so many actions and sub-components that the FFA diagram would be so complex as to be useless. The more significant reason is that *we now seek to look at the strategic problem in a wholly fresh light* as, unless we do so, we shall not do a valid check on the strategic thinking. Changing the viewpoint is a stimulus to imaginative thought, whereas merely copying items from earlier analyses on to a new piece of paper would be no more than a clerical exercise.

To be sure, the TOWS congruence and resource analyses will be an input to FFA, but only in a general sense. One might start the FFA by reviewing the earlier results to refresh one's memory, and that might help to get the first few arrows on to the page, but the key step is to *change the mindset* to enable one to think afresh. To be specific, the TOWS mindset generates action plans from thought about the interplay of four sets of factors, some internal to the organisation and others in its environment. Congruence analysis deals with the political factors in organisational change and the standpoint of resource analysis is a gap-analysis calculation to identify what is needed to get from *here* to *there*. FFA, by contrast, requires visual thought about how two sets of forces bring about, or inhibit, movement on a scale of achievement. There is, therefore, no simple correspondence between the results from the TOWS and resource analyses and the force field diagram and, though the diagram can usually be *started* by checking back to previous work, imagination and insight should swiftly be turned loose to think about what restraints exist and how actions might overcome them, if they can. If they cannot, can the actions be changed so that they will overcome the restraints? Are additional actions required? What has been overlooked in earlier **ACTIFELD** steps?

> The key to force field analysis is to change your mindset.

Group discussion in front of a whiteboard will usually easily show which actions and restraints to include, and how they are to combine. When differing opinions emerge, it is usually effective to adopt the stance of a Delphi discussion (Chapter 3) by debating the reasons for extreme views about, perhaps, the relative widths of arrows, rather than allowing a dominant individual or majority opinion to dictate the result.

Figure 7.2 gives some suggestions for showing how arrows combine, how a restraint can be shown as negating an action, or vice versa, or how one action supports others, and other possibilities. It is, however, important not to use these suggestions too slavishly. They do not cover all imaginable possibilities and you must feel free to invent your own conventions where necessary; the only thing that matters is that all members of the group,

> Develop your own conventions if they help.

Width of arrow can show strength of effect

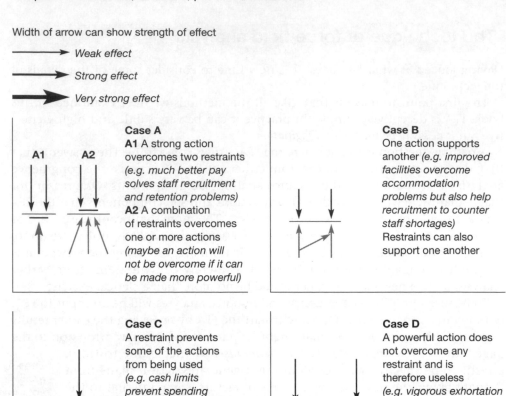

Case A
A1 A strong action overcomes two restraints (*e.g. much better pay solves staff recruitment and retention problems*)
A2 A combination of restraints overcomes one or more actions (*maybe an action will not be overcome if it can be made more powerful*)

Case B
One action supports another (*e.g. improved facilities overcome accommodation problems but also help recruitment to counter staff shortages*)
Restraints can also support one another

Case C
A restraint prevents some of the actions from being used (*e.g. cash limits prevent spending on people, facilities*) or an action abolishes restraints (*e.g. a change in the law prohibits strikes and restrictive practices*)

Case D
A powerful action does not overcome any restraint and is therefore useless (*e.g. vigorous exhortation may not counter union opposition and staff conservatism*)
Even a powerful action may need support from another action

The difference between case A and case C is that, in A, the restraints operate, but are overcome by actions; in C, the restraint wipes out the actions so that they cannot take place.

These tips should not be followed slavishly; but **must** be used **with flexibility**: In case A1, an action does not always have to be strong to overcome two restraints. An action might reinforce a restraint – in case D, exhortation could annoy people and *increase* opposition and that might be shown by a + instead of an X.

Above all, do not make the diagram too complicated!

Figure 7.2 Some tips for drawing force field diagrams

and the people to whom a report is made, should know what the conventions are. It can be useful to draw the agreed conventions at the side of the board as an aid to memory.

It is also important not to let the diagram become too complicated. For instance, when using different widths of arrows to show the relative power of actions and restraints, it might be useful to have at most three possibilities: weak, strong and very strong. It is also easy to be tempted to have too many branching arrows from, say, funding. To be sure, the presence or absence of funding does affect practically everything but the idea is to depict the principal effects.

If the diagram is allowed to become over-complicated, with too many details and too many lines crossing over, it loses its virtue which, as we said earlier, is to provide a highly visual check of the robustness and apparent holes in the ability of an organisation to achieve its desired goal.

The force field diagram must be developed by group discussion round a board. It will probably need to be redrawn to make it as clear as possible, the end result being recorded using a software package (Appendix I).

> Above all, don't let the diagram become too complicated.

The outcome of force field analysis

The end result of FFA is to pose five key questions:

1. *Which actions or policies are likely to be effective?*
2. *How can they be combined?*
3. *Which restraining forces might be critical?*
4. *Are any of the restraining forces so utterly dominant that nothing can be achieved?*
5. *Is there any cunning way of overcoming an apparently dominant restraint?*

Whatever the answers, FFA will have fulfilled its purpose of being a highly visual check, from a fresh, balance-of-forces, viewpoint on the viability of repositioning the organisation within the VFM. If the answers are encouraging, a corporate plan, in as much detail as necessary, will show what has to be done to implement the strategy in practice.

Producing a corporate plan

The last item in **ACTIFELD** before **D**, the decision on whether or not to go ahead with the indicated strategy of repositioning the organisation within the VFM, is the development of a corporate plan. This can involve some detailed work, as we have to draw together the resource analysis and new ideas from the force field results. However, without the corporate plan to tell people what they need to do and what resources they will have to do it with, all the previous work will do no more than fill a filing cabinet.

The corporate plan covers the *milestones to be achieved* and the *resources required*, to ensure the transition from one configuration to another in the viable firm matrix. In practice, this is likely to be no more than an *acceptable* result; perfection is usually unattainable in the real world.

Table 7.1 illustrates the general layout of a corporate plan. The time periods may be months, years or whatever, depending on the problem. The milestones will depend on the level of the plan so, for an overall plan for the chief executive, they could be related to the VFM configuration. If the aim is to move to a new configuration by the end of period 2, the period 1 milestone would be some sort of halfway position. It would probably make the plan too complicated to put all six or seven elements of the VFM configuration in the space for the milestone so a short phrase might be developed that summarises the configuration in question.

> The milestones are derived from the viable firm matrix.

Table 7.1 An illustrative corporate plan

Time phasing	Milestone to be achieved	Required availability of:				
		People	**Technology**	**Money**	**Political actions**	**Any other factor(s)**
First period	M_1	P_1	T_1	£1	A_1	X_1
Second period	M_2	P_2	T_2	£2	A_2	X_2
And so on						

For a lower-level plan, such as for the marketing director, the milestone comes from the VFM. For example, in the case of the oil consultancy, PAI, in Chapter 5, the marketing actions for the management buy-out involved moving from 'M_6 Rely on reputation and contacts to bring in work', to 'M_2 Actively seek business wherever it can be found but only if it fits a selected range of skills', and eventually to 'M_5 Constant monitoring of both markets to exploit established reputation'. These are clear targets the achievement of which, or lack of it, should be easily recognisable. Similar ideas apply to other functional responsibilities.

The review milestones will be crucial to the unfolding of the plan. As time passes they raise issues such as 'What should have been achieved by now?', 'What has been achieved by now?', and especially 'What adjustments need to be made to the plan?' It might even be that the plan has become unviable, in which case one needs to go back at least to the force field and think about what new restraints might have arisen.

> The VFM milestones enable the plan to be monitored as time passes.

The requirements for the availability of people, perhaps in one or two broad categories, of technology to be acquired or developed, of money and so forth, come from the totals in the resource analysis tables *and* any additional factors derived in FFA. (Political actions might mean persuading a regulatory authority to do, or not to do, something.) Leave a cell blank if nothing is required.

It would almost certainly be silly to carry the plan down to the last detail. For instance, Table 6.5 was PAI's full resource analysis, one element of which was development of better recruitment brochures. Producing an explicit plan for such details is the kind of thing that gets corporate planning a bad name. Such tasks are best left to the appropriate senior manager to supervise, perhaps using the resource analysis table as a checklist to ensure that the necessary improvements are being achieved.

The decision stage

ACTIFEL**D**

Drawing up a plan is a waste of time and effort unless its feasibility is evaluated, and that is the decision stage; the **D** in **ACTIFELD**.

The questions to be asked are, for example, will P_2 people be available in the second period? If not, are there any adjustments that can be made, such as recruitment or redeployment? Will the firm's cash flow or line of credit generate the required finance? Can equipment delivery be speeded up? And so on.

If the review of the corporate plan shows that it will probably be feasible but there are some shortcomings, then one has some rather precise indications of the business risks being run: 'We might not have quite enough people in period 2 but, if we make the effort, there may be time to recruit some more', or whatever it is. This is the 'Yes, but ...' answer mentioned in Chapter 1.

> The plan should make the business risks very clear.

Of course, if the risks multiply and become too great the plan is infeasible and one can only go back to an earlier stage. Perhaps the FFA can be revisited to see if there is some cleverer way of overcoming the restraints. Maybe the resource gaps have been overestimated, though it is vital to avoid wishful thinking and the Delphi style of debating assessments can be a safeguard against that. One might have to revisit the VFM to see if there is some less demanding configuration. Of course, such reiterations are by no means always necessary but they can happen. It seems to be a benefit of the **ACTIFELD** methodology that it not only gives clear indications of when reiteration is needed but also provides a structure for the process, in the sense that one can work back step by step and it is not always necessary to go straight back to the beginning and do everything again. Naturally, reiteration is a great nuisance, especially if it is triggered at a late stage in the process, but it is better than going ahead regardless of clearly identified problems.

Herrington-Jones's force field analysis

CASE STUDY

Figure 7.3 is the force field diagram for *Herrington-Jones* that summarises, as all force fields do, the thought processes of a group of people as they reach the end of using the tools for practical strategy on a particular problem. By this stage, they are thoroughly immersed in the *Herrington-Jones* case and have formed a strong gestalt appreciation of the firm's problems, prospects and strategic objectives. They have an intuitive grasp of the patterns in the business, and the force field has enabled them to express their ideas from a fresh viewpoint.

Let us see where that takes us.

First, Figure 7.3 has only two levels on the vertical scale, labelled, though clearly not to scale, with configurations from the *Herrington-Jones* VFM. The reason why Figure 7.3 has two levels, while Figure 7.1 had three, is that, for *Herrington-Jones*, the VFM has identified what seems to be a feasible target. As ever, we bend the tool to fit the problem, not the problem to fit the tool.

The object of the FFA is to see what, if anything, might prevent that being achieved. It is a matter of personal style whether one uses the VFM acronym and subscripts, as in Figure 7.3, whether one reproduces the text from the corresponding cells in the VFM (which might make the force field diagram very wordy), or whether one writes a short phrase to summarise the VFM configuration.

Secondly, although ideas from the resource analysis appear in Figure 7.3, there is no exact correspondence. Certainly, aspects such as requirement for capital, which figured in several places in the resource analysis, also appear in the FFA, as do supply channels, e-commerce and other factors, but they are now in a more aggregated and

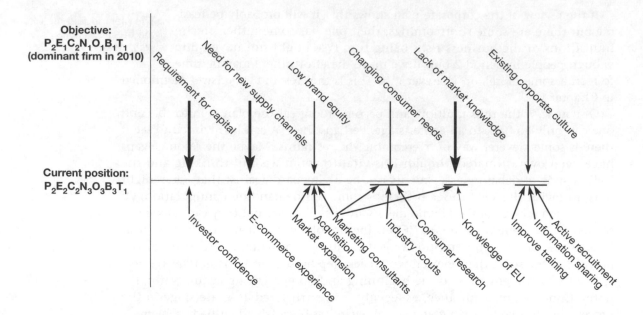

Figure 7.3 *Herrington-Jones's* **force field analysis**

highly visual form. It turns out that this new viewpoint sheds fresh light on the actions required to achieve *Herrington-Jones's* aim of becoming the leading European retailer by 2010 (in what follows, restraints and actions from the force field are shown in italics and in a different type face).

The team have judged that requirement for capital and the need for new supply chains are such powerful restraints that it is unlikely that the countervailing forces of investor confidence and *Herrington-Jones's* e-commerce experience will overcome them; something else will be needed. Similarly, expansion into Europe is severely restrained by lack of market knowledge and *Herrington-Jones's* in-house knowledge of the EU is far too weak to deal with that on its own. However, if knowledge of the EU can be combined with the use of marketing consultants, the restraint can be overcome – note the use of the convention of drawing a horizontal line to show two or more actions overcoming a powerful restraint.

To illustrate the practical results that can emerge when FFA is followed through to its conclusions, we note that marketing consultants turned out to be an action against three restraints: low brand equity, changing consumer needs and lack of market knowledge, particularly in the EU. These are three rather different things so, instead of saying 'we need to appoint marketing consultants', *Herrington-Jones* management now know why the consultants are needed and what they have to do. It goes further than that because the force field shows, for instance, that to overcome the obstacle of changing consumer needs, the consultants will have to collaborate with, or provide, industry scouts and consumer research – the brief to the consultants can be made rather precise. Moreover, the corporate plan that will emerge at the end of the force field process will set milestones and allocate the necessary resources, both of money and of *Herrington-Jones* management effort, to ensure that the consultants fulfil that brief. Finally, since there are three somewhat different tasks, it raises the issue of whether one firm of consultants can be expert in all these areas or whether *Herrington-Jones* should commission different firms for the various tasks. By identifying this issue, the force field analysis should help to ensure that the consultants are well chosen, thoroughly briefed and properly managed. That will be valuable, as it is all too easy for consultants to get out of hand.

Of course, we hope that you have been developing your own force field for *Herrington-Jones*, just as you produced your own versions of all the earlier steps in analysing this case study, though your final version is probably not the same as this, as you will necessarily have had to assume much of your 'data'. That does not matter; the aim of the revisions was to give you practice in the techniques, whereas the team that analysed *'Herrington-Jones'* had the time to find and use a lot of public information about food retailers.

As we come to the end of the *Herrington-Jones* case, let us draw together the threads of the analysis.

Recall that, in Chapter 1, we suggested a strategic question for *Herrington-Jones*, though you were asked to revise it and pose your own question. The suggested question mentioned the ageing population (changing consumer needs includes that, but is broader) and possible growth of electronic shopping (also implied by changing consumer needs). The opening steps of the mind map, futures research with field anomaly relaxation (FAR), and TOWS generated a set of actions (among which was the need for new supply chains), and, in turn, those actions helped to identify the required transition from one configuration to another in the VFM. The resource analysis investigated that transition in more detail and the FFA has summarised, in an intuitive, vivid and constructive way, the balance of forces.

Herrington-Jones's decision

After the resource analysis step, the **E** in **ACTIFELD**, *Herrington-Jones* seemed to have a reasonable plan for achieving a dominant position by 2010 but the force field viewpoint has identified two risk factors: the need for new supply chains, and investor confidence to improve availability of capital. The existing mechanisms that can be used to counter these two remaining barriers appear to be weak, and hence substantial remedial action is required now in order to avoid undesirable future consequences. We suggest that the analysis of *Herrington-Jones*, which we have used to illustrate the tools for practical strategy described so far, would provide a very good basis on which to approach the banks or the market to improve investor confidence and raise the additional capital. A search will now have to start to discover what else can be done to overcome the restraint of need for new supply chains.

In view of these factors, perhaps the answer is 'Yes, **but**...'; though perhaps the risks are looking serious and iteration back to an earlier step might be needed. That would be a choice for *Herrington-Jones* management to make but the reasons for it are very clear.

Chapter summary

Force field analysis is, like almost everything else in this book, an exceedingly simple idea that is very easy to explain but which requires an imaginative step for its application. That step is to realise that, though there are broad connections to the earlier steps, especially congruence and resource analysis, there is much to be gained by thinking about the VFM configuration shift from a different viewpoint, which is the visual balance of forces in FFA as opposed to the tabulated 'calculations' of resource analysis. There is a further aim, which is that resource analysis tables can extend over several pages whereas FFA summarises the force balances on one piece of paper. That summary will usually aggregate factors thought about when resource analysis was applied, but it is likely to express them in different terms, and it will often generate ideas that did not emerge at earlier stages. Finding new ideas is never a bad thing and is a valuable outcome of changing one's viewpoint.

The change of viewpoint cannot be achieved by simply copying from earlier work. Before starting the force field you can refresh your memory by looking at the resource tables, but you must then very firmly put them away and think again. The discipline of having to put the ideas on to one piece of paper is immensely valuable – it concentrates the mind on the essentials. It is also a good communications device; a busy executive board might not be impressed by having to wade through pages of resource analysis, but the force field diagram might engage their attention, after which questions can be answered from the earlier steps in the methodology.

The end result of this deceptively simple technique is not only a vivid display, it is also a final, and essential, check on the whole practical strategy process. It identifies risks, such as the existing level of investor confidence being insufficient to meet the requirement for capital. On top of that, it allows tasks such as the role of the marketing consultants to be specified in some detail.

All told, force field analysis is a vital stage in the use of the tools for practical strategy.

Finally, though, you might want to have a go at practising your skills by developing a force field for the management buy-out for the oil consulting firm, PAI, in Chapter 6, and corporate plans, on the lines of Table 7.1, for PAI and for *Herrington-Jones*, using information from Web sites or company reports, or just inventing your own.

Sorting out the practical strategy toolbox

What this chapter is about

- A review of the ideas so far.

- The tools for practical strategy from another point of view.

- A checklist for using them.

- Judgement in practical strategy.

- Some topics to which the tools have been applied.

- Topics for you to try for yourselves.

- A bridge to other tools for practical strategy.

Introduction

Anyone who does jobs around the home knows that it is necessary to sort out and tidy up the toolbox from time to time. It's easy to use the same hammer every time and to forget that there's another that might be more effective for the current job. Sorting out can also reveal a tool that one had forgotten was there, the purpose of which seem obscure until one remembers what it is for, and recalls its relationship to other tools. One might even rearrange the tools into two groups: the standard, commonly used, set, and those which are for more specialised tasks.

Much the same is true of the tools for practical strategy. They need to be sorted out in one's mind and, since we have studied them in series in the preceding chapters, it will now be as well to see them as a whole. This chapter therefore aims not only to review the practical strategy process but also to see it from another point of view and to give you a checklist for using the tools for thought.

> We now need to see the tools as a whole set.

As we shall see on its last page, this chapter and the next one are like a hinge between the earlier and later chapters of the book:

■ this chapter looks back at what we have done so far with the **ACTIFELD** methodology

■ the next looks forward to more specialised tools for practical strategy.

The joint theme of Chapters 8 and 9 is that, though the **ACTIFELD** approach works well, is easy to apply once you have grasped the trick and is effective for *many* problems, it is not necessarily appropriate for *all* strategic issues. The variety of strategic challenges is so large that we have to provide additional tools that can supplement, or even replace, the **ACTIFELD** approach. The next chapter will, therefore, be a preview of, or a bridge to, other tools for practical strategy. Please, then, bear in mind while we review **ACTIFELD** that it is not the only pebble on the analytical beach.

First, we must review what we have done so far.

The ACTIFELD methodology

The purpose of the **ACTIFELD** structure is to give a basic procedure with a standard set of steps that will cope with many, if not most, strategic issues. Its name is also an *aide-mémoire* for questions to be asked as one works through such a problem. The **ACTI** reminds us of finding actions to solve the problem, while **FELD** suggests the steps needed to make the actions work in the field.

The outline for the process was shown in Figure 1.1, reproduced as Figure 8.1. Now that you have worked through all the steps, you will understand them more clearly and, above all, you will have seen the distinction between the left- and right-hand sides of Figure 8.1.

There are six points to bear in mind:

1. The mental world
Where problems exist.

1. The left-hand side of Figure 8.1 is the world of the mind. It is where a problem is perceived, where steps are taken to address it, where thinking takes place and where the brain absorbs, interprets and controls the successive stages of problem-solving. The mental world is also where imagination, stimulated by the results of using the tools, creates new ideas for strategic action.

2. The toolbox
For steps in the problem.

2. The right-hand side is the analytical world containing the **ACTIFELD** tools for practical strategy – though remember that there are other tools that we have not yet covered. The connection between the two sides is that when, for instance, we wondered about obstacles in the mental world we reached for the tool of force field analysis.

3. One tool to the next
Changing the viewpoint is essential.

3. Practical strategy requires a good deal of imagination and there is no automatic connection between the output of one tool and the input to the next. It is not only necessary, it is also *vital*, to change one's point of view, as we saw with force field analysis, for example.

4. Iteration
Go back as needed. Revising the question can be vital.

4. Tackling strategic problems is rarely straightforward and it may sometimes be necessary to go back to an earlier stage in order to find a 'good' solution. That is emphasised by the dashed lines at the left-hand edge of Figure 8.1. The key aspect is constant review of the

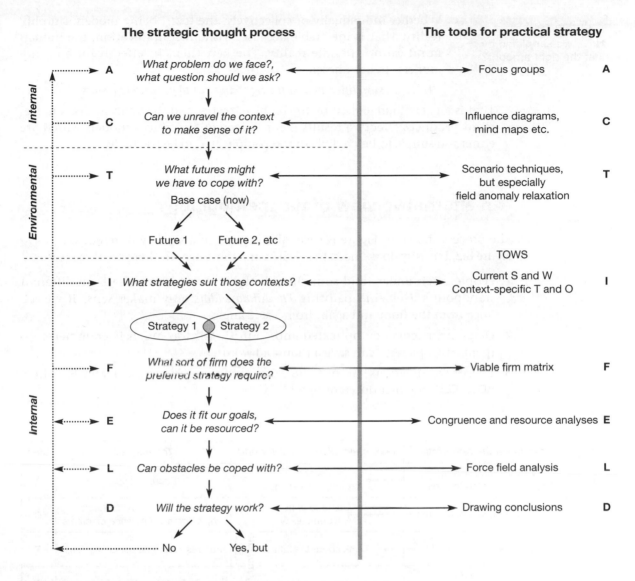

Figure 8.1 The practical strategy process

strategic question, either to confirm it or to restate it. Restating the question does not necessarily involve wasted effort as TOWS, perhaps, might not need to be repeated. Even if earlier work has to be redone, that is a necessary evil as it is far more important to answer the right question than to answer the wrong one.

5. Each technique simplifies reality to give a tool for thought about an aspect of the problem. It is, as we saw in Chapter 1, a *model* to support that step in the process and the tools as a whole provide a model for the process of practical strategy.

> **5. Tools are models**
> All models simplify reality.

6. Judgement

Have we simplified by just the right amount?

6. Whether individually or collectively, the tools, being models, simplify reality. That is inevitable because, without simplification, the human mind cannot handle reality. The key, then, in effective use of any model is to ask oneself:

'Have we simplified by just the right amount to get usable results?'

That is an act of judgement by the problem-owner and the analyst. Good judgement produces effective results. Poor judgement produces models which are either too simple to be credible or too complicated to be tractable.

An alternative view of the methodology

The process shown in Figure 8.1 can also be seen in a slightly different way, as in Figure 8.2, but why do we need to see the same thing again? There are three reasons.

1. People often understand something better if they see it twice from different standpoints. Holbein's painting *The Ambassadors* only makes sense if viewed once from the front and again from a side angle.

2. Diagrams become complicated and confusing if too much is crammed into them – two pictures can save a thousand words.

3. These two diagrams are not the same thing and Figures 8.1 and 8.2 show **ACTIFELD** in rather different lights.

Step	Questions in the real world	Task in simplified (model) world	Technique?	Step
A	What is our problem, what should our strategy be?	Ask a good strategic question	*Focus groups*	A
C	Do we understand the system?	Come to grips with complexity	*Mind maps, impact wheels, why diagrams, influence diagrams*	C
T	Is the future a foreign land?	Think about the future	*Futures methods, especially FAR*	T
I	What do we do about the scenarios?	Identify required actions	*TOWS and actions*	I
F	How do we implement those actions?	Find a viable organisation	*Viable firm (or other organisation) matrix*	F
E	Can we make those changes?	Evaluate acceptability and resource needs	*Congruence analysis Resource analysis*	E
L	Are we sure?	Look for obstacles and remedies	*Force field analysis (FFA)*	L
D	Is it go? No Yes, but	Decide if the risks are acceptable		D

A shortcut?

Figure 8.2 Another view of the methodology

On the one hand, Figure 8.1 shows how the steps in the mental process on the left-hand side match with the eight parts of **ACTIFELD**. The main point is, though, on the extreme left-hand side, stressing the idea of looping back to an earlier step if the analysis is not generating a viable solution to the question.

Above all, that diagram drives home the point that the initial strategic question is not sacrosanct. In practice, any of the ensuing **ACTIFELD** steps can add so much understanding of the issues that one is led to rephrase the question *and that can only add value to the analysis*. Answering the right question is the key to getting practical and believable results of which senior managers take notice, as opposed to writing a report for the filing cabinet. Rephrasing the question usually does not mean that work has been wasted. Neither the complexity, nor the future nor the TOWS necessarily change because the question has changed!

Figure 8.2, on the other hand, expresses **ACTIFELD** in a subtly different way. Instead of the two columns of Figure 8.1, we now have three (ignoring the **ACTIFELD** labels at the extreme edges). From left to right they connect the successive questions in the real world, the tasks in the simplified world of the models, and the techniques that are likely to be drawn into play.

Notice particularly that the heading of the third column has a '?'. To be sure, the techniques listed there usually work very well and have been tested in numerous cases. They give a nice flow to analysis, with one leading to another, provided one makes the mental leaps and changes viewpoint as one proceeds. Complexity is complex, so having four tools available for **C**, unravelling it, can be valuable, and you don't have to use all of them, only those that usefully contribute to answering the strategic question. However, as we mentioned earlier, the **ACTIFELD** techniques are not the only tools available for strategic analysis and Chapter 9 will preview, while Chapters 10 to 13 explain, some other approaches that are useful in other cases (another, specialised, tool is on the website).

The ladder of arrows leading back and forth between the question and task columns is the *usual* flow of **ACTIFELD**. Looping back to earlier steps is *not* shown, for simplicity, though the idea is vital and must not be forgotten. What is, however, shown in the middle column is the possibility of *shortcuts in the methodology*.

Shortcuts can arise because, although Figures 8.1 and 8.2 almost suggest that **ACTIFELD** is a discipline and that, having done **A** and posed a question, one *must* do **C**, *follow that* by **T**, and so on, there is, in practice, no such thing as a standard strategic problem that has to be dealt with in a rigid way. For instance, the issue for the petroleum consultants in Chapter 5 was so clear-cut – possible collapse of their business – that in their case one could go straight from recognition of the problem to the viable firm matrix. Other shortcuts might be possible in different problems. If a problem is urgent, there may be no point in using FAR to look 10 years ahead. Even the sequence in **ACTIFELD** is not fixed; you might do TOWS after you've done the VFM, just to be sure that the strengths and weaknesses of the new firm have been thought about.

Of course, shortcuts should not be taken unthinkingly. They can save effort but they can also lead one to miss some important step; missing out **C** because it's assumed that the context is simple can be a bad move. Taking items out of sequence needs careful thought. Overall, then, it's probably better to stay with the 'standard' process until you are really comfortable with the full **ACTIFELD** approach.

A checklist for ACTIFELD

Diagrams are a good way of showing how one thing connects to another but it is also useful, even at the expense of some repetition, to have a written checklist of things to do and think about. In this section, each item of **ACTIFELD** is summarised in a few words, with some added detail in the rest of the paragraph. Key points are given in the marginal boxes. As you read this, try to rewrite it in your own words.

A – Why is this the question?
If there is time, trace the issue's history.

■ **A** – the *strategic question* (Chapter 1). The key point is why the question has arisen, which is the reason for '*why?*' being part of the parsing of the question. Discovering why may not be as simple as it seems and, if time allows, exploring the issue history can be fruitful. The concept of *issue history* will be covered in Chapter 11, and that is an example of the hinge between the two parts of the book. *Never* be afraid to reformulate the question!

C – Do we know what's going on?
Use at least one tool to sort out the system.

■ **C** – *unravelling the system's complexity* (Chapter 2). Things are rarely as simple as they seem and sorting out interactions between aspects of the problem can help one to see why it has arisen – a check on A – and to make sense of the problem in its context. Sense-making is vital and at least four tools are available for the task: why diagrams, mind maps, impact wheels and influence diagrams. Using a why diagram and the issue history is a good check on the question. Mind maps are a good way to sort out one's initial thinking and kick-start the analysis. Impact wheels are good for thinking about consequences, while influence diagrams are the preferred tool for tracing feedback and dynamics. *Always* try to use at least two tools. Each supports sense-making in its own way and two views illuminate better than one.

T – Is the future a foreign land?
Understanding what the future *might* be should reduce risk.

■ **T** – thinking about *the future* and building scenarios (Chapter 3). Any decision, even to do nothing, unfolds into the future so its 'effectiveness' will be affected by what the future might be. No human mind knows what the future *will* be, but intelligent thought is possible about what it *might* be, and developing scenarios, or stories about the future, can be a powerful stimulus to practical strategy – the future does not have to be a completely foreign land. Field anomaly relaxation, FAR, develops scenarios from internally consistent 'fields' of socio-economic, political, technological and other sectors appropriate to the issue's context. **T** might be omitted if urgent action is needed about an imminent problem.

I – What should we do?
TOWS can generate action plans.

■ **I** – getting ideas about what might be done by using *TOWS and strategies* (Chapter 4). It's all very well to have a question to answer, to have understood its complexity, and to have peered into the future (however imperfectly) but what are we to do? The traditional SWOT analysis does not help as it can create useless argument about whether X is a weakness or an opportunity and does not say what is to be done when the SWOT table is completed. The TOWS *and* strategies technique avoids those problems by ensuring that X will get considered no matter where it is placed in the table and consideration of all the Xs, in pairs, triples, or all together, generates a set of actions. When the actions are examined, common themes are usually found and can be grouped into broad strategic areas. Remember that the table of strategic areas has to be read not only from left to right but also from right to left. Of course, the elements of TOWS should not be placed in the table without any thought as to what they are, but this approach avoids much wasted argument and gives effective and quick results.

■ **F** – evaluating what the organisation needs to be in order to implement those actions, using the *viable firm matrix* (Chapter 5). The firm in which the strategic question has arisen is viable in the sense that it is a combination of factors such as skills, assets and objectives that work together in a given market. 'Viable' does not necessarily mean 'successful': it just means that the firm is in business. Similar ideas apply to other organisations, and *firm* in the VFM can be any other word such as charity, policy, R&D department, or whatever is suitable. The strategies found in step I may require changes to the firm and the aim of the VFM is to find a mutually consistent set of attributes – skills, assets and so on – that will be feasible with those strategies. Of course, the strategic question may be that the firm is not going to be viable for much longer, for some reason.

> **F – Is the new firm viable?**
> How do we change to implement the strategies? Is the new organisation feasible?

■ **E** – evaluating the required changes against the interests of stakeholders and the resources likely to be needed using *congruence analysis* and *resource analysis* (Chapter 6). Step F involves changing the firm from one VFM to another, or sometimes trying to keep it at its existing configuration, either of which has two effects. The first is on the values, ambitions and expectations of stakeholders such as owners, employees, customers, suppliers and regulators. This is one of the strongly political aspects of strategic analysis and is dealt with by congruence analysis; ignoring it is a virtual guarantee that the report will end up in the filing cabinet, not on the chief executive's agenda. The second aspect is to appraise the resources required to bring about the change, and thereby to assess the difficulties of making it (resources may be needed even to maintain a current position). If the changes are politically unacceptable, or resource requirements cannot be satisfied, it may be necessary to change the question and then go back and find a less demanding configuration in the VFM.

> **E – Do they like it? Can we do it?**
> Will stakeholders accept it? Can we resource it?

■ **L** – checking that obstacles have been thought about and that they can be overcome, using *force field analysis* (Chapter 7). The results so far are a conceptual plan of action from TOWS, an intention to change the configuration in the VFM so as to implement those actions, an assessment of the political acceptability of change in the organisation and an estimate of the resources required. However, it is virtually certain that there will be obstacles to change and these will have to be overcome. It is also possible that, no matter how much care was taken in the previous steps, something might have been overlooked. The force field analysis is a final 'sanity check' on the work and should lead to a time-phased corporate plan. Portraying obstacles and actions as a set of competing forces calls for a change of viewpoint but, without that alteration of the mindset, imagination cannot truly be unleashed.

> **L – Have we thought about obstacles?**
> Change the viewpoint and portray actions and obstacles.

D – Is it a go?

If it is 'no', loop back to an earlier step. If it is 'yes, but ...', risks have been identified.

■ **D** – finally, some person or group has to decide whether or not to take action on the proposals that have emerged. If the conclusion is 'no', there are two outcomes, neither of which is fully satisfactory. The worse of them is that the project is shelved, the report goes into the shredder and there is recrimination about wasted effort. That, of course, still leaves the original strategic question unanswered by rigorous thought, though it will still have to be answered somehow. The second outcome is somewhat more likely to get a good answer to the strategic question even though the analysis has to go back to an earlier step and some work has to be repeated. The key to getting that second outcome is strict attention to ensuring involvement of the problem owners throughout the work, perhaps to the extent of them doing much of the work, with expert facilitation. That is why we have laid emphasis on the concept of the focus group as managers of the strategic analysis process. Note that the decision choice will rarely be an unqualified 'yes'. A much more realistic decision is 'yes, but ...', where the 'but ...' shows that risks have been identified and can, therefore, be managed. It is evident that this final choice cannot be supported by any analytical techniques and is fundamentally an act of judgement. We shall have more to say about *the art of judgement* in Chapter 11.

Judgement about the tools for practical strategy

The real message from the preceding sections is that using the tools for practical strategy calls for a good deal of judgement, not only by the analyst but also by the problem owner, or the focus group managing the exercise. There are four issues to be balanced:

■ Have we really posed the most useful strategic question? Not getting the question right first time is not a sign of incompetence; it is a symptom of the complexity, difficulty and subtlety of strategic analysis.

■ Does the changed question mean that we need to loop back to an earlier stage, and if so, how far? Having to redo earlier work is unusual, but it can happen and, if it does, the wasted work must be accepted as the price for answering the right question.

■ Is the full **ACTIFELD** process, in our particular problem, a sledgehammer to crack a nut? Can we take a shortcut, and if so, what can we omit? What is the risk that by skipping some analysis we shall miss something really important? In short, and this is question 6 on page 158, might we be simplifying to a rash extent?

■ Finally, since the **ACTIFELD** techniques are not the only possibilities, are we on the right lines? The **ACTIFELD** techniques are powerful but might it be more fruitful to tackle this particular problem using one or other of the approaches described later in this book?

Those are the main judgements but, to make them, it is necessary to bear in mind the essential nature of the tools, in the sense of what they are supposed to do and what they do not do.

The first thing to realise is that the tools for practical strategy – both those to be considered later and those embodied in **ACTIFELD** – are a facilitating process, not a magic wand. They exist to help analysis and cannot be expected to provide some ultimate 'answer'; *the final step, **D**, is an act of judgement and all the preceding analysis is intended to illuminate that judgement, not to supplant it.*

> The tools for practical strategy are a facilitating process, not a magic wand.

Secondly, it is easy to get carried away with enthusiasm while using these tools. Most people (though not all, as mentioned later under 'success factors') thoroughly enjoy using the tools, whether in a class assignment or in a real project. Some caution is called for and that can be summarised in three key points:

1. Have we oversimplified this problem? A clear test is whether what is being done is a good deal better than guessing.

2. The **ACTIFELD** tools were earlier described as being 'a good way to turn an argument into a discussion'. If we are arguing rather than discussing then either we are not using the tools properly or we have somehow lost the plot of the problem. If that happens, the best thing is to take a break, go for a walk to clear the mind, and come back refreshed.

3. For some problems, full-scale rigorous application of the tools may be overkill. On the other hand, a partial application with shortcuts may be so incomplete as to be imprudent, with the likelihood of producing unreliable recommendations and action plans. The test is continually to ask 'For *this* problem, where do we lie on the overkill/simplistic spectrum?'

A small sample of applications

The examples we have used to explain the tools for practical strategy – *Herrington-Jones* and PAI for instance – are business orientated but you should not think that the tools are only applicable to business problems. Table 8.1 is a list of some recent applications of **ACTIFELD** by MBA students, usually working in teams of about four people. They drew their information from their own practical experience, websites or, since the aim was to practise using the tools, not to analyse real problems, sometimes made reasonable assumptions. In all cases, the team assumed that they had a client such as the chief executive of a business, a government minister or a political party, and were required to present recommendations to that client at the end of the project.

This is only a sample of many cases but, even so, the variety is surprising. There have, of course, been other cases from my consultancy, though only one is mentioned in this book, with permission and impenetrably disguised.

Topics for you to try

We analysed *Herrington-Jones* at some length, Chapter 14 has two more case studies, and there are more on the website. Nonetheless, the only real way to master

Table 8.1 Some illustrative uses of the practical strategy tools

Regeneration of a country's decrepit mining industry	An outsourcing company for software applications in the Asian market	Strategies for a national airline that is struggling to survive
Crime and safety in a European country	Immigration systems for a country (not the UK)	Should one low-cost airline buy another?
Operating a call centre	Fire protection in the Amazon rain forest	A nation's foreign policy
Border controls between a central European country and its neighbours	The growth and development of a two-person chiropody practice	Grand Tours of the Scottish highlands in classic cars and staying at luxury hotels
Promotion of sport for young children	An environmental consultancy for the Great Barrier Reef	A supplier of components for factory automation
Pollution in Mexico City	Security strategies for a hospital maternity unit	The use of e-commerce by watch retailers
Lifestyle strategies for high-profile celebrities	Survival strategies for a failing political party	Developing world-class strategies for a nation's procurement systems

these techniques is to practise them, preferably in a syndicate group. Here, then, are some possible topics, which can also serve as class exercises.

Before you tackle a topic, pose a strategic question and identify a client to whom you are to report.

- We made *Herrington-Jones* into a supermarket chain and we chose to concentrate on its food retailing activities. Of course, *Herrington-Jones* also sells other products and there are similar chains such as household goods, clothing, do-it-yourself and home improvement, vehicle maintenance, and several other retail sectors.

- All such retailers deal with customers on a regular, even weekly, basis but what about firms that interact with customers only occasionally? Some examples are a local car dealership, a chain of travel agents, and a group of tourist hotels.

- By contrast with MoveStuff in Chapter 5, there are much smaller haulage firms that operate locally or regionally and there are others specialising in house and office removals. Yet other transport firms concentrate on regular runs between, say, Manchester and Milan carrying whatever customers want to send between those places.

- Local and regional/county governments always have a myriad of issues to deal with: traffic management, town planning, policing, care of the elderly and providing schools are some examples.

- What might be the strategic issues for Overseas Carers in raising and spending money?

■ In Britain, the National Trust is a voluntary organisation that receives no government money but endeavours to acquire stately homes that can no longer be maintained by their owners so that the houses can be preserved and opened to the public. The Trust has also acquired large tracts of countryside and coastline to protect them from development. There are similar bodies in at least Australia and Canada. What might their strategic issues be?

■ Many stately homes that are open to the public are still in ancestral ownership and are run as businesses. How might such a place remain viable? (Both this example and the previous one relate to business issues in what amounts to the provision of a public good.)

■ What might be the problems of the emergency services in dealing with 'routine' fires and accidents as well as planning to cope with much larger events? Are fire, ambulance and police services different from the lifeboat service, the coastguard and mountain rescue?

■ What would be a good command and control strategy for a city's emergency services?

■ Does the organisation you work for have any strategic issues?

Now think widely and make up some topics of your own, but it might help you to see the full flow of an application by studying the cases in Chapter 14 before you tackle any problems.

Success factors in practical strategy

We close this chapter by reviewing what seem, from experience, to be success factors in using these tools.

The *first*, and much the most important, is to involve the problem owners, certainly in managing the project, and possibly in doing at least some of the thinking. The concept that an analyst can go away, solve the problem and come back with the 'answer' is naïve, outdated, and practically a guarantee of failure.

> **Success factor 1:** Involve the problem owners.

The *second* is the need to be comfortable with soft data and techniques; some people are and some are not, but there seems to be no rhyme or reason to that. On the face of it, one might assume that people trained in mathematics or the hard physical sciences would not be at ease with these

> **Success factor 2:** Get used to soft data and tools.

very soft approaches. Equally, one might imagine that people whose backgrounds are in, say, history would find these essentially verbal techniques easy to use. On the same grounds, it might be thought that people whose first language is not English would find difficulties with a language-based approach to practical strategy.

The only observation is that some people do fit into these stereotypes, while many others do not. In general, though, teaching experience suggests that, out of a class of 16 to 20 MBA students, a few people initially have difficulty adjusting their minds to these approaches. Regardless of their previous academic training and their language skills, the reason always seems to be that some people look for hard numbers, or even formulae, when none exist in practical strategy, nor can they exist in such a domain. I usually advise such people to get on with the prescribed steps, but to suspend their disbelief, as one does when watching a stage play. The effect is that, for the vast majority of people, their minds become attuned to the pattern of thought after a couple of days, the difficulties vanish, and they can use the tools for practical strategy with as much confidence and mental dexterity as anyone else.

Success factor 3: Be patient with the softness.

The *third* success factor is, then, a little patience, until the tools become familiar. That familiarity mainly comes through use, but it is valuable to study real cases as guides. The *Herrington-Jones* case, and those in Chapter 14, may be helpful.

Success factor 4: Be honest in assessments.

The *fourth* success factor is scrupulous honesty of thought. For instance, when using TOWS, it is important to avoid complacency about weaknesses and over-optimism about strengths. Similarly, there should be neither panic nor myopia about threats, and a little scepticism can guard against over-enthusiasm about opportunities.

Success factor 5: Disciplined imagination is vital.

Disciplined imagination is the *fifth* success factor and is both required for, and supported by, the tools we have described. FAR and the VFM are examples of this trait as both require the creation of 'filing space' for all possibilities. Don't get locked into the obvious! If the imagination gets stuck, a mind map will often get it moving again.

The *sixth* success factor is the proper use of domain experts. Of course, the people who run the National Trust, for instance, have a vast amount of knowledge and experience about how it works, what its problems are and so forth, and that will be invaluable in posing strategic questions, when unravelling complexity, in TOWS and, in fact, at every stage of the analysis. The trick is to use that knowledge without allowing them to dominate the process. The focus group will, and should, contain domain experts and that group will, and should, be managing the exercise. The facilitating analysts will, therefore, have to manage *them* in subtle and unobtrusive ways, so as to trigger their imagination when using their knowledge and to prevent them getting stuck in what everyone already 'knows' is the solution to the problem.

Success factor 6: Use domain experts but don't let them dominate.

Success factor 7: Be aware of limitations and strengths in the tools.

The *seventh* success factor is to develop a mature awareness of the limitations as well as the strengths of these tools and techniques. Those characteristics are not absolutes but are with respect to different problems. That, I am afraid, really only comes with practice, though the study of cases helps to develop a balanced assessment.

Some people complain that the **ACTIFELD** approach, even with shortcuts, takes time to apply, with the implication that it needs too much time. The comment is hard to understand as, given the importance of a strategic issue and the magnitude of the benefits of getting it right, it does not seem to be an unreasonable investment for a few people to spend perhaps two or three weeks to sort out how a real *Herrington-Jones* might be the Number 1 retailer in its sector by the year 2010. The magnitude of the consequences of getting it *wrong* because no one was prepared to spend some time beggars belief. The *final* success factor is, therefore, to be prepared to make an effort.

Success factor 8: Be prepared to make enough effort.

Nonetheless, urgent problems sometimes arise to which an answer is needed in, perhaps, two days and even the limited effort required by **ACTIFELD** is simply not possible. To provide for such cases, and to foster the art of judgement, we will describe the so-called mini-methods of Neustadt and May in Chapter 11.

That comment is to remind you of an earlier remark that the **ACTIFELD** tools are not the only ones available. It serves as a bridge to other practical strategy tools that will be previewed in Chapter 9 and explained in the following chapters.

Broadening the practical strategy toolkit

What this chapter is about

■ Why we need additional tools for practical strategy.

■ The proliferation of tools under different names.

■ Four themes for which extra tools are needed:

1. *Innovation* – its stimulation, relevance, and assessment.
2. Fostering *the art of judgement*.
3. Tools for use o*n the back of an envelope*.
4. Creating and dealing with *wish lists*.

Introduction – why we need more tools

The previous eight chapters have been a balance between two somewhat conflicting ideas.

> ACTIFELD does not deal with all problems so we need additional tools.

The *first* is that there is a formal methodology – **ACTIFELD** – that gives a straightforward approach to strategic problems. It offers a sequence of steps, each leading to the next after a slight mental jump, that takes one through a thought process from strategic question to force field analysis and that is likely to give a good, workable solution to many strategic issues. The *second* idea is that strategic issues come in all sorts of guises and contexts and that the **ACTIFELD** methodology, effective though it usually is, is simply not going to be all-conquering in every imaginable case. We resolved the conflict by presenting the **ACTIFELD** steps in 'this is how to do it' style, while frequently mentioning the need to adapt the process to the problem and even to adapt the steps themselves.

We now have to deal with the aspects of practical strategy that **ACTIFELD** does not handle particularly well and we will preview the four themes mentioned in the box above and addressed in detail in the next four chapters. You should not, though, think that these themes are highly specialised or very esoteric; they are perfectly valid members of the practical strategy toolbox for dealing with issues for which the **ACTIFELD** tools are not particularly effective and they might be used to complement the **ACTIFELD** tools or to replace them. For example, there is nothing in **ACTIFELD** about stimulating innovation so, if a problem involved that, one might digress from **ACTIFELD** at some stage and use the tools for innovation in Chapter 10. Similarly, it is true that even a partial **ACTIFELD** takes some time and, for some problems, time is simply not available. In such a case a quick answer – sometimes called quick and dirty – is needed and the tools in Chapters 11 and 12 might be used in place of **ACTIFELD**. Wish lists are universal and means for dealing with them are covered in Chapter 13.

In short, this relatively brief chapter will, as mentioned in Chapter 8, serve as a bridge or hinge between the two parts of the book. The first part was 'standard' **ACTIFELD**, the second is other tools and thought processes. These are not, though, merely a collection of extras that might come in handy; they are powerful ways of dealing with the four specific strategic issues listed at the head of this chapter.

The proliferation of tools

One of the problems with the 'soft' – verbal and diagrammatic – methods that are the subject of this book is that there is little agreement on terminology. By contrast, in operational research everyone knows what linear programming is and one would be seen as a fool if one said that a pay-off matrix is the same thing as a linear program. The two things are distinctly different and are precisely and formally defined.

However, as we discussed at length in Chapter 1, these precise, exact tools do not handle the imprecise squishiness of strategic issues and for that we need soft methods. The trouble is that there are many soft approaches – we have even challenged you to invent your own if **ACTIFELD** does not work – and there is little agreement about what they are called. For instance, what we have called an influence diagram (in Chapter 2) is also called a causal loop diagram, though the two are not exactly the same. A cognitive map looks like an influence diagram, though it is not quite the same thing, but I have also seen a mind map called a cognitive map. Some workers would draw an impact wheel using hexagons and call it a hexagon map.

I mean no disrespect to my colleagues who use different terminology, and certainly not to those who find that other techniques work well with strategic problems. This problem of the variety of names and the number of techniques is inherent in the challenging domain of practical strategy and you will just have to be alert in your wider reading for a given technique with different names or for the same name being used for rather different things.

Rather than trying to describe all the different techniques used in practice or mentioned in the literature, which would probably be impossible, and in preference to trying to explain the difference between techniques X and Y, where none might exist, I have chosen four themes to complement the **ACTIFELD** techniques. They deal with innovation, the art of judgement, the military appreciation (which, despite its name, is highly applicable to many other types of problem), and the handling of wish lists. We can now preview those themes.

Theme One – innovation

To innovate is to invent or begin to apply new methods, ideas etc. It is one of the most important aspects of strategy and, in sympathy with this book's concept of tools for practical strategy, this theme introduces some seminal techniques for stimulating innovation. They were developed by Professor Fritz Zwicky and are called *morphological methods*. We have used morphological ideas earlier in FAR and the VFM but in Chapter 10 we shall see them in their full rigour and in three variants. The idea is to explore all conceivable possibilities for a technology with the aim of identifying radically novel, and hopefully better, technological options.

Theme One deals with innovation and its consequences.

Identifying options is valuable but we also need to pick out routes by which a new technology might most effectively be developed from things that now exist. That idea is called *morphological distance*. Of course, a technology may have all sorts of effects on human affairs and we shall examine *relevance trees* as a way not only of tracing impacts, but also of reversing the train of thought and trying to identify new technologies needed to meet some management need or human goal. Finally, Chapter 10 will draw on the technique of congruence analysis to assess the *benefits of technological change* to different stakeholders.

Theme Two – the art of judgement

A slightly pompous phrase sometimes heard in meetings is *in my judgement*. We compliment people by saying that they show good judgement and criticise them for the opposite. How, though, is judgement exercised? Can the art of judgement be learned? How can the process of judgement be managed by a group of decision-makers and their advisory staffs, especially when they are faced with an urgent issue, or even a crisis?

Theme Two is about the idea of judgement and how it can be applied in urgent issues and crises.

Chapter 11 draws on two remarkable texts to address these questions. The first is Vickers' *The Art of Judgement*, which uses its author's vast experience in very senior management, and his subsequent research, to provide some theoretical concepts to help us to understand this mysterious property of judgement. Secondly, Neustadt and May's *The Uses of History for Decision Makers* presents a series of *mini-methods* which can be applied very quickly, and even under great pressure of events, to help a group of senior decision-makers and their staffs to keep track of the judgements they make about the importance of whatever information is available, the assumptions they are making, and the analogies they have in mind. The purpose of the mini-methods is to develop viable options for action in the face of an urgent issue, or even a crisis.

Theme Three – making plans under pressure

Of course, having an option for action, or an aim to be achieved, is one thing but achieving it might be something else. How, in fact, can one make a plan to achieve a given objective and, especially, how can one make a feasible plan under great pressure of time or under unfavourable circumstances?

To answer that, we shall turn, in Chapter 12, to the military world. The reason is that, in many countries, the armed forces are rightly admired for their ability to get things done under pressure, not only in combat, but also in all sorts of crises and problems. A recent example was the use of the British army to sort out a horrific logjam of slaughtered animals during the outbreak of foot and mouth disease in 2001, but there are many other instances. In the UK, and elsewhere, some retired officers make a good living from teaching their skills to business managers. What, though, are the thought processes used in the military approach to problem-solving?

> Theme Three has three techniques that can, if necessary, be applied *very* rapidly.

Chapter 12 will describe the so-called *military appreciation* which is a logical sequence for analysing the factors involved in achieving a given aim – perhaps to implement the action option derived by using the mini-methods – making deductions from those factors, and arriving at a workable action plan. Every military officer in the world, whether army, navy or air force, is taught to appreciate situations (though the name of the technique and some of its steps can vary considerably from place to place and change from time to time). Practice makes appreciation almost automatic so that it can be applied *very* quickly and under extreme pressure of time and circumstances. Despite its name, it is highly applicable to non-military problems and some civil servants are also taught to think in this way.

That chapter also discusses the *principles of war*, which give a checklist for the viability of a military plan. Again, despite the name, they are applicable to other domains and we suggest how they can be adapted to business use. Finally, the chapter explains *fishbone diagrams* as a quick technique for diagnosing the causes of a problem.

Theme Four – wish lists

A wish list is simply all the things that one might want to buy, the required changes of procedure and culture, or anything else that seems to be necessary to bring about improvement in a problem situation. The term is commonly used in defence planning to mean all the equipments needed to bring a force up to some level of capability, but it also includes a myriad of aspects such as personnel to be recruited and retained, training needs, stocks ranging from ammunition to boots, research and development projects and so on and so forth. Such lists usually contain several hundred items at any one time and they are called *wish* lists because, in the practical world, there is no realistic prospect of being able to do all the things on the list in any reasonable time. An obvious reason is money but there are also practical limits on how many acquisitions can be handled at any one time.

> Theme Four handles 'wish lists' – all the things an organisation would like to do, but probably cannot.

Although the term is of military origin, wish lists arise in just about every walk of life (not least in spending one's own money). The list for improving a country's ground transport system will contain, probably, hundreds of road improvement schemes, many proposals for new bus and train systems and services, yet further requirements to connect with airports, and no doubt many other things. In the practical world there is no hope of implementing all these proposals in a reasonable time, if ever. The organisation for which you work no doubt has a wish list, perhaps under another name.

Chapter 13 shows that dealing with wish lists requires two steps: *mission-orientated analysis* – for choosing which items from the list are to be implemented, and another – the *conceptual planning framework* – for creating valid wish lists. For completeness, the website also explains an advanced technique – the analytic hierarchy process (AHP) – for assessing the relative importance of alternative actions (the AHP is an exception to the rule about 'soft' methods as it involves some mathematics).

Chapter summary

ACTIFELD works well but does not do everything. There are additional tools for special needs.

The theme of this short chapter is that the techniques within **ACTIFELD** work very well for many cases, but not all, so we need some additional tools. These extra tools are far from being esoteric; they are effective ways of applying rigorous thought to important issues:

- Innovation is fundamental.

- Judgement is universally used – it has a strong role at the end of **ACTIFELD** when someone has to decide whether or not to accept the action plan.

- Judgements about action options often have to be made under pressure of time.

- Quickly making a workable plan to implement an action option is a valuable skill.

- The handling of wish lists arises in any organisation.

The ensuing chapters will cover all this in detail but, before reading further, it might help you to go back and read Chapter 8 again to remind yourself of the connection between the two parts of the book.

Stimulating innovation: possibilities, relevance and impacts

What this chapter is about

- The development of technology is sometimes a critical aspect of a practical strategy problem.

- How, though, can technology be explored so as to envisage all possibilities in order to help us to plan for the best options?

- The chapter covers three variations of *morphological analysis* – a method of technology exploration.

- Morphological analysis can be applied to any other innovation and is not limited to technology.

- We also explore *morphological distance* as a way of identifying routes for technology improvements.

- *Relevance trees* help us to assess the importance, or otherwise, of technologies.

- The effects of technological change are studied using *impact wheels*.

- Technological developments can have significant effects on stakeholders and we use *congruence analysis* to assess those and to decide whether a technology is a breakthrough or a disruption.

Introduction

This chapter will cover three topics:

1. The first is *processes* for generating new ideas about how a task might be accomplished, or seeing previously unrealised technological possibilities. These topics are of immense importance in practical strategy as they lead one's thought into hitherto unrealised realms and that can be where strategic gold is found. These processes go by the forbidding name of *morphological methods*, but that cannot be helped.

2. Secondly, we shall consider *relevance trees*, as a means of linking factors together according to their relevance to goals and objectives.

3. Finally, we will look at ways of assessing the *possible impacts* of new ideas and their effects on stakeholders.

For example, Table 4.8, page 99, mentions the development of 'safer' delivery vehicles and 'safe' delivery points, but what might those be? If we could imagine all the conceivable types of 'safe' vehicle we might be able to make a better choice than if we simply used the first idea to come along. The essence of these approaches is, then, to *help to stimulate imagination about innovation.*

| Morphological methods deal with innovation in any area, not just technology. |

When morphological methods, relevance trees and impact analysis are used in conjunction with one another they are valuable additions to the tools for practical strategy. Although they are highly applicable to technology innovation and forecasting, that, as we shall see, is by no means their only role.

One difficulty is that, unlike almost everything else in this book, the morphological methods are *not* simple to explain and are sometimes not user-friendly. The effort expended in grasping them will, though, be repaid by their utility.

Introduction to morphological methods

The background

| Morphology means the study of shape and form. |

Morphology means 'the study of the whole form and structure of anything'. It has a very long lineage and Wills (1972) quotes Aristotle's *Politics*:

> If we are going to speak of the different species of animals, we should first of all determine the organs that are indispensable to every animal [mouths, stomachs and so on]. Assuming that there are only so many kinds of organ but that there may be differences in them [different mouths, say] the possible combinations of these differences will necessarily furnish many varieties of animal, for animals cannot be the same which have different kinds of mouth or ear. When all the combinations are exhausted there will be as many different sorts of animal as there are combinations of the necessary organs. The same, then, is true of the forms of government …

This is the root of morphological analysis. By identifying the main aspects of an entity (mouths, say), by enumerating all the possible conditions for each aspect (shapes of mouth) and by finding all combinations of aspect and condition, one discovers all conceivable possibilities. The number of possibilities can be enormous and, indeed, there are very many types even in a limited class such as mammalian quadrupeds, as diverse in form and habitat as the elephant and the mouse, and even in those cases there are many species and subspecies.

Morphological analysis is, as one would expect, widely used in the life sciences, and in linguistics to study the form and structure of language and languages. A search of the Internet showed more than 220,000 references to morphology and many websites, most of which seemed to be devoted to biology and language.

From our point of view in practical strategy, there are obvious attractions in this idea. One might imagine a zoologist saying, 'Morphological considerations suggest that there could be a hitherto unknown animal of *this* sort living in *that* habitat, so let us go and seek it.' By the same token, the strategic thinker could systematically conceive of all the possible ways of accomplishing some task, all possible ways of building a machine, or whatever, with the aim of discovering novel possibilities, and with the hope that the new concept would be superior, in some way, to current methods or techniques.

> **Morphological methods help us to find new ways of doing things.**

In modern times, morphological analysis (MA, for short) has been strongly espoused by Professor F. Zwicky and this discussion of MA will largely follow his treatment of the subject. We have, of course, already encountered variants of morphological ideas in field anomaly relaxation and in the viable firm matrix. In this chapter we will first discuss 'classical' MA, considering later how FAR and the VFM are both similar to and different from that.

Zwicky's book

Professor Fritz Zwicky (1898–1974), Bulgarian by birth, Swiss by education and American by adoption, was an extremely distinguished astrophysicist, engineer and all-round polymath. His book, *Discovery, Invention, Research* (1969), now out of print but available through inter-library loan, seems to be the source for subsequent authors, such as Wills (1972).

It is a fascinating read, with some entertaining sideswipes at incompetent directors of observatories and scientific committees unwilling to entertain new ideas. It describes three variants on MA, which we will consider in later sections, and gives numerous summaries of the applications of MA to a wide variety of problems, including new concepts in cosmology (corresponding to the zoologist's search). Much of the notation is over-complicated and confusing and we will simplify it. He calls for the development of the profession of morphologist, which seems not to have happened. Unfortunately for some of us, many of his references are in German.

Before we turn to the method, we will set the scene by briefly summarising two of Zwicky's applications of MA, the first of which is the more remarkable.

Very early in the Second World War, Zwicky realised that there would be great damage to the libraries of universities and research centres and that, when the war ended, it would be necessary to restock their collections. That would help education and research to resume so that the institutions could contribute to post-war recovery. Working entirely part-time and with the help of dedicated volunteers, but without any funding, Zwicky set about building a collection of scientific publications, within the USA, to be distributed when the time came. His first step in what might have seemed to be an impossible task was to conduct a morphological analysis of all the possible paths a journal or book might follow, through individuals, libraries, scientific companies and so on, so as to work out the best points at which spare copies could be intercepted and added to his collection. One result of this achievement by a truly remarkable person using an effective method was the eventual despatch of more than 15 *tons* of material to libraries in Korea and what was then Formosa (Taiwan). Far more was sent to European destinations, resulting in a personal letter of thanks from the then President of the Federal German Republic.

The second example (Zwicky 1947) deals with all the possible types of jet engine, and what they should be called; jet engines, now commonplace, were then in their infancy and there was confusion in distinguishing correctly between different types of engine. By carefully examining six aspects of an engine, such as the chemical reaction it uses, and listing all possibilities for each aspect, such as four different types of chemical reaction, Zwicky showed that there were no fewer than 576 conceivable types of jet engine. Of course, not all 576 are useful or feasible, but knowledge of what the options are is a tremendous stimulus to truly radical innovation as opposed to progressive improvement of existing engines. With such a large number, a naming convention is important, and he was able to provide one.

> The morphological techniques are aimed at truly radical innovation.

I have been unable to trace the reference (it may or may not be Zwicky) but it seems that the idea of MA has been used in aeronautical engineering to imagine all possible types of aircraft by considering combinations of engine type, numbers, power, airframe shape and all the other aspects of an aircraft. That led to a very large number of hypothetical aircraft, many of which would, literally, never be able to get off the ground. There was, however, a valuable residue of new concepts in aircraft design that had not previously been imagined.

It is now time to turn to how to do morphological analysis, and Zwicky developed three methods.

The method of systematic field coverage

The essence of MA is to seek out all the possible ways in which a task might be accomplished or a problem might be solved. Zwicky illustrates this by examining all the possible regular polyhedra. A regular polyhedron has sides made from regular polygons (triangles, squares and so forth), so a tetrahedron can be made from four equilateral triangles, whereas a cube has six square sides. These two cases are easy to visualise, but how many regular polyhedra exist? At first sight this seems to be an intellectual exercise in solid geometry but, as we shall see, it can be of considerable practical importance. It turns out that the answer, somewhat surprisingly, is that there are five, and only five, regular polyhedra (if you want to know, they are the tetrahedron, the cube, the octahedron, the icosahedron and the dodecahedron).

> Systematic field coverage explores all possible solutions to a problem.

Zwicky's morphological approach then asks one to think about all the possible ways in which a cube, say, can be made and some of the options are shown in Figure 10.1. Each shape in that diagram represents a sheet of cardboard or thin metal that can be folded along the marked lines, and it is obvious that A cannot be folded into a cubical box with a lid. On the other hand, B, C and D can be made into boxes and it turns out that there are eight other ways in which a box can be made: a total of 11 possibilities that work and many others that do not. As we have seen, A cannot be made into a box by folding the edges and neither can six squares laid end to end.

The practical significance of this is in the box-making industry. In a box factory, a very large sheet of cardboard could be printed with hundreds of B, C or D shapes fitted closely together (the 'legs' of the Cs would point alternately to the right and left). Except round the edge of the large sheet, there would be no waste material.

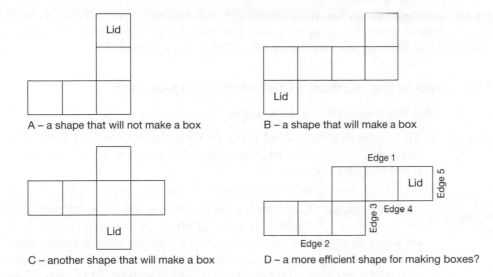

A – a shape that will not make a box

B – a shape that will make a box

C – another shape that will make a box

D – a more efficient shape for making boxes?

Figure 10.1 The morphology of boxes

Source: Zwicky (1969)

The difficulty comes when the marked sheet has to be cut to make the separate boxes. Shapes B and C are very inefficient, as very many small cuts will be needed to separate the box outlines. With D, however, two cuts from one end of the sheet to the other along the edges 1 and 2 need only three cuts along edges 3, 4 and 5 to separate the box outlines. The benefit of this seemingly purely theoretical exercise is that, by knowing that there are 11 ways of making a box by folding, the most efficient cutting pattern can be found, the savings to the box-making industry being very considerable.

Similar ideas apply to the most efficient way of packing polyhedral boxes into larger containers, a cube not always being the most suitable shape for what is being shipped.

Of course, the idea of field coverage is not limited to cardboard boxes and Zwicky used it to identify all the factors in building and operating an astronomical observatory. These range from optics to foundations, with very many others, both human and technological. He asserted that observatories were, at that time, fulfilling only a small fraction of their potential, and that enormous improvements could be achieved by what he termed *integral engineering*; what we would now call systems engineering.

Field coverage examines all possible solutions to a problem. In order to deal with *combinations of solutions*, we turn to the second morphological method.

The method of the morphological box

The basic idea of the morphological box

This is the form of morphological analysis that we have already encountered in field anomaly relaxation (FAR, Chapter 3) and the viable firm matrix (the VFM, Chapter 5). It consists of identifying all the significant

> The morphological box gives all *combinations* of solutions.

aspects of a problem and all the possible variations in the aspects. These form the morphological box and it gives the totality of conceivable solutions to the problem (FAR and the VFM use the box somewhat differently, as discussed later).

The steps in the method of the morphological box

Zwicky states that the method has five steps.

Step 1: Define the problem.

1. The problem to be solved must be formulated concisely and unambiguously. What, for example, are the conceivable solutions for developing jet engines?

Step 2: Select the significant aspects, or parameters.

2. All of the parameters that might be of importance in that problem must be thought of, and their possibilities analysed. We referred above to 'aspects', a term which is appropriate for a problem in which the infinitely fine-grained nature of a socio-economic field has to be aggregated into broader categories for tractability (such fields are described under FAR in Chapter 3) but, for technological uses of MA, 'parameter' is more correct as it means something that can have a few, or several, clearly distinct values. There are, for instance, some clearly different ways in which an engine can work.

Step 3: Create a matrix with all variations of the aspects.

3. The morphological box or matrix of all the parameter variations is constructed.

Step 4: Evaluate the combinations to find desirable or unattractive solutions to the problem.

4. All the conceivable solutions to the problem – the totality of the parameter combinations – are studied and evaluated with respect to the purposes to be achieved. The evaluation might show that some of the potential solutions are undesirable, perhaps for social or environmental reasons. As far as technological forecasting is concerned, these correspond to unfavourable developments, were someone to bring them about, so these are sometimes referred to as *disruptive technologies*. On the other hand, some possibilities might be so attractive that, if they could be brought to fruition, they would be *breakthrough technologies*. Note that, at this stage, we are not considering feasibility, only attractiveness, and, as far as research and development planning is concerned, one would seek to divert resources from potentially disruptive outcomes and direct them towards the breakthrough possibilities. We shall examine this again later when we consider the impact of innovations.

Step 5: Select the most attractive and feasible solution.

5. Finally, the most attractive solutions are selected and applied in practice, if it is feasible to do so. If they are not currently feasible, appropriate research and development activities might be set in train.

An example of the morphological box

Table 10.1, adapted from Zwicky (1947), is the morphological box for all conceivable forms of jet engine. Note how wide-ranging is its thinking, even allowing for engines that use water as a propellant (chemicals such as liquid sodium–potassium alloys react violently with water), or use earth as a propellant (that reaction would require some as yet unknown chemical).

Table 10.1 Zwicky's morphology of jet engines (bold represents an 'aerojet')

Character of chemical reactions	Mechanical character of propulsion system	Method of thrust augmentation	Physical state of propellants	Operating mode of propulsive power plant	Reactivity or reaction speed of the propellants
Self-contained – carries all chemicals necessary for activation and operation	No motion	No thrust augmentation	Gaseous state	**Continuous operation**	Propellants are self-igniting
If air-propelled, carries only fuel and uses atmospheric oxygen	**Translatory motion**	**Internal thrust augmentation**	**Liquid state**	Intermittent (pulsating) operation	**Artificial ignition is necessary**
If propelled through or over water, uses water as propellant reacting with an on-board water-reactive chemical	Rotary motion	External thrust augmentation	Solid state		
If propelled through or over the earth, may use earth as propellant reacting with an on-board earth-reactive chemical	Oscillatory motion				

Source: Adapted from Zwicky (1947).

Breadth of visionary thought is the key to MA. One has to be prepared to conceive of *all* the logically possible cases, especially those which have not previously been envisaged, as one of them might represent a genuine advance, or even a breakthrough. Of course, one of them might be potentially harmful and hence to be avoided or protected against.

> The key to morphological analysis is breadth of imagination.

The morphological box in Table 10.1 contains 576 combinations of the parameters. The bold combination represents what Zwicky termed an 'aerojet'. His chosen problem was to develop an unambiguous naming scheme for jet engines, and this particular combination is a specific form of ram jet; other types of ram jet are identifiable from his matrix.

Zwicky likens these combinations to drawers in a filing cabinet of conceivable jet engines, and we used much the same words to explain FAR and the VFM. Some of the combinations are self-contradictory: a mechanism that is oscillatory cannot provide continuous power, so that drawer is empty. A drawer corresponding to a disruptive technology should, metaphorically, be sealed or guarded. Another, which contains a potentially valuable technology which is not yet attainable, might be labelled 'open as soon as possible'.

A key point is that each drawer should contain either one possibility or none. If a drawer contains two or more possibilities, the analysis is incomplete and additional parameters need to be introduced to discriminate precisely between the individual cases. That is a useful check on the validity of the thinking.

One aspect of the morphological box is that it can easily generate hundreds or even thousands of possibilities. That is both the strength and the weakness of the method. The strength lies in the comprehensiveness of the results: everything has been taken into account and the resulting combinations will show previously unimagined possibilities, some of which will be either genuinely beneficial or seriously damaging options. Discovery of those cases can only be of value and the proof of that is that Zwicky held no fewer than 14 US patents as a result of morphological thought.

The drawback is the need to investigate these large numbers of combinations. Eliminating the infeasible combinations, as we did with FAR, makes the problem more tractable, and computer support will help. The emphasis, though, must be on computer *support*; the essence of the morphological box is to be a *tool for thought*, and the computer must not replace the intellect.

Other applications of the morphological box

Out of respect for Zwicky's seminal work, we have explained morphological analysis largely in terms of technology, adapting from his publications, but it is manifest that MA is not limited to technology. Indeed, Aristotle hinted at the underlying ideas being used to study forms of government, and Zwicky himself used MA on problems as diverse as restocking war-damaged libraries, a legal framework for space exploration, and in cosmological research. Gordon (2000) reports a case of the use of MA to stimulate technological innovation in a US business and cites other cases. A very recent development is the establishment of the Swedish Morphological Society. Their website, www.swemorph.com, describes current applications to a wide variety of problems.

One obvious and powerful application is in systems engineering. Zwicky wrote of 'integral engineering' for making the most efficient use of exceedingly costly assets such as astronomical telescopes. He refers to a range of factors such as the quality of the optics, the skill of the maintenance, the ability to manage the allocation of time on the instrument, electronic and computer support, and other factors. As an exercise in MA, imagine what some of the other factors might be and draw up a morphological box for this problem. You should keep the number of parameters to not more than about seven and you should not assume that the parameters in the second sentence of this paragraph should be used exactly as they stand; you may need to combine them in some way. You may need more than one attempt to get a matrix that seems to be useful. If you prefer, develop a box for any other systems engineering problem that interests you.

Morphological analysis, field anomaly relaxation and the viable firm matrix

In this book, we have used morphological ideas in field anomaly relaxation and for the viable firm matrix and we must briefly explain the differences between those cases and the formal use of MA, described above.

> FAR and the VFM use morphological ideas, but in different ways.

The first difference is that, in the problems that FAR and the VFM address, we cannot rely on there being distinctly different 'parameters', such as the chemical reaction and the operation of the power plant in Table 10.1. By contrast, FAR and the VFM have to aggregate an infinitely fine-grained socio-economic 'field' into broader categories – in Chapter 3 we had to ignore Aunt Mabel's cat! Similarly, we cannot depend on parameters having clearly different 'values', as in the clearly separable ways in which a power plant might operate. In a VFM we are forced, for instance, to use several definitions of the possible competence levels in a firm. These are fairly easily distinguishable one from the other, but they are not as precisely and explicitly different as are the power plants. The same applies to the definitions in the rows of a FAR matrix.

The second difference between FAR, the VFM and Zwicky's formal morphological analysis lies in what they aim to do. The Zwicky concept is to identify *all* the parameter combinations with the aim of finding a new way of doing something – he refers to this as *totality research*, which is exactly what it is. To be sure, some of the combinations will be inherently infeasible and can be eliminated, but the whole emphasis is on discovery, not on rejection. In FAR, on the other hand, the stress is placed on eliminating configurations that, in a gestalt, whole-pattern, sense, correspond to impossible 'worlds', so that the surviving coherent configurations can be used to generate time lines into the future, which will be genuine story scenarios. The viable firm (or anything else, such as an observatory) matrix is different both from MA and from FAR. While it uses a FAR-type matrix, the aim is not so much to eliminate infeasible firms and see what is left, it is to discover a feasible design which does not involve impossibilities but which can satisfactorily implement the actions that emerge from the TOWS analysis.

Nonetheless, both FAR and the VFM owe a clear debt to Zwicky's ideas.

We must now turn to a more difficult, but potentially very powerful, notion for assessing the prospects for, and even 'designing', technological developments.

Morphological distance and technological routes

Introduction

The underlying ideas in this section are due to Ayres (1969, summarised in Wills 1972), though we have extended them to incorporate the idea of 'designing' technological improvements. We have also adapted the terminology.

Ayres' idea is that, when only one or two of many possible combinations have actually come to practical fruition (there are only one or two types of jet engine in operation), they provide a relatively small 'springboard' from which further

Existing technologies or systems are the springboard for further developments.

advances might be made. On the other hand, if all possible combinations have been built, no further advances can be made. The greatest prospect for *further* advances is when a fair number of technological possibilities have been turned into reality. Like all good ideas, it looks very obvious after someone has thought of it.

Of course, if *none* of the conceivable combinations yet exists, there is the greatest possibility of a development as all of them are, as it were, open to research. That, however, is only of theoretical interest as a morphological study of all possibilities only starts once someone has developed the first one, such as Whittle's first jet engine. It seems that we humans can only imagine further possibilities from what we can already see; Zwicky's jet engine morphology does not consider plasma propulsion as that concept had not been thought of in 1947.

Ayres goes further and thinks of what we will call the 'morphological distance' between one technology and another.

Morphological distance

The ideas behind morphological distance are shown in Figure 10.2. It might help you to follow the argument if you photocopy that diagram for easy reference.

For simplicity we imagine a technology defined by three parameters, A, B and C, each of which can have three possible values, A1, B2 and so on. We must, though, make it absolutely clear that A1, A2 and A3 are drawn from left to right purely for convenience and it is *not* implied that A3 is harder to attain, or is 'better', than A2 and A1 simply because it is further to the right on the page. The shaded cells, such as A1, are the morphological possibilities actually in existence. Other cells, such as A2,

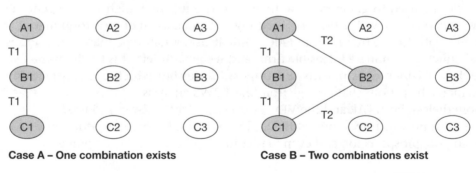

Figure 10.2 The concept of morphological distance

Source: Author's own, based on Ayres (1969)

are those logical possibilities from the morphological matrix that have not yet been achieved in reality. The links between, for instance, A1, B1 and C1 indicate that these separate possibilities have been made to work together as a coherent system.

There are 3^3 or 27 possible combinations for this technology (or any other case, such as a form of government) and, in Case A, one of those, T1 – technology 1 – is A1B1C1 and already exists so there are a further 26 logically possible combinations still to be brought into being. One of them is A2B1C1 and involves only one change from A1B1C1. On the other hand, A2B2C1 would require two changes, whereas A3B2C3 would need three.

Depending on the circumstances, a change such as the addition of A2 may happen by evolution from A1, which already exists, or it may have to be brought about independently by developing A2 from scratch. In practice, there is almost always some degree of evolution; lessons learned from A1 in metallurgy, say, might be applicable in A2.

With a little patience one can work out that there are six new technologies involving only one change, 12 needing two changes, and 8 calling for three. Three changes are, in a broad sense, more 'distant' from T1 than two changes, and two are more distant than one. These distances have been deduced from the morphological matrix, hence the term *morphological distance*. In Case B, with existing technologies T1 and T2, the numbers turn out to be 8, 12 and 5 for one, two and three changes respectively. Note that in this example the number of changes and the number of existing technologies always add to 27.

> The idea of *morphological distance* is to see the options for further advances.

What are we to make of these results? Ayres makes the broad assumption that making two changes will be twice as hard as making one, while making three will be three times as difficult. What we might call the 'morphological scope' of case A is then roughly estimated as 6 + 12/2 + 8/3 = 14.7 (if two changes are twice as hard as one, a two-step development has half the scope of a single step). Case B comes out to 15.7, and case C (ignore the dotted line for the moment) is 18.5.

These numbers have no objectively real meaning; they simply give one a feel for the possibilities so that, if we had to choose to invest either in a technological area with a scope of about 15, or in another area with a scope of 19, the numbers tend to suggest that 19 could be a better prospect.

Competing technological routes

Now look at the dotted line in case C and suppose that it represents a desirable technology, if it could be achieved. We already have a basis in the sense that A1, A2 etc. already exist, so what is the best route to achieve the required development?

It is immediately obvious that B1 and B2 can be ignored, leading to the 'route map' in case D of Figure 10.2. There are three options for A3, by evolution from A1 or A2 (and recall that the sequence A1, A2, A3 does not imply increasing difficulty in going from A1 to A3, it is drawn like that simply for convenience), or development of A3 from scratch, as shown by the arrow coming in from the right. The question marks indicate the decision as to the best development route.

It might, of course, turn out that A3B3C3 cannot be achieved but that A2B3C3 can be attained. Will this be good enough?

Summary

Carefully handled, the notion of morphological distance is helpful. The distance 'numbers' are not to be taken too seriously but they give a rough indication of the relative maturities and scope for improvement in different technological areas. The rationale that led to case D in Figure 10.2 is considerably more powerful as it gives guidance on research and development options for technology and, indeed, for planning almost any kind of evolution, whether it be of a business organisation or the evolution of a military force.

> **Don't take the numbers seriously; they are only indications.**

It would be difficult to make these ideas work for a problem with many parameters, each of which has numerous possible values, because of the large number of combinations – even as few as five parameters, each with five possible values, gives more than 3,000 combinations. However, attempting to handle large problems in this fashion would not only be intractable, it would also miss the point. The whole purpose of the ideas in this section is to obtain broad, high-level, views of the issues and, in practice, the key is to aggregate the detail from data such as Table 10.1, which has 576 possibilities, to a level that better supports practical strategy.

The method of negation and construction

> **Defying accepted wisdom can yield remarkable results.**

The last of Zwicky's morphological methods goes by the slightly cumbersome name of *negation and construction*. The idea is that once one denies the truth of accepted ideas, or axioms – or defies accepted wisdom – and builds on the result, considerable possibilities may be opened up. He states that the classical example of this is in geometry. In ordinary Euclidean geometry all triangles enclose 180°, a property arising from the axiom that 'parallel lines never meet', and this property of triangles is of great practical value in surveying. However, in the nineteenth century mathematicians such as Lobachevski (immortalised in song by Tom Lehrer) denied the truth value of the parallel lines axiom, leading to the development of non-Euclidean geometry, without which, Zwicky states, much of modern physics would be impossible.

Zwicky's own use of this method was in the development of new types of explosive. A normal chemical explosion has three interesting parameters: p1, the explosive charge is changed into other chemical forms and energy is released; p2, the transition from the original explosive to the reaction products is very fast; p3, there is a large expansion of volume because much of the original explosive substance is transformed into gas. This is the standard method used in mining, the military, and other applications. Apart from its practical utility, it yields spectacular results and, provided one exercises the right skills – not to mention a good deal of care, blowing things up is immensely enjoyable.

Zwicky's concept was that there might be an explosive such that p1 and p2 still applied, but p3 did not. An explosion of that type would generate very hot reaction products, but it would not fly apart. Such a substance, which Zwicky called a corruscative, would have numerous uses in shaped charges for all manner of applications but that theoretical possibility would only be a practical reality if one could find chemical substances capable of creating a corruscative reaction. The method of negation and construction suggests the idea, and that stimulates research into new uses for existing chemical substances. The end result is Zwicky's US patent on corruscative explosives.

The method of negation and construction is, implicitly, a powerful source of beneficial change in human affairs. It might be said that the United States is the eventual product of negation of the idea of rule from Britain and construction of the Constitution. Religious divisions arise when one group negates an article of dogma and constructs its own theology. Political parties arise in much the same way. Social change occurred in nineteenth-century Britain when the idea that it was acceptable for women and young children to work in coalmines was negated and new laws constructed.

> Negation and construction has had major effects on human affairs.

A business example is, perhaps, the growth of telephone and Internet banking. The availability of the technology made it *possible* but what made it *happen* was abandonment of the idea that banks had to close at 4.30 p.m. in order to balance that day's books.

It is unlikely that the originators of any of these ideas used the term 'negation and construction', but, nevertheless, that is what they were doing. Doing negation and construction formally and explicitly, as we have described, is an effective discipline for creating new ideas and methods, rather than leaving them to chance.

In short, this concept of thinking the unthinkable *and then developing a new basis* can be exceedingly powerful. Construction is, though, an essential part of the process; the worst kind of revolutionary wishes to negate what he sees as an abomination, but simply assumes that something better will happen. Unhappily, that seems rarely to be the case.

> Thinking the unthinkable is a powerful basis for new developments.

The morphological methods and technology forecasting

In Chapter 3 we reviewed the Delphi method of organised debate about technological possibilities (though Delphi has many other uses). These debates draw out the opinions of people presumed to be knowledgeable about technological prospects and, provided that they explore the reasons for extreme opinions and do not simply average out the differing views, or ignore the extremes, can be very valuable. One downside, however, is that a full Delphi exercise can be rather time-consuming. Much more serious disadvantages are that there is no way of knowing how much effort the respondents have put into their judgements, and no way of knowing what framework they used to organise their knowledge so as to arrive at their judgements. Finally, there is no guarantee that respondents have stayed within their areas of competence in making their judgements and have not been tempted to stray into domains of which they are ignorant.

It seems obvious that the morphological methods, by contributing to overcoming those drawbacks of Delphi, should have a powerful role to play in technological forecasting. That will involve four main steps.

The first stage is to use the Delphi panellists to draw up the morphological box. The parameters (column headings) could be chosen by the

> Morphological methods can help to overcome some of the weaknesses of the Delphi approach.

Delphi organisers, from their own technical knowledge or with the aid of a small team of panellists. The members of the main Delphi team are then asked a very plain question – 'What are the theoretical possibilities for each of the parameters of which you have specialised knowledge?' That should not require much input of time, or multiple Delphi rounds, and would give the entries in the rows of the morphological box. The end result of step one is a table along the lines of Table 10.1, p. 179.

The second step maintains respondents within their areas of competence and involves two precise questions. The first is to ask them which of the parameter possibilities exists now – the highlighted cells in Figure 10.2. The second question is to ask which of the unshaded cells is deemed to be physically impossible or very unlikely to happen within a chosen time horizon. The essential feature of this step is only to allow respondents to answer questions from the column in the matrix that corresponds to their deep expertise in chemistry, for instance. With proper opportunity to debate reasons, this second step should be easy to do on the Internet. It should be *much* less time-consuming than standard Delhi with multiple rounds, and ensures a common basis for judgement. The end-product of this stage would be a much-reduced morphological box – we can call it the *feasible* box – with many fewer combinations than the box from step 1, which we can call the *imaginable* box. The feasible box might be yet further reduced by pairwise comparisons similar to those in field anomaly relaxation in Chapter 3, provided one used carefully chosen pairs of domain experts.

The third stage is for the Delphi organisers, perhaps with help from a small group of respondents, to represent the feasible box in the form of Figure 10.2, possibly with some aggregation of parameters to keep it to a manageable size. The diagram will look something like case D, say, and should identify and list the combinations which are potentially realisable but do not yet exist, as with Zwicky's jet engines. Calculation of the morphological scope might be helpful as long as it did not generate futile debate about the weightings to be used.

These three initial steps overcome the main disadvantages of Delphi – they require less work, they ensure that respondents stay within their competence, and they provide a common framework for thought. The final stage will, though, be the most productive.

The fourth step involves the kind of reasoning shown in Figure 10.2 case D. There is a feasible, but not yet existent, technological combination, such as A3B3C3, and that generates a range of questions:

- What might give rise to it or inhibit it?
- How difficult, or easy, would it be not only to create A3 and C3 but also to link them, as a system, with B3?
- Would the consequences be beneficial or harmful (a topic to be considered below with the aid of relevance trees, impact wheels and congruence analysis)?
- What are the policy implications?
- What actions might be called for?

No doubt further questions would arise as these are discussed, so the preferred format for stage four is a concentrated, and skilfully facilitated, study period or workshop, lasting for a couple of days and held in a congenial location. The session should use syndicate groups, and we shall have more to say about syndicates in Chapter 15.

Summary on the morphological methods

This discussion of the three morphological methods – complete coverage, the morphological box or matrix and negation and construction – has suggested that they are remarkably effective at stimulating thought about innovation. We have explained them mainly in terms of technology but they are capable of being applied to almost any domain: Aristotle used it to consider forms of government, and morphological thinking is, it seems, a mainstay of linguistics, the life sciences and, probably, palaeontology. Despite their promise, and their use in other disciplines, morphological methods seem to have been little used in management or organisational strategy: Gordon (2000) cites little literature later than about 1969 and a search of the Internet was not productive. How is this to be explained?

Undoubtedly, it is because a morphological box usually generates so many combinations, often hundreds and perhaps many thousands, that it is assumed that the results are too numerous to be dealt with. We suggest that this is not, in fact, an insuperable obstacle and that there are several possible ways of getting the benefit of the morphological stimulus to innovation without being swamped by data.

The first is the use of human judgement and inspiration. Some of the morphological combinations will be more 'interesting' than others, perhaps in the sense of their feasibility, novelty, potential pay-off, or whatever. Clearly, one cannot go through a list of thousands of possible combinations looking for the interesting ones but the process is reversible. For instance, in Table 10.1 there are 576 ostensible combinations – too many to inspect. If, however, the judgement was that combinations involving an air-propelled vehicle using translatory motion were inherently interesting, then there are only 18 combinations left to inspect. It would be easy to do such searches on a PC.

The second approach is not to look for the interesting cases but to discard the uninteresting ones and see what is left. If, say, the combination B3C2 in Figure 10.2 is physically impossible, then discarding it reduces the number of combinations from 27 to 24. In a larger morphological box, discarding even one combination will reduce the total number of combinations by hundreds (review second footnote of Chapter 3, p. 68). This pairwise elimination is, of course, the basis of field anomaly relaxation in Chapter 3 and its use would vastly improve the tractability of the morphological box method.

Undoubtedly, though, the potential power of the morphological methods is too great for them to be allowed to remain unused simply because they appear to be too laborious. There is room for some intelligent research into the best ways to generate complete coverages, create and use the morphological box, exploit the concept of morphological distance, and stimulate completely new, even heretical, ideas by negation and construction.

We have devoted a good deal of effort to examining ways in which innovation can be stimulated, though we remind you that innovation does not occur only in technology. In fact, you are challenged to use any or all of the morphological methods to innovate in domestic postal services, farming, criminal justice, health care, pensions and air traffic control, to mention only a few of the issues of concern in the UK in 2002. You will also have your own ideas for topics to consider.

However, we know that innovation without regard to its relevance or consequences has sometimes turned out to be unwise. We must, therefore, look at some techniques for evaluating those aspects of innovation.

Relevance trees

Relevance trees connect technology to a purpose.

It is evident that a technological development is of no more than intellectual interest unless it is relevant to some higher purpose, and the *relevance tree* is a device for understanding such connections.

The illustrative tree shown in Figure 10.3 has six levels down its left-hand edge, ranging from the overall objective, defence against terrorism in this example, through four sub-levels, to specific technologies. The level below the objective shows the principal ways by which an objective can be achieved. Each of these, in a complete tree, would have its own sublevels, but we will concentrate on protection. That is expanded, in turn, to categories of things to be protected, followed by the means of doing so: making it harder to damage; hiding it; pretending that it is something, or somewhere, else and, perhaps, in other ways. Below that again we have techniques of hardening and, finally, some specific technologies; the empty branches at that level imply that additional technologies exist or might need to be developed.

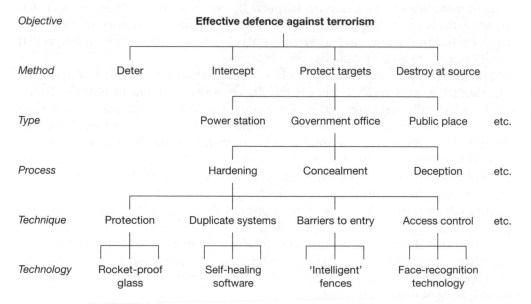

Figure 10.3 Illustrative relevance tree

The tree works both upwards and downwards. Working from the bottom level, self-healing software, if it existed, would feed up through a series of steps to the highest objective. There might, indeed, be trade-offs. If 'intelligent fences' to warn of, and prevent, attempts to get within range exist, then rocket-proof glass may be unnecessary, and so forth. Of course, a given technological item might have more than one application; perhaps intelligent fences would help to deter attacks. Working down from the top, it is easy to see what needs to be done to achieve an objective.

Wills (1972) and Jones and Twiss (1978) suggest the calculation of 'relevance numbers' to indicate the relative merits of competing solutions to the overall problem, though the latter give the very sensible advice (with which I agree) that these numbers might be little better than window-dressing. The analytic hierarchy process (on the website) would produce more reliable weightings, if numerical indicators of relevance seem likely to be useful.

The tree might even suggest policy options such as the balance of investment between deterrence, interception, protection and destruction. The whole value of the relevance tree is in clearing the mind and supporting imaginative practical strategy.

Clearly, one has to use the technique sensibly, and not all factors need to be included. It would be hard, in this example, to conceal a power station or to deceive terrorists into believing that the Tower of London is somewhere else. It is equally important not to use obvious categories. Perhaps, in this case, it might have been better not to have been specific about target types but, instead, to have referred to high-value/low-value targets or difficult and easy ones. That might add another layer to the diagram. It will usually be as well to invest the effort to get two groups each to draw their own tree and then draw it again to get the best of both views.

The main handicap of relevance trees is that, unless the process is well controlled, they can rapidly become impossibly complicated, even with software support; the complete version of Figure 10.3 would probably include hundreds of items. The process needs to be managed, and the keys to exploiting the considerable utility of this technique are to realise what it is for and to keep it simple.

The aim of the tree is to clear the mind and to suggest possibilities, not to produce a vast catalogue of every possible factor. The tree is a model of relationships and, as with any model, it must simplify reality if it is to be a useful tool for thought. In practice, if a tree cannot be drawn on a whiteboard clearly enough for people to see it and discuss it, it will serve

> The tree is a model and needs to be as simple as the purpose requires.

no purpose. To keep the complexity under control one might draw sub-trees for aspects such as hardening.

This method has strong relationships with those considered in Chapter 2 for unravelling complexity, but it goes a little further by stimulating thought, such as 'What if there were "intelligent fences"?' If such ideas have merit, research and development can be started with a clear idea of what is to be achieved, perhaps using TOWS and strategies as we did with the unmanned ground vehicle in Chapter 4. Further ideas might emerge from a morphological box for, say, hardening.

Figure 10.3 is only an illustration, chosen for its topicality, and, as usual, you should now try out your skills on that tree or one of your own choosing. One suggestion is to go back to the **Herrington-Jones** case which, you will recall, required the development of new distribution channels. The objective might be 'efficient distribution to *Herrington-Jones's* stores'. It might be 'efficient operation of electronic shopping'. Try some ideas of your own.

Relevance trees show the effect that innovations have on an overall objective. However, we should also look at the wider impacts of an innovation, and the impact wheel, which we studied in Chapter 2, helps us to analyse the effect that an innovation might have on other aspects of society or technology.

The impacts of technology

Let us suppose that the technology A3B3C3 from Figure 10.2 is a new diesel engine that makes heavy vehicles, such as trucks and farm machines, cheaper to run (thus reducing distribution costs), more reliable, cleaner, harder to steal and opens up the possibility of further improvements to vehicle design. Figure 10.4 is a signed and structured impact wheel showing some illustrative effects. Some of the impacts are within a sector, while others lie on boundaries, suggesting joint impacts. (This diagram is similar to, but simpler than, Figure 2.4.) Most of the plus and minus signs are self-evident but note the use of '??' for the effect on crime. One might assume that vehicles that are harder to steal will reduce such thefts but there is some recent evidence that thieves have become more violent as they now need to get the vehicle keys from the owner.

Impact wheels can show the effects of an innovation.

You might revise Figure 10.4 to improve the suggestions it contains, and add your own ideas, such as other impacts (it is obviously not essential for a structured wheel to have six segments). You could consider tertiary impacts, such as increased tax revenues from the improved business profitability, and increased tax needs for rural social services. At what point would the diagram become too complex to be useful?

There is a clear possibility of feedback effects: rural viability affects agricultural production which, in turn, probably supports viability. Increased rural viability creates an increased need for rural social services but, if those are not forthcoming, rural viability might be adversely affected. As we saw in Chapter 2, an influence diagram is the preferred tool for thinking about feedback and it is always beneficial to switch one's point of view and use another tool for unravelling complexity when the one you started with has reached the end of its usefulness.

An impact wheel for an innovation can best be built with the Delphi-type approach from Chapter 3 and also mentioned on page 185; each respondent assessing the impacts within an area of expertise. Its main value is to provide a sense-making device, as we saw in Chapter 2.

In this chapter it helps us to make sense of the consequences of an innovation, which might be one that has happened, something that is being developed (what insights might have emerged from an impact wheel when Concorde or the Channel Tunnel were being contemplated?), or a development that might occur – perhaps beyond one's control.

The sense-making can, and often should, be done from more than one point of view. What, for example, might be the effect on terrorists of implementing the actions described in Figure 10.3? It is rash to assume that a problem has been solved just because *you* think so.

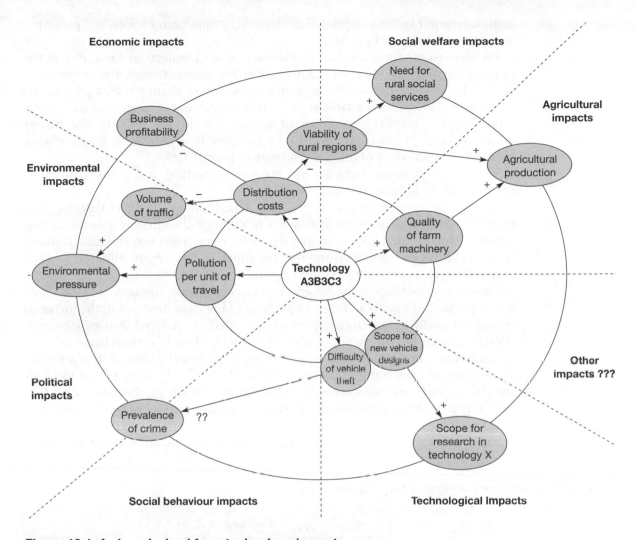

Figure 10.4 A signed wheel for a technology impact

An impact wheel for an innovation – technological, political, legal, or anything else – raises the clear question, 'Are the consequences benign or harmful?' Is it, as we mentioned on p. 178, a breakthrough or a disruption? To that final issue we now turn.

Assessing innovations

It is clear from the impact wheel that A3B3C3 has a number of primary and secondary consequences and that these will be felt, perhaps for good or ill, by a variety of stakeholders. There is, therefore, no single indicator of whether A3B3C3 might be a breakthrough or a disruptive technology, so we must look at the question from a wider point of view and a suitable

> Congruence analysis can show the social effects of innovations.

approach might be the congruence analysis technique from Chapter 6. The matrix could be laid out as in Table 10.2.

We have to use the secondary and tertiary (if any) impacts in Table 10.2 as the primary 'impacts' are merely a restatement of the inherent properties of the innovation. The stakeholders are the segments of the wheel, slightly rephrased, and the first use of the congruence table is to ask if the stakeholders have been adequately represented. Given the mention of crime, should we include the justice system/police? Do not have too many stakeholders; aim for a good balance between representation of interests and ease of interpretation.

The plus and minus signs are simply for illustration, but seem reasonable, though you should alter them as you see fit.

The '??' denote two areas of uncertainty. One is about the effect that the difficulty of theft will have on the prevalence of crime. If the effect is positive – crime becomes worse – what are the consequences for the farmers and the rural community? What can be done to ensure that the inherent property of difficulty of theft is actually realised, making the signs negative?

The other uncertainty is the net effect on environmental pressures of reduced pollution per unit of travel – an inherent property of the technology – and the increased volume of traffic arising from the inherent property of reduced distribution costs. Will the balance be positive or negative? What can be done to make it negative?

Congruence analysis, despite its simplicity, or perhaps because of it, is a sophisticated way of assessing innovations. In this illustration it suggests that the only stakeholders who will unequivocally benefit from A3B3C3 are the auto industry, as they can now develop technology X, though that, in turn, may be a mixed blessing. Depending on the crime issue, the farmers and business might benefit. Even then, we will imagine that neither the government nor the green lobby necessarily

Table 10.2 Congruence analysis of an innovation

Secondary impacts	Stakeholders					
	Government	Business	Auto industry	Farmers	Rural community	Green lobby
Business profitability	+	++				
Volume of traffic					– –	– – –
Environmental pressure	??				??	??
Prevalence of crime	??	??		??	??	
Scope for technology X			++			
Agricultural output	–			+++	+	–
Need for rural social services	– –			++	+++	
Viability of rural regions	?			++	+++	+++

want increased agricultural output, preferring, instead, farmers to be paid to look after the countryside.

As Table 10.2 implies, it is very unlikely that a given innovation will be unambiguously a blessing or a curse, and it is probably overly simple to refer to breakthrough and disruptive technologies when wider impacts are considered. There is much more likelihood of a mixed pattern of advantages and drawbacks and congruence analysis displays them clearly. Of course, the signs are no more than the opinions and judgements of informed people, they cannot be otherwise, but the views are organised and can be debated and revised, most usefully at a study period away from the office. The debate should turn on two questions:

1. What can be done to ensure that benefits are reaped and drawbacks avoided?
2. To the extent that they cannot be reaped or avoided, what risks are being run?

Chapter summary

The overall theme of the chapter is that innovation, whether it be of technology or anything else, is too important to be left more or less to chance and serendipity. To be sure, those are welcome guests but the potential benefit of systematic thought is likely to be an even greater help in achieving real innovation. The topic of stimulating and managing innovation is, perhaps, not as well covered in the strategy texts as it deserves to be, which is why it has been included in this book.

> Innovation, in technology or anything else, is too important to be left to chance.

Zwicky's three morphological methods are potentially powerful for the vital task of exploring technological combinations and visualising genuinely new possibilities. Their limitation is, paradoxically, their very power; a morphological box can generate thousands of possibilities, far more than can easily be handled: this tool for practical strategy has the potential to smother thought in a welter of ideas.

The key to success with morphology is to use a well-managed discussion, especially using the Delphi concept of exploring reasons (p. 185), to find the combinations involving interesting possibilities or, and more fruitfully, by eliminating uninteresting or infeasible combinations.

> The key to success is well-managed discussion.

Of course, finding an attractive new technological idea is only a very small part of dealing with innovation problems in practical strategy. There are four more issues to deal with:

- Finding the most effective route by which the attractive technological novelty can be reached. The concept of morphological distance is one method of looking imaginatively and realistically at that question but the *key to success* is to keep it simple and work at an aggregated level to identify broad development strategies, dealing with the details as a separate step, also kept simple.
- It is also necessary to look at the relevance of a given technology to some overall aim or objective. That can be reversed to search for technologies to support that objective. That is the domain of the relevance tree but, as with the morphological box, the tree can 'explode' into unmanageable detail. Yet again, the *key to success* is to keep things simple. A full-scale tree, as in Figure 10.3, can be aggregated into

a simple tree of the top two levels, the objective and the method. A Delphi discussion could pick out the key methods so that they can each be explored in a method/type tree. The steps from method down to technology can then be explored in series of two-stage sub-trees, homing in on the significantly relevant items at each stage.

■ We also need to examine the wider impacts of a technology and the impact wheel does that without too much explosion of detail. The *key to success* is to use sensible domains, such as environmental impacts in Figure 10.4, so that expertise in each domain can be exploited.

■ Finally, though, the concepts of breakthrough and disruptive technologies are overly simple, as they do not ask the question 'a breakthrough from whose point of view?' The simple technique of congruence analysis, Chapter 6, handles that quite well. The *keys to success* are intelligent choice of the stakeholders to be included and ignored, and scrupulous honesty in attempting to assess their preferences. In some cases, of course, openness is possible and they can state their own views as an input to a government decision.

This whole question of stimulating innovation in a manageable way, of assessing its relevance and impacts, and appraising its effects on those people who have to live with, or might benefit from, its effects is, though, an aspect of the tools for practical strategy that is ripe for intelligent research.

References

Ayres, R. U. (1969), *Technological Forecasting and Long Range Planning*. McGraw-Hill, New York, pp 94–142.

Gordon, T. J. (2000), in J. C. Glenn and T. J. Gordon, *State of the Future*. American Council for the United Nations University, Washington, DC.

Jones, H., Twiss, B. (1978), *Forecasting Technology for Planning Decisions*. Macmillan Press, London and Basingstoke.

Wills, G. (1972), *Technological Forecasting*. Penguin Books, London.

Zwicky, F. (1947), Morphology and nomenclature of jet engines. *Aeronautical Engineering Review*, June, 20–3.

Zwicky, F. (1969), *Discovery, Invention, Research* (translated from German). Macmillan, Toronto.

The art of judgement: concepts and methods

What this chapter is about

- Dealing with top-level issues, whether in the public service or any other organisation, depends fundamentally on *the art of judgement*.

- That art relies on a mental *appreciative system* and the concepts of appreciation are explained.

- Sometimes the issue is an *urgent matter* and the pressure of events can preclude detailed analysis.

- Fortunately, there are some simple and quick *mini-methods* that use the issue's history to illuminate, and perhaps improve, judgement.

- The mini-methods can also be used when the problem is not urgent.

Introduction

This chapter is addressed to people in the public service, business, non-governmental organisations, or anywhere else, who have to make policy at the highest level in the organisation to deal with what we can therefore describe as top-level issues.

Some issues arise almost overnight and policy has to be decided swiftly. For example:

- For many years Argentina and Britain had argued about the possession of the Falkland (Malvinas) Islands. The dispute had simmered at a diplomatic level; a status that was satisfactory, or not of much concern, to British policy-makers. Early in 1982 intelligence suggested that Argentina might be preparing to occupy the Falklands and, indeed, Argentina did so in April of that year. The situation has now become unsatisfactory from Britain's standpoint. What are the options? What is to be done?

- Between 1967 and 2001 there had been no serious occurrence of foot and mouth disease in farm animals in the UK. In February 2001, an outbreak was reported, initially on a few farms. What should policy be on controlling it by slaughter or vaccination, compensation for farmers, and so forth?

- Barings Bank was, for more than a century, the epitome of financial solidity but was brought down by one person. The catastrophe emerged practically overnight. Some immediate action is needed.

In other cases, the issue develops more slowly; the state of affairs steadily deteriorates until the issue rises to the top of the agenda. For instance:

- The UK's National Health Service, for decades a source of pride, is widely perceived to have slipped into decline, to the point where the NHS is seen to be 'in crisis'. What is to be done?

In yet other instances, the problem is seen to be some distance into the future but calls for action fairly soon. For example:

- Increasing numbers of older people mean that current systems for funding pensions, which have worked well for decades, may be unable to provide for a decent old age in 20 or 30 years' time. What changes need to be made?

Such issues have some features in common.

- The first is that a state of affairs that was *previously* satisfactory, or not of concern, is *now* unsatisfactory, a cause for complaint, or even a 'crisis'. Pension systems were fine, now they are not. People felt that they could rely on the NHS, now they are not so sure. The Falkland Islands were not a serious concern, now they have been invaded.

- Secondly, there is a cry for something to be done, and sometimes to be done quickly.

- In the urgent cases, the staff assistants have practically no time for analysis when formulating options.

- Whether or not the case is urgent, decision-makers must draw on judgement, experience and, perhaps, analogies with other cases, to develop options and decide between them.

- Sometimes, the outcome is favourable, or at least acceptable, but not always. The Falkland Islands were recovered by Britain (albeit at great cost in lives and money), but the response to the foot and mouth disease outbreak in 2001 was widely seen as disastrous.

This chapter will discuss ways of handling such problems, drawing on two remarkable books: Vickers (1983) *The Art of Judgement*, and Neustadt and May (1988) *Thinking in Time: The Uses of History for Decision Makers*. The connection between them is that Vickers lays a conceptual foundation for the art of judgement while Neustadt and May provide some supporting techniques for getting the best out of that art. Neither book makes mention of the other, which is unfortunate as there are some remarkable similarities between them, as well some notable differences.

Both books run to 300 pages or so, and we shall have to summarise quite sharply. If you have time, you will find it worth while to read the originals. First, we deal with what Vickers has to say about underlying concepts.

Vickers and his book

Sir Geoffrey Vickers (1894–1982) enjoyed four careers. He served with distinction in both world wars, winning the Victoria Cross in 1915. As a lawyer between 1923 and 1940 he was described as being 'almost dangerously brilliant'. In 1947 he became legal adviser to the body set up to manage Britain's nationalised coal industry and was involved in the legal and management tasks of bringing more than 600 separate companies into one ownership. He also served on some major governmental committees, continuing to do so after he 'retired' in 1955. Retirement saw his fourth career as a thinker and writer, with eight books and 100 papers to his credit (Adams *et al.* 1987). His theme, to the extent that it can be summarised in a few words, was the connections between policy-making, socio-economic systems and human behaviour.

The Art of Judgement first appeared in 1965 and is still in print. It develops Vickers' best-known concept, that of the *appreciative judgement* (it is one of the drawbacks of practical strategy that there are no standard terms, and 'appreciation', as Vickers uses the word, has nothing at all to do with the 'military appreciation' described in the next chapter). The prose is elegant, the case studies are still illuminating, despite their age, and, overall, it is one of the best books on management in the literature.

The subject of the book is the mental processes by which we make conscious policy choices; an act that Vickers calls 'judgement'. That is addressed in four parts covering policy-making as: a mental skill; an institutional process; in the context of actual situations; and in the human ecological system. He illustrates those themes with various examples, including three Royal Commissions (the highest form of enquiry into an issue in the UK).

One of the examples is a Royal Commission enquiring into capital punishment and Vickers remarks that the commissioners had to deal with all sorts of evidence: statistics and estimates; opinions, often conflicting; and legal and ecclesiastical authorities, past and present. In a typically resounding phrase he writes that 'all of this, and more, goes into the [mental] mill and out comes the judgement, balanced, coherent, urbane, a mental artefact which only familiarity robs of the wonder which is its due'. The human mind is, indeed, capable of truly wondrous achievements, and the art of judgement is one of them, but how does judgement come about? Vickers offers a concept for the process.

The skills of appreciation

Vickers' approach is rooted in control theory. For instance, the domestic thermostat receives a signal that the room is not warm enough; the room temperature has departed from the 'norm' of comfort that the householder desires. The system takes action by supplying heat and the norm is satisfied again. If that proves to be too expensive, the thermostat norm may be reset to a lower level. Norms – as standards to be achieved or qualities, such as justice, desired for themselves – are, Vickers says, just as much the root of policy-making as they are of central heating.

For example, the Royal Commission on capital punishment was not set up as a result of a spate of murders but because of public concern about official killing of murderers. Previously, execution of murderers had been seen as normal, but the norm of what was acceptable had changed. Norms are easy for a machine to operate, but how does the human mind, or a group of minds, apply them to policy-making? Vickers' idea is deceptively simple.

- A 'signal' emerges that *'something is the matter'* (public unease – in the 1960s – about capital punishment

- that poses the problem *'what is the matter?'* (the judicial process seemed to be undermined as about 50% of condemned murderers were reprieved by the Home Secretary, an elected politician in Britain);

- the answer that *'this is the matter'* (judges had no option but to impose a death sentence in most cases)

- sets a new problem *'what to do about it?'*.

Vickers explains all these steps in terms of what he calls *'mental appreciation'*, a process that he divides into three aspects. Two of them are:

- the *reality judgement*: what are the facts of the case? (recognising that 'facts' may also be opinions)

- the *value judgement*: which of these facts is important or relevant and shows departures from previous norms?

He makes the profound point that facts and values are intertwined and calls this the *appreciative setting*, by which he means the readiness of a person or group to see things, to value them, and to respond. It is what allows us to distinguish between some aspects of a situation and others. It is a little like one's state of mind – a judge in 1910, say, probably had a different appreciative setting and might have been baffled by the very idea of ameliorating capital punishment.

The third aspect is

- the *instrumental judgement*: what is to be done about these facts and values?

It is at this stage that innovation and imagination have their place. What solutions to the problem can be envisaged? Vickers says potential solutions are appreciated in terms of

- *reality* – what will be the anticipated effect of this solution?

and

- *value* – will that expected result satisfy our norms?

The policy-maker needs to use two criteria.

Vickers calls the first of these the *balancing criterion* – is the solution feasible within the constraints of time, money and so forth? That is, of course, exactly the point of the action plan described at the end of Chapter 7.

The second he names the *optimising criterion* – is this the best solution available, when judged by our numerous, and probably inconsistent, ideas of value? Notice that this is much more subtle than the idea of optimisation used in the mathematical techniques of operational research, where the aim is often to minimise some measurable factor such as production cost. Vickers' idea is, in fact, close to the concept of congruence analysis in Chapter 6.

We need to return, briefly, to the Royal Commission on capital punishment to see how balancing and optimisation operated for their instrumental judgement. Abolition of the death penalty was ruled out by the Commission's terms of reference (and all policy-making has implicit or explicit terms of reference). Redefinition of the categories of murder was a legal minefield. Restricting the powers of the Home Secretary would increase executions. Allowing juries more latitude to find extenuating circumstances requiring a lesser sentence was halfway to abolition. There seemed, then, to be no solution that the commissioners could recommend; the constraints of conflicting norms were too severe. The importance of this is to emphasise that sometimes policy cannot be made unless norms are changed.

The subsequent abolition of the death penalty in Britain has produced both a new appreciative setting and a new set of problems, such as how best to deal with murderers of different categories. Capital punishment has been abolished in many countries, but some US states have restored, and inflict, the death penalty. Can you interpret that in terms of reality, value and instrumental judgements?

There is, of course, very much more to *The Art of Judgement* than this brief summary can cover. If you have time, read it yourself, but we must now turn to the relationships between Vickers' thought and that of Neustadt and May.

The difference between them is that Vickers discusses at illuminating length the mental processes of appreciation. The great value of his concepts of reality, value and instrumental judgements is to give some basis for the otherwise slightly mysterious things that happen in the head of a person or, more commonly, those of a group such as a board of directors. Understanding what one is doing in one's mind may help one to do it better. However, Vickers gives us no guidance on how, for instance, to organise the 'facts' in the reality judgement, whereas Neustadt and May's mini-methods are, as we shall see, an excellent basis for working through a policy issue and arriving at options for action – the instrumental judgement. They, though, lay little theoretical basis for the process.

The first connection between these two sources is, then, to keep Vickers' ideas firmly in mind when you work through Neustadt and May's mini-methods.

For the second connection we can do no better than quote Vickers' own words: 'Few would deny that time is the dimension in which we objectively and subjectively live; but even fewer have yet acquired the habit or drawn the conclusion of taking it sufficiently seriously.' That is exactly what Neustadt and May's *Thinking in Time: The Uses of History for Decision Makers* aims to help us to do.

Judgements about issues, or, is history bunk?

Neustadt and May's most basic point is that the sorts of problems mentioned in the introduction to this chapter all have an *issue history*. For example:

- Foot and mouth disease in farm animals is not new and there had been an outbreak in 1967.

- The status of the Falkland Islands had been a bone of contention for more than 100 years.

- Problems in the National Health Service have not arisen overnight.

- The Royal Commission on capital punishment was set up, not in response to a spate of murders, but because public opinion on the effectiveness of, and justification for, the execution of murderers had changed with the passage of time. The 'norm' had altered and what had once been acceptable to opinion was no longer so.

The theme of Neustadt and May (N and M, for short) is that thought about the *issue history* can illuminate options and decisions. To make that idea practical they propose what they call *mini-methods* that, if practised regularly and made a normal part of staff procedures, can support policy-making. In urgent cases, the mini-methods can be applied very swiftly and could make at least a marginal improvement to the quality of top-level issue management. They suggest that even a marginal improvement will usually be well worth having.

In short, they assert that issue history is not, as Henry Ford is alleged to have said, 'bunk' but is a vital source of insight for developing action options and arguing the case for or against one option or another. The development of options uses the issue history for analysis; arguing the case for or against the possible actions uses the history for persuasion. They are not, though, referring only to 'capital H' History, for which Marwick (1989) *The Nature of History* is excellent, but rather to how the issue history relates to the wider context of History.

Before summarising the mini-methods, we must first briefly review Neustadt and May's book, as this chapter draws heavily on, and fully acknowledges, their work.

Neustadt and May's book

Neustadt and May, professors at the Kennedy School of Government at Harvard, had also, as is common in the USA, held senior posts in government service and frequently been consultants to government people and agencies. They were incredibly well acquainted with people at the very highest levels in the various branches of the US system of governance.

From their experience, their contacts, and access to documents written both at the time and subsequently, they were in an excellent position to know in some detail how, for example, President Truman's team reacted to the sudden invasion of South Korea by North Korea in 1950. They illustrate each mini-method with similarly authoritative case studies.

It has to be admitted that, although the book is beautifully written, it is not an easy read (though the effort is worth it). The reason is that the very strength of the authoritative case studies is also their weakness for anyone who does not have a good grasp of US history (N and M bemoan that this includes all too many Americans). The case studies will mean little to anyone who is too young to have lived through the Cuban missile episode, does not remember the era of President Carter, cannot recall the Vietnam years and has never heard of Robert McNamara.

Because most readers will not be familiar with N and M's case studies we shall give only some brief examples from some relatively topical themes to illustrate the successive mini-methods. As usual in this book, the ideas are simple; because of that they are highly effective, but you need to practise them for yourself.

The mini-methods

Introduction

N and M describe a series of steps for the analysis of a concern that has arisen. The purpose of these steps is not only to help to set objectives but also to identify viable options for achievement of those objectives. The underlying aim can be expressed no more clearly than by a slight variation on their own words:

> *'developing proposals for the future, taking account of the constraints of the present as inheritances from the past'.*

What's happening? The K/U/P mini-method

When an issue arises, sorting out the 'facts' is important. Some things are *known* for certain, other things may be *unclear* while yet others are simply unknown and have to be *presumed*. However, the 'facts' of an issue cover a wide range of factors and go far beyond simple numbers. For instance, when the foot and mouth disease outbreak occurred it was **known** that some cases had been detected. It was, however, **unclear** whether vaccination could be used to control the outbreak or what the policy of the powerful National Farmers Union would be. It had to be **presumed** that there were further cases of the disease waiting to be found. It was probably also presumed that the public were either not interested in foot and mouth disease, or were confident that the Ministry of Agriculture could deal with it.

> The K/U/P mini-method. Write down what is *known*, what is *unclear*, and what is *presumed* about the situation.

Of course, there was much more to the foot and mouth disease outbreak than that, but N and M's point is that it is invaluable to clarify a problem by taking a few minutes to jot down the 'facts' under these headings. The distinctions are profound. The unclear 'facts' might become certain with some research, and the immediate question is whether unclear fact X is important enough to justify the time and effort. An essential point is that the presumptions will play a powerful role in decision-making and it is as well to make them explicit, which might open them up for debate. We shall have more to say about presumptions later.

The significant items in the K/U/P are those that make the current situation different from before, when it did not need attention. The aim is to identify why some kind of decision seems to be called for. If, for example, it could be presumed that foot and mouth disease would die out of its own accord, then that is different from a presumption that it will have serious effects.

> The aim of K/U/P is to identify why something needs to be done.

Now put yourself in the shoes of a senior government minister, the Chief Veterinary Officer, the President of the National Farmers Union, or whomever, and jot down what you think that *their* K/U/P might have been about this issue. Don't worry if you don't know much about foot and mouth disease; just use your imagination. Try it again for any other problem; like many other of these tools for strategic thought, it becomes easy once you've practised it a couple of times.

The seductive power of analogies: the L/D mini-method

| The L/D mini-method. Don't be seduced by analogies. Write down *likenesses* and *differences*. |

It is nearly inevitable that analogies come to mind when an issue or a crisis arises. President Truman, faced with the invasion of South Korea, resolved to fight, as his memories of the 1930s led him to believe that failure to withstand aggression had led to the disaster of the Second World War (what does that tell you about his norms?). As this book is being written, commentators suggest that the USA risks being sucked into another Vietnam in Afghanistan, but are the cases comparable? What are the similarities and contrasts?

The **likenesses/differences**, L/D, mini-method calls for caution with analogies, especially those expressed as catch phrases: '*never again!*' implies an analogy with some past event.

| The PESTLIED acronym might help you to organise likenesses and differences for a business issue. |

Table 11.1 suggests some L/D between Vietnam and Afghanistan in the first few months of US involvement. Note that the main aspects are from the big political picture, not from the military details. An L/D list for a business issue should similarly first focus on the wider competitive, regulatory and economic aspects before the details of products and processes. The PESTLIED acronym (political, economic, social, technological, legal, international, environmental and demographic aspects) might be useful in drawing up a list of likenesses and differences.

The purpose of L/D, which should take only a few minutes, is two-fold. *First*, it helps to eliminate invalid analogies and to find better ones. Is Vietnam relevant to Afghanistan? Are there other cases in which an attacked nation has sought to punish the transgressor? *Second*, good analogies may help in setting objectives. Will what was a realistic aim then be sensible/foolish now?

L/D for foot and mouth disease is instructive. One difference is that the 1967 outbreak affected cattle and pigs, but in 2001 the victims were sheep. I have been unable to think of any likenesses between the two cases, so why don't you try?

The likenesses and differences need to be reviewed as more K/U/P emerge.

The issue's history: building time lines

| Goldberg's Rule – What is the story? How did these concerns arise? |

An option for action has to be related to the objective. What is the action supposed to achieve? In what ways must the future be different from the present? The National Health Service is generally perceived not to be delivering effective and timely care. Such care ought to be available in the future but will the action of spending more public money on the National Health Service achieve that? To think about such questions requires use of the issue history because, as N and M elegantly put it, 'understanding what used to be is essential for any realistic definition of what needs doing', and that starts with Goldberg's Rule.

Table 11.1 Likenesses and differences: Vietnam and Afghanistan

Vietnam	Afghanistan
Likenesses	
Major power (France) previously defeated.	Major powers (Britain, Russia) previously defeated.
Fanatical enemy.	Fanatical enemy.
Adjacent nation (North Vietnam) already involved and a potential belligerent	Some support for Taliban within Pakistan
And so on	
Differences	
No direct threat to USA	Serious attack on USA
No coalition of support	Some coalition support
Domestic dissent	Passionate domestic commitment
Warsaw Pact and Cold War	Russia quiescent/supportive
Established government in S. Vietnam	Weak Afghan government
Hundreds of thousands of troops committed, many dead	About two thousand troops, thirty dead
Easy access	Access very difficult
Airpower a blunt instrument	Airpower sophisticated and accurate
And so on	

Mr Goldberg was CEO of the US equivalent of *Herrington-Jones*. When his managers came to him with problems he made it a rule to say, 'Don't tell me the problem, tell me the story.' The rule is implemented by drawing a time line, and experienced people dealing with, say, health policy should have no difficulty in doing so in, perhaps, half an hour.

The time line should start with the first significant event and should continue into the future, so that planning and background will be thought about simultaneously. N and M stress the importance of getting the key trends and major changes first, with detail being added when it helps. They also emphasise the importance of the 'political' events – which means not only national politics but also company/institution politics.

> **Time lines.**
> Go back as far as necessary. Identify key trends and big changes.

Simply marking events on a piece of paper will not make the most of them so a related step is to ask the six questions a journalist uses in building a story, which Kipling called his 'honest serving men'. If time is tight, at least ask what and when. If time allows, how and why add value. Where and who can be left to last. In the future, planning, part of the time line, the who, what and when questions are tantamount to an action plan.

> **The journalist's six questions:**
> What? When? Where? How? Why? Who? Kipling's 'honest serving men'.

How do you know what is the right history and the first significant event? The answer is that you don't, except from common sense, the shared experience of the staff team, and whether or not the time line is illuminating the issue.

To extend N and M's mini-methods, we suggest that a key trick, if time allows, is to plot the time line from another point of view. The reason is that most issues of concern involve another party, perhaps more than one. In conflict, the

A useful trick is to plot the time line from someone else's point of view.

other party is the enemy or a competitor. In political or commercial negotiations it is the other side of the table. In the foot and mouth disease outbreak the Ministry of Agriculture had to work with the Farmers Union, other government agencies (the carcasses of slaughtered sheep could not be buried on archaeologically valuable ground), and various organs of the European Union. To say to oneself, 'If I were the European Commissioner for Agriculture, how would I see the issue history?' can do nothing but good.

N and M accept that the result of time-line analysis will be less than perfect, but one can only agree with them that it is better than ignoring how we came to be at the current undesirable position.

Another way of analysing time lines might be the trend dynamics wheel described in Chapter 2, p. 26.

Testing presumptions: bets and odds, and Alexander's question

Presumptions are a significant part of the problem: they influence the choice of objectives and affect the options being considered and the choices to be made. It is therefore vital to test presumptions, but how can one do so? Before answering that, we have to look at three different sorts of presumption.

Types of presumption:

- maybes,
- truths,
- causal statements.

N and M call the *first* sort 'maybes'. They are essentially factual and can change as time passes. It might, for instance, have been presumed that there would be only a few more cases of foot and mouth disease. It subsequently became clear that such was not the case and it had to be presumed that there might be many tens of thousands. A maybe presumption might be turned into an unclear or a known by straightforward questions or research.

The *second* sort is more insidious as it is so value-laden that it has the status of a truth. Presumptions that a state-run health service is the best way to deliver health care, or that market mechanisms are 'good', are very hard to debate.

The *third* type of presumption is, N and M argue, the most dangerous of all. It is the causal presumption that doing X will bring about Y. N and M mention the presumption that bombing North Vietnam would inflict so much pain that its leaders would come to terms and cease to support the Vietcong. These X→Y presumptions, as we shall denote them, can have such a powerful effect that they should be scrutinised as closely as possible.

At the very least, it will be helpful to jot down the presumptions from the K/U/P stage under these three headings, but let us now look at four tests, three from N and M, and one of our own.

The bets and odds test is quick and easy. As the panel shows, the questions are plain. A variant on the odds question is, 'If I told them that the odds were 3 to 1, would I be wrong?' However, we have to realise that the simplicity of the questions belies their subtlety. The real value arises when one person says that the odds are 10 to 1 but another thinks that they are no better than evens. This is a classic case of the Delphi debate from Chapter 3 to explore the reasons for these divergent views.

Bets and odds – How much of your own money would you bet on that presumption? As a bookmaker, what odds would you give?

N and M's second test is Alexander's question, named for Dr Alexander who was a very senior public health official during a suspected outbreak in 1976 of swine flu (despite its name, this is a potentially serious illness for people). After 13 army recruits had been infected, the presumption was that it would be necessary to prepare to immunise all Americans against the disease. Alexander asked what new data would change that presumption: many new cases, a hundred, sporadic outbreaks, or what? N and M say that the question was the right one but was never answered. One wonders what Alexander's question should have been for the 2001 foot and mouth disease outbreak and what effect an answer might have had.

> **Alexander's question.**
> What new information would make me change a presumption?

The final test is for the X→Y presumptions and N and M's mini-methods are listed in the box.

The first answer, that X caused Y in a prior case, is an analogy and should be tested as one would for any other analogy. For example, the presumption that bombing would break the enemy's will in North Vietnam invites comparison with the bombing of Britain and Germany in the Second World War, where neither will had been broken. The likenesses/differences mini-method can be applied: a previous causal effect might happen again, or, of course, it might not. L/D should help to tease out the respective reasons.

> **Why will X cause Y?**
> - Because it did before in situation Z (analogy and L/D).
> - For these reasons (testable theory).
> - Because I say so (Stalinism).

The second answer, testable theory, is exactly that. It does not require time-consuming research but might be clarified by something known, even unclear, or by another, *tested*, presumption.

The third reply would only work in the most hierarchical organisation and, even so, would invite derision, either open or covert.

All three types of presumption can be tested by 'bets and odds' and Alexander's question, if there is no time for research into maybes.

To supplement N and M's tests, we suggest that the 'why?' diagram in Chapter 2 might be renamed the 'because' diagram. The first box is the presumption that X will cause Y, probably with an added qualification such as 'within 6 months'. The descending chains are now 'because Z has already happened', 'because some fact is known', or 'because it is also presumed that …'. The process stops when one can make no further valid 'because' statements. A 'because' diagram could probably be drawn in a short time.

> **The 'because' diagram.**
> Start with 'X will cause Y' 'because …'. Trace, and debate, chains of reasons.

If there is no initiating 'because', the initial presumption is unjustified. If the because diagram involves other presumptions, the starting presumption that X→Y starts to look rather shaky. Its aim is not so much a fully justified chain of formal logic, but a gestalt appreciation of the arguments justifying the initial presumption.

Refining stereotypes: placing people

N and M make a powerful case that, since all policy issues involve dealing with people – colleagues, competitors, opponents, or even downright enemies – it is as well not to base one's dealings on crude stereotypes of them. As one example, they state that people who saw President Reagan as 'only a cowboy actor with no idea of what a president did at the office'

> **Placing people.**
> Relating public history and personal detail to refine stereotypes.

were sadly in error. They propose the mini-method of 'placement' as a means of making stereotypes less crude and hence more useful as a basis for understanding what another person might be willing to do, or how that person might best be persuaded to do, or not to do, something. This is really a more sophisticated version of the adage that 'communication takes place at the receiver, not the transmitter'; there is no point in transmitting unless you understand what the receiver is willing and able to receive and can comprehend.

Placement works by drawing up a table with a time line of public events and a related time line of the history of the person in question (Mr Reagan, as well as being a screen actor, had also been the head of the actors' union and Governor of California). The time lines should start reasonably far back, probably in the lifetime of the parents of the person being placed. The idea is shown in Table 11.2 for John Jones, who has worked for XYZ Industries for some years and has now applied to be deputy to Mike Green, the sales manager of XYZ Industries.

From Jones's CV, and having met him a couple of times, Green sums him up as 'just a steady plodder – a safe pair of hands'. That stereotype will be important as it will influence what Green asks Jones to do, how he persuades Jones to do it, and how they work together.

N and M's point is that the process of 'placing' Jones might enrich Green's view of him and hence produce more fruitful and effective working relationships. Table 11.2 shows how this might look for a purely imaginary 'Jones'.

The placement view now suggests that Jones may be somewhat embittered by his parents' experiences, his childhood poverty and by losing his job, possibly disdainful of people without first-class degrees from top universities, resentful of such

Table 11.2 'Placing' John Jones

Dates	Public events	Jones's personal history
1930s	Economic depression	Prosperous grandparents with established business
1939–45	Second World War	Business hit by war
1950s	Labour government, nationalisation, austerity	Parents inherit business, go bankrupt and live in reduced circumstances. Jones born 1955
1960s	Greater prosperity, independence for many former British Colonies	Happy, but impoverished, childhood
1970s	Large expansion of university access	Scholarship to top university, first-class degree in history. Active in hard-left student politics. Job in public utility, active member of Labour Party
1980s	Conservative government and privatisation	Marries, two children. Career developing but made redundant. Retrains as MBA
1990s	'Big bang' in the City, electronic age, the 'me' generation	Joins XYZ. Steady, but slow, progress up ranks
1997– 2003	'New Labour' government. Private financing of some public services. 'Crisis' in National Health Service	Disillusioned with politics. Worried about job security

people if they pass him on the corporate ladder, disappointed about his political beliefs, very cautious, and risk-averse because he is terrified of losing his job again.

The deeper insight from placement may, N and M suggest, help Green to understand what Jones can and cannot do, and what he might support or oppose, better than the 'steady plodder' stereotype does. It might reveal that Jones is not a steady plodder but someone resentful that his abilities have not been used. He is far from being a safe pair of hands – someone whom one can trust to carry a task to completion. Jones is actually ultra-cautious and unwilling/unable to exercise any initiative if difficulties arise in the task.

Placement is, as N and M point out, only another guess, but it should be better than the unplaced guess. Jones might, of course, be well advised to 'place' Green, and I am convinced that placement would be a big help when interviewing job candidates, providing a nice complement to the CV.

How does one find out the personal history? The CV is a start, but one can also use casual conversation with the person, discreet telephone calls to others, and a candidate's references, especially if one can read between the lines.

Placing organisations

N and M make a very profound point when they suggest that the best way for a newcomer to get a fair picture of an organisation is to find out how its present objectives, powers, resources and personnel system compare with those of the past, and especially by asking *why* those changes occurred. This is the notion of organisational placement. Its purpose is to help one to understand what an organisation does now – how it ticks, so to speak – and what it might do, or be unlikely to do, in the future.

Organisational placement works in the same way as the placing of people, with two parallel time lines. The public history will be whatever is relevant to the type of organisation. For Overseas Carers, the non-governmental organisation in Chapter 1, we might be interested in past events affecting fund-raising, previous notable disasters, etc. For XYZ Industries, the public background might involve technology, regulation, taxation, employment legislation, competition and so forth. The 'personal' history is how the organisation has changed in parallel with the public events. How, for example, did Overseas Carers react to the drought in Ethiopia and the later floods in Mozambique? Try it for your own organisation.

> **Placing organisations.** What changes have occurred in an organisation's power, resources and personnel policies?

Organisational placement has numerous, and potentially *extremely* useful applications.

- The obvious one is for a newcomer, whether trainee or chief executive, trying to understand his or her new job. It might help that person to understand how the organisation came to be where it is in the viable firm matrix (Chapter 5).

- If corporate sensitivities can be avoided, placement would be a valuable addition to an induction programme.

- Competitor analysis is another clear use and it might be done twice: once by *us* to place *them*, and again, by us, to try to see how *they* place *us*.

- Understanding the 'best in class' in a business sector, and how they got to be that, would be a valuable use of placement.

- An organisation awarding a contract could 'place' the actual or potential contractors, while the competing contractors could place the awarding body, and each other, in the hope that the understanding thus gained will improve the chances of winning the contract.

Summary on the mini-methods

Neustadt and May's mini-methods have been summarised rather severely and you would do well to read the original, though you might need a handbook of US history and a dictionary of US public figures fully to grasp all their points. If you have time, the effort will be worth while as this is a truly remarkable book.

We stress again that the vital aspect of N and M's mini-methods is that they can be applied quickly – almost certainly in a good deal less time than will be wasted in arguing about what to do without at least first having sorted out why anything needs to be done (the K/U/P stage) and clarified analogies (L/D). Interestingly, Neustadt and May report that their students, who are experienced people from government and business, find organisational placement to be about the most useful of the mini-methods. That is probably because they work in environments in which persuasion of other government departments to do, or not to do, something is likely to be a vital part of their jobs. In such bureaucratic organisations, placing both the organisation and its head might be useful. For application to the management of issues or concerns in business or other environments, I recommend that all the methods need to be used.

The outcome of the mini-methods is one or more viable options to deal with the issue. The chosen option becomes an aim to be achieved by the people on the ground and planning how best to achieve an aim is the subject of Chapter 12, 'On the back of an envelope', dealing with the so-called *military appreciation*. We shall show that, despite its name, it is strikingly applicable to non-military problems.

Chapter summary

Making policy for top-level issues seems to be something of a black art. The pronouncements of some politicians about the policy of their party for dealing with a current issue sometimes make one wonder about the depth of thought that has gone into their selection of that 'policy'. The message of this chapter is that policy-making can become a little more sophisticated by understanding the art of judgement and using the history of an issue.

The ideas that Vickers so lucidly explained (and I fear that I did scant justice to them) are a deceptively simple, but utterly profound, analysis of the thought processes underlying policy-making. The interplay between reality, value and instrumental judgements is a valuable basis for understanding what policy-makers do; the drawback is that he does not explain how to do it.

Neustadt and May admirably fill that gap with their mini-methods. For instance, sorting out the 'facts' into known, unknown and presumed powerfully strengthens the reality judgement, especially when some of the presumptions are about the norms. Almost inevitably, we think of analogies and may make wrong choices based on past success or failure, and N and M offer the simple test of like-nesses and differences to test analogies.

The *key to success* is, then, to bear in mind Vickers' theoretical underpinnings when using Neustadt and May's mini-methods. The end result may be improvements to policy choices, marginal maybe, but nonetheless worth having. The unfortunate aspect is that one never knows if the policy is 'right', as the effects may in many cases not be seen for 10, 20 or 30 years. That, though, is just part of life and the hope is that better policy, based on the sophisticated art of judgement described by Vickers and by Neustadt and May, might avoid, even if only at the margin, painful long-term consequences for our children and grandchildren.

References

Marwick, A. (1989), *The Nature of History*. Macmillan Education, London.

Neustadt, R. E., May, E. R. (1988), *Thinking in Time: The Uses of History for Decision Makers*. The Free Press, a Division of Simon and Schuster, New York.

Vickers, G. (1983), *The Art of Judgement*. Harper and Row, London.

On the back of an envelope: tools for rapid analysis

What this chapter is about

- Sometimes it is necessary to make a plan very rapidly in order to achieve an aim.

- All military officers are trained to do this, not only in combat but also in any other task, such as civil aid.

- Their method is the *military appreciation*.

- The appreciation is highly applicable to practical strategy in many other fields.

- The *principles of war* are a checklist for a military plan, but also work for non-military problems.

- *Fishbone diagrams* are a simple way of sorting out the possible causes of a problem.

- The common feature of all three approaches is that *they can be applied rapidly* when there is no time for formal analysis.

- The *capability for rapid analysis is a powerful supplement* to the **ACTIFELD** methodology. The appreciation can be a quick and useful check on the plan.

Introduction

Sometimes it is necessary to make plans very rapidly, perhaps in the face of difficulties or opposition. The plan may be for the relatively short-term future, the next few months, perhaps, but it is likely to have *strategic effects*, in the sense of leading to a basis for longer-term consequences.

This chapter therefore covers techniques for dealing with a particular type of practical strategy:

- An aim has to be achieved, but there are difficulties and, possibly, opposition.

- A plan has to be made very quickly.

For example, during the first half of 2001, the UK suffered from a serious outbreak of foot and mouth disease (FMD) affecting sheep and cattle. The authorities chose to deal with this by slaughtering all infected animals and, in addition, animals on neighbouring farms on the grounds that even animals not apparently infected with FMD might pass it to others. Despite objections that the policy was excessive, the government persisted with the policy and within a short time hundreds of thousands of animals had been killed.

The only feasible method of disposing of the carcasses was to burn them on huge pyres but the logistical problems of digging the fire pits, assembling the fuel for the pyres, transporting the carcasses, supervising the incineration and disposing of the remains proved to be vast. Within days there were huge numbers of slaughtered animals lying in the fields waiting to be burnt. At this point, the Army was called in to organise the logistics and, within a short time, the backlog was under control.

The officer in charge said that he had worked out his plan in his car 'on the back of a fag [cigarette] packet'. This is a fairly common, though now not politically correct (few officers smoke), phrase in the British armed forces meaning that the plan can be made swiftly, often under extreme pressure, and is clear and simple. As the FMD case shows, such problem-solving is clearly very effective, so this chapter will cover some analysis tools that can be applied very quickly and still give productive results.

To preview, we will cover three approaches: the military appreciation, the principles of war, and fishbone diagrams.

The two military analysis methods are included here for three reasons.

1. To show military readers that their discipline of thought can be useful in other domains.

2. Civilian analysts of defence problems should know how their military colleagues think.

3. Analysts in business and government will also find these concepts to be effective in their own spheres.

Their role is not limited to planning battles, as the FMD example shows, and the style of structured thought that they support is widely applicable. There is, in fact, an increasing tendency for military ideas to spill over into business strategy; the very word *strategy* originated in the military domain. There have been attempts to distil the writings of military gurus, such as the ancient Chinese commander Sun Tzu's thoughts on the art of war being used as the basis for management books.

Fishbone diagrams originated in manufacturing industry but have widespread applicability as a technique for organised thought about the causes of problems and the formulation of action plans.

The military appreciation

Introduction

The appreciation is a structured approach to decision-making. It is applicable in all domains.

Every military officer is taught the military appreciation as a logically structured approach to decision-making. The precise details, and even the title of the appreciation (it is also called the military estimate), vary somewhat between countries and services and attempts have been made to streamline the process. We will discuss the appreciation first from a military point of view but we stress that it is applicable to any type of problem area.

The version discussed here is rather traditional but it covers the thought processes in some detail and it is useful to know what those are before attempting shortcuts.

What is an appreciation?

An appreciation can be defined (slightly adapting from military terminology) as:

a logical sequence of reasoning leading to an effective solution to, and a detailed plan for coping with, a problem.

Like the ACTIFELD tools, the appreciation is a disciplined thought process.

It is a disciplined thought process designed to examine all relevant factors, make deductions about the factors and produce a detailed and effective plan to achieve an aim. The essence of an appreciation is a blend of logical reasoning and critical examination.

An appreciation is sometimes a written document for presentation to higher authority. The advantage is that the higher commander knows that the problem has been analysed in a reliable fashion which is consistent with military practice. Nine fully written appreciations were made during the voyage of the Task Force to the Falkland Islands to test all options for their recovery. In military use, where plans often have to be made under acute pressure, it is more commonly a rapid mental process since the main steps have been memorised, and practised so that they have become second nature. For non-military use, a written appreciation, at least in outline, may be more effective at communicating reasoning to other people in the organisation.

Main stages in the appreciation

An appreciation has seven main steps.

An appreciation is carried out in seven main steps:

1. Study the existing situation.
2. Specify the aim to be attained.

These two steps are exactly what Neustadt and May's mini-methods in the previous chapter help us to do, especially in urgent cases or crises, so the appreciation is also valuable in swiftly working out a plan to achieve that aim. It is a follow-on stage to the mini-methods. If the aim is given, the appreciation makes the plan in the remaining five steps:

3. Examine all relevant factors and make reasoned deductions about the effect that they might have on the ability to achieve the aim.

4. Consider all practicable courses of action. Usually, three courses are sufficient to explore the problem and to keep discussion manageable.

5. Decide on the best course to attain the aim.

6. Make a plan to implement that course.

7. Check all the reasoning and the practicability of the plan.

Of course, junior commanders/managers may have to start at step 3 as the aim will have been given by a higher authority. (Experience teaches me that Second Lieutenants are usually told *very* precisely what they are to do.)

Stage 7 is not a formal step in the British services but it is used in the United States Marine Corps where plans are scrutinised by subordinates. This is an example of the variability of practice in the military. In non-military cases, step 7 would be essential, since the course of action chosen is likely to unfold over a very long period of time.

These main features of the appreciation will now be discussed.

The aim

The aim should be checked against the following list:

1. Will it achieve a definite result in one's favour?

2. Does the wording say what is to be achieved and make any restrictions (such as time for completion) crystal clear?

3. For those with the authority to select aims, is it in accordance with one's instructions and responsibilities?

4. Is there a reasonable chance of attaining the aim?

5. Is it the utmost that can be done?

Questions 4 and 5 make it clear that the appreciation can sometimes be an iterative process since it may not always be clear at the outset whether the aim can be achieved, or even if it is the most productive aim to select. Such matters may become clearer as the appreciation proceeds and a military officer might *sometimes* have to seek approval for a modified aim from higher authority. That authority would have to consider knock-on effects from modifying the aim given to a subordinate. In non-military cases, the aim may need to be rigorously reviewed (just as we stressed the importance of verifying or revising the strategic question), precisely because of the long lifetime of the courses of action and the plans.

An aim must be expressed in positive language and should not be qualified except, perhaps, by time and space. For example,

To complete the design work on Product X by 31 December

is clear, positive, and explicit.

On the other hand,

To carry out the research programme so as to complete the design work in
order to introduce the product

is vague. It introduces an intermediate step (the research programme) and links the aim of completing the design work with the ulterior aim of introducing the product. If the aim is to introduce the product by a certain date, then the research programme and the design work are factors to be included in the plan.

Factors

A factor is

**a circumstance, fact or influence that affects the chances
of achieving the aim.**

A factor may be a known fact or it may be information supplied which is treated as a fact, such as military or competitor intelligence. It may even be a 'fact' that we do not know the enemy's strength, and that would clearly be an important factor in subsequent stages of the appreciation. Of course, the K/U/P mini-method from Chapter 11 could be used very quickly to sort out the 'facts'.

The mandatory factors for military problems are: Time and space; Weather; Surprise and deception; Comparison of forces; Logistics; Communications; Morale; Ground; Endurance and bases; Vital points; How would an enemy attack on a vital point affect the achievability of the aim? (The last three factors, affecting the availability of bases, are more typical of air force thinking than of the army's.) Not every factor is relevant to each problem but military practice takes them in a standardised order so that their relevance can be decided.

It is difficult, and might be misleading, to stipulate 'standard' factors for non-military applications of the appreciation since the diversity of problems encountered in business firms, government departments and non-governmental organisations is so great. It would, however, be an important step in its own right to set up some standard factors to be considered in a given organisation, regardless of whether or not that body used an appreciation procedure.

Deductions

The point of listing the factors is that each should be used as the basis for deductions. It may, for example, be a fact that a defence contractor is in a weak financial position. From that one might deduce that it is liable to go bankrupt and that, in turn, may lead one to deduce something about to whom a contract might be awarded. Significant factors usually lead to many deductions.

The key point is that each deduction should be followed by the question: *So what?* If the answer is 'nothing', then the deduction adds nothing to the appreciation and is not valid. In some cases, the deduction is blindingly obvious and is simply a restatement of the previous step in the argument. In the example above, the 'deduction' that the supplier is liable to go bankrupt is really no more than a restatement of the fact that it is in a weak financial position. It would be better to discard the 'fact' that it is in a weak position, and start with the 'fact' that it is liable to go bankrupt.

Enemy courses

The courses of action open to the enemy (competitor, other departments within the same organisation, supplying company etc.) are really factors in the situation, but are so important that they are considered as a separate category. They are considered in relation to one's own courses of action under the following headings:

1. Courses of action open to the enemy
2. Courses of action open to oneself
3. Enemy's most probable course of action
4. Own best course of action.

If the enemy (competitor) has the initiative or has many courses open, his courses must be considered first, and the deductions should relate to the effect that they might have on our ability to achieve our aim. If we have the initiative, items 1 and 2 are reversed as it is essential to consider our possible courses first, and the deductions about the enemy's possible courses will relate to their possible effects on the courses open to us.

In all cases, the aim of making deductions about the enemy is to assess his or her most likely course of action. It may, or may not, be easy to deduce which of the enemy's courses he or she is most likely to choose but the key principle is not to jump to conclusions and to remember that he or she is likely to be acting rationally and in his or her own interests. He or she, enemy or competitor, is certainly not acting in our interests!

Own courses

The main points about one's own courses of action are that:

1. They should be expressed as broadly as possible.
2. They should not be based on events too far ahead, though a subordinate commander/manager may have a time horizon specified in the aim given to him by higher authority.

Having gone through this chain of reasoning, one's own best course of action, which might have several phases, will probably be fairly clear. If it is not clear, there is likely to have been a slip in the logic, or the aim may require revision.

Plan

To implement the chosen course, a plan is drawn up. For military applications of the appreciation there are standard forms for writing orders. For commercial applications, the plan may be more free form. In both cases, the plan should specify:

1. the resources to be applied
2. the tasks to be accomplished by the resources (forces) in as much detail as is needed to avoid confusion and error
3. results required and the times at which they are intended to be achieved
4. support available, such as intelligence, logistics, reinforcements etc.
5. the arrangements for command and control and the delegation of responsibility.

This is, of course, exactly the purpose and structure of the corporate plan described in Chapter 7.

Testing

While going through the logical process of the appreciation it is essential that the sequence of argument and deduction be tested. The criteria are:

1. Is the reasoning valid?
2. Is the sequence logical?
3. Are the results precise, unambiguous and objective? (There is always a danger of 'proving' at great length what has already been decided on. This is known as 'situating the appreciation'.)
4. Are the facts accurate?
5. Will the plan achieve the desired aim?

For testing, the appreciation of a problem, whether military or not, could usefully be followed by a force field analysis. That is a good example of how these apparently specialised techniques fit into the **ACTIFELD** framework. The strategic question specifies the aim, an appreciation is used to make a quick plan, the plan is checked using FFA and a time-based action plan is made. That whole process would probably not need even a working day.

Summary

It is worth restating the main steps in the appreciation which are:

1. Study the existing situation.
2. Specify the aim to be attained.
3. Examine all relevant factors and make reasoned deductions about the effect that they may have on the achievement of the aim.
4. Consider all practicable courses of action. Usually, three courses are sufficient to explore the problem and to keep discussion manageable.
5. Decide on the best course to attain the aim.
6. Make a plan to implement that course.
7. Check all the reasoning and the practicability of the plan.

The appreciation is an extremely easy method to apply once one has practised it; it becomes virtually instinctive. It is a useful and effective method for supporting decision-making, though it is important not to let the form become the substance.

The principles of war

Introduction

It is evident from even a glance at military history that some commanders tend to be more successful than others (for at least most of the time). Napoleon, Frederick the Great, the Duke of Wellington and Alexander the Great are some of those who are often called 'The Great Captains'. Much ink and fury have been expended in deciding who is, and who is not, a Great Captain, in the search for the reasons for their success and even for some 'formula' to guide the less talented or less experienced.

It is fair to say that no such formula for success has been found but some 'principles of war' (POW) have been deduced and, broadly, agreed on. Because they have been worked out by much thought by many people and over a long time, they are a powerful checklist that can be applied rapidly.

However, as with the military appreciation, the terminology differs from one country to another so do not treat the following list as being Holy Writ.

The ten principles

The principles of war are *sometimes* listed as follows in italics. The comments are abbreviated from the discussion in British military doctrine, though some of the POW are fairly self-explanatory.

1. *Selection and maintenance of the aim.* Depending on his level of command, a commander may be given an aim from higher authority or he may have to select it himself. The key idea is to keep that aim firmly in mind and to ensure that forces are deployed to achieve that desired outcome. Plans must continually be checked to ensure that they are consistent with the aim and that the aim remains valid.

2. *Maintenance of morale.* This has to do with leadership and all the myriad of other factors conducive to good morale. Regular delivery of personal mail to troops in the field is often cited as a significant aspect of this. Montgomery is alleged to have said that he would rather fight without his artillery than without his chaplains (though presumably he did not say it to a group of artillery officers).

3. *Offensive action.* This confers the initiative on the attacker and is the chief means of influencing a campaign or battle. Even when one is on the defensive, overall, tactics can still be offensive to disrupt the enemy's attack.

4. *Security.* This means to protect one's own assets and deny information to the enemy so as to enable one's own forces to achieve their objectives despite the enemy's interference.

5. *Surprise.* This can relate to timing, place, or strength of one's own actions or to the hitherto unrevealed capabilities of one's own weapons systems or platforms. The aim is to confuse the enemy's chain of command and destroy the cohesion and morale of his military units.

6. *Concentration of force.* This is in some ways the most difficult to pin down. Essentially, it means that the maximum effort should be applied to the vital point at the right time. German thinking refers to this as the *schwerpunkt*, which might roughly be interpreted as the point in time and place at which the outcome can be decided in one's own favour by the devastating use of force. It must be the most difficult judgement that a battlefield commander and his staffs can be called upon to make.

7. *Economy of effort.* Since it is impossible to be strong everywhere, there must be no wasted effort.

8. *Flexibility*. A plan should never be so rigid that the unexpected cannot be coped with, bearing in mind that the enemy is also applying the POW for his own benefit.

9. *Cooperation*. Components of the force should not, as it were, be doing their own things. Nowadays this is usually taken to mean joint operations by army, naval and air assets.

10. *Sustainability (formerly called administration)*. This one is said to have been added by Montgomery who demanded careful planning of logistics and thorough preparation before battle commenced so that it would not be halted by problems of resupply and maintenance.

The concept is *not* that adherence to the principles will guarantee success; it is rather that ignoring them is likely to lead to defeat. In a sense, they are to be seen as a checklist against which an operational plan can be assessed. A staff officer and commander will pose questions such as 'Am I deploying forces to meet the aim I have chosen (or which has been given to me)?', 'How does my plan ensure that morale will be maintained?', 'What has been done to ensure economy of effort?', and so on for all the principles.

The principles of 'war' in civilian problems

There are two answers to the question, 'What have the POW to do with non-military problems?'

The first is that, as with business strategy books which draw on the work of such military thinkers as Sun Tzu, there seems to be a growing willingness on the part of civilian organisations (businesses, government departments and non-governmental organisations such as charities) to admire military competence. This is based on entirely justified respect for the efficient and effective conduct of such campaigns as the Falklands and Gulf Wars, not to mention expert military assistance in disaster relief. In fact, I know some retired officers who now make good livings as consultants teaching business people how the military think and plan. It is, therefore, worth while to know what the military's thought processes are.

The second reason is that it is self-evident that a business that allows itself to be surprised by the competition or the market will be in an unhappy position. In that sense, 'security' goes far beyond having passes to enter buildings and preventing computer hacking. Similarly, a business that vacillates about its aim is less likely to do well than one that selects a good, clear aim, sticks to it for as long as it remains valid and ensures that proper and sufficient effort is devoted to achieving that aim.

However, saying that something is broadly self-evident is not sufficient for practical use in the bewildering diversity of civilian problems. To take but one example, a local convenience store competing for customers against a supermarket chain is not at all the same as two broadly comparable military forces fighting a campaign (in theory, one side would avoid combat if it did not believe itself to be at least comparable to its enemy, though military history affords some counter-examples).

Clearly, we should not blindly apply the POW to civilian problems. On the other hand, it is self-evident that they *are* applicable so Table 12.1 is suggested as a way of coping with this dilemma. The first two columns restate the POW, but slightly abbreviated and rewritten in the imperative voice. The third column is blank to give space for the problem you are dealing with and the domain in which you operate. It is suggested that you photocopy it and enlarge it so that it can be pinned to a flip chart for a discussion session or focus group.

The idea is not to copy from the military column to the civilian column, even with rephrasing. For instance, *Maintenance of morale* could pretty well be directly copied from one to the other, replacing 'troops' with 'staff'. The correct approach is to ask,

Table 12.1 Blank table for civilian 'principles of war'

Principle	Military planning	How could that be achieved for my problems in the civilian world?
Selection and maintenance of the aim	Sustain the aim and deploy forces to achieve the desired outcome	
Maintenance of morale	Keep the troops confident in their cause, their leaders, their equipment and themselves	
Offensive action	Gain the initiative as the best way of influencing a campaign	
Security	Protect own assets and deny information to the enemy	
Surprise	Confuse the enemy's chain of command and destroy the cohesion and morale of his forces	
Concentration of force	Apply the maximum effort to the vital point at the right time	
Economy of effort	Don't waste effort. Ensure everyone is contributing to the plan of action	
Flexibility	Don't be so rigid that the unexpected cannot be coped with	
Cooperation	Joint operations by army, naval and air assets	
Sustainability	Don't get halted by problems of resupply and maintenance	

'How does my plan ensure that my staff are confident ... ?' The military commander might explain the steps that have been taken to ensure the delivery of personal letters to troops in the field. The business manager's response might be that he has reassured people that they will not be made redundant if the merger with another firm goes ahead. Under *Cooperation* the question might be, 'What have I done to achieve close cooperation between departments and satisfaction of stakeholders?'

We now turn to another problem-solving approach designed to focus people's minds on what causes a problem and to help them to think about how it can be dealt with.

Fishbone diagrams

The idea of the fishbone diagram goes back to the 1940s when it was invented in Japan by Professor Kaoru Ishikawa as a way of getting factory workers more involved in decision-making and, especially, in solving production problems. The fishbone has proved to be a very effective way of organising people's thoughts about why problems arise and how they might be addressed. Like many other techniques in this book, it is a way of organising the results of thought and imagination so that effective action plans emerge.

The process is shown in Figure 12.1. It starts at the right-hand side with the name of a problem; 'Difficulties in meeting delivery promises in our transport and distribution business' might be an example. The problem may appear to be so self-evident that effort to refine it would be pointless, but it is not always wise to take things at their face value. Perhaps a focus group, as discussed in Chapter 1, might help to clarify understanding and develop consensus as to what the problem *really* is.

Regardless of how the problem was identified, discussion is then directed to four possible categories of its cause: the *techniques*, the *equipment*, the *materials* or the *people*. This gives a convenient acronym, TEMP, and makes sure that all possible sources of the problem are thought about, rather than jumping to conclusions about one 'obvious' cause. Taking the four categories in order also gives some control over the discussion, which might otherwise degenerate into confusion or even

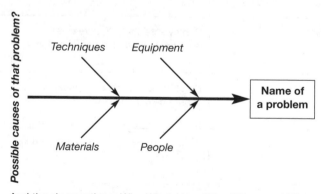

And the six questions: *Why, What, How, Who, Where* and *When*

Figure 12.1 The fishbone diagram

chaos. A why diagram (Chapter 2, page 29), perhaps restated as a because diagram (page 205), might be very helpful in working out why the techniques, say, are a cause of the problem. As ever, there is no magic formula for any of the tools for practical strategy; it is vital to adapt them to the problem and never to bend the problem to fit the technique.

For the illustration of delivery difficulties, some of the identified causes might be:

- Our *techniques* for planning delivery routes are not fast enough for same-day delivery or they don't give the most efficient routes round a set of customers.

- The *equipment* (vehicles) we use is too big to get access to customers' premises/too small to carry the volume of deliveries/too slow or whatever.

- The *materials* (things we are asked to deliver) are badly labelled/too heavy for the driver/not ready when we call for it, etc.

- The *people* are badly trained/poorly motivated/don't stay with us long enough to learn the routes, and so on.

Of course, some of these may be interrelated. Perhaps larger vehicles would be able to carry power-lifting equipment to overcome the heavy loads. *As with all the techniques in this book, it is essential that an imaginative approach be taken and that the process does not get bogged down into some formal ritual.*

Having identified a collection of the sources of the underlying problem, and there may be many, attention moves to the age-old issue of 'so what do we do?' That could be tackled by, say, the TOWS and strategies technique from Chapter 4, but it can also be addressed by using the journalist's six questions encountered in Chapter 11.

The journalist uses the questions in a slightly different order to make sure that a story is coherent and checked. We can use them to help to develop a comprehensive plan of action.

- *Why* do we need to do this? is answered from the analysis of the problem cause.

- *What* do we need to do? might come from TOWS – which is also a rapid analysis technique – but usually the Why? question gives the What? almost automatically. If poor staff training is the Why then the What is to improve staff training. *As with many of the approaches in this book, the technique is easy to explain, but harder to do, and the answer looks obvious, but only **after** the thinking has been done.*

- *How* do we go ahead?, *Who* needs to do it?, *Where* should it be done? and *When* should it be completed? give a very definite action plan with clear allocation of responsibility and time lines.

No technique should be seen in isolation or as a full solution to a problem. In the case of improving staff training, a resource analysis (Chapter 6) might help to identify the degree of improvement needed in the various components of training. Alternatively, a second-order fishbone might be done starting with, say, 'Poor/Insufficient training' in the problem box. That might show that the training techniques need to be improved, or that the training manuals (the materials) are deficient. In fact, the fishbone can be repeated as often as necessary and the repetitions will provide an audit trail for the action plan. If there are obstacles to be overcome, a force field analysis (Chapter 7) might be helpful.

Finally, although fishbone analysis is based on the four-factor TEMP acronym, one or more of the factors may not be applicable or not be a problem cause. The fishbone will, however, make sure that all four categories are at least considered and that none is arbitrarily discarded.

As an exercise, the reader might try to develop a fishbone for the UK FMD crisis. It doesn't matter if you don't know the details – make things up if you have to – the important thing is to practise using these tools for practical strategy.

Chapter summary

This chapter introduced three approaches which are, perhaps, not as widely known in business, government and NGOs as they deserve to be. Their main value is that they can be used rapidly when there is no time for even part of **ACTIFELD**.

The military appreciation is a systematic procedure for inferring a course of action to give good chances of achieving an objective in the face of opposition and difficulties. It does not matter whether the 'opposition' is another military force or competitors, or whoever. The appreciation works by considering the factors that might affect the achievement of the aim, making reasoned deductions about those factors, considering the courses of action open to both sides in the situation, and hence coming to a conclusion about one's own most satisfactory course of action. Its great strength is that, once it has been memorised and practised, it becomes second nature and can be applied very quickly and easily, under great pressure, while still giving some guarantee that nothing has been overlooked. When the appreciation is written, it gives a clear audit trail of the reasoning.

The principles of war are *not* a guarantee of success but are a checklist of significant factors, neglect of which might cause a plan to fail. They can be expressed reasonably unambiguously for military operations but the wording of their application to non-military problems will depend very heavily on the nature of the business and the domain in question.

Fishbone diagrams are, like most of the techniques in this book, a simple yet effective framework for structured thought by a group of people. Their basis in an easily memorable acronym, TEMP, and a simple diagram makes them easy to understand by the participants in a problem-solving exercise. They usually give quick and effective results and can, if necessary, be taken to successive layers of problem-solving to work out action plans in as much detail as needed, though there is no virtue in pursuing detail simply for the sake of it. The use of the journalist's six questions gives a structure for the action plan.

What all these methods have in common is that they can be applied quickly, which explains the chapter's title. They can, though, also give a written audit trail of the steps in the appreciation, the checks done against the 10 principles of 'war', or the thinking supported by the fishbone. As with all the techniques in this book, none of them is necessarily a complete solution to a problem. They can, indeed, often complement one another. For example, if there are difficulties in ensuring the principle of economy of effort, one might use a fishbone analysis to see how they might be overcome.

Dealing with wish lists

What this chapter is about

- Adjusting the capabilities of an organisation to those required by its strategic objectives is a *feedback cycle*.

- Balancing current capabilities against requirements generates *wish lists*.

- *Mission-orientated analysis* helps us to choose which items from the wish list to implement so as to get the maximum benefit.

- Wish lists can rarely be satisfied, and that creates *risk*.

- The items in a wish list need to be justified, and the *conceptual planning framework* does that.

- The set of techniques helps us to *assess eventual risks*.

Introduction

All organisations have *wish lists*, or collections of things to be acquired in order to match the organisation's capabilities to its needs. This issue arises very prominently from TOWS analysis, Chapter 4, the whole purpose of which is to arrive at a list of things to do. In the **FELD** steps of **ACTIFELD** we used the TOWS wish list to look at the organisational implications of those actions (the viable firm matrix in Chapter 5); we evaluated the congruence and resource implications (Chapter 6); and we studied the potential obstacles to building the necessary organisation (force field analysis in Chapter 7). The end result of **ACTIFELD** is a corporate plan to implement a set of TOWS actions.

> All organisations have *wish lists* – the things they would like to do to improve their capabilities.

Sometimes, though, an organisation has to face up to constraints such as finance or available time and has to decide specifically which items from the wish list are to be bought now, and which are to be deferred until later.

For example, an oil company's list might include not only the need to build refineries in new places as demand patterns change but also the development of new types of refinery so as to make new products. Not all of these can be afforded and the staff can only deal with relatively few major projects at any one time, so what is to be done? An automobile firm has similar problems with new models and factory facilities. Defence planners probably have the hardest task of all as there is no bottom line against which to measure the quality of their decision-making on commitments, other than the hardest test of all: the end result in combat, peace-keeping, humanitarian aid, or assistance to the civil authorities (such as replacing striking fire-fighters).

However, commitments are not restricted to long-term capital expenditure. Many other aspects are usually involved, such as recruiting, training and retaining people with different skills and at varied levels of seniority. Other examples are marketing efforts; research, design and development; acquisition or defence of patent rights; stocks of raw materials and spare parts; and so on and so forth to a perhaps bewildering variety.

The wish list is the totality of all these aspects and, while most of the items will involve expenditure, perhaps considerable and protracted, some will be virtually free of cost, such as changes in attitudes towards people – 'dress-down Friday' is only one example of many.

This chapter therefore provides techniques to complement **ACTIFELD** in order to deal with wish list problems. *Mission-orientated analysis* (MOA) focuses on wish list implementation. The other, the *conceptual planning framework* (CPF) deals with the development of wish lists so, for *some* strategic issues, you might replace the I step of **ACTIFELD** by the methods described here and then revert to the **FELD** stages for final evaluation of the strategic choices.

This chapter is the most challenging in the book, so take your time and work through it carefully, doing the suggested exercises as you go.

Managing wish lists

The problem of managing wish lists has several components, regardless of the type of organisation:

- There are always *time delays* before the decision to acquire some new asset can take effect and those delays can be long. An oil field takes years to develop and delays of 10 or 20 years are not uncommon in defence procurement. In business and government, major computer systems have long development times, as did the Channel Tunnel. Disposing of unwanted assets can also take a long time.

- There is obviously no point in acquiring, say, new machinery without recruiting the people to run it, so managing commitments involves decisions to be made now so as to ensure some required *balance of capabilities in the future*.

- Wish lists *nearly always include many items*; it is not uncommon for the list to include two or three hundred entities.

  - The reason why *wish lists* are so called is that there is, in practice, *no reasonable chance of being able to acquire all of those items*. The obvious reason is budget limitations but there is also the very practical fact that an organisation can only cope with a limited number of projects at any one time.

There is no prospect of implementing the full wish list.

Commitment management can therefore be seen as involving two issues:

1. How do you decide what is to be on the wish list?
2. How do you decide which items on the list should be made into firm commitments now, and which should be left until later or even abandoned as unlikely ever to be achieved?

This chapter will put forward very simple methodologies for dealing with both of those questions. Because the main technique to be described, *mission-orientated analysis* (MOA), was developed for defence planning, the principal example in this chapter is from that field (Coyle (1989), though this chapter includes all the most recent developments in the techniques). That is not only a further instance of the broad range of applicability of these tools for practical strategy, it is also a recognition of a very important field of application. The UK alone spends about £10 billion per year on defence acquisition, though that is dwarfed by the US defence budget. The management of wish lists is universal so, while we will show some examples from health care and business, you are, as usual, urged to try out the concepts in their own domain. First, though, we need to understand the process of commitment management in a little more depth.

> Wish lists are universal to all organisations.

The structure of commitment management

It is self-evident that the management of commitments is a feedback process. In an ideal world a wish list item is identified and, as it is acquired, the need that it represents is met and hence the wish is satisfied. That is clearly the same as the negative, or goal-seeking, feedback loops discussed in Chapter 2 and shown in Figure 13.1, though, to keep things simple, we have dispensed with the normal conventions of plus and minus signs.

> Managing commitments is a *feedback process*.

The 'drivers' at the head of the diagram represent the reaction of a government to the external world. The classic example is, of course, the Cold War in which the governments of the NATO nations perceived a context of threat and hostility from the then Soviet Union and resolved that, in the event of aggression, they would fight. Owing to a wide combination of factors, that event happily did not come to pass but, for 40 years, that was broadly the basis of Western defence planning (things were never quite that simple, but the illustration serves our purpose).

In more recent times, matters have become rather less clear-cut and the problem of defence acquisition management is bedevilled by the fact that the 'drivers' rarely seem to stay steady for long enough for the corrective loop to have its effect. Even in the apparently stable political environment of the Cold War, constant changes in defence technology – the so-called arms race – demanded inevitable changes to capabilities, by both sides, and their corrective loops never seemed to achieve a balance (Miller 1998).

> The drivers of commitment management can change quite rapidly.

It is clear, though, that the fact that the drivers change, perhaps quite rapidly, is at least as relevant in business and other domains as it is in defence. We shall show that in more detail after we have discussed Figure 13.1.

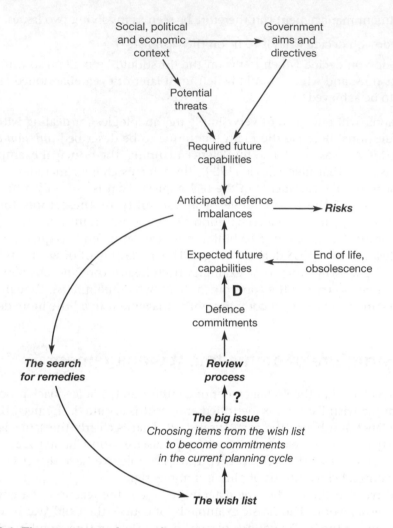

Figure 13.1 The structure of commitment management

Figure 13.1 has five key features, shown in bold italic type:

1. The first is **risk** – the defence imbalances mean that the policy requirement cannot be met, even to the extent of the risk of military defeat. Later in the chapter we shall show how risk can be identified and 'measured', though not numerically.

2. The imbalances drive a **search for remedies** which, in turn, produces the wish list. It is, however, all too easy for the wish list to be governed too much by wishes and not enough by logic. An example of that is so-called 'technology push' – because it is *possible* to develop some new system, that system becomes part of the list.

3. The large **D** is the **inherent and inevitable delay** in converting a decision to acquire something into hardware (or other assets) available for use.

4. The main item is the large **?** to show **the big issue** – how do we choose items, or packages of items, from the wish list? Much of the chapter deals with that.

5. Finally, there is the matter of ***the review process***. The planning and analysis required in the big issue may be done at fairly senior level but it is always reviewed at top level, with questions such as 'Can the recommended acquisitions be afforded?' and 'Do these proposals fit in with the internal politics of the organisation?'

Before we leave Figure 13.1, notice that if we changed some of the wording as in Table 13.1 the diagram would apply equally well to business. It would be easy to amend it again for any other case, such as railways, hospitals, the Murray/Darling Basin in Chapter 14, the charity Overseas Carers, or whatever. Try it for your organisation.

Methodologies for commitment management

The aim of this book is to provide a structured approach and supporting techniques for dealing with the issues of practical strategy. Commitment management topics are no exception and Figure 13.2 is a preview of the techniques described in this chapter, showing how they relate to the feedback loop.

The techniques described in this chapter are shown in boxes with thick borders. To correspond to the *logic of their use* they will be described in the following order: threat profile matrix; mission-orientated analysis (MOA); risk assessment techniques; and conceptual planning frameworks. The other four boxes with narrow borders are, of course, techniques we have already dealt with and are shown here to indicate how steps from the **ACTIFELD** methodology have application outside that process, just as the specialised techniques described in Chapters 10 to 13 might substitute for steps in the 'standard' **ACTIFELD** process.

Table 13.1 The equivalence of defence and business commitment management problems

Defence terminology	Business terminology
Social, political and economic context	Social, regulatory, economic and competitive context
Government aims and objectives	Corporate mission and objectives
Potential threats	Potential threats and opportunities
Anticipated defence imbalances	Anticipated business (or core competence) imbalances
Defence commitments	The company investment plan

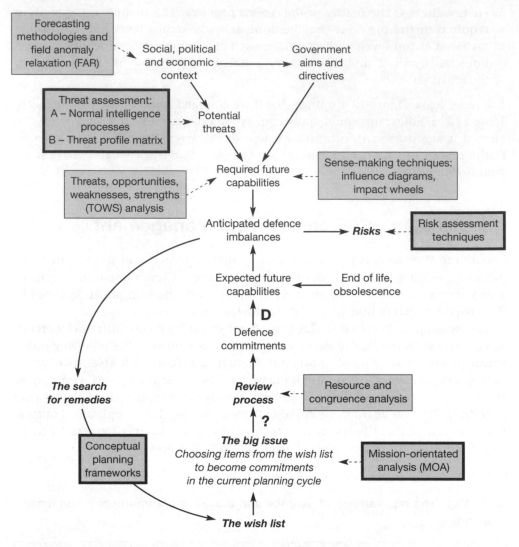

Figure 13.2 Methodologies for managing commitments

The concept of the threat profile matrix

Assessing and describing patterns of threat, whether in military planning or in business competition, can be dealt with by using ideas from the morphological methods for scenario-writing (FAR in Chapter 3) and organisational design (the viable firm matrix in Chapter 5). As in those cases, the concept is to develop a table, the columns of which represent aspects of the threat, while the rows provide 'filing space' for all reasonably conceivable possibilities. The first example is for military planning, after which we will illustrate a threat profile matrix (TPM) for a manufacturing company.

Describing patterns of threat.

The Republic of Tethys is somewhere to the East of Suez.* It is an archipelago of many islands and is a developing nation with modest natural resources. Its sea area includes the Straits of Tuna, a major international seaway. Tethys faces a variety of threats to its stability and economy, including, among others, foreign support to secessionists and theft of its littoral resources such as fish and coastal crops. The complete range of threats is summarised under six headings in Table 13.2, making, as we did with FAR and the VFM, a convenient acronym: SIPFET in this case. As usual, up to about seven columns can be used so as to maintain the idea of gestalt appreciation.

Consider piracy, for example. This is described as having five possible levels, from that capable of disrupting Tethysian national life, P_1, down to risks to tourists, P_5. This idea of 'worst' down to 'best' is seen in all the columns and is the important difference between the TPM and the similar-looking matrices in FAR and the VFM. Recall that in FAR we sought to eliminate anomalies so as to develop logically consistent scenarios and in the VFM we looked for organisational designs capable of implementing strategies. In those cases the entries in the rows did not have to be in any particular order of importance; indeed it is often hard in FAR and the VFM to say that one row entry is more 'important' than another. In the TPM, by contrast, we intend to use the severity of threat patterns to provide assessments of military or business risk, as was indicated in Figure 13.2. That requires a ranking order so that in a TPM, the rows in a column provide not only filing space for all reasonable possibilities but also *rank the possibilities in order of severity*. Thus, P_1 is clearly a far more severe threat than P_5.

> In a threat profile matrix the rows are ranked from 'most serious' to 'least dangerous'.

In the next sub-section but one we will show how these ideas apply to business issues, but first we must discuss how a TPM can be developed.

Developing a threat profile matrix

It is obvious that a threat profile can be described by selecting one row from each column, exactly as we did with the viable firm matrix, but how do we know which cells to select?

One approach is to use the TPM simply to summarise the assessments made by normal intelligence procedures. In that way, the TPM can provide senior decision-makers with a gestalt summary of what might otherwise be a mass of data and reports. That, though, would be a picture of the current situation, whereas, in order to deal with the time delays inherent in acquisition, what we need is a picture of the threats that might arise at some point in the future.

That can be handled by making a link back to the futures methods discussed in Chapter 3 and, since Tethys is somewhere to the East, we can use Figure 3.5, p. 71, the futures tree for the South China Sea. That tree lays out four logically consistent estimates of what might happen there by about 2010. One condition was α, a catastrophic future, while another was γ, the Asian community being recognised as an equal by the rest of the world. It would, no doubt, involve much discussion, but careful thought (drawing on the documentation of the ESPARC profiles describing worlds α and γ which we were at pains to stress is a vital part of the FAR process) might lead us to describe the respective threat patterns for those worlds as shown in Table 13.3. The structure of the TPM itself, with its categories of threat and its array of all reasonable possibilities, should help to make a discussion out of what might easily become an argument.

---

*In Greek mythology, Tethys was a sea goddess and the wife of Oceanus.

Table 13.2 An illustrative threat profile matrix

Smuggling S	Illegal immigration attempts I	Piracy P	Foreign support for secessionists F	Evasion of traffic tolls E	Theft of littoral resources T
S_1 Volume damaging to national interest, smugglers defiant and combative	I_1 Waves of refugees. A major national problem	P_1 Inter-island traffic seriously restricted. Major problems for international traffic in Straits of Tuna	F_1 Determined and blatant attempts to bring in large volumes of supplies and weapons	E_1 Widespread defiance of collection of tolls	T_1 Widespread and defiant
S_2 Large volumes, smugglers armed and dangerous	I_2 Organised and armed gangs seek to bring in large groups	P_2 Sporadic raids on coastal villages/small towns for supplies, plunder and 'recruits'	F_2 Small shipments of supplies and weapons at isolated places	E_2 Most vessels make serious attempts to avoid payment by evasion or fraud	T_2 Widespread but avoiding contact with authorities
S_3 Moderate volumes – non-violent	I_3 Widespread, but unorganised, attempts by family groups	P_3 Occasional attacks on large vessels even when crews are armed	F_3 Occasional infiltration of small teams	E_3 International traffic will pay tolls but only if actively intercepted by coastguard	T_3 Fairly frequent in remoter areas
S_4 Small amount of 'traditional' smuggling	I_4 Small groups of people at secluded spots	P_4 Risky for fishing vessels not working in large groups	F_4 Single individuals moved in or out	E_4 Small vessels evade tolls where possible	T_4 Occasional 'poaching'
		P_5 Occasional attacks on isolated small craft			

Table 13.3 Two threat profiles (α in *bold italic*, γ in bold)

Smuggling S	Illegal immigration attempts I	Piracy P	Foreign support for secessionists F	Evasion of traffic tolls E	Theft of littoral resource T
S_1 Volume damaging to national interest, smugglers defiant and combative	***I_1 Waves of refugees. A major national problem***	***P_1 Inter-island traffic seriously restricted. Major problems for international traffic in Straits of Tuna***	***F_1 Determined and blatant attempts to bring in large volumes of supplies and weapons***	***E_1 Widespread defiance of tolls***	***T_1 Widespread and defiant***
S_2 Large volumes, smugglers armed and dangerous	I_2 Organised and armed gangs seek to bring in large groups	P_2 Sporadic raids on coastal villages/small towns for supplies, plunder and 'recruits'	F_2 Small shipments of supplies and weapons at isolated places	E_2 Most vessels make serious attempts to avoid payment by evasion or fraud	T_2 Widespread but avoiding contact with authorities
S_3 Moderate volumes – non-violent	I_3 Widespread, but unorganised, attempts by family groups	P_3 Occasional attacks on large vessels even when crews are armed	F_3 Occasional infiltration of small teams	E_3 International traffic will pay tolls but only if actively intercepted by coastguard	T_3 Fairly frequent in remoter areas
S_4 Small amount of 'traditional' smuggling	**I_4 Small groups of people at secluded spots**	**P_4 Risky for fishing vessels not working in large groups**	**F_4 Single individuals moved in or out**	**E_4 Small vessels evade tolls where possible**	**T_4 Occasional 'poaching'**
		P_5 Occasional attacks on isolated small craft			

When we come to MOA we will show how wish lists can be dealt with to take account of the two very different circumstances represented by α and γ.

Finally, we can point out that, in this case, it has just happened that the threats are straight across the rows but, in practice, the threat profile might have any shape such as $S_2I_3P_4F_4E_2T_3$.

A business threat profile matrix

The same concepts can be applied to other problem areas and Table 13.4 is a TPM for a manufacturing company such as XYZ Industries. In this case, we have not developed an acronym because, as the etceteras imply, we want to challenge you to develop a similar matrix for your own organisation or for any other case that interests you.

Where do the column headings in Table 13.4 come from? There are several possibilities:

■ Common sense and experience in the organisation.

■ Business monitoring and intelligence collection.

■ The strategy literature such as, say, Porter's well-known five forces (Grant, 2002) or the PESTEL framework (Johnson and Scholes, 2002, pages 99–103).[*]

■ However, the first three approaches might lock your thinking too much into the current world, so the fourth option is to use any relevant scenarios, or FAR

Table 13.4 A threat profile for a manufacturing company

Competition in established markets	Barriers to entry in new markets	Technological change	Finance	Labour supply	Regulation/ government bureaucracy	Etc.
Competition very aggressive	Barriers are almost insuperable	Change very rapid in all applicable areas	New money very hard to obtain. Banking sector generally hostile to manufacturers	No intelligent people want to work in manufacturing	Etc.	
Severe competition	Very difficult to enter genuinely new markets	Rapid change in customer needs	Money is available but only at poor terms	Some good people available but vacancies very hard to fill within a reasonable time		
Competition can be serious but not all the time	Etc.	Technology generally stable, but spasmodic developments in some aspects	Etc.	An adequate supply but endless problems of keeping good people		
Etc.		Etc.		Etc.		

[*]PESTEL is not, perhaps, ideal as an acronym as it contains two Es, but it is easy to pronounce and is widely used.

analyses – for instance, if XYZ has an operation in Singapore or Malaysia, Figure 3.5 might be highly relevant to assessing the business threats. The conflict threat profile might, of course, also be significant to XYZ (Singapore). If no scenarios, in the sense of stories about the future, are available, you might be well advised to spend a small amount of time developing suitable scenarios using simplified FAR (p. 73).

We must now move on to developing a structure for developing and handling wish lists. This will give me some difficulties, as it will be necessary to discuss the principles before showing the detail of how those concepts work in practice, and that will involve several promises that things will be explained later. That is inevitable as we are dealing with what is probably the most complex technique in the book, so you are asked to be patient and follow the explanation as it evolves.

The mission-orientated analysis hierarchy – a structure for wish list problems

Key components of the structure

The difficulty with wish lists is that they contain specific things to be evaluated – they are usually called 'line items' – but we are not, paradoxically, concerned with the things themselves, we are interested in the extent to which they contribute to overall performance.* To illustrate, imagine two oil refinery projects, A and B, each costing £X million. There is only £X million available, so which project contributes more to business performance? (Of course, wish lists are, by definition, far more complex than that, but this example shows the issue to be addressed.)

> The aim is to see how wish list items contribute to overall performance.

There is no simple way to calculate that project A is 'better' than B and the answer is certainly not self-evident so, to address such issues rationally and effectively, *we will need four components.*

1. *A hierarchy of planning levels* to show how the specific items on the wish list contribute to ultimate operational or organisational performance. In essence this will be a 'model' of the operation or business, though, as with the other techniques in this book, it will be a 'model' in words, not in equations. Since we will use this later in the chapter for mission-orientated analysis, we will refer to it as *the MOA hierarchy.*

2. The object is to measure whether or not refinery A is better than B, so we will need a *measurement scale* which will be provided by a set of definitions of *possible* degrees of operational or business performance at each level in the hierarchy.

3. We will need to *assess how capability at one level in the hierarchy contributes to performance at the next*, and that can be done using expert business or military judgement or, indeed, any other information.

4. Finally, MOA is a structured judgement method and, though human judgement is a powerful tool of which we have made much use in the **ACTIFELD** steps, there is always a risk of someone 'adjusting' (or fiddling) the judgements to get

---

*The line items may involve capital expenditure on hardware, or they may involve management effort, perhaps considerable, such as making improvements to employee satisfaction.

the answer they want. We will therefore use *simple arithmetic to trace the assess-ments through the hierarchy to overall performance*. That cannot make the judgements 'right' but it does mean that judgements made in good faith are traced to their logical consequences and there is no possibility of fiddling the process to get a politically desired answer.

The rest of this section will concentrate on the first point to explain the hierarchy. The other three components will be discussed in full when we come to mission-orientated analysis. Finally, we will show how the hierarchy can be used to develop rational wish lists.

The hierarchy of planning levels

The hierarchy of planning levels is shown in Figure 13.3. The ideas in it are quite subtle so it will actually help if we explain it in a conceptual order rather than from top to bottom, or bottom to top. This will seem to involve some jumping about, so please be patient and refer to the diagram as we go. At this stage we are only concerned with the principles underlying the hierarchical *structure*; detailed examples will emerge as we proceed.

The top item is a short statement of the *overall objective or mission*. For a business this might well be the mission statement. For the UK's National Health Service it

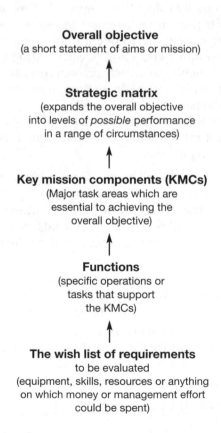

Overall objective
(a short statement of aims or mission)

↑

Strategic matrix
(expands the overall objective
into levels of *possible* performance
in a range of circumstances)

↑

Key mission components (KMCs)
(Major task areas which are
essential to achieving the
overall objective)

↑

Functions
(specific operations or
tasks that support
the KMCs)

↑

The wish list of requirements
to be evaluated
(equipment, skills, resources or anything
on which money or management effort
could be spent)

Figure 13.3 The MOA hierarchy

might be as succinct as 'to care effectively, swiftly, and efficiently for the ills of mind and body'. For Tethys it could be 'to protect the integrity of Tethys against a particular range of threats' (summarised in Table 13.2). It is vital to spend some effort to get this statement right, as *it is essential to say what is to be achieved, without saying how that is to be done*. Some business missions have been known to mix 'what' with 'how'.

> The overall objective specifies what is to be achieved, but without saying how.

The bottom of the page has the *wish list* and the whole object of the exercise is to be able to select those items from the list that, within constraints of money and time, best satisfy the overall mission.

To take us forward in that aim, we have to allow for the fact that the overall mission might have to be achieved under distinctly different circumstances; Tethys, for instance, might face a greater or lesser degree of threat. Meeting the objective of the health care system in winter might not be the same as achieving it in summer. The Mont Fleur scenarios (p. 61) are distinctly different business opportunities and threats. We must also have a measuring scale since different packages of items from the wish list might improve strategic performance to differing extents.

Both these aspects of different circumstances and degrees of performance are expressed in the *strategic matrix* next to the top of Figure 13.3. That matrix has as many columns as are necessary to cope with the range of different circumstances (up to about four is manageable) and four rows to represent performance levels ranging from 'very poor' to 'fully satisfies the overall objective'. There is no magic about having *four* levels except that it is enough to discriminate between different cases and to give a gestalt appreciation of trade-offs.

> The strategic matrix is a scale for assessing how the wish list items contribute to the overall objective in different circumstances.

To connect the wish list to the strategic matrix requires two steps.

The best way to see this is to start from wish list items. Suppose that Tethys has to choose between buying radios and acquiring warships. The first would improve the specialised task, or *function*, of communications while the second would enhance the function of the ability to react to events, such as piracy or fish theft, or even to prevent them. Communication and reaction are, however, specific military tasks – the functions near the bottom of Figure 13.3 – they are not ends in themselves.

> The functions are specialised tasks.

The final step in the hierarchy is, then, to connect this functional ability to do specific tasks to the essential aspects of the mission, the *key mission components (KMCs)*. These are exactly what the name says:

> The key mission components are the major factors in achieving strategic performance.

- They are broad and general capability areas such as the ability to control the sea. That will, of course, contribute to countering all aspects of the threat but it is important to express the KMC in broad terms and not, at this level in the hierarchy, get involved in specific factors.
- They are components of the overall mission of ensuring the political, social and economic integrity of Tethys.
- They are *key* in the sense that deficiencies in satisfying them are likely to undermine the ability to satisfy the top-level mission.

In the next section we will develop a practical example of these ideas, and later we will show illustrations from business and health care, but before we go into those technical details it is first necessary to show the ideas behind how the hierarchy works and what it does.

Using the hierarchy

Figure 13.3 implies very clearly that selecting an item, or in practice a package of items, from the wish list will improve the ability to perform one or more of the func-

MOA can use all the available information.

tions. The extent of improvement can be assessed by expert judgement, by using operational research models, as a result of tests or experiments, or by employing any other source of information. In fact, it is one of the great strengths of MOA that it can make use of *all* relevant sources and is not restricted only to judgement, numerical data or any other single type of information.

Obviously, improvements in functional capabilities will enhance the ability to discharge the KMCs. Finally, the improved KMC performance is reflected in the

MOA uses a traffic-light display of performance.

achievability of different performance levels under the variety of circumstances shown in the strategic matrix. That ultimate effect is shown using a traffic-light display in which the cells in the strategic matrix are coloured as red for unachievable, green for OK and amber if there are some deficiencies. That can also be amber/green if the deficiencies are not serious or amber/red if they are.

Judgements made in good faith are traced to their logical conclusions.

It is very important to realise that these two stages of assessing the effect that items from the wish list have on KMC performance and the consequent impact on ability to meet the overall objective in the circumstances shown in the strategic matrix *are calculated using some simple arithmetic* (to be explained a little later). That is why it is impossible to fiddle the assessments of the effects of wish list items in order to 'prove' some pre-chosen opinion that such-and-such a wish-list line item will be a valuable enhancement. As we stated earlier, that cannot make the judgements and assessments 'right' but it does mean that judgements made in good faith are traced to their logical conclusions.

This process might be called bottom-up analysis as it works from the wish list to the strategic performance. However, planners might also look at the red and amber cells in the strategic matrix and ask what needs to be done to reduce risk by turning a given cell from red to amber or green. That would be top-down analysis and the power of the arithmetic is that top-down planning is very easy and quick.

A hierarchy for Tethys

The basic picture

We now need to make all this more specific by developing an MOA hierarchy for Tethys, as shown in Figure 13.4. This will need a little explanation so a photocopy of the diagram might help you to follow the argument.

Down the left-hand side are the five components of the hierarchy from *Overall objective* down to *the wish list* and emphasised in that typeface. The overall objective is a short statement of what is to be achieved and it is useful, in practice, if

Overall objective   *Protect integrity of Tethys against this range of threats*

Strategic matrix

Performance level	Deal with γ-world threats	Deal with α-world threats
1	Maintain constant surveillance of seas and territory and prevent all infractions	Prevent damage to national life and maintain sovereignty
2	Maintain some surveillance of most areas and react to events within 12–24 hours	Inflict damage to threatening forces and limit their freedom to operate
3	Deal with the most blatant incidents	Harrass threatening forces and protect essential infrastructure
4	Maintain some degree of law enforcement	Protect vital points and receive assistance from allies or United Nations

Key mission components (KMCs)

	Sea control	Territorial defence	Reaction capability	Command, control and intelligence
1	Ability to operate at will in all areas and defeat any plausible opposition	Be able to defeat hostile forces and regain occupied locations	Deploy significant land and/or sea forces to any required area within 24 hours	Maintain positive control of all forces and surveillance of all areas
2	Ability to gain sea control of threatened areas, if necessary against some opposition	Be able to contain hostile forces and limit damage	Deploy significant land and/or sea forces to key areas within 48 hours	Positive command and control of forces in active operations. Surveillance of most other areas
3	Ability to achieve sufficient sea control to deter serious violations and protect key approaches	Be able to exert national sovereignty against light opposition	Deploy smaller forces to vital points within 24 hours	Maintain communications with major units and sweep area every week
4	Ability to intercept and detain after minor violations	Defend vital points such as main government centres	Deploy locally based forces within their areas of responsibility	Detect and report incursions and violations of sovereignty

Specific functions

	Maritime capability	Land force capability	Surveillance capability	Communications	Command and staff	Training	Bases and facilities	Logistics
1	Operate throughout all sea areas in all weathers and successfully engage significant enemies	Ability to dominate required areas and destroy hostile elements	All-weather, day and night capability to detect, identify and track intruders in approaches to Tethys	Maintain continuous contact with all forces in all areas	Ability to anticipate events and seize and maintain the initiative	All forces maintained at high level of individual and collective training	Extensive network of well-equipped bases with good training facilities	Maintain all forces at full scales at intensive rates for sustained periods
2	Operate in main sea routes in most weathers to intercept and detain hostile violators	Ability to sweep required areas and intercept/detain intruders	In most cases, locate, monitor and acquire targets for interception or engagement	Ensure contact with forces in operational circumstances	Ability to plan rapidly and effectively for new events	Most forces at moderate level of individual and collective training	Scattering of bases throughout islands. Some well equipped and with modest training facilities	Maintain key forces at full scales. Ensure rapid resupply to other forces in emergency
3	Operate in coastal areas to enforce traffic rules and collect tolls	Ability to patrol selected areas and detain intruders	Ability to detect and monitor intruders after they have arrived	Maintain communications between major headquarters	Well-developed and rehearsed contingency plans for most eventualities	Infrequent joint exercises	Bases sited to cover main sea routes	Maintain supply of key items to all forces but with occasional shortages
4	Lightly armed operations in coastal waters to protect fishing	Ability to assist civil authorities in border control	Limited coast watch for frequently threatened areas	Maintain communications for key functions	Ad hoc planning as events unfold	Basic training with some specialised skills	Bases only near main centres. Basic facilities	Provide basic support in limited areas

The wish list   *The line items arranged against the functions to which they are relevant*

Figure 13.4 An MOA hierarchy for Tethys

that short statement is amplified by some documentation, though we shall not do so for this example. We will suppose that the line items of the wish list have been arranged against the functions to which they apply. The three items of the **Strategic matrix**, the **KMCs** and the **Specific functions** are all defined in matrices and we will start with the first of those.

The strategic matrix

The strategic matrix has, for this example, two columns, as we need to deal with the two extremes of the dangerous α-world and the relatively benign γ-world. (Depending on the case, a strategic matrix might have only one column or it might have several, though four columns are about the maximum for a gestalt appreciation of its traffic-light display.)

Let us explain the ideas by looking first at the γ-world column and reviewing the threat profile matrix in Table 13.3, p. 231. The top level, labelled 1, has a definition of what Tethys needs to be able to do to satisfy its overall objective in this calm world. That degree of capability, *if it could be achieved*, would clearly be able to defeat the minor piracy (and piracy still exists in some parts of the world), cope with low-level illegal immigration and so forth. If the Tethysian armed forces can achieve that, all will be well. Now look at level 4.* That is a minimal level such that, if the forces *cannot even manage to do that*, they would not be a realistic proposition and are essentially a waste of money. The two levels in between are precisely that; they are intermediaries between the ideal and the barely adequate. At the end of this section we will explain where these definitions come from.

| The definitions are *potential* levels of performance. |

Note, then, that these definitions are of *potential* levels of strategic performance. The aim of MOA is to analyse the wish list to see what needs to be implemented in order actually to achieve some desired level of capability and thus to minimise risks. Although we are at present discussing a military planning case, we shall see later that precisely the same ideas apply to business and health-care planning and, indeed, to any other wish-list problem.

It is a key point that if a given level, 2 perhaps, can be achieved then all the levels below that, 3 and 4 in that case, could also be achieved.

Drawing on the earlier explanation of the hierarchy, it is now obvious that, if it turns out, say, that levels 4 and 3 are green, but levels 2 and 1 are red (when we apply the MOA technique) then Tethys faces risks and the government must decide whether to accept those risks or to increase defence spending to ameliorate them.

The definitions for the more challenging α-world are clearly quite different for the very simple reason that the two worlds, and the corresponding threat profiles, are by no means the same things.

The key mission components

| Each KMC contributes to strategic performance. |

The KMCs for Tethys are also labelled from 1 to 4 with the same meaning of ideal and minimal capabilities. Notice that these are broad tasks to be accomplished and are not directly related to the specific threats in the threat profile matrix. It is a temptation to use the TPM column names as

---

*Some people prefer to number the levels from 4 – highest – down to 1. I prefer the format in Figure 13.4 as 1 implies First Class down to 4, Barely Acceptable, which is roughly the same as degree classifications.

KMCs, but it runs the risk of getting too embroiled in detail at too early a stage in the analysis. We shall see later how the specific risk of not being able to cope with, say, piracy can be assessed.

The solid lines connecting the KMCs to the strategic matrix are intended to show that each KMC has a contribution to make to the accomplishment of strategic performance in the variety of circumstances shown in the strategic matrix.

How, though, do we know what a given level of KMC capability will contribute to strategic performance? This is a key aspect of MOA.

For instance, suppose that the KMC of sea control can be achieved at level 3 – serious violations can be prevented and the key approaches are protected. A senior naval officer judges that, *as far as sea control is concerned*, that would be sufficient to meet level 2 of the strategic matrix in the γ-world, but would only satisfy level 4 in the α-world. Of course, the other KMCs would have to make their appropriate contributions but, if

> The connection between KMC capability and strategic performance is a key aspect of MOA.

sea control was the only thing that mattered, the strategic matrix would be green for level 2 in the γ-world and green for level 4 in the α-world. All higher levels in the strategic matrix would be red, unachievable.

How do we know, though, that sea control level 3 will be sufficient for strategic level 2 in the γ-world, but not adequate for level 1? The answer is that we do not *know*, as such; the judgement is that of an experienced senior officer, such as an admiral, whose responsibility it is to execute the task of sea control. At this stage, we have only previewed the point, but this idea of the level of KMC capability needed to achieve given levels of strategic performance is a key factor in MOA. It will be discussed in more detail when we come to the MOA procedure.

The functions and their connections to the KMCs

Finally, the specific military functions are also defined in four levels, with the definitions also meaning 'ideal' down to 'barely adequate'. The dotted arrows between the function and KMC matrices imply that every function does not necessarily contribute to every KMC. For example, the specific function of logistics is not *directly* involved in the KMC of command, control and intelligence. The diagram would become illegible if we drew an arrow from each of eight functions to show which of the four KMCs they supported and it is easier to show the connections in Table 13.5, in which the ♦ symbol shows a direct involvement of the function in the KMC, with some abbreviations of the function names.*

It is tempting to think that every function is involved in all the KMCs, and that, to some extent, is true – for example, if the land force cannot protect the bases, the navy could not operate. We need, though, to avoid that level of detail and concentrate on the *direct, clear and immediate relationships*.

Who decides what these connections are? In this instance, it is the business of military officers to know how things interact. For a management example, it would be the intrinsic expertise of the management team to know how the business works. For the hospital example, which we will consider later, it would, again, be decided by the practical knowledge and experience of health professionals and managers.

The table can be read down its columns or across its rows. For example, reading downwards, the function of maritime capability contributes only to the KMC of sea

---

*Of course, this hierarchy is specific to the case of Tethys and a hierarchy for the UK or US forces would be very different.

Table 13.5 The KMC/Function interactions

The KMCs	The specific functions							
	Maritime capab	Land force capab	Surveill capab	Comms	Cmd and staff	Train	Bases and facils	Logs
Sea control	♦		♦	♦	♦	♦		♦
Territorial defence		♦	♦	♦	♦	♦		♦
Reaction capability				♦	♦	♦	♦	
Command, control, intelligence			♦	♦	♦	♦		

control, whereas the command and staff function has a role to play in all KMCs. Reading across, six of the functions combine to achieve the KMC of sea control.

This is a useful check on the realism of the thinking. The connections in Table 13.5 are a 'model' of this particular defence problem. In practice, the table would be based on a good deal of discussion, preferably in the Delphi style of debating the reasons for extreme views. The issue would be whether or not the model is reasonably realistic, is neither too simple nor too detailed, and whether it is a useful tool for thinking with. Once the table is accepted as an 'official' view, it might help people to understand how their particular role fits into the bigger picture – something which is called 'jointery' in military parlance.

> Check for *acceptability* with a KMC/Function interaction table.

There is a second check on the *validity*, as opposed to the *acceptability*, of a table such as Table 13.5. Suppose that we had a ♦ which is the only one in its column and also the only one in that row. That would mean that we had a function that is also a KMC – that would confuse the specifics of a function with the generality of a KMC, and would be a serious error in the hierarchy.

> Check for *validity*. Have KMCs and functions been confused?

Building MOA hierarchies

Introduction

We have had to do a good deal of explanation of the ideas in the hierarchy, and we are nearly ready to deal with the working of the MOA process, but first we need to clear up three final questions about the hierarchy:

■ How do we derive its structure?

■ Where do its definitions come from?

■ How do we arrange for the traffic-light display of capabilities?

The structure of the hierarchy

This particular hierarchy has two columns in the strategic matrix, four KMCs and eight functions, but where does that structure come from? Why, for instance, are there eight functions, and not seven, ten, or some other number? As with all the techniques in this book, there is no simple formula and probably no single 'right' answer – much depends on common sense, supported by technical knowledge and practical experience of the problem domain, whether it be defence, health, professional service firms or whatever. We can, though, show the general lines of thought which help us to develop a sound, usable and acceptable hierarchy. That will be illustrated by the case of Tethys, though the process applies to any other problem area.

The first step is to select the *number of columns in the strategic matrix* by deciding on the number of distinctly different circumstances that must be provided for. In the Tethys case, the threat profile matrix defines two clearly different contexts: the γ-world and the α-world. Sometimes, then, this best-case/worst-case approach will work. That is rare as there are usually no evidently best and worst cases and you might have to think in terms of the end states of story scenarios (Chapter 3) and use those. Essentially, though, you just have to think through the problem, talk to relevant people and then decide on the number of cases.

> **Key step 1:**
> Decide how many distinctly different circumstances must be catered for.

The next stage is the *number of key mission components*. We have put that in full, rather than abbreviating to KMCs, to remind you that these are precisely what it says: key areas of broad capability, deficiencies in which might undermine the ability to meet the overall objective in the selected circumstances.

> **Key step 2 :**
> Think about the *essential* task areas.

In this instance, we know that Tethys faces threats by sea and by land – pirates, for instance, might attack shipping or raid villages and even small towns. It is therefore self-evident that the Tethysian forces need to be able to control the sea and defend the land. However, they won't be able to do that without command and control. Finally, they cannot be everywhere all the time and will have to be able to react to, or still better, to anticipate, events and that gives us a total of four KMCs. Just as a suggestion, KMCs for a business hierarchy might be Retain existing customers, Develop new customers and Internal management. Notice that these do not involve organisational aspects, such as marketing, product development, finance and so on. They will be involved as functions, which are the final stage in building the hierarchy. What, though, do you think are suitable KMCs for your problem area? What might they be in a city government?

Now, develop a *relevant* set of specific functions. This is the danger area as there can be a strong temptation to have too many and to go into too much detail. In fact, it is not that difficult, as the functions will follow from the KMCs, just as the KMCs were derived from the strategic matrix columns.

> **Key step 3:**
> Identify the relevant specific functions.

For instance, we already have a KMC for Territorial defence. Even a little military knowledge suggests that, to satisfy that key component, we need land forces, we need to know where the enemy is (surveillance), information and orders must be communicated, the command and staff people must plan and control, the troops must have been trained, and they will need supplies (logistics). Similar thought about the other KMCs will add one or two additional functions together with those we already have, so we easily arrive at eight as a reasonable number.

The final step is to build a table of the KMC/function interactions, as in Table 13.5, revise if necessary and gain acceptance of the model.

Key step 4 :
Check your reasoning with a KMC/Function interaction table (see Table 13.5) and revise if necessary.

The definitions of capability

Where, though, do the capability definitions in the three matrices come from? The broad answer is that they flow downwards from the strategic matrix, but let us make that a bit more explicit.

The strategic matrix

This has to reflect overall policy with respect, in this case, to the γ-world and the α-world. The same is true for a business, a hospital, or any other domain. The highest, level 1, definition must be whatever would fully satisfy the overall objective in the given circumstances. Thus, in Figure 13.4 the level 1 definitions reflect the military capabilities that would be needed to meet the overall objective in the two very different worlds of the α and γ scenarios. There are higher levels of potential capability, such as that needed to invade and conquer another country, but that is not what is required by the essentially defensive objective of maintaining national sovereignty.

The strategic matrix definitions reflect the overall policy.

The level 4, barely acceptable, definitions are those below which sovereignty, or the business, could not, in any reasonable sense, be said to exist. Figure 13.4 has some *very* low performance capabilities at that level so the development of the strategic matrix and, indeed, the whole hierarchy hinges on this definition; while the level 1 definitions are relatively easy to develop, level 4 needs a good deal of thought.

In short, the trick, for all matrices, is first to formulate the level 1 definitions, then to develop level 4, and finally to choose levels 2 and 3 as intermediate capabilities. This applies to all problem domains, not just to defence. These definitions are essentially political in that they reflect what the civil authority, or the board of directors, wants to be able to achieve in these two worlds, in terms of the best that is required and the worst that is acceptable, with the two intermediate levels completing the measuring scale. Whether or not the armed forces can achieve these levels remains to be seen. If they cannot, finding the wish list items to be acquired, within the constraints of time and money, in order to enable them to improve their capabilities and hence reduce risk, is the whole purpose of MOA and the hierarchy is the first stage of that analysis. Because the hierarchy is both subtle and critical we have had to discuss it at length, but we will soon come to MOA itself.

Always define level 1, then level 4. The other two levels will follow fairly easily.

The KMC definitions

These are developed from the strategic matrix. In a military problem, senior officers and planners would develop the KMC definitions as their responsibilities are to deal with the bigger picture and key tasks, and that is what KMCs are. In any other domain it would be the responsibility of the people who have to develop strategy to meet overall objectives.

The level 1 definitions correspond to the degree of, say, sea control that would be needed *to satisfy strategic level 1 in the most demanding case* (the α-world in the Tethys example). The level 4 capabilities are those that would be *enough for level 4 in the least demanding case* (the γ-world). The subtlety of the whole hierarchy lies in this distinction between 'best required' and 'least needed'.

> The KMC definitions are related to the strategic requirements and are
>
> ■ best required
> ■ least needed
> ■ two intermediate cases.

Each KMC's level 1 matches α level 1 and its level 4 deals with γ level 4, but what about its levels 2 and 3? These are more difficult as they not only have to be reasonable intermediate states between levels 1 and 4 but they also have to bear some relation to the remaining cells in the strategic matrix. This usually involves some editing and revision of the KMC matrix to get a satisfactory result.

The function definitions

We can complete the hierarchy by explaining the function definitions. We can do so relatively briefly as the underlying principles are identical to the KMC definitions.

These definitions are the responsibility of technical experts. For example, an experienced signals officer of about the rank of Lieutenant Colonel would formulate the definitions for the function of communications.* When we deal with MOA for a hospital later in the chapter we will see functions such as surgical procedures, general nursing and transportation and it is obvious that the relevant health care experts would develop those definitions. In a business case, the marketing manager, the head of research and development, and so forth, would derive definitions for their specialist areas. Naturally, in all these cases, there would in practice be a good deal of discussion between comparably qualified people in order to get a satisfactory and acceptable collection of definitions. That could only add value to the hierarchy, especially if the Delphi-style debate of the reasons for extreme assessments is adopted, rather than an opinion poll or the pulling of rank.

Table 13.5 also shows that the capability definitions of the functions must match those of the KMCs. This means that the level 1 capability in, say, the communications function must be the performance required to enable the KMCs to which it contributes – all of the KMCs in this case – to reach their level 1 performances *in the most demanding KMC*.

One final point

Let us recall that senior people define the relationships between KMC and strategic performance whereas technical experts cope with the function definitions. This separation of judgements is another reason why, as we mentioned before, it is impossible for any person or interest group to fiddle the process to 'prove' that what they have already decided to implement from the wish list is the right choice.

> Separation of judgements makes it impossible to fiddle the process to get some preconceived result.

This discussion of the MOA hierarchy has necessarily, and regrettably, been quite long. As we mentioned at the beginning of the chapter, MOA is probably the most difficult technique in this book and the hierarchy is a subtle and novel idea. However, we are now ready to put all this into action and deal with wish list problems.

---

*I have found in many cases that less senior officers such as majors and captains usually come up with very good definitions that are readily accepted by their higher-ranking officers. Perhaps majors and captains are closer to the practical detail.

Mission-orientated analysis (MOA)

Introduction

To get us started, let us remind ourselves that the aim of MOA is the use of a system based on expert judgement to:

- Identify the strategic capabilities achieved by chosen improvement packages. That is bottom-up planning.
- Alternatively, we might want to identify improvement packages that will achieve target levels of strategic capability. That is top-down analysis.

Although MOA is applicable to any wish list problem in any domain, it is important to grasp what the technique can do and what it cannot.

- The first thing that MOA *does* is to use the hierarchy of definitions to give broad indications of which items on a wish list are likely to be cost-effective solutions to the achievement of desired levels of strategic performance, and which are not. In that sense, it directs the attention of planners to the areas where more detailed work is most likely to be beneficial.
- The second valuable part of MOA is the hierarchy itself. Much like the sense-making techniques of Chapter 2, it puts on to one piece of paper a high-level view of the interactions in a problem. In the real-world applications of practical strategy, it is hard to overstate the benefits of doing that.
- What MOA does *not* do is *fully and completely to solve in every detail* the problem of which items from a long wish list are to be implemented. That is too hard for any single technique to do, but, as we shall see, MOA's ability to identify the items from the wish list that make the greatest contributions to strategic performance can save a vast amount of work wasted in the wrong parts of the list.

In practice, MOA can be used at two levels of detail, just as FAR (Chapter 3) can be used at full scale or as simplified FAR:

1. *Simplified MOA* is used when all that is required is broad-brush analysis to identify key planning issues. That only requires an understanding of the nature of the MOA hierarchy and the connections between functions and KMCs, as shown in Table 13.5 and the basic principles of the relationships between KMCs and the strategic matrix, which we shall discuss in a moment.

2. *Full-scale MOA* is used when there are numerous detailed items on the wish list. The mode requires some calculation using the arithmetical scores just described. It is fully explained, with a worked example, in Coyle (1989, on the website).

The whole theme of this book is to present simple approaches to practical strategy – though most of them are deceptively simple – so we will illustrate simplified MOA for Tethys.

Simplified MOA for Tethys

The analysis is shown in Figure 13.5 and it will help you to follow the explanation to have a photocopy of that. The text definitions of capability have been deleted from Figure 13.5 to leave space for the red and green traffic-light display, so a photocopy of Figure 13.4 will also help you. The matrices have been duplicated to give two halves in the diagram, separated by the vertical dotted line and labelled base case and improved case. The links in Figure 13.4 between the strategic and KMC matrices and between the functions and the KMCs have been omitted for clarity, though they still operate. This example has been deliberately simplified for non-military readers and has been developed to show the concepts of MOA as clearly as possible.

It is essential to be clear that the base case corresponds to Tethys' existing capabilities and is *before* any of the line items from the wish list have been acquired. The whole purpose of the base case will be to give us pointers as to which line items will provide useful improvements to strategic capability.

Where, though, do the colours in Figure 13.5 come from and how are the improvements assessed? Those questions are the key issues in this example and, to answer them, we start with the base case on the left-hand side, and with the function capabilities at the bottom of the diagram.

The base case

The base case function capabilities

Tethys already has armed forces and they have capabilities that have been built up since the country gained its independence. Of course, those capabilities are neither satisfactory not perfectly balanced – no nation's are – and that is shown by the green and red symbols on the function matrix in Figure 13.5. Green shows that maritime capability reaches band 3, so the Tethysian navy can operate in coastal waters to enforce traffic rules and collect tolls, but it cannot reach band 2 and operate in the main sea routes in most weathers to intercept and detain hostile violators. The other functions also have their red and green capabilities. A thick line has been drawn at the green/red boundary to emphasise that capabilities are not, as the result of previous defence investments, evenly spread. That is very typical of real cases but how do we know what the colours should be?

For the functions, the answer is that they are assessed by expert knowledge, practical experience, exercises, or analytical models, but the simplest answer is the best; naval officers know very well what their ships and crews are capable of doing. The same applies to the other functions.

The base case KMC capabilities

We now move up Figure 13.5 to assess the green/red display for the KMCs and for that we need Table 13.5, which gives the interactions between KMCs and functions.

Using the KMC of sea control as an example, Table 13.5 shows that six functions contribute to that KMC. The heavy black line in the base case function matrix shows that four of those are green at band 2 but two reach only to band 3.

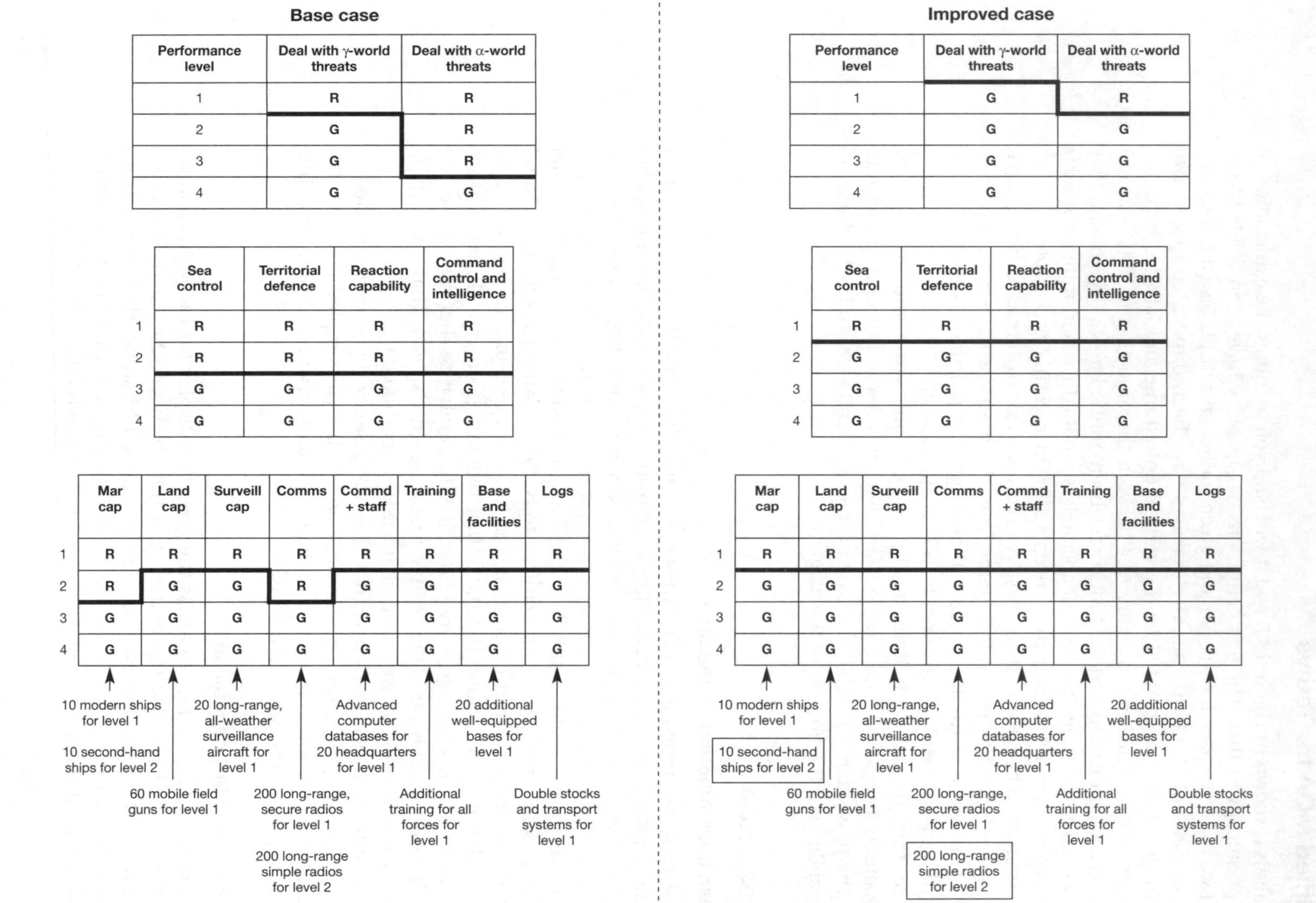
Base case
10 modern ships for level 1
10 second-hand ships for level 2
60 mobile field guns for level 1
20 long-range, all-weather surveillance aircraft for level 1
200 long-range, secure radios for level 1
200 long-range simple radios for level 2
Advanced computer databases for 20 headquarters for level 1
Additional training for all forces for level 1
20 additional well-equipped bases for level 1
Double stocks and transport systems for level 1
Improved case
10 modern ships for level 1
10 second-hand ships for level 2
60 mobile field guns for level 1
20 long-range, all-weather surveillance aircraft for level 1
200 long-range, secure radios for level 1
200 long-range simple radios for level 2
Advanced computer databases for 20 headquarters for level 1
Additional training for all forces for level 1
20 additional well-equipped bases for level 1
Double stocks and transport systems for level 1

Base case

Performance level	Deal with γ-world threats	Deal with α-world threats
1	R	R
2	G	R
3	G	R
4	G	G

	Sea control	Territorial defence	Reaction capability	Command control and intelligence
1	R	R	R	R
2	R	R	R	R
3	G	G	G	G
4	G	G	G	G

	Mar cap	Land cap	Surveill cap	Comms	Commd + staff	Training	Base and facilities	Logs
1	R	R	R	R	R	R	R	R
2	R	G	G	R	G	G	G	G
3	G	G	G	G	G	G	G	G
4	G	G	G	G	G	G	G	G

Improved case

Performance level	Deal with γ-world threats	Deal with α-world threats
1	G	R
2	G	G
3	G	G
4	G	G

	Sea control	Territorial defence	Reaction capability	Command control and intelligence
1	R	R	R	R
2	G	G	G	G
3	G	G	G	G
4	G	G	G	G

	Mar cap	Land cap	Surveill cap	Comms	Commd + staff	Training	Base and facilities	Logs
1	R	R	R	R	R	R	R	R
2	G	G	G	G	G	G	G	G
3	G	G	G	G	G	G	G	G
4	G	G	G	G	G	G	G	G

Figure 13.5 Simplified MOA for Tethys

MOA is, like all else in this book, intended to be simple and the rule it applies is that the worst function determines the KMC performance. The reason for that is common sense: the level 2 performance from surveillance, for instance, cannot be exploited if the ships can only operate in coastal waters. The same reasoning applies to the other KMCs. The net effect is to show what the KMC performance is in the base case, emphasised by the thick black line separating green from red (we shall encounter some ambers later).

> The rule is that the worst function determines the KMC performance.

The base case strategic performance

To *assess* the strategic performance, senior officers have to judge the KMC capability required to meet given levels of strategic performance. That might seem to be subjective but it is what admirals and generals are paid to do and they have spent their lives studying and practising their professions so it is better to regard it as the exercise of their seasoned judgement.

> Strategic performance is governed by how well the pattern of KMC capabilities matches the required pattern for each cell in the strategic matrix (Table 13.6).

In its simplest form, the idea is shown in Figure 13.6. To get into the ideas we will use the example of the connection between the KMC of sea control and strategic performance, though the same ideas apply to the other KMCs.

Part 1 of Figure 13.6 simply restates the definitions of the possible levels of KMC capability for sea control and the potential degrees of strategic outcome for the α- and γ-worlds.

In Part 2 of the figure, we suppose for illustration that the KMC is capable of reaching level 2 (the definition of which is in Part 1). The connection between that capability and strategic outcomes is shown in the remaining two columns for the α- and γ-worlds. Thus, if the KMC can reach level 2, then strategic level 1 can be achieved for α while level 2 is reachable for the more hostile γ-world. Recall that if a given level can be achieved, as shown by green, then all levels below that in the matrix can also be achieved.

Part 3 of the figure shows that if the KMC reaches only level 3, then there is a somewhat reduced outcome in α and a very much poorer outcome for γ. This is an illustration of the very non-linear effects that can occur in the handling of wish lists.

We have to repeat that these relationships stem from the judgement of very senior officers. They are *not* arbitrary and subjective; they are the product of a lifetime of experience and training, perhaps supported by exercises and analytical studies. Of course, since they are explicit, they can be debated and refined until an agreed view is reached.

We chose to explain Figure 13.6 in terms of the KMC of sea control but it is obvious that similar judgements have to be made for the other KMCs. It then follows – and this is the root of MOA – that if all the KMCs reach the capabilities required for level 1 in the α-world, then that level will be fully green. If none of them do so, it will be red. What happens if some reach the required capability, but others do not? The answer is that level 1 in the α-world will be neither red nor green, but can be seen as amber. This particular hierarchy has four KMCs so, if only one KMC had the capability required for level 1 in the α-world, then we would say that it was amber/red. If three had the required capabilities, it would be reasonable to call that amber/green, and so on.

Part 1 – A reminder of the definitions of performance

	Sea control	Deal with γ-world threats	Deal with α-world threats
1	Ability to operate at will in all areas and defeat any plausible opposition	Maintain constant surveillance of seas and territory and prevent all infractions	Prevent damage to national life and maintain sovereignty
2	Ability to gain sea control of threatened areas, if necessary against some opposition	Maintain some surveillance of most areas and react to events within 12–24 hours	Inflict damage to threatening forces and limit their freedom to operate
3	Ability to achieve sufficient sea control to deter serious violations and protect key approaches	Deal with the most blatant incidents	Harrass threatening forces and protect essential infrastructure
4	Ability to intercept and detain after minor violations	Maintain some degree of law enforcement	Protect vital points and receive assistance from allies or United Nations

Part 2 – Strategic effects of ability to achieve sea control level 2

	Sea control	Deal with γ-world threats	Deal with α-world threats
1	**Red** cannot be achieved	**Green** can be achieved	**Red** cannot be achieved
2	**Green** can be achieved	**Green** can be achieved	**Green** can be achieved
3	**Green** can be achieved	**Green** can be achieved	**Green** can be achieved
4	**Green** can be achieved	**Green** can be achieved	**Green** can be achieved

Part 3 – Strategic effects of ability to achieve sea control level 3

	Sea control	Deal with γ-world threats	Deal with α-world threats
1	**Red** cannot be achieved	**Red** cannot be achieved	**Red** cannot be achieved
2	**Red** cannot be achieved	**Green** can be achieved	**Red** cannot be achieved
3	**Green** can be achieved	**Green** can be achieved	**Red** cannot be achieved
4	**Green** can be achieved	**Green** can be achieved	**Green** can be achieved

Figure 13.6 Connection between KMC and strategic performances, for example of sea control

A sanity check

It is always valuable to make an independent check on an analytical procedure, but how might that be done? One way is to ask someone who not only understands MOA but is also knowledgeable about the domain in question, whether it be defence, business or, as we shall discuss below, a hospital system, to colour the strategic matrix from that general knowledge but *before* the MOA analysis is done. That can then be compared with the results *after* the analysis, and the reasons for any differences fully explored.

The policy issue for Tethys

The issue for the Tethysian government is whether or not this base case strategic performance is adequate for their objectives. They can achieve green at level 2 in the γ-world – 'Maintain some surveillance of most areas and react to events within 12–24 hours' – but not level 1 – 'Maintain constant surveillance of seas and territory and prevent all infractions'. In the more hostile α-world, they can only 'Protect vital points and receive assistance …'. Whether or not those performances are adequate is a political judgement. It might be assessed that the α-world is unlikely to arise or that, if it does, there will be adequate warning. On the other hand, it might be judged that level 2 in the γ-world is not acceptable and that something must be done, and that is where the wish list comes in.

The wish list

The wish list exists in the base case (at the foot of the left-hand side of Figure 13.5) because, as part of normal staff work, the heads of the various technical specialties identify improvements that they would like to achieve. For instance, the army commander knows that 60 mobile field guns would bring land defence capability up to its level 1. It is clear that the 60 guns are a very specific item, the cost of which is known.

> The wish list items are very specific and their costs are known.

The naval commander's case is not quite so clear-cut. Buying 10 modern ships would reach level 1 but there is the option of buying 10 second-hand ships from another nation, and that would reach level 2. The chief of communications has a similar choice.

There are, therefore, 10 line items in the wish list (in practical cases, these tend to be packages of improvements, not single items as in this simplified case). Buying all the items on the list, including the modern ships and secure radios, would reach level 1 in all functions, level 1 in all KMCs, and hence green in all the cells of the strategic matrix, but that cannot be achieved given the limitations of budgets. That is why a wish list is so called – it can never be fully satisfied. Which, then, are the most cost-effective acquisitions? That will determine strategic performance in the improved case.

The improved case

First principles

Reasoning from common sense, it is clear that improving, say, the command and staff function to level 1 would be likely to be a waste of money. There would be no point in having superb capabilities in that function if the communications function could not provide reports and transmit orders. It is evident from the base case in Figure 13.5 not only that attention needs to be focused on maritime capability and communications but also that the first step in an improvement programme is to bring them up to level 2, recalling MOA's reasonable assumption that the worst function will determine the capability of the KMCs to which it applies.

That much is blindingly obvious from Figure 13.5 but is only obvious *after* the hierarchy has been developed. It would not be obvious simply from discussion of a wish list problem, and one of MOA's virtues is to help to avoid simplistic assertions that 'we are over (under) invested in function X'.

> MOA guards against simplistic assertions.

Two cases of working with the wish list

Since we can identify the maritime capability and communications functions as the limiting factors, and since there is no point in increasing them beyond level 2, we can first try the effect of acquiring the second-hand ships and the simple communications, identified in boxes on the right-hand side of Figure 13.5. All functions and all KMCs now reach level 2 and, by applying the rules in Figure 13.6 we can obtain the colours in the improved case strategic matrix. This is a very worthwhile strategic improvement; achieving full capability in the benign γ-world has led to a major improvement in the event that the harsh α-world comes about.

The dramatic improvement in α-world strategic performance is less surprising than it seems, as the improvements in the maritime and communications functions have enabled the hitherto somewhat wasted capabilities in the other six functions to have their effect.

Let us now suppose that when the *review process* in Figure 13.2 takes place, the Ministry of Finance decides not to fund the second-hand ships but will agree to pay for the communications equipment.

Maritime capability does not improve so, on the basis that the worst function dominates the KMC, sea control remains at level 3. The effects are shown in Figure 13.7.

Using Figure 13.6, sea control level 3 is not sufficient for strategic level 1 in the γ-world, though all the other KMCs are capable of satisfying that performance level. That cell is nearly green, but not quite, so it is coloured A/G for amber/green. Similarly, sea control is not enough for α-world level 3, though the other KMCs are, so it is coloured A/G. However, if there are deficiencies at level 3 in that world, they must be more serious at level 2, so that is coloured amber. Level 1 remains at red. The investment in radios, while helpful, has not enabled the other functions to fulfil their potential.

Marginal returns to investment

> MOA assesses the benefits from investment or the damage done by spending cuts.

The significance of the difference between the base case and improved strategic performances in Figure 13.5 is what economists refer to as *marginal return to investment* (MRI): the extra strategic performance achieved by the spending of the extra cost of the second-hand ships and the simple radios. One of the roles of MOA is to give pointers to where MRI is likely to be greatest so that more detailed work can be carried out.

Improved case

Performance level	Deal with γ-world threats	Deal with α-world threats
1	A/G	R
2	G	A
3	G	A/G
4	G	G

	Sea control	Territorial defence	Reaction capability	Command control and intelligence
1	R	R	R	R
2	R	G	G	G
3	G	G	G	G
4	G	G	G	G

	Mar cap	Land cap	Surveill cap	Comms	Commd + staff	Training	Base and facilities	Logs
1	R	R	R	R	R	R	R	R
2	R	G	R	R	R	R	G	G
3	G	G	G	G	G	G	G	G
4	G	G	G	G	G	G	G	G

- 10 modern ships for level 1
- 10 second-hand ships for level 2
- 60 mobile field guns for level 1
- 20 long-range, all-weather surveillance aircraft for level 1
- 200 long-range, secure radios for level 1
- 200 long-range simple radios for level 2
- Advanced computer databases for 20 headquarters for level 1
- Additional training for all forces for level 1
- 20 additional well-equipped bases for level 1
- Double stocks and transport systems for level 1

Base case

Performance level	Deal with γ-world threats	Deal with α-world threats
1	R	R
2	G	R
3	G	R
4	G	G

	Sea control	Territorial defence	Reaction capability	Command control and intelligence
1	R	R	R	R
2	R	R	R	R
3	G	G	G	G
4	G	G	G	G

	Mar cap	Land cap	Surveill cap	Comms	Commd + staff	Training	Base and facilities	Logs
1	R	R	R	R	R	R	R	R
2	R	G	G	R	G	R	G	G
3	G	G	G	G	G	G	G	G
4	G	G	G	G	G	G	G	G

- 10 modern ships for level 1
- 10 second-hand ships for level 2
- 60 mobile field guns for level 1
- 20 long-range, all-weather surveillance aircraft for level 1
- 200 long-range, secure radios for level 1
- 200 long-range simple radios for level 2
- Advanced computer databases for 20 headquarters for level 1
- Additional training for all forces for level 1
- 20 additional well-equipped bases for level 1
- Double stocks and transport systems for level 1

Figure 13.7 Reduced investment by Tethys

The difference between the improved cases in Figures 13.5 and 13.7 might be called the *marginal penalty* of the budget cut. MOA can direct attention to where that penalty is least severe.

A vital caveat

It is important to realise that simplified MOA *is valid only for simple cases such as this*. This example only had one wish list item, or a choice between two *mutually exclusive* items, in each function. That is, in fact, a powerful way to use MOA for broad-brush thinking and it helps to guard against naïve simplifications such as 'we are over-invested in land capabilities'. However, for detailed staff planning, it is common for there to be several *competing* wish list items for each function. In such a case it is necessary to use the full-scale MOA technique, which is described in a separate paper on the website.

> Simplified MOA only deals with the broad outlines, not the details.

Strategic performance and threat assessment

Earlier in this chapter we discussed the idea of the threat profile matrix and, in Table 13.3, we highlighted the TPM for the α- and γ-worlds. That table is reproduced in Table 13.6 to save you searching back. We now need to see how the MOA results relate to the TPM and we will use the base and improved cases of Figure 13.5 to illustrate that.

The base case in the relatively peaceful γ-world is green at level 2 which means, from the definitions in Figure 13.4, that some surveillance can be maintained over most areas and that events can be reacted to within 12–24 hours. Looking at Table 13.6, we might conclude that such a performance would allow Tethys to cope with threats $S_4I_4F_4E_4T_4$. P_4 could probably not be handled as the slow reaction time might mean that the damage had been done before the navy could respond. That is consistent with red at level 1 in the γ-world. The base case for the α-world is only green at level 4, which is consistent with practically nothing being able to be done about the $S_1I_1P_1F_1E_1T_1$ threat pattern.

The improved case in Figure 13.5 shows green at level 1 in the γ-world and green at level 2 in the α-world. Looking again at Table 13.6, that seems to mean that threats at $S_2I_2P_2F_2E_2T_2$ can be handled, which is more than sufficient for the γ-world and nearly good enough for the α-world, which is consistent with red at level 1 in that situation.

This line of thought not only transfers the broad definitions of Figure 13.4 and the colouring in Figure 13.5 into more detailed planning terms, it is also a further sanity check on the MOA analysis.

MOA and improvement programmes

Improvement programmes

In practical planning, in all domains, it is rare for it to be a matter of a single improvement to capability, such as acquiring ships and/or radios or hiring more

Table 13.6 Reproduction of Table 13.3

Smuggling S	Illegal immigration attempts I	Piracy P	Foreign support for secessionists F	Evasion of traffic tolls E	Theft of littoral resources T
S_1 *Volume damaging to national interest, smugglers defiant and combative*	I_1 *Waves of refugees. A major national problem*	P_1 *Inter-island traffic seriously restricted. Major problems for international traffic in Straits of Tuna*	F_1 *Determined and blatant attempts to bring in large volumes of supplies and weapons*	E_1 *Widespread defiance of tolls*	T_1 *Widespread and defiant*
S_2 Large volumes, smugglers armed and dangerous	I_2 Organised and armed gangs seek to bring in large groups	P_2 Sporadic raids on coastal villages/small towns for supplies, plunder and 'recruits'	F_2 Small shipments of supplies and weapons at isolated places	E_2 Most vessels make serious attempts to avoid payment by evasion or fraud	T_2 Widespread but avoiding contact with authorities
S_3 Moderate volumes – non-violent	I_3 Widespread, but unorganised, attempts by family groups	P_3 Occasional attacks on large vessels even when crews are armed	F_3 Occasional infiltration of small teams	E_3 International traffic will pay tolls but only if actively intercepted by coastguard	T_3 Fairly frequent in remoter areas
S_4 Small amount of 'traditional' smuggling	I_4 Small groups of people at secluded spots	P_4 Risky for fishing vessels not working in large groups	F_4 Single individuals moved in or out	E_4 Small vessels evade tolls where possible	T_4 Occasional 'poaching'
		P_5 Occasional attacks on isolated small craft			

surgeons. Far more common and realistic is the need to develop a programme of improvements to be carried out over a period of some years. It is not easy to do that using simplified MOA because each function will usually have several items on its wish list so the function capability improvement will be incremental rather than all at once, as was the case with Tethys.

Improvement programmes can, though, easily be dealt with using the full-scale MOA technique explained in the paper on the website. This is somewhat more specialised so we will merely illustrate the results, so that anyone needing to develop an improvement programme can see what can be achieved. Again, although the example is military, the same ideas would apply to an oil company, *Herrington-Jones*, a hospital, or to any other wish list problem.

An MOA improvement programme case study*

Let us suppose that, during the Cold War, one of the NATO nations contributed a relatively lightly armed infantry force to the common defence plan. It was judged that the force would not be able to make an effective contribution in the event of conflict and the country undertook to upgrade its contribution to an armoured division, fully equipped with heavy tanks and all other necessary equipments. Clearly, such a change will take some years, so an improvement programme is needed and that has to take account of three factors:

- The country's defence budget could only afford about two major new acquisitions in any given year.
- The army could only cope with a limited amount of new equipment at any one time, given the need to train to use it and to integrate it into the force structure.
- Some items in the programme could be acquired quite quickly while other elements might have to be spread over two or more years.

The end result is shown in Table 13.7. The requirements in the middle column are very specific; not just 'heavy trucks' in general but 'X number of heavy trucks, costing Y amount of money', and similarly for all the other line items. Thus, knowing broadly what the acquisition budget is likely to be and what each item costs, one can make an initial estimate of what is affordable at each stage in the programme. Similarly, the judgement was that only two major acquisitions could be managed at any one time.

So, down the centre column are the specific items in the programme, with the left-hand column giving the year in the programme. The implication is that the first two items in year 1 will take two years to acquire so the next *relevant* entry in the left-hand column is year 3, to show which items will start to be acquired at that stage in the programme. There are similar details elsewhere, for instance heavy tanks will take three years to pay for, manufacture, and absorb into the force structure.

The right-hand column refers to three cases, A, B and C, which are the tasks the new division might be called on to undertake – don't worry about what they are. These are the columns in the MOA strategic matrix, though, since we are dealing with a division as a component of an army, it is more correct to call it the 'operational capability matrix' in this case. Whatever the top MOA matrix is called does

---

*This is based on a Master of Defence Administration dissertation and is not an official analysis for any actual country.

Table 13.7 An illustrative improvement programme

Year	Requirement implementation	Operational capability
1	Heavy trucks, Combat engineer vehicles	Case A, Level 4
3	Mobile air defence systems, Heavy tanks	Cases B and C, Level 4
5	Heavy tanks, Advanced radio equipment	Case C, Level 3
6	Reconnaissance vehicles, Light helicopters	Case A, Level 3
7	Reconnaissance vehicles, Transport helicopters	Case B, Level 3
9	Decontamination systems, Attack helicopters	Case C, Level 2
11	Heavy artillery, Sensor systems	Case A, Level 2
13	Mobile bridges, Multi-launch rocket systems	Case B, Level 2

not matter; the main point is that Figure 13.7 shows the progressive capability increases as the improvement programme gradually takes effect.

A key factor is that, once the MOA hierarchy for this problem had been created, developing Table 13.7 took *one afternoon*. Such speed of analysis means that it would be very easy to try numerous different sequences for the improvement programmes, such as the heavy tanks in year 1, in the space of a couple of days.

> MOA allows many alternative improvement programmes to be tested very rapidly.

Of course, the best result from such an exercise does not give *the* definitive improvement programme but it very quickly shows where detailed planning effort should be focused.

MOA has been applied to numerous defence problems but we now turn to non-defence examples.

MOA for a large hospital

Introduction

Figure 13.8 is an *initial* MOA hierarchy for a large hospital and Table 13.8 is the KMC/function interaction matrix. As always, you are challenged to improve it, but a brief explanation may help you to get started, ignoring for now the 'developing nation' column in the strategic matrix.

The basic assumption is that this refers to a large hospital serving an urban and rural community in, say, the UK. Ideally, it should reach level 1 and provide superb care. That is described in one paragraph in Figure 13.8 and it might be helpful in practice to have some supporting documentation, perhaps half a page, to state more precisely what is meant by that. It is always a temptation to have too much detail in the MOA cells but, as with FAR, it is better to err on the side of brevity and back that up with reasonable documentation. The same is true for KMCs and functions.

> Keep the definitions relatively brief, with some supporting documentation.

Overall objective   *Without guaranteeing immortality, cope with the ills of mind and body*

Performance level	For an advanced, Westernised nation	For a developing nation
1	Provide swift, cost-effective, top-quality care for urban and rural populations, in all age groups to maximise life expectancy and minimise infant mortality. Contribute to coping efficiently with a national disaster	???
2	Provide delayed, costly, good-quality care for urban and rural populations, in most age groups, achieve normal life expectancy and infant mortality. Cope efficiently with a local disaster	???
3	Provide delayed, costly, moderate-quality care for urban and rural populations, in most age groups, achieve sub-normal life expectancy and infant mortality. Manage to cope with a major accident	???
4	Treat potentially fatal ailments, long delays for non-urgent cases, alleviate suffering and cope with minor incidents and accidents	???

	General health care	Geriatric care	Paediatric care	Emergency care
1	Waiting list less than 2 months. Success rate for treatment at least 80%	Hospital care for 90% of those needing it. Cures for some ailments. Life expectancy male 75, female 85	90% live births healthy when discharged. Facilities for all illnesses and birth complications. Excellent surgical facilities	Advanced and prompt emergency treatment. 80% survival rates. Urban population 20 minutes from emergency ward. Excellent disaster facilities
2	Waiting list less than 6 months. Success rate for treatment 70%	Hospital care for 50% of those needing it. Cures for few ailments. Life expectancy male 70, female 80	80% live births healthy when discharged. Facilities for some illnesses and birth complications. Some surgical facilities	Good treatment after some delay. 60% survival rates. Area ambulances. Epidemic facilities
3	Waiting list more than 6 months. Success rate for treatment 60%	Only severe cases in hospital. Some help at home. Life expectancy males 65, female 70	70% live births healthy when discharged. Limited facilities for illnesses and birth complications. Emergency birth facilities	Surgery for severe cases. Others to general ward ASAP. Area ambulances for near-death cases. Limited disaster facilities
4	Emergency care only. Success rate 50%	Relief from pain and acute distress	Home births encouraged. No guarantee for sick babies. Very limited surgical facilities	Survival only if no complications. Limited surgery. Regional ambulances. No disaster facilities

	Referrals to hospital	Administration	Surgical procedures	General nursing	Intensive care	Transportation	Specialist nursing
1	Prompt consultation, local tests and swift access to specialist advice, referrals are accurate and timely	Instant access to patient notes, effective management of clinics and beds, all resources used to best effect, internal bureaucracy minimised	Four theatres per hospital with high ratio of surgeons, anaesthetists and nurses, excellent post-operative care, research and training	Excellent standards of hygiene and personal care, 24-hour pharmacy, extensive use of electronic equipment and good access to social/psychiatric services	High ratio of trained and experienced nurses/bed, latest high-tech equipment, two patients per room, 80% success rate	High-tech ambulances readily available for all needs, most crews are para-medics, bus transport for elderly, electric cars within hospital	Staff for wards for cardiac, paediatric, and transplant patients, para-medic nurses for ambulance and casualty, recovery and bereavement aid in all wards
2	Urgent cases seen immediately, some tests available and some access to specialist advice, some referrals unnecessary	Access to notes in 1 day, fairly effective management of clinics and beds, some resources wasted, acceptable bureaucracy	Three theatres per hospital with sufficient staff and good post-operative care, some research and training	Reasonable standards of hygiene and personal care, 24-hour pharmacy, some use of electronic equipment and some contact with social/psychiatric support	Good ratio of trained and experienced nurses/bed, good equipment, four patients per room, 70% success rate	Ambulances for emergency and transfer only, some life-saving equipment and para-medics, buses for elderly, some electric cars in hospital	Staff for wards for surgical and paediatric patients, para-medic nurses for casualty only, recovery and bereavement team in hospital
3	Patients seen within a few days, few simple tests and slow access to specialist advice, many unnecessary referrals	Slow access to notes, poor management of clinics and beds, resources wasted, paperwork a burden to clinical staff	Two theatres per hospital but barely adequate staff and post-operative care. Some testing of new techniques	Adequate standards of hygiene and personal care, 12-hour pharmacy, limited use of electronic equipment, psychiatrist in emergencies	Acceptable ratio of nurses/bed, but not all fully trained, some equipment dated, six patients per room, 60% success rate	Ambulances for emergencies with surplus for transfer, no transport for elderly, ambulance crews can prevent drastic deterioration, porter and wheelchair in hospital	Some surgically trained nurses, most nurses have paediatric training, some para-medic nurses
4	Patients first seen within a week, limited facilities and access to advice, delays in referrals, many patients have deteriorated	Inefficient handling of records, wasteful use of resources, a bureaucratic nightmare	Two theatres per hospital but low ratio of staff, post-operative care on general wards and no use of new techniques	Minimal standards of hygiene and personal care, pharmacy 8 hours/day, traditional equipment, very poor access to social/psychiatric support	Minimal nursing coverage per bed, all equipment dated, ten-bed wards. 50% success rate	Ambulance strictly for emergency only, with basic equipment and limited training. Do-it-yourself for all other needs. Nurse and wheelchair in hospital	Nurses have initial training and can do a little of everything

Figure 13.8 An illustrative MOA hierarchy for a large hospital

Table 13.8 The hospital KMC/Function interactions

The KMCs	The specific functions						
	Refer	Admin	Surg procs	Gen nurse	Intens care	Transp	Spec nurse
Gen health	◆	◆	◆	◆	◆		◆
Paediatrics	◆	◆	◆	◆	◆		◆
Geriatric	◆	◆		◆		◆	
Emergency care	◆	◆	◆	◆	◆	◆	◆

Most of the KMC and function definitions are self-explanatory except, perhaps, 'referrals to hospital'. That presupposes a system in which, except in emergency, one first sees a local doctor (in the UK this is a general practitioner, GP, whose office is called a surgery) who is often able to treat the ailment locally. Tests, such as blood samples, might be done at the surgery or they may have to be sent to the hospital. In some cases, a patient is referred to hospital and the definitions mention 'unnecessary' referrals. These can arise either because the GP's facilities cannot diagnose a case that could otherwise have been treated locally, or because delays in treatment (such as levels 3 and 4 in that function) mean that the patient has deteriorated. Such distinctions would be clarified in the supporting documentation.

As an exercise

You might now try your hand at simplified MOA by assessing where you think your local hospital scores on these definitions and where you think improvements are needed. Where might money be spent to get the greatest effect?

Of course, you might not be happy with the hierarchy. How would you change it? How might it be modified to allow for the role of small, or 'cottage', hospitals in the area's small towns? How would it apply to a developing nation? Would the strategic objective be appropriate in such a case? Would the KMC and function definitions still apply to that instance?

However you choose to refine Figure 13.8, one aspect will be to develop a wish list and that is the topic to which we now turn.

Conceptual planning frameworks

Introduction

The wish list for Tethys was developed by normal military staff work and that is usually how wish lists emerge in all domains. How, though, do we know that the wish list is the correct one? There is always a risk that the list has been affected by 'technology push' or, forgive the pun, wishful thinking.

The conceptual planning framework (CPF) offers a rational approach to drawing up justifiable wish lists, thereby avoiding both of those problems.

An illustrative conceptual planning framework

Table 13.9 is part of the CPF for the large hospital. It shows only some of the functions and only part of the analysis for each of those functions.

The first column in the table is a basic requirement in the function, such as being able to get access to a GP and the doctor's ability to identify when a patient does, and does not, need to be referred to hospital. Similarly, it is a fundamental

Table 13.9 A fragment from a conceptual planning framework

Functional requirement	Deficiency (if any)	Wish-list line item
Diagnosis		
Access to GPs	GPs overloaded in inner cities	Better conditions for inner-city GPs to attract more doctors. Encourage more responsible behaviour by patients. Etc.
GP ability to identify need for admission	**NONE**	(ensure GPs maintain continuing education)
Etc.		
Administration		
Catering in wards	On 1 out of 10 days there is only sufficient food for 90% of patients	Closer monitoring of patient numbers.
Monitoring of patients	10% readmitted within 2 months	Better quality tests before discharge.
Surgical procedures		
Surgical capabilities	Difficult to deal with X, Y and Z types of case	More research but closely directed at those types.
Theatre maintenance	**NONE**	(but ensure standards do not slip)
General nursing		
Drug dispensing	**NONE**	(but keep up standards)
Contact with Social Services	Social Services not always aware of deliberate injuries	More meetings to discuss cases **Some better system??**

requirement to be able to feed patients in hospital, maintain operating theatres (operating rooms in the USA), dispense drugs to patients and so on.

The second column is the assessment of any deficiencies in satisfying the functional requirement. In this example, it is assessed that inner-city GPs are overloaded. However, they are still able correctly to identify the need for hospital admission so there is no deficiency in that aspect.

The final column contains the candidates for the wish list: the items that *might* overcome the given deficiency. In the first row, methods to recruit more GPs are an obvious, but expensive, possible solution. Unhappily, a minority of inner-city patients make matters worse by behaving badly, such as by not turning up for appointments, being abusive, arriving drunk and so on. Perhaps solving that issue would improve the situation relatively inexpensively. There may, though, be other solutions, suggested by the etcetera. What do you think those might be?

The real work of the CPF takes place in this column in that thought must be given to the ways of solving the problem. The Delphi style of debate might be used; in some cases all or part of the **ACTIFELD** process (TOWS, perhaps) might be used. The aim is to arrive at the most satisfactory method, or balance of methods, for removing the deficiency and the end result will be a good candidate for the wish list, not something dreamt up or obvious. For example, the obvious solution of more meetings to discuss cases appears at the foot of the table, though it is well known that meetings can be an excellent way of wasting the time of a lot of people. Who should attend those meetings? How should they be organised? Is there some better way of eliminating that deficiency?

The whole point of the CPF is to find the 'best' solution, because that should be the real wish list item, not the obvious things. Develop the wish list for your local hospital.

> The purpose of the planning framework is to find the ideal wish list items, not to 'prove' that the obvious solution is the best thing to do.

Even where there is no deficiency as such, a management action might arise, such as ensuring that GPs maintain their continuing education and that the standards for dispensing drugs do not slip.

Note the *very* wide range of items that has emerged, even in this simple illustration, including:

- *more* inner-city doctors
- *research* closely aimed at specific targets, enabling us to solve identified surgical problems
- improved *management practices.*

The CPF picks out the variety of things that are needed in the wish list.

However, with eight functions to consider, and some MOA problems have more than eight, the CPF table might become quite long, very diverse, and might call for some effort to develop. That is, paradoxically, one of the virtues of the CPF in that it ensures that nothing has been overlooked. It also ensures that where there is no deficiency there is no line item for the wish list. In short, the important consequence is that the wish list *is exactly as long as it needs to be, and no longer.* The significance of that in the practical world is hard to overstate. It might, for example, make it easier to spend wisely the resources made available by the government or by private finance.

Who makes the assessments of deficiency? Usually, the deficiencies are fairly obvious and are detected by the expert knowledge and experience of the people concerned. They might also arise from complaints by customers and patients, through military exercises and from any other useful source. They must, though, be identified objectively and dispassionately, not as a result of special pleading or the pulling of rank.

Business applications of MOA

Introduction

MOA has been widely used for military problems, which is not surprising since it was invented to deal with a particular issue in that domain. Its use in business and other problem areas has been less widespread. There is no reason for that since, as the hospital example has shown, the technique is perfectly easily used in non-military areas. In this section we will, therefore, mention a particularly interesting business application, suggest how MOA might be applied to *Herrington-Jones* and challenge you to complete that exercise.

The 'millennium bug'

During 1999, practically the whole world was worried that the so-called 'millennium bug' might inflict great commercial and social damage if computers failed to recognise the change to the year 2000. Huge amounts of money and effort were devoted to checking and replacing software and hardware and, in the event, the transition at midnight on 31 December 1999 was trouble free. However, during 1999 no one knew that such would be the case and plans had to be made to cope with the impending problem. How could a given business be sure that its plans were good?

MOA was used to help an international business to assess its millennium bug strategy. Let us be clear, though, about exactly what was at issue. The firm had a legal duty of care to its suppliers and customers to show that it had done its best to avoid the bug problem and not only might the law vary from one country to another in which it operated, different categories of customers might have different needs. The question, then, was not whether the millennium bug plans would actually solve the problem; no one could assess that as no one knew what the problem really was or might be. The real issue for the company was to be able to show that it was satisfying its duty of care, and that meant that it had to show that its bug plans measured up to best practice, and satisfied any guidance issued by advisory authorities in the various countries. Where no guidance had been issued in a country, authoritative guidance from other countries was used.

The end result of the MOA assessment was that the company's plans were excellent in some areas, though not all, but the necessary adjustments could be made in the time available.

| MOA and *Herrington-Jones and Co* | CASE STUDY |

We have used *Herrington-Jones* as a running case to show the **ACTIFELD** steps as they emerged in earlier chapters. Recall, though, that *Herrington-Jones* aims to be the leading grocery retailer in Europe by the year 2010. That will take time and might involve many actions, and that is similar to the improvement programme in Table 13.7, p. 255. Perhaps MOA might shed more light on that and thereby complement, or verify, the action plan for *Herrington-Jones* that emerged at the end of Chapter 7.

How might that be done? We shall pose some questions and suggest possibilities, but you will only really grasp MOA by working out the details for yourself, using Figures 13.4 and 13.7, together with Tables 13.5 and 13.8, as guidance only. You should aim to get to the stage where you can apply simplified MOA to get a broad improvement programme.

The *Herrington-Jones* strategic matrix

The strategic matrix has to represent distinctly different circumstances which *Herrington-Jones* might have to cope with. We already have three scenarios for *Herrington-Jones*, developed using simplified FAR in Chapter 3, giving a strategic matrix of three columns. Define four performance bands for each of those cases. It doesn't matter if you make assumptions – the aim is to learn about MOA – and, in any case, there is much information available on company websites.

The *Herrington-Jones* KMCs

Earlier in the chapter we suggested that Service existing customers, Develop new customers, and Internal management might be suitable KMCs. What do you think might be suitable? Bear in mind that a KMC is a key capability area, deficiency in which will undermine the ability to achieve strategic performance. Do not confuse that with the detail of specific tasks and skills – that is the role of the functions. Do not have too many KMCs – five or six is about the sensible maximum.

The *Herrington-Jones* functions

What might these be? A good guide is to remember that, as far as an MBA is concerned, this book is intended to be a complement to the core strategy course. The standard strategy texts usually deal with the key business competences, and other MBA modules will have dealt with operations management, human resources, purchasing, distribution, marketing and so forth. Even if you are not doing an MBA, and this book is also intended for use on degrees in operational research, management science, decision sciences and the like, a little reading and a dose of common sense will take you a long way in developing a good hierarchy.

Chapter summary

This has necessarily been a long chapter as MOA is a subtle technique calling for explanation of its theoretical background and illustration from several points of view. The military case was discussed at length, partly because that is where MOA originated but also because that is an important application area for these tools of practical strategy.

What, though, are the keys to success in MOA?

Think at high level, don't get into the fine detail.

The *first* is that MOA is not intended to be a magic wand for the full solution of a wish list problem. Those problems are too complex to be handled by any one technique, so MOA is designed to indicate where the leverage points in the problem are so that more detailed analysis can be done, or staff attention directed. That is necessarily a high-level task and calls for an overall view of the problem, via the hierarchy, so keep that high-level viewpoint and don't get into too much detail by having, say, too many functions.

Take time to get the hierarchy right.

The *second* is that the formulation of the hierarchy is the key first step, without which nothing else can happen. It is *very* unlikely that the first hierarchy will be satisfying and acceptable so it is necessary to take time to revise and adapt it as necessary.

Always check the hierarchy for acceptability and validity.

Thirdly, don't forget to check the hierarchy in the KMC/Function interaction table. That is actually an important part of MOA. It gives a gestalt appreciation of how the KMCs and functions play against each other and where knock-on effects might occur, such as the large improvement in the α-world strategic performance shown in Figure 13.5.

Educate the client to know what MOA is about.

The *fourth* point is that MOA is usually very attractive to potential users who will be enthusiastic about getting involved. That's fine, as long as the client staff know what they are about. It is vital to educate the client staff, perhaps by the study of examples, and lead them gently into this subtle and powerful technique. Don't overemphasise the wish list aspect at first, but concentrate on how the hierarchy gives a high-level view of the whole problem, showing where all the parts fit together.

Don't let the hierarchy get too big.

Finally, don't let the hierarchy get out of hand and become too detailed. In special cases, I have seen some large hierarchies but, as a rules of thumb:

■ Have not more than about four distinctly different circumstances in the strategic matrix.

■ Don't have more than five or six KMCs, but why five or six? A KMC is what it says: a key component of strategic performance, and you are aiming at a truly high-level view. It is not likely that there are more than six really critical aspects of a problem and four might be nearer the mark in many cases.

■ Functions are the danger area as it is easy to get sucked into too much detail. The hierarchy for Tethys has eight functions and that should usually be about sufficient.

The best way to learn MOA is to do it, using the examples of Tethys, the hospital and the indications for **Herrington-Jones** as guides. Try it for a problem that interests you, or have a go at the Murray/Darling River Basin case after you have read Chapter 14.

References

Coyle, R. G. (1989), A mission-orientated approach to defense planning. *Defense Planning*, 5(4), 353–67.

Grant, R. M. (2002), *Contemporary Strategy Analysis*. Blackwell Publishers, Oxford.

Johnson, G., Scholes, K. (2002), *Exploring Corporate Strategy*. Financial Times Prentice Hall, Harlow, Essex.

Miller, D. (1998), *The Cold War: A Military History*. John Murray, London.

14 Two case studies in practical strategy

What this chapter is about

- The chapter has two case studies to show the flow of the **ACTIFELD** process.

- That will make you confident with its tools and techniques.

- The cases do not show how **ACTIFELD** *must* be used – they are only examples!

- They are not complete, so you will have to do some of the work yourselves.

- The two cases are very different:

  – The Murray/Darling River Basin case embraces ecology, agri-business and government.

  – The case of Littleworth and Thrupp combines a business problem and stakeholder aspirations.

- Having seen how **ACTIFELD** worked for these problems, you can tackle the suggested topics in Chapter 8.

- Always bend the tool to suit the problem and not the problem to fit the tool.

- You can also read this chapter, after Chapter 1, as a precursor to the book, as suggested in the Preface.

Introduction

The case studies in this chapter show the application of the **ACTIFELD** tools for practical strategy to two very different problems. The case of the Murray/Darling River Basin (MDB) deals with a wide-ranging social, economic, agricultural and ecological problem with a time span of 20 years. As mentioned in the Preface, its use of the tools is summarised to give you a preview of them as a precursor to the book. The case of Littleworth and Thrupp is an urgent business problem, with powerful stakeholder interests. Other case studies are on the companion website.

The cases are intended to help you to grasp the style of the approach, but not to be definitive in the sense that they show how the tools *must* be applied. In fact, you will find that the tools are not always used consistently, and that is an important point. The reason is that there is no such thing as a *standard* strategic problem and the tools have to be adapted to the case and used as its nature demands. In addition, none of the analyses is really complete and that is deliberate to give you the chance to use the cases as exercises and to alter and refine some of the work. That will be useful practice and you should feel free to invent facts and data. Indeed, in one of the cases, there are question marks in some of the matrices, which are there to force you to add information and make your own deductions.

The cases have been placed here, rather than immediately after the completion of the coverage of the **ACTIFELD** process, to encourage you to consider using some of the more specialised tools, especially in the Murray/Darling River Basin case.

I gratefully acknowledge the help of numerous students from the Universities of Oxford, Bath, New South Wales and Queens (Ontario) who have helped to develop some of this material by taking part in the one-week practical strategy course mentioned in Chapter 15 and discussed in detail on the instructor's website.

The Murray/Darling River Basin*   CASE STUDY

Introduction

Figure 14.1 shows the drainage basin of the Murray and Darling Rivers (the MDB for short) and their many tributaries, in the south eastern 'corner' of Australia. The basin covers some 1 million square kilometres, which is about 14% of Australia, and about the same size as Germany, France and the UK, or Texas and Arizona, combined. The basin extends over parts of the States of Queensland, New South Wales, Victoria and South Australia. All of the Australian Capital Territory lies within the basin. It is home to some 2 million people, 11% of the national total, its irrigated area is 70% of Australia's total and it produces about 41% of the national agricultural output from both grazing and crops. The Basin is also home to substantial manufacturing industries and has considerable leisure use.

In short, the basin is of very great economic importance to Australia in many ways, but it is also of great environmental value. It has many wetlands, some recognised as being of international significance, which maintain the health of the rivers and, as it has only one exit to the sea, it is an unusually complex biophysical system. Over the past 100 years major water storage systems have made it possible to manage the water supply during wet and dry periods.

Unhappily, all is not well in the MDB. The developments that made it so productive and important have also damaged the biophysical environment. The storage systems and the extraction of water for irrigation have reduced the seasonal variability in river flow (which is, of course, what the storage systems were

---

*The factual information in this case study is derived from the Murray/Darling River Basin Commission's Web site at www.mdbc.gov.au.

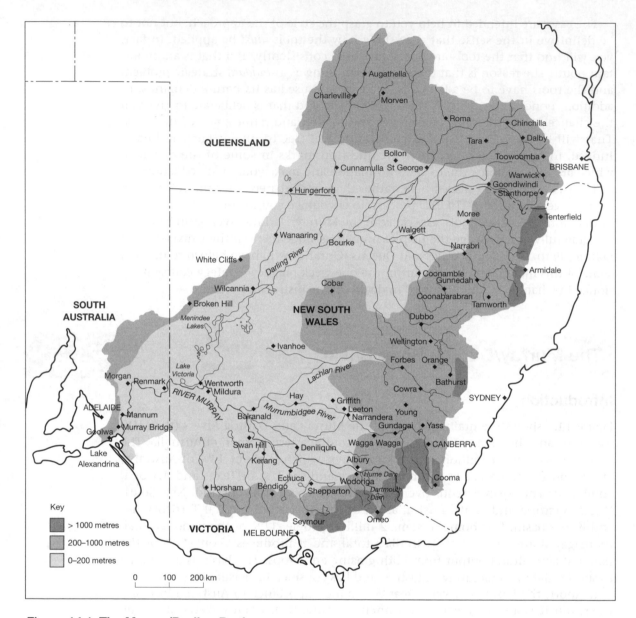

Figure 14.1 The Murray/Darling Basin

Source: MDBC (www.mdbc.gov.au)

supposed to do) but they have also affected the ecology of the region (which is not what was intended). Clearance of native vegetation has altered the rainwater leakage systems, hence raising groundwater levels, causing serious salinity problems, and reducing the habitat for native plant and animal species. These problems are of great concern as there are fears that the rivers might effectively be dead within about 20 years.

The Murray/Darling Basin Commission has the unenviable task of trying to reconcile the tensions between economic and environmental demands and the competition between different economic interests such as crop-growing, animal grazing and tourism. It has to work with four State governments and with many community and voluntary groups.

We will now take this problem through the **ACTIFELD** methodology, challenging you at every step to check and, where you think it appropriate, to revise and improve the analysis. For instance, it might be illuminating to develop a time line for this issue history, and to 'place' the MDB Commission, using Neustadt and May's mini-methods, Chapter 11. There are numerous websites for the MDB, as well as *The Australian* newspaper.

The MDB strategic question

The question for the MDB might be, 'Can the MDB be regenerated to a sustainable state within the next 20 years?' Applying the standard test for a question, that can be parsed as: *Why*, by implication, the MDB is, or is becoming, unsustainable; *When*, within 20 years; *What*, to regenerate to a sustainable state; *How*, by developing an action plan to achieve sustainability. Of course, it might turn out that no such plan can be developed, the problem might be just too difficult, and that might cause the question to be redefined as 'Take swift action to prevent further deterioration', which parses as: *Why*, the condition of the MDB is getting worse; *When*, as soon as possible; *What*, prevent things getting worse; *How*, a rescue plan. It is obvious that a rescue plan would not be the same as one for regeneration.

We will now summarise the practical strategy steps for the MDB problem, using a number of tables and diagrams with some connecting text. The text should give you the thread of the argument and lead to each successive stage in the **ACTIFELD** process but you will need to study the tables and diagrams quite closely to see the structure underlying the analysis. Unfortunately, the page layout means that a diagram may appear a few pages after its descriptive text.

Unravelling complexity

Even the very brief summary of the MDB's problems given above makes it clear that the complexity of the biophysical system, and the possibly conflicting interests of the numerous stakeholders, involve many factors and we have to try to make sense of them before we can go further. Figure 14.2 is a mind map, which you will need to study in the light of the discussion of the MDB, above, perhaps checking further with appropriate websites, and reviewing the explanation of mind maps in Chapter 2. You may, of course, want to revise the diagram to reflect your own thoughts.

You might also try redrawing it as an impact wheel or Why diagram (Chapter 2). If time allows in a practical strategy exercise, it is always worth while to unravel complexity using at least two techniques. In a syndicate of four people it might be useful for two of them to work together using one sense-making device, while the other two do it another way, finally redrawing a diagram of one type or another to get the best of both efforts.

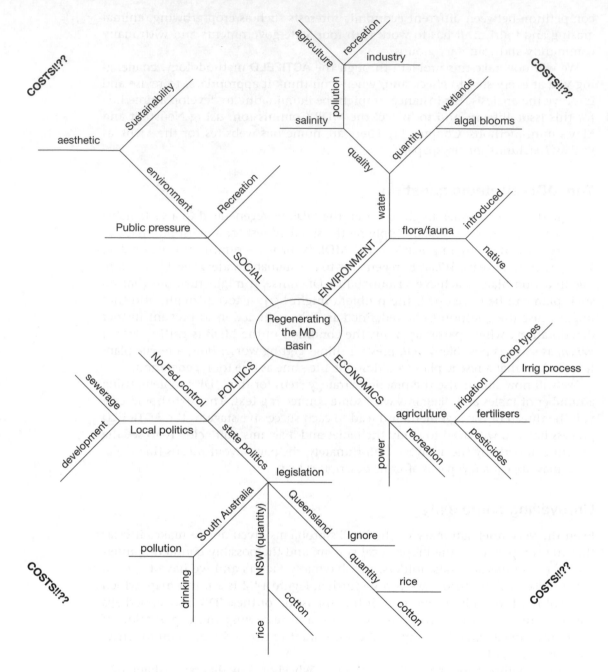

Figure 14.2 Mind map for the Murray/Darling Basin

Scenarios for the MDB

Armed with the insights from the mind map, the MDB study group formulated the FAR sector/factor array shown in Table 14.1 (p.266). This uses the acronym THECARP which is memorable, pronounceable and meaningless, though with suitably fishy overtones for a river basin problem.

Table 14.1 A FAR sector/factor array for the Murray/Darling Basin

The influence of the environmental movement T	StakeHolder cooperation H	Long-term Economic potential E	Condition of the river C	Agricultural impact on the river A	Recreational usage R	Palliative measures P
T_1 Strong at all levels	H_1 All parties agree	E_1 Flourishing growth	C_1 Pristine	A_1 No usage, no pollution	R_1 Unrestricted	P_1 Effective and vigorously applied
T_2 Heard at most levels	H_2 Majority cooperate	E_2 Steady growth	C_2 Sustainable	A_2 Sustainable pollution and usage	R_2 Low regulation	P_2 Applied without drive
T_3 Heard in some areas	H_3 Half the parties agree	E_3 No growth	C_3 Borderline	A_3 Mild pollution, restricted usage	R_3 Moderate regulation	P_3 Partially effective
T_4 Heard in one area	H_4 Less than half cooperate	E_4 Negative growth	C_4 Poor	A_4 Moderate pollution and usage	R_4 Highly regulated	P_4 Would be effective if applied
T_5 Not heard at all	H_5 No cooperation	E_5 Collapse	C_5 Unusable	A_5 Heavy pollution and usage	R_5 Banned	P_5 No effort applied
						P_6 Makes it worse

Using simplified FAR, that produced the 10 feasible configurations shown as time lines in Figure 14.3, in which solid lines are transitions about which the team felt confident and dotted lines others which seemed to them to be less likely, though not impossible. The time lines have been spread across the page from 'bad' to 'good', with only one end state being truly satisfactory.

TOWS analysis for the MDB

The first step in the TOWS analysis is shown in Table 14.2 (p. 268). As we have frequently mentioned, *all* the techniques in this book need to be used flexibly and there is no standard method. It seems strange to say that in a textbook which is supposed to explain *the* answers, but it is just the nature of practical strategy; there are no 'standard' problems and hence there cannot be 'standard' approaches.

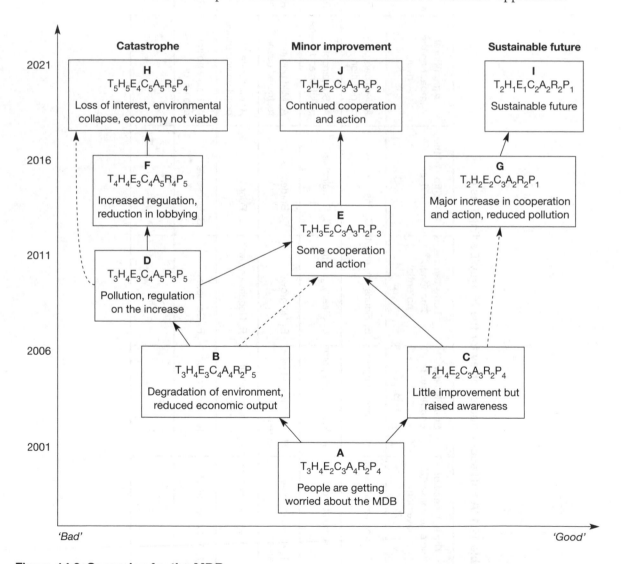

Figure 14.3 Scenarios for the MDB

Table 14.2 First step in TOWS analysis for the MDB

Threats	Opportunities
T_1 Conflicting interests (e.g. political conflict)	O_1 Local action groups/volunteers
T_2 Recreational activity	O_2 Popular opinion
T_3 Irreversible degradation	O_3 Good state of the economy
T_4 Reluctance to fund	O_4 Tourism/recreation
T_5 Complacency	O_5 Less dependence on resource-intensive
T_6 Reduction in water quality	industry
T_7 Reduction in water quantity	O_6 Availability of international research
T_8 Increased land clearance and degradation	O_7 Potential for new industries
T_9 Introduced flora and fauna	O_8 Alternatives to hydro power
T_{10} Increased population	O_9 Coordinated government effort
T_{11} Unintended consequences of remedial	
measures	
Weaknesses	**Strengths**
W_1 Lack of consensus	S_1 Visibility of consequences
W_2 Conflict of interests	S_2 Number of interest groups
W_3 Number of interest groups	S_3 Increased environmental concern
W_4 Regulatory conflicts/inconsistencies	S_4 Health concerns
W_5 Limited water volume available	S_5 Memory of prior condition
W_6 Limited funds for research and development	S_6 Existing research base
W_7 Insufficient implementation of	S_7 Improved agricultural practices
remedial measures	S_8 New low water-use practices
W_8 Extent/size of the problem, required	S_9 Wetland development
financial resources	S_{10} Landcare and other initiatives
	S_{11} Conflicting urban/rural views

In Table 14.2, the threats and weaknesses cells derive from thought about the MDB and, especially, the mind map (and perhaps the issue history) as these are the factors which, if unchecked, will drive the system in an unfavourable direction. The opportunities and strengths are aspects identified as having prospects for reversing the decline, if only they can be marshalled effectively. Recall from Chapter 4 that this way of using TOWS gets round the arguments about whether X is a weakness or a threat as all factors will be considered in the second stage of TOWS, shown for the MDB in Table 14.3 (p.272).

Table 14.2 needs a few words of explanation. T_1 means the conflicts of interest between States within Australia whereas W_2 refers to conflicts between, say, graziers and crop farmers on the one hand and environmental campaigners on the other. W_3 and S_2 are an example of 'common elements' in TOWS analysis – a particular item is both a weakness and a strength. S_2 indicates the strength of concern; W_3 suggests the possibility of confusion. You should, as a means of improving your skills, now create your own TOWS table for this problem.

Table 14.3 takes the analysis forward by using the factors in the TOWS to deduce actions and Table 14.4 (p.272) is the important step of grouping the actions into strategic areas of emphasis, of which there are four in this case. Note that action 12 appears twice and it is perfectly legitimate for actions to appear as often as necessary. As we saw in Chapter 4, tables such as this are of great value, simple though they seem.

Table 14.3 Actions identified from MDB TOWS analysis

	Threats	Opportunities
Weaknesses	1. Develop procedures to plan on long-term basis (W_2,W_4,T_1,O_9) 2. Increase public awareness ($W_1,W_2,W_3,W_5,T_1,T_2,T_5,S_1,S_2,S_3,S_{11}$) 3. Encourage community involvement ($O_1,O_2,O_4,T_1,T_3,S_1,S_2,S_3,S_4,W_2,W_3$) 4. Encourage private investment in sustainable industries (O_5,O_7,W_5,W_6,S_3,T_4)	8. Fund/support sound environmental practices and research ($O_3,W_6,W_7,W_8,S_7,S_8,S_9,S_{10},T_6,T_7,T_8,T_9$) 9. Promote new industries using international research to reduce water usage and improve quality ($O_6,O_7,T_6,T_7,T_8,T_9,W_5$)
Strengths	5. Capitalise on existing research base by increased support/funding for its application ($W_6,S_6,S_7,O_7,T_4,T_6,T_7,W_5$) 6. Encourage alternative energy sources ($O_6,O_7,O_8,W_5,S_3,S_4,S_9$) 7. Foster new practices to counteract immediate problems ($S_7,S_8,S_9,S_{10},T_2,T_3,T_6,T_7$)	10. Use improved agricultural practices and international research to improve quality of the river (O_6,O_7,T_6,S_6,S_7,S_8) 11. Enable interaction between interest groups to reduce conflicts of interests ($O_1,O_9,S_2,S_{11},W_1,W_2,W_3,W_4$) 12. Promote eco-tourism to increase awareness and provide revenue for research (S_3,T_5,O_4,W_6)

Table 14.4 MDB strategic areas and related actions

Grouped actions	Broad area or strategy
2. Increase public awareness 3. Encourage community involvement 12. Promote eco-tourism to increase awareness and provide revenue for research	**A** Promote awareness
5. Capitalise on existing research by increased support/funding for its application 8. Fund/support sound environmental practices and research 10. Use improved agricultural practices and international research to reduce water usage and improve quality	**B** Promote research and capitalise on knowledge
1. Develop procedures to plan on long-term basis 7. Foster new practices to counteract immediate problems 11. Enable interaction between interest groups to reduce conflicts of interests	**C** Increase coordination of funding, support and planning
4. Encourage private investment in sustainable industries 6. Encourage alternative energy sources 9. Promote new industries using international research to reduce water usage and improve quality 12. Promote eco-tourism to increase awareness and provide revenue for research	**D** Promote new industries

They tell us several things:

- First, it shows that, for this problem, there are *four* specific areas, as opposed to any other number. To regenerate the MDB, all four will have to be attended to, and simply doing one, D for instance, might be a waste of effort if D is not balanced and supported by the others. Identifying the correct number of strategic areas is usually of great value in itself.

- Second, it demonstrates that area D, say, requires four specific actions, while each of the other areas also has its own collection of actions. The implication is that doing only action 6, say, will not be sufficient to achieve D; all four must be done. If one or more is omitted, those which are implemented may prove to be a waste of money and effort as D will be incomplete.

- Finally, and most importantly, the table can be read from right to left. This shows that area B, for example, involves actions 5, 8 and 10. In terms of implementation, the actions for B can be mapped onto State (or Federal) departments of scientific research, finance and agriculture, and similarly for the other areas.

In short, TOWS, even though it involves only organised intelligence and not advanced mathematics, has now told us what needs to be done, and who needs to do those things, in order to make progress with the MDB. Unhappily, because there are 12 distinct actions ranging across a multiplicity of agencies, it also suggests the scale of the MDB problem.

Viable policy for the MDB

Basic ideas

The next stage in **ACTIFELD** is to design a feasible organisation to implement the output from the TOWS analysis. In Chapter 5 we discussed the idea of a viable firm matrix but, in this instance, it will obviously be a viable policy matrix, the first step in which is shown in Table 14.5 (p. 274).

Before studying that, it will be useful to remind ourselves that although a VFM looks rather like a FAR sector/factor array and, indeed, the author developed the idea for the VFM from the sector/factor concept of providing 'filing space' for all possibilities, the VFM is subtly and powerfully different from a FAR array. In FAR, the idea is to eliminate impossibilities and then to develop time lines from what is left. In a VFM, on the other hand, impossibilities rule out certain options for a firm, as we saw in Chapter 5, but the impossibilities are also combinations that cannot achieve corporate objectives. For example, in Chapter 5 we studied a VFM for consultancy firms and saw that five people in one office cannot be BigLeague, but they could still be a perfectly viable consultancy. If, however, those five people aspired to be on a par with BigLeague, there were gaps to be filled and changes to be made. The VFM is a tool for designing organisational capabilities, not a forecasting technique.

Developing the VPM for the MDB case study

How, though, do we make the transition from TOWS to a suitable VPM?

There is no simple answer as, in essence, the step is one of imagination and insight, though supported by the framework of tools for practical strategy. That

Table 14.5 A viable policy matrix for the MDB problem

Human resources H	Incentives I	Development, research and applications D	Financial resources F	Regulation R	Awareness A	Coordination and planning C
H_1 Large number of trained experts, volunteers, administrators etc.	I_1 Wide range of incentives	D_1 Dedicated R&D effort effectively applied	F_1 Fully funded by government and private enterprise	R_1 Absolute power to regulate relevant activities	A_1 Intensive educational and media-based campaign	C_1 Effective plan with high level of consensus
H_2 Sufficient number of trained experts, volunteers, administrators etc.	I_2 Consciously chosen but limited number (>4) of incentives	D_2 Dedicated and shared R&D, adequately applied	F_2 Fully funded by government	R_2 Sufficient power to regulate	A_2 Educational and media-based campaign	C_2 Effective plan with medium level of consensus
H_3 Barely adequate number of trained experts, volunteers, administrators etc.	I_3 2 to 4 incentives	D_3 Shared R&D adequately applied	F_3 Partially funded	R_3 Strong influence with regulators	A_3 Educational and print media campaign	C_3 Adequate plan with medium level of consensus
H_4 Not enough trained experts, volunteers, administrators etc.	I_4 1 or 2 incentives	D_4 R&D inadequately applied	F_4 No funds	R_4 Mixture of regulation and persuasion	A_4 Print media campaign only	C_4 Inadequate plan with little consensus
	I_5 No incentives	D_5 Piecemeal, unfocused. Dedicated R&D and application		R_5 Laissez-faire	A_5 No campaign	

was the case with TOWS; there were no formulae for identifying the TOWS themselves, for deducing actions from them, and for grouping actions into strategic areas, but the steps flow naturally from asking intelligent people to, as it were, fill in a blank form. The same is true for the VPM, but the toolkit stimulates the imagination. In this case study, thinking about Table 14.3 suggests ideas such as the importance of volunteers and human resources, and providing incentives to stimulate new industries. Note that the word 'incentive' does not appear in Table 14.3, but it is an obvious means of bringing in new business. Think through the other sectors in the VPM for yourself.

With those notions, study Table 14.5, a VPM to give 'filing space' for all conceivable possibilities for the MDB, based on the acronym HIDFRAC. It is very obvious that a Murray/Darling Basin with policies such as $H_4I_5D_5F_4R_5A_5C_4$ is a recipe for disaster and is manifestly *not* going to solve the MDB's problems. Note that Table 14.5 does not apply to all river basins; the Amazon and the Thames probably have quite different strategic questions.

Analysis with the MDB VPM

The VPM now moves towards analysis of the gaps between existing and desired policy structures.

The existing case is $H_2I_3D_4F_3R_4A_{2/3}C_4$. As with FAR, factors can be combined as in $A_{2/3}$, in this case meaning that Awareness is somewhere between being fully media-based and only print-based.

It is then a matter of further rigorous thought to see that the actions that emerged from the TOWS analysis require a different policy set-up. This is shown in Table 14.6 (p. 276) in which the existing case of $H_2I_3D_4F_3R_4A_{2/3}C_4$ is shown in bold while the required case of $H_2I_1D_2F_1R_2A_1C_1$ is in bold italics.

There are two points to notice:

- The first is that perfection is judged not to be required; there is no need to go as far as $H_1I_1D_1F_1R_1A_1C_1$. That is somewhat of a relief as the move from $H_2I_3D_4F_3R_4A_{2/3}C_4$ to $H_2I_1D_2F_1R_2A_1C_1$ could well be hard enough to achieve without adding further demands.

- This VPM is a little unusual in that the human resources dimension must not be allowed to slip below H_2. That might lead one to neglect that aspect but, as we shall see, it will require consideration in the next stage, resource analysis.

Resource analysis for the MDB

In Chapter 6 we studied the ideas of the congruence of strategy with the objectives of stakeholders and of resources needed to make improvements. In this case study, we shall omit the congruence analysis, leaving you to do that as an exercise. Who might the significant stakeholders be? In some cases, the mid-line of a river is also a boundary between Australian States; each 'owns' half the river.

The resource analysis matrix is shown in Table 14.7 (p. 277). It breaks each of the HIDFRAC sectors into subcomponents and uses the simplest ranking system of a scale from 1 to 4, with 1 meaning a virtually non-existent capability and 4 denoting an excellent capability. As we explained in Chapter 6, these rankings do

Table 14.6 Viable policy matrix with MDB's current (bold) and required (*bold italic*) situations

Note: H_2 is current state and must not be allowed to deteriorate

Human resources H	Incentives I	Development, research and applications D	Financial resources F	Regulation R	Awareness A	Coordination and planning C
H_1 Large number of trained experts, volunteers, administrators etc	I_1 *Wide range of incentives*	D_1 Dedicated R&D effort effectively applied	F_1 *Fully funded by government and private enterprise*	R_1 Absolute power to regulate relevant activities	A_1 *Intensive educational and media-based campaign*	C_1 *Effective plan with high level of consensus*
H_2 Sufficient number of trained experts, volunteers, administrators etc.	I_2 Consciously chosen but limited number (>4) of incentives	D_2 *Dedicated and shared R&D, adequately applied*	F_2 Fully funded by government	R_2 *Sufficient power to regulate*	A_2 Educational and media-based campaign	C_2 Effective plan with medium level of consensus
H_3 Barely adequate number of trained experts, volunteers, administrators etc.	I_3 2 to 4 incentives	D_3 Shared R&D adequately applied	F_3 *Partially funded*	R_3 Strong influence with regulators	A_3 Educational and print media campaign	C_3 Adequate plan with medium level of consensus
H_4 Not enough trained experts, volunteers, administrators etc.	I_4 1 or 2 incentives	**D_4 R&D inadequately applied**	F_4 No funds	**R_4 Mixture of regulation and persuasion**	A_4 Print media campaign only	**C_4 Inadequate plan with little consensus**
	I_5 No incentives	D_5 Piecemeal, unfocused. Dedicated R&D and application		R_5 Laissez-faire	A_5 No campaign	

Note: H_2 is current state and must not be allowed to deteriorate

Table 14.7 Resource analysis for the MDB

Aspect	From	To	Gap
Human resources	H_2 **Sufficient number of trained experts, volunteers, administrators etc.**	H_2 **Sufficient number of trained experts, volunteers, administrators etc.**	
Training	3	3	0
Recruitment	3	3	0
Incentives	3	4	1
Specific skills	3	4	1
Incentives	I_0 **2 to 4 incentives**	I_1 **Wide range of incentives**	
Adequate funding	2	4	2
Free access to relevant organisations	2	4	2
Access to expert advice	3	3	0
Appropriate tax legislation	1	4	3
R and A application	D_4 **R&D inadequately applied**	D_2 **Dedicated and shared R&D, adequately applied**	
Adequate funding	2	3	1
Skilled scientists	3	3	0
Infrastructure	1	3	2
Commercial sponsors	1	3	2
Financial resources	F_3 **Partially funded**	F_1 **Fully funded by government and private enterprise**	
Access to all levels of government	1	4	3
Funding	1	4	3
Access to private organisations	1	3	2
Regulation	R_4 **Mixture of regulation and persuasion**	R_2 **Sufficient power to regulate**	
Access to relevant government levels	1	3	2
Strength of regulatory base	1	3	2
'Deputy sheriff' to enforce	1	3	2
Awareness (PR)	A_2 **Educational and media-based campaign.** A_3 **Educational and print media campaign**	A_1 **Intensive educational and media-based campaign**	
PR skills, access to media	2	4	2
Ability to galvanise volunteers	2	4	2
Encourage eco-journalism	1	3	2
Encourage environmental education	1	3	2
Commercial sponsors	1	3	2

▶

Table 14.7 Continued

Aspect	From	To	Gap
Coordination/planning	C_4 **Inadequate plan with little consensus**	C_1 *Effective plan with high level of consensus*	
Involvement of unions	1	3	2
Involvement of agricultural organisations etc.	2	4	2
Highly skilled planning team	1	4	3
Detailed, well-coordinated plan	1	4	3
Involvement of all levels of government	2	4	2
Net effect of gaps			50

not have precise meanings but do give a feel for where particular improvements are needed and roughly how much needs to be done in each case. The total gap of 50 'points' is not mathematically exact in any way but it suggests that the overall problem is pretty extensive. You might reassess the gaps using one of the other scaling systems described in Chapter 6.

In some cases, no improvements are called for. In R and A, the scientists are already in the high class required. On the other hand, coordination and planning is rather poor and much needs to be done. The human resources sector is in good shape but, to prevent any deterioration, a little needs to be done in skill development and incentives, not necessarily financial.

We can now address the final analytical step in **ACTIFELD** – obstacles and actions.

Force field analysis for the MDB

In Chapter 7, we encountered force field analysis (FFA) as a tool for identifying obstacles to improvement and testing how the proposed actions could overcome or bypass those barriers. In a very real sense it is a *sanity check* on the whole analysis as it helps to verify that nothing has been missed out.

The principle of FFA is, like much else in this book, very simple; the practice is rather harder and, as with everything else in this book, needs imagination and team discussion.

FFA *has* to be done on a board with room for the team to walk round and stand back, add, erase and redraw. FFA *cannot* be done on a computer, though the end result should be drawn with a graphics package for legibility.

It is worth reminding you of the comment that these tools for practical strategy are collectively a good way of turning an argument into a discussion. FFA is an excellent example of that adage.

The FFA diagram in Figure 14.4 has on its vertical scale the base case of $H_2I_3D_4F_3R_4A_{2/3}C_4$ and the required case of $H_2I_1D_2F_1R_2A_1C_1$ as the movement from one to the other is what the actions are supposed to bring about and what the

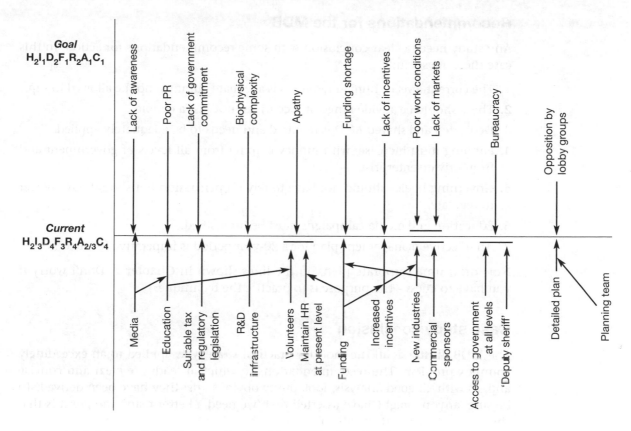

Figure 14.4 A force field diagram for the Murray/Darling Basin

obstacles might prevent. However, that scale does not measure the magnitude of the difference between the two HIDFRACs, it simply gives space in which to draw, as does the horizontal scale. The length of the arrows is not significant.

The obstacles broadly derive from earlier steps such as the TOWS tables and the FAR futures contexts but there is no exact one-for-one correspondence. Further thought has refined and summarised earlier ideas but there is an overall equivalence. The actions come from the TOWS and strategies, the resource analysis and, above all, from the VPM.

The conventions from Chapter 7 have been used with a bar to show combined actions and diagonal arrows indicating supporting actions. You should redraw Figure 14.4 using some of the other conventions, such as different widths of arrows to indicate what you think might be powerful and weak actions and obstacles. In short, you should experiment with this diagram.

The conclusion from the FFA is the last step in **ACTIFELD**, the '*decision*' as to whether or not the overall plan seems to be workable. What do you think? If you do think this will work, what is the 'but'?

Recommendations for the MDB

Any study needs a clear conclusion with some recommendations for action. In this case there are seven:

1. The current level of human resources is adequate but must not be allowed to slip.
2. There should be a wide range of incentives, not just a couple.
3. Dedicated and shared R&D is required and needs to be adequately applied.
4. Funding must increase, with money coming from all levels of government and from private enterprise.
5. Governing bodies should not have to rely on persuasion but should have power to regulate.
6. Education and media campaigns must be intensified.
7. An effective management plan for a 20-year period is imperative for success.

Now draw up a corporate plan, on the lines shown in Chapter 7. Don't worry if you have to guess – the purpose is to practise the technique.

Case study conclusion

The MDB illustrates all the tools for practical strategy as applied to an exceedingly complex problem. The recommendations to which it leads are clear and concise and, as with all good analysis, look pretty obvious *after* they have been derived. To be sure, anyone might have asserted that 'we need a better plan'; the point is that the study shows that we also need six other things, that the plan has to be for those six aspects, not just a vague plan for something undefined, and, *above all*, the chain of steps gives an explicable audit trail leading to, and justifying, the seven final recommendations.

Of course, this is not a definitive study of the MDB and some checking, verification and perhaps rework would be required in a study for real clients as opposed to an academic exercise. Nonetheless, this case shows how far it is possible to get in an intensive week and I am grateful to the group of bright, experienced and hard-working students who helped to develop it.

We can now turn to a completely different type of problem but, now that you have seen the full use of the strategic tool set in the Murray/Darling case, you will have to do more for yourself. The gaps will be shown by ??? so you will have to treat this as an exercise as well as a case study.

 CASE STUDY | ## Littleworth and Thrupp (L&T) – Solicitors

Introduction

Mr Littleworth and Ms Thrupp are the senior equity partners in a firm of solicitors. Littleworth is about 63 years old and owns 55% of the equity. Thrupp is only about 50 and owns 35%. Mr Tubney, who is 35, owns the balance of the equity.

His equity stake gives him little power but he hopes that one day the firm will become Thrupp and Tubney, or even Tubney Associates. The firm also has about 20 qualified solicitors who are salaried employees. Mr Littleworth and some of the employed solicitors are nearing retirement. Ms Thrupp and Mr Tubney are far too young to retire.*

Over the past 20 years or so, the two senior partners have developed an excellent practice specialising in compensation for motor accidents. Sometimes, L&T act on behalf of the person seeking compensation, on other occasions they defend against the claim. Some of the accidents they deal with are relatively trivial but others are vastly more serious. Their primary aim is either to get as much compensation as possible, or to ensure that the minimum reasonable payment is made. In practically all instances, they are retained by, and eventually paid by, an insurance company. Littleworth, Thrupp, Tubney and their employees work hard and skilfully and, while not mega-rich, the partners make a good living. The partners enjoy practising law and may, perhaps, get too involved in cases and not enough in management. For further discussion of this type of business, see Maister (1993).

Most of L&T's accident clients are so impressed with the firm that L&T are sometimes asked to take on other legal work and some of the staff are qualified to do so. L&T have tended to see this as a small sideline and have generally not actively sought non-accident work.

Unhappily, all this is now threatened as the leading insurance companies, in a very competitive market, are moving to set up their own in-house litigation departments and L&T's established market might vanish, or be seriously diminished, within a couple of years.

L&T's strategic question

In Chapter 1 we discussed the important idea of the strategic question and suggested the following question for L&T:

> 'What strategies should Littleworth and Thrupp adopt to continue to prosper given the possible, and relatively imminent, collapse of their traditional legal market?'

That parses to: *Why*, threat to established business; *When*, within the next year or so; *What*, continue to prosper; *How*, an action plan for development of new legal business.

We did, though, mention in Chapter 1 that a practical strategy study may, *and often should*, lead to the question being changed if no feasible action plan can be found. Perhaps L&T will not be able to maintain their prosperity and might have to retrench or even sell out, and it is obvious that plans for those possibilities

---

*Littleworth, Thrupp and Tubney are actually villages near Oxford. The names seemed ideal for a firm of solicitors. For non-English readers, solicitors in England and Wales are lawyers who, *very* broadly, deal with family law, such as wills, property and trusts, compensation matters and minor litigation cases in the lower courts. For more serious matters which have to be heard in higher courts, a solicitor will brief a barrister who is qualified in advocacy at the higher levels. Suitably qualified solicitors now have rights of advocacy in the higher courts. A firm of solicitors acts as a partnership, with the equity held by the senior members. When one of them retires he/she hopes to sell the equity to a new partner.

would not be at all the same as a plan to develop new legal business. We shall have to see how the analysis turns out.

Sense-making and futures

Although the **ACTIFELD** methodology involves eight steps, they do not necessarily apply to all cases. For L&T, futures studies seem now to be irrelevant; the potential collapse of their market is clear and imminent.

Their current context also seems to be very simple; since they cannot make accidents happen, they can do little to generate new business in their traditional market apart from making sure that insurers still see them as being a very cost-effective solution to accident claims. However, the future context may be very different if the insurance companies take the work in-house. You might try to develop an impact wheel (Chapter 2) to see if it illuminates the problem. If it does not, you should abandon it – there is absolutely no point in applying ACTIFELD steps just for the sake of it. We shall move on to the TOWS analysis.

Littleworth and Thrupp's TOWS analysis

A suggested set of TOWS is given in Table 14.8, though that table is no more than a suggestion and you may wish to add some more items of your own, as implied by the '???'. Apart from that, two points need to be noted. The first is that W_3 and O_1 are identical concepts. We pointed out in Chapter 4 that it is pointless to debate whether X is a weakness or an opportunity or whatever; it is both possible and perfectly legitimate for X to be two or more things at once and it should be

Table 14.8 Stage 1 of Littleworth and Thrupp's TOWS analysis

Threats	Opportunities
T_1 Pressure to reduce costs of legal work	O_1 A partner and some senior staff near retirement
T_2 Insurance companies may move in-house	O_2 Solicitors now allowed to appear in higher courts
T_3 Barriers to entry in other branches of legal work	O_3 Human Rights Act brings more litigation
T_4 ???	O_4 Emphasis on health and safety matters
	O_5 Possibly increased personal litigiousness
	O_6 Local university has strong department of law
Weaknesses	**Strengths**
W_1 Firm has traditionally worked in one legal area	S_1 Good list of clients
W_2 Hard to recruit good people	S_2 Recent investment in modern IT
W_3 Some senior people approaching retirement	S_3 Strong financial position
W_4 ???	S_4 ???

Source: Coyle (2003)

shown as such in the table. The second point is that a TOWS table should always be carefully checked. For example, if two items (O_3 and O_5 for instance) are the same thing under different names, they should be merged into one. If they are genuinely different, they should be kept separate. A TOWS analysis has a momentum of its own and it is always worth while to pause and take stock and not allow that momentum to get in the way of careful thought.

When you have revised Table 14.8 – and you should feel free to invent reasonable TOWS for the sake of the practice in practical strategy – you will be able to draw up your own version of Table 14.9, the actions indicated by the TOWS comparisons. Perhaps the triple comparison of O_1, W_3, W_1, O_2, O_4 and T_3 points to bringing in new lawyers with skills in health and safety law. Does that link with action 4? There may be other possibilities, as suggested by the '???'.

Table 14.9 is only a suggested outline and your version may be somewhat different if you have treated this case study as an exercise. Simple though Table 14.9 is, it leads fairly easily to Table 14.10, postulating relationships between actions and broad strategic areas. As we pointed out in Chapter 4, all actions in an area are needed to

Table 14.9 Outline of Stage 2 of Littleworth and Thrupp's actions matrix

	Threats	Opportunities
	T_1 Pressure to reduce costs of legal work	O_1 A partner and some senior staff near retirement
	T_2 Insurance companies may move in-house	O_2 Solicitors now allowed to appear in higher courts
	T_3 Barriers to entry in other branches of legal work	O_3 Human Rights Act brings more litigation
	T_4 ???	O_4 Emphasis on health and safety matters
		O_5 Possibly increased personal litigiousness
		O_6 Local university has strong department of law
Weaknesses W_1 Firm has traditionally worked in one legal area W_2 Hard to recruit good people W_3 Some senior people approaching retirement W_4 ???	1. Market firm as active in new areas of expertise (W_1,T_2) ???	4. Offer promotion/partnership chances (W_3,O_1,S_3) 5. Use part-time academic lawyers to broaden expertise (W_1,O_6) 6. Develop links with local university to attract staff – offer work experience? (W_2,O_6) ???
Strengths S_1 Good list of clients S_2 Recent investment in modern IT S_3 Strong financial position S_4 ???	2. Reduce fees (T_1,S_2,S_3) 3. Use contacts for more active promotion of the firm (S_1, T_2) ???	7. Offer better pay and training (S_3,O_1,O_5) 8. Use client base to develop work in health and safety compensation S_1,O_4) ???

Source: Coyle (2003)

Table 14.10 Littleworth and Thrupp's actions and strategies

Grouped actions	Strategic area
1. Market firm as active in new areas of expertise 3. Use contacts for more active promotion of the firm	*Promote new image of firm*
5. Use part-time academic lawyers to broaden expertise 8. Use client base to develop work in health and safety compensation	*Develop portfolio of skills*
4. Offer promotion/partnership chances 6. Develop links with local university to attract staff – offer work experience? 7. Offer better pay and training	*Attract new people with wider skills*

achieve it and, when the table is read from right to left, it gives specific tasks to be undertaken and identifies which agencies or departments have to do them.

Note that action 2, reduce fees, does not appear in Table 14.10 as it would be an act of desperation given L&T's strategic question of continuing to prosper in the changed circumstances.

The viable firm matrix for L&T

The step from TOWS to the VFM is not automatic. The one should lead reasonably logically to the other but it requires further imagination and thought and there is no 'formula'.

In this case, the chain of argument is on the following lines:

The traditional market may (or may not) collapse, but L&T's strategic question is about continuing to prosper so they need to develop new work. Hitherto, they have not bothered much about other work so now they will have to market themselves differently and they will need to do something about their capabilities and human resources.

That reasoning implies that the VFM will need columns relating to two markets, L&T's objectives and marketing, and their reputation, human resources and portfolio of skills. Table 14.11 (p. 285) is a VFM for the possibilities for legal firms, especially L&T. As with the FAR sector/factor matrix, it gives filing space for all logical possibilities. You should, of course, modify this in the light of your own thinking.

Their present position is $S_4L_2O_{2/3}M_1A_4R_3C_3$. By contrast, a leading City firm of lawyers is at S_1 (which includes accident work so L can be ignored), uses M_3 and has A_1, R_1 and C_1, so its owners can achieve O_1, which is why they have £million incomes.

The VFM is more subtle than the FAR matrix. It can be used in this way and does not have to be read from left to right across the columns.

Table 14.11 Littleworth and Thrupp's viable firm matrix

| | | Practice objective and strategy | | Practice characteristics | | |
| | Traditional accident Litigation market **L** | Strategic **O**bjective **O** | **M**arketing policy **M** | Corporate reputation and **A**ttitude **A** | Human **R**esource position **R** | Skill and **C**apability base **C** |
Scope for expansion in other markets **S**						
S₁ Excellent. Seen as having excellent legal expertise in a wide range of cases	L₁ Increased litigiousness brings some growth in market	O₁ Aim for rapid growth in size and value	M₁ Concentrate on a well-established client base. Rely on reputation and contacts to bring in work	A₁ One of the very few firms seen as a lawyer of first recourse for most types of problem	R₁ Highly qualified people see employment with firm as a good career step. Very high quality of work. High motivation and pay	C₁ Wide range of skills at cutting edge. Skill base retained by recruitment of people with those skills
S₂ Very good. Seen as having very good legal expertise in a range of niche markets	L₂ Steady flow of work at about present level	O₂ Aim for good growth in size and value	M₂ Careful attention to existing clients, some effort at getting new ones	A₂ A well-known and respected firm with a good client base in both market areas	R₂ Fairly easy to recruit and retain good people. Consistently good work quality. Above average motivation and pay	C₂ Planned and actively managed portfolio of skills with strong attention to training for skill development
S₃ Reasonable. Expertise acknowledged but serious competition from other firms	L₃ Volatility (up and down) in frequency and volume of work for next few years	O₃ Aim to remain pretty much the same size and value	M₃ Constant monitoring of market to exploit established reputation	A₃ Reputation and client base growing steadily but not yet in the big league	R₃ Not easy to recruit and retain good people. Some variation in work quality. Average motivation and pay	C₃ Consciously chosen, but limited, portfolio with recruitment of people with those skills
S₄ Limited. Some cases because of personal contacts	L₄ Some use of insurance companies' in-house lawyers leads to significantly reduced level of work	O₄ A smaller firm, designed to be survivable in difficult and changed circumstances	M₄ Promise anything to a few existing clients	A₄ Good reputation but not widely known outside its traditional market	R₄ A few highly expert individuals. With good support	C₄ Concentration on 1 or 2 skills areas with no skill development
S₅ Poor. Limited legal expertise outside traditional base	L₅ Widespread use of insurance companies' in-house lawyers leads to collapse of market	O₅ Seek survival (and possibly some growth) by merger/partnership with complementary firm	M₅ Actively seek clients in a selected range of legal fields	A₅ One among many small firms of reasonable quality	R₅ Filling slots with warm bodies	C₅ No real portfolio – just doing what they can get
		O₆ Struggle to save the firm		A₆ A doubtful quantity which may not last much longer		

Source: Coyle (2003)

It is clear that if L moves to L_4 or L_5, L&T will only be able to maintain $O_{2/3}$ if they can move to about S_2 within a reasonably short time. If they cannot, they will sink to S_5 (the smaller accident market will bring them even less work on other cases). That will probably force them into $M_4A_{5/6}R_5C_5$ with the likely outcome of $O_{5/6}$ being the best that can be hoped for. (You should experiment with this idea. How could an R_4 firm still achieve O_2, relative to its size?)

The picture for L&T is starting to look gloomy because of the magnitude of the challenge but we proceed with Table 14.12 (p. 287), the strategic position to be achieved if L&T wish to stay at $O_{2/3}$. The gaps in the table lead to the resource analysis in Table 14.13 (p. 288) and to the force field in Figure 14.5. You really *must* check these steps for yourself, revising as you see fit!

The conclusions I draw from this are as follows (but you may have different ideas):

1. The resource gaps in Table 14.13 are numerous and substantial – L&T have a fight on their hands.

2. The force field suggests that control of costs, a natural reaction for a firm in trouble, can be overcome by achieving higher fees, but that will only happen if people with wider skills can be attracted, and cost control would prevent that.

3. L&T have financial reserves so it comes down to almost throwing caution to the winds (something lawyers hate) and spending that money on recruitment and marketing to try to achieve a breakthrough.

4. However, that money is effectively Mr Littleworth's pension fund as he controls the firm and he could retire if he chose. In his position, I would sell out while I still could and if anyone was prepared to buy my share.

5. However, Ms Thrupp and Mr Tubney, to say nothing of the salaried solicitors, are not in that position and may want to struggle on at O_4 or try O_5.

Case study conclusion

It has become pretty clear that the original strategic question cannot be answered and the analysis has to be changed to meet the new problem posed by Littleworth's departure, with whatever money he can get, and Thrupp and Tubney's new problem of survival. In this case, very little of the analysis has to be redone, apart from a new version of Tables 14.12 and 14.13 and a new force field. The final thought is that L&T probably got into this mess because they failed to heed Chapter 3 and treated the future as a foreign land.

Table 14.12 Littleworth and Thrupp's ideal strategy? (current – bold, future – *bold italic*)

Market characteristics		Practice objective and strategy		Practice characteristics		
Scope for expansion in other markets S	Traditional accident Litigation market L	Strategic Objective O	Marketing policy M	Corporate reputation and Attitude A	Human Resource position R	Skill and Capability base C
S_1 Excellent. Seen as having excellent legal expertise in a wide range of cases	L_1 Increased litigiousness brings some growth in market	O_1 Aim for rapid growth in size and value **contacts to bring in work**	**M_1 Concentrate on a well-established client base. Rely cn reputation and types of problem**	A_1 One of the very few firms seen as a lawyer of first recourse for most quality of work. High motivation and pay	R_1 Highly qualified people see employment with firm as a good career step. Very high with those skills	C_1 Wide range of skills at cutting edge. Skill base retained by recruitment of people
S_2 Very good. Seen as having very good legal expertise in a range of niche markets	L_2 Steady flow of work at about present level	O_2 Aim for good growth in size and value	M_2 Careful attention to existing clients, some effort at getting new ones	*A_2 A well-known and respected firm with a good client base in both market areas*	*R_2 Fairly easy to recruit and retain good people. Consistently good work quality. Above average motivation and pay*	*C_2 Planned and actively managed portfolio of skills with strong attention to training for skill development*
S_3 Reasonable. Expertise acknowledged but serious competition from other firms	L_3 Volatility (up and down) in frequency and volume of work for next few years	**O_3 Aim to remain pretty much the same size and value**	M_3 Constant monitoring of market to exploit established reputation	A_3 Reputation and client base growing steadily but not yet in the big league	**R_3 Not easy to recruit and retain good people. Some variation in work quality. Average motivation and pay**	**C_3 Consciously chosen, but limited, portfolio with recruitment of people with those skills**
S_4 Limited. Some cases because of personal contacts	*L_4 Some use of insurance companies' in-house lawyers leads to significantly reduced level of work*	O_4 A smaller firm, designed to be survivable in difficult and changed circumstances	M_4 Promise anything to a few existing clients	**A_4 Good reputation but not widely known outside its traditional market**	R_4 A few highly expert individuals. With good support	C_4 Concentration on 1 or 2 skills areas with no skill development
S_5 Poor. Limited legal expertise outside traditional base	L_5 Widespread use of insurance companies' in-house lawyers leads to collapse of market	O_5 Seek survival (and possibly some growth) by merger/partnership with complementary firm	*M_5 Actively seek clients in a selected range of legal fields*	A_5 One among many small firms of reasonable quality	R_5 Filling slots with warm bodies	C_5 No real portfolio – just doing what they can get
		O_6 Struggle to save the firm		A_6 A doubtful quantity which may not last much longer		

Table 14.13 Littleworth and Thrupp's resource analysis

Sector	Sub-category	From	To	Gaps
		C_3 Consciously chosen, but limited, portfolio with recruitment of people with those skills	C_2 Planned and managed portfolio of skills with strong attention to training for skill development	
C Skills and capabilities	Numbers and pressure of work	2	3	1
	Individuals' range of skills	2	4	2
	Training effort	1	3	2
	Equipment	3	3	0
	Buildings and facilities	3	3	0
	Effectiveness of Principals' time management	2	4	2
	Support systems	2	4	2
		R_3 Not easy to recruit and retain good people. Some variation in work quality. Average motivation and pay	R_2 Fairly easy to recruit and retain good people. Consistently good work quality. Above average motivation and pay	
R Human resources	Recruitment techniques	2	4	2
	Work quality and consistency	2	3	1
	Pay and conditions	2	3	1
		A_4 Good reputation but not yet widely known outside its traditional market	A_2 A well-known and respected firm with a good client base in both market areas	
A Attitude and reputation	Corporate visibility	1	3	2
	Internal culture	2	4	2
		M_1 Concentrate on a well-established client base. Rely on reputation and contacts to bring in work	M_5 Actively seek clients in a selected range of legal fields	
M Marketing	Contact list	2	4	2
	Marketing staff	1	3	2
	Marketing skills	1	3	2
	Promotional techniques	2	3	1
Net effect of gaps				24

Source: Coyle (2003)

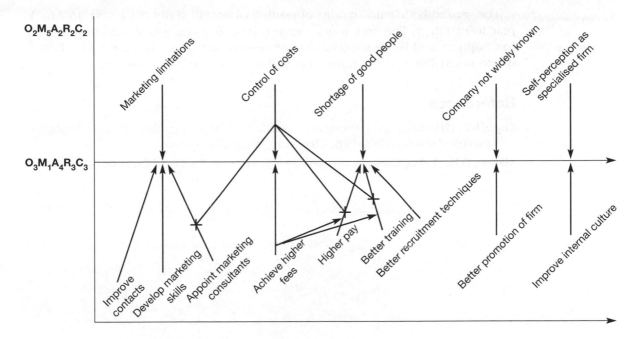

$O_2M_5A_2R_2C_2$

$O_3M_1A_4R_3C_3$

Figure 14.5 Littleworth and Thrupp's force field analysis
Source: Coyle (2003)

Chapter summary

The aim of this chapter is to make you familiar, and comfortable, with the *flow* of practical strategy. That should also make you more confident with the details of the various tools.

The two cases are very different. The MDB case is so wide-ranging and of such long duration that it virtually demanded the use of the full **ACTIFELD** process. L&T, on the other hand, faced a more imminent, and apparently simpler, problem so we used the shortcuts of not unravelling the complexity and not doing a futures exploration.

These cases are not definitive analyses of the respective problems. They are designed to make you do some of the work and you should now examine them fairly closely. Some of the questions you should think about are:

■ To what extent do you disagree with some of the steps in the analyses? Were the TOWS analyses complete? Would you revise the VFMs? In what ways would you change the resource analyses? And so on.

■ Do the action plans seem to be feasible?

■ Should the strategic questions have been revised?

This chapter has, though, *two key lessons*.

The first is that there is no such thing as a 'standard' practical strategy case. Do not, therefore, see these two cases as templates that *must* be followed. Always bend the tool to fit the problem and don't force the problem to fit the tool!

The second is that no amount of reading cases will really teach you how to do practical strategy. The only way to learn is by doing and you should now go back to Chapter 8 and tackle some of the suggested topics. You can use the list of previous topics in Table 8.1 to create other problems for you to practise on.

References

Coyle, R.G. (2003) Scenario thinking and strategic modelling. In Faulkner, D. and Campbell, A. (Eds) *Oxford Handbook of Strategy*, Chapter 11, vol. 1. OUP, Oxford.

Maister, D.H. (1993), *Managing the Professional Service Firm*. Free Press Paperbacks, New York.

Practical strategy in action

What this chapter is about

- *Reviewing* the tools and techniques.
- *Managing* their application to real problems.
- Making *syndicates effective*.
- *Presenting* results and conclusions.
- *Comparative approaches* to practical strategy.
- Suggestions for *further reading*.

Introduction

In working through this book you will have learned most by having applied the tools to some of the suggested exercises, such as those in *Topics for you to try* in Chapter 8. The greatest learning value lies, though, in having tackled a problem of your own choice, either because it interested you or because it was relevant to your own work.

In applying the techniques, as opposed to reading about them, it would be most unusual if you did not conclude that, although the techniques are easy to understand, it is not always straightforward to adapt them to the messy reality of an actual problem. That has generally been the experience of those who have trodden this road before you, so you are not alone. This final chapter will, therefore, try to give some guidance on applying the techniques for practical strategy to the real-world problems encountered either within your organisation or in consultancy practice. You must, though, recognise from the outset that it will not be possible to give prescriptive 'rules' that will always work. The enormously wide variety of problems *and the great diversity of the people involved in them* preclude a 'formula', so that all that can be offered is some general tips and hints, and you will have to adapt them, and develop your own, as you tackle successive problems.

First, though, it will be as well to review the tools for practical strategy. That will involve some repetition of what has gone before but that is usually a good way to learn and absorb ideas.

The whole theme of the book is that there is a set of tools and techniques that come together to give a systematic process for developing practical strategic action. Chapters 1 and 8 referred to the *strategic toolbox*, which seemed to be a good way of describing the aim of the book. Like all toolboxes, though, it has items that the craftsperson uses regularly because they will handle most jobs, and others that are designed for more specialised tasks.

Review of the 'standard' toolbox

The **ACTIFELD** process is in the first category. Its stages will take you through most practical strategy problems effectively and systematically. The main reason is that, as was mentioned in Chapter 1, **ACTI** suggests the *actions* that are needed to address the strategic question in the light of the situational complexity and the future's uncertainties. **FELD** comprises the extra steps to make sure that those actions can work in the *field* of the real world. Figure 15.1 is the same as Figure 8.2 and should be reviewed at this point to refresh your memory about the separate steps and the way that they relate to the questions and tasks. However, as was pointed out in Chapter 8, it is *not* mandatory to use all the steps in **ACTIFELD**. Shortcuts can be used when a given problem does not need a particular step, or if time is not available.

Step	Questions in the real world	Task in simplified (model) world	Technique?	Step
A	What is our problem, what should our strategy be?	Ask a good strategic question	*Focus groups*	A
C	Do we understand the system?	Come to grips with complexity	*Mind maps, impact wheels, why diagrams, influence diagrams*	C
T	Is the future a foreign land?	Think about the future	*Futures methods, especially FAR*	T
I	What do we do about the scenarios?	Identify required actions	*TOWS and actions*	I
F	How do we implement those actions?	Find a viable organisation	*Viable firm (or other organisation) matrix*	F
E	Can we make those changes?	Evaluate acceptability and resource needs	*Congruence analysis Resource analysis*	E
L	Are we sure?	Look for obstacles and remedies	*Force field analysis (FFA)*	L
D	Is it go? No Yes, but	Decide if the risks are acceptable		D

A shortcut?

Figure 15.1 A review of the ACTIFELD methodology

The range of applicability of **ACTIFELD** is virtually unlimited. Three very different cases have been used to illustrate that: *Herrington-Jones* is a major international business seeking to expand; Littleworth and Thrupp combine problems of survival with very significant differences in stakeholder expectations; the Murray/Darling River Basin is an important part of a national economy, not to mention the vital human and ecological implications. In addition, Table 8.1, p. 164 gives a further sample of applications ranging from lifestyle strategies for celebrities, via managing an airline and many other examples, to government procurement. Study and practice of those will hone your skill and understanding.

The specialised tools for practical strategy

The specialised tools for practical strategy handle four additional tasks:

> The specialised tools deal with important topics.

- Chapter 10 explored some ways of stimulating technological innovation. That is an important issue in its own right but recall that the TOWS analysis might well call for an action to 'develop new technology'. Zwicky's approach supports thought about doing exactly that.

- The art of judgement in Chapter 11, and especially the idea of using the issue history, is powerful for dealing with sudden 'crises', but its approach to examining the background to a problem might be very useful in asking a good strategic question. It would not replace the focus group but could give a disciplined framework for it, especially by forcing the group's members to be clear about their assumptions.

- The military appreciation in Chapter 12 gives a useful way of producing an action plan by systematic thought, often under extreme pressure of time or circumstances. Not all practical strategy problems in the non-military environment can afford the luxury of the time needed to apply even part of **ACTIFELD**, so the appreciation is a back-up method. The 'principles of war', and their business equivalents, are an effective checklist for plans. The fishbone diagram in that chapter is a rapid means of focusing people's minds on the root causes of a problem.

- Mission-orientated analysis and related techniques in Chapter 13 deal with selection from 'wish lists', or deciding which of a myriad of things that are needed will have the most impact on performance, recognising that, in the practical world, not everything that is needed can be acquired. This technique was developed for military planning but works perfectly well for any other domain; it might, for instance, have a role to play in advanced resource analysis.

Do not, though, see these 'advanced' methods as anything esoteric. They are no more complicated than anything in **ACTIFELD** and, while they have specialised uses, they might well replace or complement parts of **ACTIFELD** when the problem calls for it.

Managing real problems

Introduction

This is, in many ways, the most difficult area in which to try to give guidance. The reasons are simple:

- People sufficiently senior to be entrusted with practical strategy in a real organisation will have their own well-developed ideas about how to run a project and don't need advice from me.

- Every organisation has its own practices and procedures, which presents the paradox that, while practical strategy calls for people to *think* outside the box, they have to *work* inside the organisational box and present their results in a way that the organisation can recognise and be comfortable with.

- The office politics can bedevil a project or crown it with success, so managing a project if there is powerful opposition is entirely different from managing one when there is enthusiastic support.

- Finally, of course, there is the sheer variety of strategic questions that can arise.

You will have to take account of these factors when you set up and run your own project, but never forget the politics. The whole purpose of **ACTIFELD** is to bring about change in an organisation and that is *fundamentally* a political process, not an analytical one. To be sure, the analysis has to be as good as human ingenuity can make it, but all the thought, imagination and effort will be wasted if the politics do not work.

We can, however, offer some general guidance.

The people

Practical work needs three groups of people.

A practical strategy project involves three groups of people: the steering group (SG); the working group (WG); and the facilitator(s).

The SG is a small group of senior people who are the problem owners. Their obvious purpose is to monitor the whole process, ensuring that the rest of senior management know what is going on, making sure that deadlines are met, that resources are available to the WG, and protecting them from political interference. More importantly, though, they focus on the strategic question, constantly asking whether the results from each stage of **ACTIFELD** (or one of the four specialised methods) are really relevant to the question. Even more importantly than that, they should be on the alert to change the question as insight deepens. Practical strategy becomes highly practical and very strategic when someone on the SG says, 'I've just realised that *this* should be the question and not *that*'. There may be some waste of previous work, though usually not much, but that is a small price to pay for solving the right problem.

The steering group works as a focus group (Chapter 1) and meets as often as is necessary but its members need to make it a high priority to attend. Its work will be wasted if it is too hard to arrange meetings or there is partial attendance.

The working group is a team of not fewer than four or more than about six middle managers or staff assistants. They need to be fully familiar with the organisation and its problems and must be able to have access to whatever information or people they need. Bear in mind that information, in the form of statistics, data or reports, is usually far less useful than what people have in their heads by way of experiences, ideas and suggestions.

The WG team will need to be assigned practically full-time to the project for as long as it takes, and that commitment will be justified by the significance of the strategic question. The time allowed has to be long enough to handle the problem, but not so long that 'paralysis by analysis' sets in. A good first estimate of the time needed in a real problem, as opposed to an MBA project (guidance on managing MBA work is given in the instructor's website) is about two weeks. In that time, a good deal of progress should have been made – probably as far as the viable firm matrix – and that should give a good guide to how much additional effort is needed. If, on the other hand, progress is not being made – the WG may not be working well together, information may be hard to obtain, there may be political interference – it may be time to call a halt. Such are the facts of life in the messy real world. The argument that 'we haven't time for strategy, we're too busy with problems' is as silly as it sounds, but may kill a practical strategy project.

The WG will usually operate as a syndicate; that is not as easy as it sounds and we shall have something to say about organising syndicates in the next section. The WG team members do *not* need to be expert in the techniques; that is the role of the facilitator. They *do* need to be imaginative and prepared to challenge the organisation's orthodoxy and, for that reason, they may need to be protected by the SG against threats to their career prospects arising from having questioned a senior manager's plans or concepts.

The facilitator (F) has to be knowledgeable about the techniques, perhaps from having studied them on an MBA, *and* having used them on at least one non-academic problem. F will provide training to the WG, keep them on track, and be a sounding board for what they do.

It might be thought that, since the techniques of **ACTIFELD** are simple, a facilitator is not needed. That is not the case as, in a sense, F is the WG's analytical conscience, making sure that they are rigorous about what they do, that they justify their assumptions, and do not skip steps in **ACTIFELD** without good reason. In some cases, F might suggest the use of one of the specialised tools.

The facilitator should ideally be external to the organisation, thereby having no axe to grind and no career aspirations within it. In short, *F's role is vital and do not even think about not having one*! F must, however, always remember that facilitators support work, but they do not do it.

Naturally, the SG and WG meet from time to time and F should be present but only as an adviser. Generally, F should keep quiet during these meetings, though it may be necessary to ask occasional questions to make sure that the SG and WG members have not missed something.

If it suits the organisation's style and is not perceived as a waste of time, it can be useful for the WG to write an occasional, and succinct, 'working memorandum'. This is *not* a report; it simply says 'this is what we have done so far'. Its value is in allowing people outside the WG, and maybe beyond the SG, to keep abreast of progress, maintain interest in the project, and perhaps inject new ideas. The working memo should always have the strategic question prominently displayed on each page.

The physical arrangements

It is essential for the WG to have a room dedicated to their use. It needs to have large whiteboards all round, and an endless coffee supply. There must be plenty of room to walk around and talk – extra tables can be brought in if needed for meetings with the SG.

It is vital always to have the strategic question on the boards. Other results, such as a mind map or an influence diagram, the FAR context, the TOWS table, and so on, will gradually fill up the boards and should be kept visible if at all possible so that the SG can see how the project has evolved.

I always try to persuade teams not to have a computer in the room but to go elsewhere when results need to be typed up or recorded in the **ACTIFELD** software. The reason is that the room is for thinking and the laptop is for recording and the two activities are quite different. On top of that, the person with the laptop is typing, not working on the problem. WG members often object that it is a waste of time to write down what is on the board and then to type that into the machine. My view is that the two steps of writing something down and then typing it up force one to look at the material in detail, and that often reveals errors or, and more importantly, creates fresh ideas. I generally lose the argument.

The mental skills needed

Successful practical strategy needs four mental skills.

Throughout the book we have referred to tools and toolboxes to stress that practical strategy is rather closer to a craft skill than it is to a science. Fortunately, though, the techniques of this craft can be learned from a book rather than through a long apprenticeship, but applying them successfully calls for four mental skills:

1. knowing, of course, how to apply each of the techniques and their limitations and strengths

2. being flexible in how you use them, adapting where necessary, or even inventing new tools of your own to handle some special problem

3. remembering to change one's mental viewpoint from one step to another, and abandoning any thought that there is any automatic and exact connection between steps, let alone a 'formula'

4. above all, being willing to revise the strategic question as your understanding of the problem deepens.

A key factor is that it is scarcely possible to do good strategic thinking for a real problem on one's own. The working group *is* a group and it will work in syndicates. That is an art in its own right and is not as easy as it sounds.

Making syndicates effective

The working group has to be a team but, paradoxically, that does *not* mean that its members have to be good team players, in the sense of loyally implementing the organisation's policy. In fact, the WG's whole purpose is to challenge and help to redesign the policy with the aim of answering, as best they can, the strategic question. To avoid what might be argument – certainly fruitless and possibly heated – the essence of **ACTIFELD** is to help *to turn an argument into a discussion* so as to reach an answer to the strategic question that will be accepted and used by the problem owners. The key interpersonal skill for a syndicate member is, therefore, to be able to disagree without being disagreeable.

> **ACTIFELD is intended to help to turn an argument into a discussion.**

In practice, syndicates usually comprise between four and about six people, preferably from a variety of backgrounds in terms of academic training and organisational role. In some cases, a few more people might be brought in from time to time to create a second syndicate on a given **ACTIFELD** step; a syndicate needs four people for a good debate. The two groups do not work in competition but on the basis that two groups of heads may be better than one and that the final result will combine the best of both efforts.

There are a few practical points about working in syndicate:

- Syndicate work is teamwork so it is vital not to sit behind desks as that is too much like individual effort. Each syndicate room will have large whiteboards, and the other furniture should be pushed out of the way so that everyone can gather round to take part in the discussion.

> **Syndicate work is *teamwork*.**

- Syndicate work is a group effort to which everyone contributes and no one is in charge, but syndicate time is limited and cannot be wasted on endless debate. Each team should therefore spend a couple of minutes (no more) at the start of each session deciding roughly how long they will spend on each task, allowing time for preparing a summary of what was done.

- They should then choose a timekeeper who has, so to speak, a chess players' clock and who will have to halt discussion when the agreed time has elapsed. Once that has happened, the rest of the team should accept it with good grace and get on with the next sub-task.

> **Keep careful control of time.**

- The team will also need a scribe to keep notes of what was decided or make copies of what has been written on the board.

- The timekeeper and scribe should change regularly so that everyone gets a chance at the onerous tasks.

- It saves time if progress reports are put on transparency film, and there is no need to use PowerPoint. In any case, that is usually unfair to one member who is the PowerPoint expert and does not get a real chance to be part of the working team.

- If discussion gets bogged down, there are two useful tricks:

> **If discussion gets bogged down …**

  - Draw a quick mind map for the aspect you are dealing with – the VFM, for instance.
  - Work as individuals for 10 minutes and then compare and blend the resulting VFMs.

■ It is also a fact that practical strategy is sometimes done under very intensive conditions and it is, in any case, intellectually demanding and tiring. If people start to say 'my brain's turned to mush' (and they should not be embarrassed to say so – everyone else in the team probably feels the same way), then take a break and go for a walk.

Bear these points in mind, but you have to evolve a working style that suits you, the problem, and the organisation's culture.

Presenting results and conclusions

This is where the organisation's culture and style can have their greatest effect, and failure to take account of those factors will ruin the project, no matter how good the work has been. For instance, if you do not write a report in the style and format that people are accustomed to, it will not be read. If your oral presentation is hesitant, verbose or excessively technical, you will not be listened to. All being well, the steering group will make sure that you avoid these pitfalls and it is essential that you give the SG a dress rehearsal of the oral presentation in time for changes to be made.

Adhering to the organisation's style is vital in presentation.

Beyond that, the standard rule of Keep It Simple applies. Concentrate on the strategic question throughout. Say that you will simply list the steps you did, taking questions or elaborating later. You might mention that 'we developed scenarios' (without mentioning FAR), or that 'we looked at the organisational implications' (not that 'we developed a VFM'), and similarly for the rest of the **ACTIFELD** steps. Then go to the conclusions. That is almost certain to generate a lot of discussion about the conclusions, after which you will get probing questions about how you got there. At that stage, you can go into detail.

Keep it simple!

Never mention the **ACTIFELD** acronym in the early stages of a briefing to senior executives, as, even if you don't get thrown out (more or less politely) for excessive jargon, you will spend a lot of time explaining what it is, after which you will get thrown out for wasting their time on theory.

Above all, though, allow time for dress rehearsals, one within the WG and then another to the SG. Make sure that you have time to revise and rehearse again if necessary. The aim is to get it right first time at the final briefing to senior management.

Get it right first time.

Comparative approaches to practical strategy

We have tried to show, by examples and cases, that **ACTIFELD**, and the specialised approaches, work well for a virtually limitless variety of practical strategy problems. It would, however, be quite misleading to pretend that **ACTIFELD** is the *only* way of developing practical strategy. Other schools of thought exist and **ACTIFELD** needs to be understood in relation to them.

Table 15.1 is an outline of the matches and mismatches between **ACTIFELD** and four other concepts. **ACTIFELD** is in the first column solely because it is the subject of much of this book and *not* because it is in some way 'better' than the other approaches. The column for 'standard' strategic management does not come from any specific strategic management text but is a broad summary of what they usually contain. 'Standard' does not mean 'routine', still less does it mean 'boring', and we were at pains at the outset of this book to stress the importance of MBA courses in strategic management as the intellectual precursor to a practical strategy course, using the techniques covered in this book. Similarly, the 'problem-solving' column is not from any particular source but is an amalgam of what that type of book usually teaches and the approaches sometimes used by management consulting firms. The

Table 15.1　Comparative approaches to practical strategy

The ACTIFELD process	'Standard' strategic management	A 'problem-solving' approach	The military appreciation	An intelligent child's technique
A – ask a good strategic question	Confirm mission and values External and internal environmental analyses Identify stakeholder needs	Analyse the problem, considering: Deviations from desirable Develop possible causes of deviations Test and explain probable causes Verify logic and reality	Receive an aim from higher authority	Dream about the things you'd like to do or have
C – come to grips with complexity			Analyse factors and draw conclusions	Look for clues about parental resistance or compliance
T – think about the future	Formulate objectives	Analyse the decision: What decision is required?	Consider own and enemy courses of action	When will Dad be in a good mood?
I – identify actions	Identify key resource areas	Establish objectives – essential/desirable Generate alternatives	Determine own best course	Choose what you want most
F – find a viable organisation	Generate strategic options	Compare and choose	Plan to implement own best course	Choose tactics for getting what you want – ask nicely, plead, compare with friends, throw a tantrum
E – evaluate acceptability and resource requirements	Choose preferred option	Analyse implementation: State action plan Anticipate likely difficulties and their causes Select actions to prevent difficulties/minimise their effects Provide for progress reports and triggers for contingencies	Check reasoning and practicality	
L – look for obstacles and remedies				
D – evaluate risks and decide on course of action	Implement preferred option. Evaluate and control		Issue orders Monitor outcome	If it did not work, try another tactic or choose another aim

military appreciation is covered in Chapter 12 because it is a good way of dealing with some types of problem. The final column for a child was suggested by Brooker and reinforced by my own observations; adults may use similar methods.

You will probably have your own ideas about the format of Table 15.1, the correspondence between different items, and the wording in the cells. If so, it will be an easy task, and a useful exercise, to draw up your own version. The whole point is to arrive at a gestalt, whole-pattern, appreciation of the methods of deriving practical action plans. The emphasis is that practical strategy is a task calling for imagination and insight and those faculties are essentially based on human thought, probably using some tools and techniques in the strategic management and problem-solving columns, and a disciplined, standardised, procedure for thought in the military appreciation. As we have repeatedly emphasised, the **ACTIFELD** process is also driven by imagination and insight; its *structured* techniques and steps exist to guide and organise thought and to steer it through the managerial questions on the left-hand side of Figure 15.1.

Some further reading

It would be easy to make a long list of things that you could read as follow-up material but you probably would not have time. If you are doing an MBA course, or an equivalent in any of the disciplines in which the tools of practical strategy are applicable, you will be doing that reading in any case. I have, therefore, picked out a few books that I have found to be helpful.

There are almost innumerable books on corporate strategy but one that I like is G. Johnson and K. Scholes *Exploring Corporate Strategy* (Harlow, Essex, Pearson Education, 7th edn, 1999). Like most such books, it has numerous case studies of a wide variety of business problems, and they will give additional material on which you could test the tools in this book.

A companion volume is V. Ambrosini's *Exploring Techniques of Analysis and Evaluation in Strategic Management* (Harlow, Essex, Pearson Education, 1998). This is an edited collection of chapters covering simple techniques typically found in the strategic management literature. While the material covered does not have the structural coherence of **ACTIFELD**, it is still worth reviewing.

Despite its age, C. H. Waddington's *Tools For Thought* (St Albans, Hertfordshire, Paladin Press, 1977) is, if you can find it, a joy to read. It is based on his work in operational research during the Second World War and is an early attempt to grapple with ways of thinking about complexity. It is the product of a Rolls-Royce mind and it is a pity that Professor Waddington did not live to complete a companion volume.

Equally worth reading is B. H. P. Rivett's *The Craft of Decision Modelling* (Chichester, John Wiley and Sons, 1994). This book comes from the operational research school of analysis and describes some of the many practical problems with which Professor Rivett has been involved during a long and distinguished career. It contains almost no mathematics and its great strength is its pragmatic orientation and its exhortation to 'go and look at the problem'. That is good advice from a master and you would do well to heed it. Don't do practical strategy work just in the office; get out on to the shop floor as often as you can.

Finally, if you can get it, read R. Rhyne's *Evaluating Alternative Indonesian Sea-Sovereignty Systems* (Linthicum, Maryland, Institute for Operations Research and Management Sciences, undated but about 1995). It describes a FAR study of the problem, which is interesting in its own right, but another strength is its painful honesty about all the things that can go wrong in an extended project.

Beyond this eclectic collection of books that I like, read as widely as you can. The weekly *The Economist* is an excellent source, as is the quarterly *Prospect*.

Finale

The final point is to repeat what has been said many times already. The structured tools and techniques support the development of practical strategy, but they do not *do it*. It is really done in the mind and the imagination. It is immensely enjoyable and demanding and the satisfaction of working a real problem to an accepted conclusion is considerable.

> Remember, the real work of practical strategy is done in the mind.

If you have enjoyed, and been challenged by, the ideas and tools in this book as much as I have enjoyed the hard work of writing it, I shall be well pleased. Should any reader wish to send me comments, suggestions or additional case material, they will be gratefully received and acknowledged.

Appendix
Software for practical strategy

Introduction

The results of a practical strategy analysis can, of course, be recorded with pencil and paper, on flip charts, or on transparencies (by the syndicate member with the neatest handwriting). That is quite adequate for many purposes but does not lead to a professional-looking presentation and risks some of the work simply getting lost.

For those reasons, many syndicates prefer to work with a laptop, recording their results as they go in a standard word-processing package and often linking directly to PowerPoint. It is a better method than pencil and paper, and leads to better-looking presentation material, but means that one member of the team is typing instead of working. The disadvantage of this method is that it still requires a fair amount of 'manual' work to link the successive stages of **ACTIFELD** together; it is not, so to speak, geared to the **ACTIFELD** process.

There is also the difficulty that word-processing packages do not always have good graphics facilities so that influence diagrams, for example, can be difficult to produce. (The diagrams for this book were produced using CorelDraw and then imported into Microsoft Word.)

There is, though, the greater handicap that this method does not support the calculations for full-scale FAR and MOA.

The ACTIFELD™ software

To overcome those drawbacks, the **ACTIFELD™** software has been developed to support the **ACTIFELD** process. Information on the latest functionality of the package, together with prices and delivery information is available at **www.actifeld.com**.

Briefly, though, the software leads you through the **ACTIFELD** process, maintaining the focus on the strategic question and allowing you to amend it, if necessary, as you work. There is support for the tools used in Chapters 2 to 7, such as the drawing of Why diagrams and force fields. It has excellent notebook facilities for documentation of the successive steps and links to presentation features such as PowerPoint. Later versions will include support for the advanced techniques in Chapters 10 to 13.

In short, the software is designed to eliminate the clerical and arithmetical labour of **ACTIFELD**, thus allowing you to focus on the all-important thinking.

Index